Praise for Sam Wilkin's
WEALTH SECRETS

"Sam Wilkin combs history for a provocative and well-written account of the secrets of wealth formation. Just reading this book will make you richer."

—Darrell M. West, vice president of governance studies at the Brookings Institution and author of *Billionaires: Reflections on the Upper Crust*

"An amazing read.... Get onto one of those secrets and you too can light your cigars with hundred-dollar bills."

—Marvin Zonis, professor emeritus, Booth School of Business at the University of Chicago

"Clever, entertaining.... Rich and poor will enjoy it equally, and if you have a modest entourage, I would consider getting copies for them too." —Marcus Berkmann, *Daily Mail* (UK)

"So how do our billionaires make their billions? Business analyst Sam Wilkin offers up the real scoop.... Delicious and insight-packed." —Sam Pizzigati, *Too Much*

"Illuminating.... Wilkin has good fun looking at how some fabulously rich people got to be that way.... Eye-opening."

—*Kirkus Reviews*

"Wilkin is a knowledgeable guide to the world's greatest fortunes.... Thoughtful, playful prose."

—Bryan Burrough, *New York Times Book Review*

WEALTH SECRETS

HOW THE RICH GOT RICH

SAM WILKIN

BACK BAY BOOKS

Little, Brown and Company

Back Bay Books / Little, Brown and Company
Hachette Book Group
1290 Avenue of the Americas, New York, NY 10104
littlebrown.com

Originally published in hardcover as *Wealth Secrets of the One Percent* by Little, Brown and Company, August 2015
First Back Bay paperback edition, March 2016

Back Bay Books is an imprint of Little, Brown and Company. The Back Bay Books name and logo are trademarks of Hachette Book Group, Inc.

The publisher is not responsible for websites (or their content) that are not owned by the publisher.

The Hachette Speakers Bureau provides a wide range of authors for speaking events. To find out more, go to hachettespeakersbureau.com or call (866) 376-6591.

ISBN 978-0-316-37893-2 (hc) / 978-0-316-34381-7 (int'l pb) / 978-0-316-37895-6 (pb)
Library of Congress Control Number 2015937506

10 9 8 7 6 5 4 3 2 1

RRD-C

Printed in the United States of America

For Janika Albers

Contents

WEALTH SECRETS

Introduction

LET US ASSUME, dear reader, that you are interested in one thing and one thing only: obtaining a vast fortune. I do not mean a comfortable fortune that might afford a few homes in prime locations, an elite school for your children, a supercar, a modest entourage, a live-in nanny. I mean a fortune of yachts and personal helicopters, of diamond-encrusted light fixtures, of stately homes and private islands, of your name emblazoned upon landmark buildings and a charitable foundation bravely tackling world issues — a fortune equivalent to the economic output of a small country; a fortune that ensures your name echoes in eternity. Not a fortune numbered in the millions or even the hundreds of millions, but a fortune in the billions.

If such a vast fortune were your goal, how might you set about obtaining it?

That is the question this book seeks to answer, not with abstract theory, or implausible schemes you can carry out from home, or indeed metaphors about rats and cheese (well, maybe one or two metaphors about rats and cheese). I seek to answer this question by researching the relatively small number of people throughout history who have become staggeringly wealthy and the methods that they have used to do so. One surprising conclusion I come to is that, despite superficial differences, these methods have a great deal in common.

The instinctive advice most people would give on how to become rich is not wrong—"start a business" would no doubt be most popular, perhaps followed by "go into investment banking"—but it is only partially right. An uncountable number of businesses are started every year in countries worldwide, and although many fail, there are still a great many that are successful and grow rapidly. Yet very few of the proprietors of even the most successful businesses become billionaires. And although there are many well-to-do investment bankers, perhaps·surprisingly, few are able to join the superyacht class. Indeed, of the more than 1,600 billionaires in the world today, fewer than 50—that is to say, less than 5 percent—are bankers. In fact fewer than ten of the world's billionaires—less than 1 percent—are bankers from the global financial centers of London or Wall Street. The majority of these rich bankers are, significantly, from the emerging world. One example is Roberto Gonzalez Barrera, a Mexican worth $1.9 billion, who came 683rd on the Global Rich List in 2012, and for whom *Forbes* listed as the source of his fortune "banking, tortillas."

So, if not good career choices or business success, what is it that sets the superrich apart from the merely very, very well-off?

It is the central claim of this book that behind almost every great fortune is a "wealth secret"—a moneymaking technique that, while not necessarily dirty, is not the kind of thing you would sprinkle on your breakfast cereal, give a baby to play with, or talk about in casual conversation with a member of the clergy. All of these wealth secrets involve some sort of scheme for defeating the forces of market competition. Most involve clever legal maneuvering or the exercise of political influence.

What I mean to imply is that, even in the modern day, if your goal is wealth, by all means apply yourself to the study of finance and commerce; but if your goal is vast, uncountable, truly extraordinary wealth, you need more. You need to know some wealth secrets.

You may wish to use this book as a manual to attain the opulence of your dreams. Indeed, I encourage you to do so, as this will produce more rich people about whom I can write a sequel. But I suspect there will also be readers who consider the book and its stories a critique of the world in which we live now, a world characterized by growing income inequality and the detrimental effects of that inequality upon public health and well-being. In the present day, the wide circulation of terms such as "the one percent" indicates that the general public senses something has gone awry with the rules of the game of capitalism. Yet, particularly in the United States, the self-made businessperson remains an untouchable icon. The "man on the street" tacitly understands that some financial gains of the past decade are not legitimate but would be hard-pressed to explain why. My book will satisfy this demand for explanations, giving the interested public a means to separate genuine entrepreneurs from those who are—to quote Barack Obama—"gaming the system." These narratives of success will demonstrate why it makes sense both to celebrate entrepreneurship and to condemn the cases in which lines have been crossed, cases where we can justly call into question the legitimacy of the wealth accumulated over the past decade by a fortunate few.

And, more importantly, how you can join them.

THE ART OF THE POSSIBLE

In Charles Morris's book about the U.S. robber barons, he writes: "Carnegie, Rockefeller, Gould, and Morgan would have been dominant figures anywhere." This is a commonly held view about the most successful individuals in any era. Great men, it is tempting to think, are great inevitably. Surely Carnegie and Rockefeller would have risen to the top, whether they had been born as peasants in medieval Europe, to a middle-class family in the present-day United States, or into a merchant caste in 1930s India.

I don't necessarily think that is the case. Time and place matter. So does luck. For Carnegie, for instance, an early oil-field investment that happened to pay off spectacularly (at $125 for every $1 invested), providing him with capital at a crucial time. For Rockefeller, being in the right line of work when the railroads came calling with a most unusual request. Did these individuals possess intrinsic qualities that all but guaranteed their rise to greatness? Perhaps. But that is not what interests me. This is not a book about *inevitability*; it is about *possibility*. It is about the factors that make it *possible* for some individuals (and, in the case of the bankers, an entire sector) to obtain fortunes that rise above others in their time—and indeed rank among the greatest fortunes in history.

In fact, in a well-functioning market economy, one should not be able to make hundreds of millions of dollars year after year after year (which is what is usually required to earn a billion dollars in a single lifetime). Indeed, economic theory implies that in a healthy, perfectly competitive market economy, business profits should be fairly close to zero (as we shall discover in chapter 1). Hence the profits we see all around us—those ritually reported by companies in quarterly earnings statements, those gained via brilliant hedge fund trading strategies, and even those obtained by well-meaning, deserving authors—stem from imperfections in markets. The stupendous fortunes of the world's billionaires, therefore, imply the existence not simply of a few market imperfections but of giant, gaping holes in economic reality—holes into which you can plunge your hand and extract a billion dollars.

You may have wondered, when you picked up this book, what an economist was going to tell you about wealth secrets. Economists are generally not much good with actual money. They tend to do things like prove conclusively that the global financial crisis did not exist, or win the Nobel Prize, start a hedge fund, and lose everything (another topic for chapter 1). At the level of wealth we are talking about in this book, though, you need to know about economics. There are great business strategies in this book, as well as extraordinary characters, tales of unusual upbringings, the occasional cynical betrayal, brilliant insights applied determinedly, some good luck, and perhaps even a little unscrupulousness. All these things made the fortunes described herein, but what made them possible is economics, and, more specifically, schemes to overcome the laws of economics as they typically operate in market economies.

What made these fortunes possible is, in short, wealth secrets.

WHAT'S IN THIS BOOK?

If you are a captain of industry, you may wish to skip over the first chapter. It is all about captains of industry who were celebrated by their many admirers and then fell hard and humiliatingly, and why that happened. (There is also a bit about some brilliant scholars who fell from grace, which may cheer you up.) Indeed, it turns out that it is the tragic fate of a great many successful business magnates to lose what they have gained. We will discover why famed business book authors (Jim Collins, Tom Peters), through no fault of their own, so often laud companies that end up in financial distress. In sum, in the first chapter we will learn why it is so hard to get, and stay, rich.

And yet, the superrich do exist—there are today more than 1,600 U.S.-dollar billionaires in the world. A few people not only make profits, they make huge profits. And not only for a year or two, but year after year after year, for the decades that it takes to produce a billion-dollar fortune. So the question for the rest of the book is not "Why is it so hard to get rich?" but rather "Why, for some, is it so easy?"

And: "How can I exploit their wealth secrets to become fabulously rich myself?"

To answer this question, we will first journey back to a simpler time, with two chapters covering the wealth secrets of history. First, ancient Rome. It was not, as we will discover, a simpler time to do business in — the ancient Roman economy was surprisingly sophisticated. But it was a simpler time for wealth secrets. Most of the population were slaves or illiterate, and had little capacity to object to being taken advantage of. Hence the wealth secrets of the day were employed in a refreshingly straightforward manner. Moreover, rich Romans tended to write down everything they did, good and bad, perhaps because they did not expect anyone who was not rich to be able to read.

A further excellent reason to start with the Romans is because the richest Romans were staggeringly rich — indeed, as a group, they were probably richer than the elite of any society that would arise for the next thousand years (as well as being richer than the elite of any society that had come before). This chapter will tell the story of how one of Rome's most colorful citizens, Marcus Crassus, made his money, and also why it was Crassus who ended up at the top of Roman society — rather than, say, a fish sauce merchant or an oil lamp manufacturer (although I will cover those too). Crassus's story, it turns out, contains a great many lessons for our times.

In the third chapter, we arrive in the nineteenth century, the era of the robber barons. If you are a captain of industry, you will like this chapter much more. Indeed, these men were probably the pinups on the wall of your room as a child — which is a little odd, but I do not presume to judge, as these were truly exceptional men. In his book *Outliers*, Malcolm Gladwell compiles a list of the seventy-five wealthiest people in world history, of which "an astonishing fourteen are Americans born within nine years of one another in the mid-nineteenth century." So that is another place we must go to find history's wealth secrets.

Indeed, Gladwell somewhat understates just how thoroughly

the American robber barons trounced the wealth secret contenders of other historical eras: by some measures, the wealth of these individuals has never since been equaled in the United States—not even by modern billionaires such as Bill Gates. Gladwell argues that the exceptional success of these individuals can be attributed to the years of their birth. These men came of age at a time of rapid technological advancement, and so were able to build entirely new types of business (e.g., railroads). But the robber barons had something else in common: they made their fortunes in remarkably similar ways.

From this point, we will leap forward to the modern day, with three chapters covering sectors where immodest fortunes are sprouting like weeds: the emerging markets, the financial sector, and the technology sector.

Chapter 4 covers the banking sector. The fortunes to be earned in banking are not on the same historical-epic scale as those of the robber barons, the richest Romans, or the emerging market oligarchs, but they are easier to come by. The banking sector has minted thousands of multi-million-dollar fortunes not just for the lucky 0.00001 percent (roughly speaking) of billionaires, but for the "one percent" of top income earners—relatively ordinary people, although usually clever and hardworking—perhaps yourself, your friends from school, or at least people you see daily on the street, particularly if you live in New York or London. It is a story that begins in the world of *It's a Wonderful Life*—the humble S&L sector in the United States—and ends in the world of titanic institutions that are "too big to fail," the mantra seared into the public consciousness in the wake of the global financial crisis.

But let's say merely joining the one percent does not interest you. Let's say you prefer more *selective* company. In that case, you will enjoy chapter 5, which explains why, if your goal is a fortune on a vast scale in the modern day, you are better off moving to a poor country. For it is in these countries that the combination of economic progress and weak regulation—the combination that gave rise to the U.S. robber barons—can still be found. If your ambition goes beyond the garden-variety hundreds of millions to be made in banking—as I've already said, there are very few bankers who are billionaires—your best bet is the emerging world. Indeed, Russia, India, China, Brazil, and Mexico alone are now home to almost one in every four billionaires on the planet. I'll show why this is the case, focusing on the story of Dhirubhai Ambani, a schoolteacher's son from a small fishing village in India who became one of the richest men who ever lived. If you have never heard of Ambani, that is because his company, Reliance—though one of the world's greatest by almost any measure—until recently did very little business outside India.

Our final tale of wealth secrets, in chapter 6, takes us to the world of high technology. For would-be joiners of the *Forbes* billionaire list who do not wish to relocate to India, China, or Russia, the challenges have increased. Antitrust legislation has made the methods used by the U.S. robber barons far more difficult to apply. But "challenging" is not the same as "impossible." This chapter will reveal the surprising wealth secrets of the technology billionaires of our own time, who account for about a quarter of today's twenty largest fortunes (including the largest personal fortune in the world).

I'll end by revealing seven secrets of spectacularly rich people. Having reviewed the methods used by the superrich to build their fortunes, we will take the time to pause for a moment and reflect: what does this mean for the rest of us? That is, how can we get in on the act?

To be sure, it will not be easy. As this book will show, the extremely wealthy are good at doing one thing above all else: preventing other people from doing what they are doing.

But then, if getting filthy rich was easy, anyone could do it, and having a billion dollars would not be exciting.

1

Why Is It So Hard to Get Rich?

THE FIRE SALE

As the Fortune 500 electronics retailer Circuit City staggered toward financial collapse, the vultures circled. Carlos Slim, a Mexican billionaire, made a lowball offer. Another Mexican billionaire, Ricardo Salinas, might have bought the ailing firm, but ran into trouble with U.S. regulators. A hedge fund was also interested, and a private equity firm. Blockbuster, in a desperate attempt to leap out of its own shrinking pond, contemplated a bid. But in the end, the winning offer to buy Circuit City came from a consortium led by Great American Group, a liquidation firm. It paid $900 million for a company that had been valued at more than $44 billion only a few years before. What Great American really wanted was the inventory. It was planning a fire sale.

Within twenty-four hours, the sale had begun. A crowd of about fifty gathered expectantly outside the Circuit City store on New York's Upper West Side before opening hours on January 18, 2009. A security consultant who specialized in liquidation sales explained: "You have to control it before they start lining up. You also need somebody to talk to these people while they're in line, because if there's nobody to guide or talk to them, it becomes a mob." (Only two months before, New York shoppers had trampled and killed a Walmart employee who was standing between them and some heavily discounted items.) "Entire Store on Sale!" and "Nothing Held Back!" proclaimed the banners above another Circuit City in midtown Manhattan, further inflaming the shoppers' desire.

But as the mob burst through the doors and fanned out into the aisles, it was soon clear that something was wrong. Hungry packs formed and then dissipated. The nervous energy of the crowd began to ebb. Eventually, coming down from their predatory rush, bored shoppers began to talk to the assembled media. "We came prepared to throw elbows," said one, "but there's not much on sale." Most items were discounted by a mere 10 percent. "As far as all this high-end stuff," said another shopper, "you can still probably find better [deals] online." The liquidation sale was "a scam," complained the technology bloggers later. The CEO of Hudson Capital Partners, one member of the liquidation consortium, attempted to justify the meager discounts: "How often do you see iPods at 10 percent off?" Similarly, a Circuit City employee commented, rather unsympathetically, "We had one customer buy something only to return it 20 minutes later saying that he got ripped off and it was cheaper at Best Buy. Now while that was true, there are signs that say 'no returns' ALL OVER THE STORE."

As the weeks wore on, though, the deals got better. By early March, bloggers were proclaiming the prices on software ($45 for Microsoft Office at one California store, for example) "a steal." Sections of most stores nationwide had been emptied and closed off with yellow tape. The TVs, at 40 percent off, were vanishing quickly. At another California branch, everything was up for grabs, including furniture from offices, half-empty cans of cleaning products, and a notice board that read "Cleaning fairy fired! Please clean up after yourself" (this latter item was optimistically priced at $5). At many stores, a descent into anarchy had begun, with one manager complaining that his employees had stolen nearly $400,000 worth of items in less than a week. A reporter from the *Guardian* wandered into a New York Circuit City to find that a "bearded, eccentric-looking" man had taken over the public address system, yelling repeatedly: "Buy American! If you're going to buy, buy American!" This being America, Circuit City retail employees discovered that their health insurance would be terminated within just a couple of months of the fire sale. The *Guardian* reporter stumbled across a laid-off worker who had been living in a homeless shelter for three months. Like any good New Yorker, his main concern was his failure to keep up appearances. "I'm a Rutgers University graduate," he said. "This is embarrassing."

The end finally came on March 9. By this point, the selection was limited but the discounts were extraordinary, so the buying frenzy continued. "I saw a guy with bins and bins of the first season of *Desperate Housewives*. I don't know what he's going to do with all those," said one shopper, leaving one plundered Circuit City in suburban Los Angeles to head to another. At 1 p.m. in another California store, a manager announced that everything would be 50 percent off for twenty minutes. At 4 p.m., the liquidation company's representative started filling shopping carts with random items, announcing "Whole cart for $1!" to anyone who would listen. Before long, nearly everything of value was gone. The following day the California employees assembled for one last time, to clean up. They watched a tape of one of the managers appearing on the television program *Divorce Court*. They played football in the empty store. They said their goodbyes, and left.

When most people think about wealth secrets, they probably think about some kind of business venture. The fall of Circuit City and another famous failure, the hedge fund Long-Term Capital

Management, illustrate why business, when practiced in the absence of wealth secrets, produces fire sales more often than fortunes.

THE NAPOLEON OF RETAIL

The company that became Circuit City was founded as Wards by Sam Wurtzel. Wurtzel was ambitious, clever, had married well, and was casting about for a new business idea after a venture with his wealthy father-in-law had failed. He was also something of a budding Napoleon of retail. When he saw territory, he longed to conquer it. And like Napoleon, he wanted to keep his empire all in the family. The name "Wards" was based on his family's initials — the Wurtzels, made up of Alan, Ruth (his wife), David, and, of course, Sam.

On holiday in Virginia in the early 1950s, Wurtzel was having a shave at a barbershop when he overheard that the first television broadcast station in the South was about to start in Richmond. Broadcasts would last only a few hours each day, consisting of whatever took the proprietor's fancy. No matter: up to that moment, there had been no TV signal at all anywhere in the area, so the broadcast would increase demand for television sets. Inspired, Wurtzel sold his home in New York and eventually, in 1952, opened Wards, a retail operation selling televisions in downtown Richmond.

Initially, Wurtzel and his business partners at Wards did not have much in the way of wealth secrets — which, as we shall discover, is the case for most small businesses. Other people heard about the new station and opened their own TV stores, so Wards had to make its money by hook or by crook. (Napoleon would have approved. He once said: "The surest way to remain poor is to be an honest man.") Wards salespeople attempted to charge each customer the highest possible price for every television sold (price tags on each set were written using a code only employees could read). The company also practiced what it called "step-up selling,"

The second branch of Wards, the store that would become Circuit City. Beginning in the 1970s, its stock would outperform the U.S. market average by a factor of 18.5. (Photo from the documentary *A Tale of Two Cities: The Circuit City Story,* created by Tom Wulf. Used by permission.)

luring in customers with cheap offers and then attempting to move them to more expensive items in the store (more commonly referred to as "bait and switch"). Essentially, the store survived by extracting the most money possible from any poorly informed customer who happened to wander in. To this end, the salespeople were well rewarded for every bit of margin they could eke out, and Wurtzel paid a great deal of attention to hiring the best sales force he could, including, in a departure from the customs of the time in the American South, hiring and promoting African Americans.

At first, there was nothing particularly remarkable about Wards in terms of its financial performance. It was marginally profitable, and by the end of the 1950s had four stores in Richmond but had failed in its efforts to expand further. This changed when consumer electronics sales in the United States began to take off, exploding from about $2 billion in 1960 to more than $6 billion in 1970. Wurtzel's sales began to grow accordingly.

More than anything, Wurtzel wanted an empire. Demonstrating his shrewd negotiating skills, Wurtzel managed to hitch a ride on the discount store boom (Walmart, Kmart, and Target were all founded at this time). A deal with a members-only discount store allowed Wards to become the first electronics retailer in the country to expand outside its home city, and soon it went public. Its sales grew from $13 million in 1965 to $26 million by 1968, and that year, the company joined the American Stock Exchange. Along the way, Wurtzel made an ill-judged acquisition, a 120,000-square-foot Two Guys from Harrison discount outlet (on the basis of the name alone, he should have known it was a bad idea).

That was only the first misstep. Flush with cash from his public listing, Wurtzel began a program of conquest. He bought a Connecticut-based chain that sold hardware and housewares. He bought an audio equipment retailer based in Washington, D.C. He bought independent TV and appliance dealers across the Midwest. But like all empire builders, overstretch was his Achilles' heel. ("The great proof of madness is the disproportion of one's designs to one's means," Napoleon had warned, although he didn't really lead by example on this point.) Soon, Wurtzel had reached too far. Indianapolis would be his Russia. The chain he wanted to buy was owned by Joe Rothbard, president of the National Appliance and Television Merchandisers and something of a pillar of the industry. Taking over Rothbard's chain therefore had symbolic appeal. Wurtzel marched in and conquered, but, like Napoleon in Russia, after winning the battle, he didn't have a plan for getting out. Of his acquisitions, only the audio business was reliably profitable, and the Indianapolis stores he had bought from Rothbard were soon bleeding money.

In 1969, Wards made a profit of $700,000, a margin of about

1.8 percent. That was Wurtzel's best year. (Eight percent is the approximate average for major U.S. companies today, and in this book we will meet many individuals who have done, and are doing, much better than that.) These razor-thin margins left Wurtzel very exposed, and when the economy turned down in the early 1970s, the Wards retail empire was headed for bankruptcy. Fortunately, unlike Napoleon, Wurtzel didn't have many enemies. But managing his empire of acquisitions was proving an overwhelming challenge in itself, and his operation was soon losing money. Even though sales of consumer electronics were still booming, Wards was stumbling.

Napoleon, in a fit of hubris, appointed his infant son king of Rome. In 1972, Sam Wurtzel installed one of his own sons, Alan, as CEO of Wards. It was a better appointment than Napoleon's. Alan turned out to be a world-class manager. First, though, he needed to clean up his father's mess. By 1975, despite selling off some unprofitable operations, Wurtzel junior found he had so little ready cash that the company was on the verge of going bust. But rather than declaring bankruptcy, Alan Wurtzel was able to convince the banks to back a plan for restructuring.

Alan cleaned out the deadwood ("Let the path be open to talent," said Napoleon), and before long the company had new management, a strong strategic plan, and a changing corporate culture, but perhaps more importantly, Alan Wurtzel had stumbled across some wealth secrets—advantages that freed the company from the plague of competition, albeit only temporarily.

First, Wards joined the National Appliance and Television Merchandisers group, an industry association that enhanced the buying power of its members. In addition, the members had a tacit understanding that they would not expand into each other's territories. As a result, Wards (according to Alan Wurtzel himself) faced little serious competition, leading to sales tripling and profits rising from 2.2 percent to an almost respectable 3.4 percent between

1978 and 1984. Wurtzel also changed the name of the company, from Wards to Circuit City—in part because he had by this point established a successful chain of stores with this name; in part because Montgomery Ward laid claim to the Wards brand in most of the United States.

Then, in the early 1980s, the U.S. government largely stopped enforcing a 1936 antitrust law that prevented retailers from using their size to extract better deals from suppliers. This meant that if there were two rivals—equivalent in efficiency, appeal to customers, skill of managers, and so on—the larger retailer would tend to make more money. This decision helped usher in the world of cloned shopping areas that we know today; it was also a bonanza for the newly renamed Circuit City.

In the wake of the antitrust decision, the Wurtzels' unwieldy, outsized empire became a tool for levering profits out of suppliers' pockets and into theirs. Just as Napoleon had modernized France, the Wurtzels would modernize retail, bringing grand scale and computerized management systems to a sleepy industry of small chains and mom-and-pop stores. The cozy arrangements of the National Appliance and Television Merchandisers group fell apart as members raced to expand into each other's territories. The retail equivalent of the Holy Roman Empire was falling, and Circuit City was seizing the leftovers. The company's sales and profitability exploded. Between 1982 and 1997, Wards' shares outperformed the broader market by a factor of 18.5—the best performance of any Fortune 500 company in the United States.

Despite the exponential growth, there was a problem. It was a prosaic problem—one that afflicts even the greatest of great companies: by this point, observing Circuit City's success, competitors had entered the market. Electronics retailing was not simply for pimply-faced young men with thick glasses, a pallor brought on by too many hours spent under fluorescent lighting, and a tendency to drop words like "megahertz" into casual conversation. Because there was money in it, electronics retailing was also for slick, take-no-prisoners, hit-the-ground-running executive types.

And they—like the British Empire that warred against Napoleon—posed a real threat. If you face little competition, bad management isn't a problem, and the banks were happy to give Alan Wurtzel a second chance in the 1970s. If you face serious competition, there's no room for error. By 1990, many other electronics retailers—including Highland, Silo, and Best Buy—had gone public, copying Circuit City's hard-charging, rapid-expansion model. Circuit City was still the industry leader, with twice the sales of Silo and about four times the sales of most of the others. But there was trouble on the horizon. Circuit City's 1991 strategic plan—an internal document used by senior management and the board to agree on the company's overall direction—focused on archnemesis Good Guys, which had, as the plan noted, "proceeded to copy us across the board." By 1993, the strategic plan was mixing annoyance with praise (imitation is, after all, the sincerest form of flattery): "[Good Guys,] the class act among our competitors...had the temerity to enter Los Angeles, our largest, most successful, and most profitable market."

There were bigger problems to come. The first of these was Best Buy, which initially, like Good Guys, had attempted to copy Circuit City's model. But by the 1990s, Best Buy had improved on it. Best Buy's store layouts were more flexible, which proved useful as new categories of consumer electronics (the laptop, the smartphone, the tablet) came into being. In addition, Best Buy's salespeople were paid by the hour, and thus cheaper than Circuit City's commissioned salespeople. At first, Circuit City did not worry much about this low-cost threat, because Best Buy was not profitable. But in dismissing Best Buy for its poor margins, Circuit City was ignoring the lessons of its own history. Stock market investors were willing to fund unprofitable retail operations as long as they were growing fast, in the expectation that once they achieved scale they would become profitable. By the turn of the century, Circuit City was also being pummeled by Walmart.

The company responded sensibly, if predictably: it copied Best Buy, which was by then the new industry leader, hiring away Best Buy executives to replace its own managers in four key senior roles; replacing commissioned salespeople with cheaper employees paid by the hour; and rolling out new, more flexible and pared-down store formats. A new CEO, Philip Schoonover—another former Best Buy executive—oversaw the changes. ("One must change one's tactics every ten years if one wishes to retain one's superiority," said Napoleon.)

But it was too little, too late. Circuit City had fallen from its spot as the top U.S. electronics retailer to third place. In the following year, 2001, profits roughly halved, from $327 million to $155 million. In 2003, profits nosedived to $41 million, and by 2004, the company was showing a loss. It was heading for a fire sale.

As Circuit City traced a flaming arc toward bankruptcy, media pundits vented their fury on its new CEO. The *Wall Street Journal's* Herb Greenberg wrote that Schoonover was a likely candidate for his annual Worst CEO of the Year award. Shortly thereafter, *Bloomberg Businessweek* named Schoonover one of the twelve worst managers of 2008. That year, *Workforce Management* gave the humiliated CEO its inaugural Stupidus Maximus Award, honoring "the most ignorant, shortsighted and dumb workforce management practice of the year."

These criticisms were somewhat unfair to Schoonover, as I will make clear in a moment. Circuit City's troubles were quite possibly unsolvable long before Schoonover took on the CEO role. That said, he did make one notable blunder. As a cost-saving measure, one that could easily have been conjured by a man stroking a white cat, he fired all store employees making more than $18 an hour ($36,000 per year). The accompanying press release claimed they were "paid well above the market-based salary range for their role.

New associates will be hired for these positions and compensated at the current market range for the job." For readers lacking a business school (re)education, the notion that a salary of $36,000 was indulgent did not come naturally. Especially as Schoonover's own severance package, when it came, was $1.8 million (considerably better than being exiled to Elba).

And yet, by the time Schoonover fired the company's highest-paid retail employees, the writing was already on the wall.

WHY NO ONE IS GREAT FOR LONG

This was, in essence, Circuit City's problem: it had come up with some great ideas. These ideas were then copied by others, most religiously by Good Guys, but most effectively by Best Buy. And then new competitors, notably Walmart, seized on this moment of weakness to launch their own invasions. Circuit City's problem was, in a word, competition.

The media, of course, didn't see things this way. They blamed Schoonover. Circuit City's fall was both unexpected and, for most observers, inexplicable. The company had ranked 151st in the Fortune 500 only five years previously. Only two years before that, it had been one of only eleven companies lauded as "good to great" in Jim Collins's famed business book *From Good to Great: Why Some Companies Make the Leap . . . and Others Don't.*

It is worth dwelling on this latter point for a moment, as it illustrates the inexorable power of competition to take money from the pockets of the deserving rich. Circuit City's financial performance had been phenomenal, almost up to the moment of its collapse. Collins did not give out accolades easily; companies only made his "good to great" list if their share price had outperformed the broader stock market by at least three times. Many household-name companies, including 3M, Boeing, Coca-Cola, GE, Intel, Walmart, and Walt Disney, fell short of this standard. Collins also excluded from "greatness" any company whose performance might have been a fluke, for example any that had ridden the coattails of a booming industry. Companies that had failed to sustain their exceptional performance for at least fifteen years were also excluded. Out of 1,435 firms that appeared in the U.S. Fortune 500 lists between 1965 and 1995—already an elite group of the world's largest companies—only eleven met Collins's exacting performance criteria. And among this elite eleven, Circuit City was, by some measures, the best, given that—as noted above—its stock price had beaten the market by a factor of 18.5.

Collins's "great" appellation also certified that Circuit City had an exceptional corporate culture. Collins and his research team read and coded 6,000 articles and generated 2,000 pages of interview transcripts on the eleven "good to great" companies, as well as less successful peers. They identified factors that made these firms institutionally different from the others: corporate cultures that imposed discipline rather than requiring formal hierarchies, for example, and the ability to adopt necessary changes incrementally until these changes took on a momentum of their own, rather than attempting sudden transformations. Years later, Alan Wurtzel, the CEO of Circuit City at the time its performance accelerated, would write: "when I read *Good to Great*…I realized that these were brilliant metaphors [*sic*] for many of the policies my associates and I had followed in the course of building Circuit City."

Of course, no great company, not even one with an exceptional culture and management, can avoid *all* of fortune's arrows. Some are undone by disruptive changes. Kodak, for instance, famously fell victim to the replacement of film cameras with digital cameras. Blockbuster (which had contemplated a desperate bid for Circuit City) eventually collapsed as Americans stopped renting movies from stores and started renting them online. And yet, as far as anyone could see, there was no analogous external trigger for Circuit City's troubles. While the bankruptcy took place during the global financial crisis (the Wurtzels' Waterloo), Circuit City's decline had begun years before, in the early 2000s. There was no obvious reason for this performance implosion. As Circuit City's profits were collapsing between 2000 and 2004, the U.S. retail industry as a whole enjoyed a 12 percent inflation-adjusted increase in sales. Many of Circuit City's competitors—notably Best Buy—did just fine, and are still doing fine today. It is no wonder the media blamed Schoonover.

It turned out that Circuit City was not the only one of the eleven companies profiled by Collins to collapse (the other was Fannie Mae, which appears here in chapter 7). And Collins was far from the only business-book author to have such difficulties. Take the era-defining *In Search of Excellence,* by Tom Peters and Robert Waterman. Only two years after that book was published, nearly a third of the forty-three companies profiled were in financial distress.

The problem isn't that Collins, Peters, and Waterman picked the wrong companies. The problem is systemic.

Profits are an irresistible lure for competition, and competition results in the undermining of profitability. Indeed, the higher the profits a company reports, the more would-be imitators of its strategy and methods it is going to attract. These imitators will lure away a few key personnel with generous salaries, employ consultants to study the successful company's business model intensively, and generally attempt to imitate its techniques. And soon the company is not profitable anymore. The share price will plummet. The CEO will be turfed out unceremoniously. The people he considered close friends will no longer return his calls; his archrivals from high school will toast his downfall; his waterfront property in St. Barths—the modest ten-room villa with the infinity pool—will be put up for auction.

This may come as a surprise for noneconomists, but in the world of economic theory, it is not possible to get rich. In a perfectly competitive free market, profits are zero (or close to it, as I'll explain in a moment). That is, when firms can freely enter a market and imitate existing companies without restriction, the result is that businesses end up competing on price. This implies that they will keep undercutting each other until market prices have fallen to the point where companies are selling what they produce for the same amount it costs to produce it. If someone else enters the market, prices will fall yet further and everyone will start making losses. This situation will not last, because eventually someone will go bankrupt. Prices will then bounce back up to the cost of production again. It's a stable equilibrium. Over the long term, nobody makes any real profit at all. This might sound ridiculous as a description of the real world, but the difficulty of finding "great" companies that stay "great" suggests there's some truth in it.

I should note one caveat: when economists say "profit" they mean something slightly different from what the average business-person might mean. An economist's view of the cost of doing business takes into account *all* of a company's costs, including its cost of capital (not just costs of wages, production machinery, property and so on). Hence a "profit" for an economist indicates that a company is earning returns that exceed its cost of capital. Companies need to earn some kind of return—otherwise, no one would provide the funding needed to start the company in the first place. Hence the price at which companies in perfectly competitive markets end up selling will include just enough profit to attract investors and entre-preneurs. In a country like the United States, this implies that profit margins in the low single digits are not all that surprising. Profit margins well into the double digits, by contrast, usually indicate the existence of real, economic profits—the kind of profits that would impress an economist.

It is possible to find markets that embody this vision of perfect competition in many places around the world. In New York City, for instance, just east of Citi Field (home of the New York Mets), there is an area of about ten square blocks taken up entirely by auto-parts retail stores. On the West Side, the stores are run primarily by proprietors apparently of Central Asian, South Asian, or North African origin (New Pamir Muffler, Merah Auto Glass, Aryana Collision, Sultan Auto Body). Farther to the east, owners with Latin affiliations predominate (Colombia Auto Glass, Gonzales Muffler, New Pancho Auto Glass). There are also East Asians (Ming Repair Shop) represented, as well as any number of generic names (Sunrise Used Auto Parts, Union Muffler Shop, Best Auto Plaza Mufflers and Glass). There are so many, in fact, that it is difficult to keep an accurate count. At the time I attempted it, the number reached about sixty. With this many shops offering the same or similar goods in such close proximity, competition is fierce. That is why they are all clustered there, on that single plot of land: they fully intend to pound the heck out of each other (in a commercial sense). If there is any profit to be made, it is in the skill of salespeople eking out the maximum each customer is willing to pay—not unlike the early days of Wards.

Of course, Circuit City, at least during the boom years, was not

The nightmare of (perfect?) competition—more than fifty auto repair shops cluster next to one another near Citi Field in Queens, New York. (Sam Wilkin)

operating in such a world of perfect competition. Like most major retailers in the modern-day United States, it had a few wealth secrets on its side. For instance, it had a brand, protected by law (so no one else could legally open a store called Circuit City). This is an important wealth secret, as we shall discover in chapter 6. The company's 2001 strategic plan proclaimed — rhetorically but accurately — "nothing is more important than the Circuit City brand."

The company also had another crucial wealth secret. Once the U.S. government stopped enforcing the 1936 antitrust law that prevented retailers from using their size to extract discounts, Circuit City had scale economies on its side (that is, larger operations would be more lucrative). As we shall discover in chapter 3, under certain circumstances, scale economies can be exceptionally valuable to seekers of wealth. Circuit City's CEO in the mid-1980s, Richard Sharp, was quick to understand the implications of this regulatory shift. He decreed that henceforth the company would focus primarily on markets where it had or could build a dominant share (defined as not less than 15 percent of TV and appliance sales, and at least a 50 percent larger share than its nearest competitor). Sharp wrote that a "strong market penetration makes us more cost-effective.... This and other efficiencies permit us to keep our prices low while investing in additional customer services. The result is even better values and deeper market penetration... [that] allow us to achieve above average profitability." He noted that this was a virtuous cycle, which "underwrites its own reinforcement and perpetuation."

In other words, if Circuit City was dominant in a particular market, and therefore larger than rivals, its costs would be lower than those of its rivals (because it could use its size to extract greater discounts from suppliers). If its costs were lower, it would be able to set prices lower than the competition and still make money. These lower prices would, in turn, cause customers to abandon rivals and shop at Circuit City — which would further increase the company's market share, and thus its size, and thus its cost advantage. It was a self-reinforcing cycle that could, over time, produce a monopoly. And monopoly is, without question, the most exciting word in business.

FROM GREAT TO GONE

As an economist, I was not surprised that the Wurtzels fell on hard times. Nearly all great businesspeople suffer this fate, unless they have the kind of wealth secrets profiled in this book. Nor was I surprised when Circuit City started trying to copy Best Buy—exactly the right response, if a little unimaginative. I was, however, very surprised they went bankrupt. The company's scale should have been almost a *guarantee* of profitability. The same with their brand, built up over roughly three decades (more, if one counts the Wards heritage). Perhaps not much profitability—say, a percentage point or two of "economic" profits. But there is a big difference between a little profitability and bankruptcy. For a company in Circuit City's position to go bankrupt required something to go very, very wrong.

This surprising collapse is why business books do have something useful to say about the fall of Circuit City. That great businesses shall be dragged down to mediocrity is inevitable; that they shall fail catastrophically is not. Circuit City's descent into bankruptcy required clever, motivated, and competent people to make some fairly extreme mistakes. Jim Collins, in his well-timed 2009 follow-up book, *How the Mighty Fall*, blamed issues relating to corporate culture—hubris, undisciplined expansion, denial of risks. James Marcum, the Circuit City CEO who presided over the company's bankruptcy (after the firing of Schoonover), believed that word-of-mouth regarding poor service and the company's inability to keep items in stock had destroyed the value of its all-important brand. Alan Wurtzel, in his book *Good to Great to Gone*, which detailed the rise and fall of his own company, identified many culprits, including bad management, bad luck, and strategic mistakes. Former employees interviewed for the documentary *A Tale of Two Cities: The Circuit City Story* blamed strategic missteps such as halting appliance sales, as well as errors of financial management— most notably an exceptionally ill-timed share buyback.

Although many factors no doubt played a role, one identified by Wurtzel seems particularly crucial. When the company was in its phase of most rapid expansion in the 1980s, Wurtzel opened stores using long-term (twenty-year) leases, because twenty-year leases did not appear as liabilities on the balance sheet (due to a technicality of accounting regulations). Initially, when Circuit City faced little direct competition, that was not a problem. But when competitors showed up, with stores in slightly better locations (often because an area's demographics had shifted since Circuit City had built its stores), Circuit City needed to respond either by moving its stores, shutting down old stores and opening new ones, or upgrading its stores. Unfortunately, it could not get out of its long-term leases. Making the necessary changes could be accomplished only at great expense. As the company headed for trouble in the early 2000s, management faced up to this problem, and even came up with plausible plans to resolve it on numerous occasions—but always balked at the cost (one plan, which would have relocated two hundred stores and remodeled another four hundred, had a price tag of a whopping $2.1 billion). Once the company's results had declined to the point that it was at last willing to take the plunge, it was too late. Investors (and prospective buyers) had lost confidence in the company—a company that, unlike in the 1970s, faced merciless, ravenous competitors. Circuit City was, at that point, good only for scrap.

The ultimate problem, then, is not that Alan Wurtzel was not an extraordinary leader, or that the management team of Circuit City was not extraordinarily talented. The problem is that there is a huge number of extraordinary leaders and extraordinarily talented people in the world. And worse yet, in business one does not need to be as talented as the best performers in order to rival them. One needs only to be able to understand and copy what they have done. Did Best Buy have an extraordinary corporate culture and exceptional leadership that could match that of Circuit City? Was Best Buy a "great" company? Perhaps not. But it was good enough to get the job done. If Circuit City wanted to stay ahead of Best Buy (and other copycat competitors), it needed to think of a new, market-leading strategy or innovation every year — and roll it out just as soon as its rivals had copied the last one. Or it would need to do something so extraordinary that it could not be copied.

Most rich people probably believe they are geniuses, and that their wealth comes from this kind of persistent outperformance. I admit to being skeptical, but let us for a moment take such claims at face value. Let us say that you are a genius. Or better yet, that you could gather together the greatest group of geniuses ever assembled, and go into business with them. Would you then be able to trounce all comers? Would you be able to overcome the inexorable logic of competition?

Perhaps the boldest experiment ever undertaken in this regard involved a hedge fund by the name of Long-Term Capital Management. LTCM brought individuals with an almost unmatched track record in finance together with the world's greatest experts on the economics of financial markets. They did not have any wealth secrets — at least, not that I know of. That said, when most people think about making a lot of money, a hedge fund probably sounds like a good way to go about it. And it was, quite possibly, the largest start-up business in world history.

One might therefore have expected great things: billion-dollar fortunes, Ferraris, mansions, life-size replicas of the starship *Enterprise*, including a Seven of Nine blow-up doll (these were, after all, math geniuses).

And at first, things looked pretty good.

THE LARGEST START-UP IN HISTORY

Unlike Circuit City, LTCM was not "good to great"—it was just great, right from the word go. The fund was founded by John Meriwether, a successful self-made Wall Street executive from the South Side of Chicago. The fund's core group of partners were experts in quantitative finance drawn from the team Meriwether had managed at the investment bank Salomon Brothers, including Eric Rosenfeld, a former Harvard Business School professor; William Krasker, an economist with a PhD from MIT; Lawrence Hilibrand, with two MIT PhDs; and Victor Haghani, with a master's in finance. At Salomon, this team had been marvelously successful. They made $485 million in profits in 1990, $1.1 billion in 1991, and $1.4 billion in 1992. To put this figure in perspective, in the early 1990s, $1 billion was approximately the profit earned by the entire rest of the bank. That is, Meriwether's team of about 100 employees earned about $1 billion; the other 6,000 people employed in Salomon Brothers' client business earned about the same. This kind of thing could go to one's head.

Meriwether had left Salomon Brothers following a scandal over improper trading activity (not his) and a bruising turf battle with other banking executives. As well as recruiting many of his trusted Salomon colleagues to his new venture, Meriwether convinced two academics to join the fund: Myron Scholes, of Stanford, and Robert Merton, of Harvard. Far from being just any old academics, these two men were arguably the finest minds on earth when it came to the study of financial markets. A few years after joining the fund, they would go on to share the Nobel Prize in economics.

The team's spectacular track record, combined with the presence of the (future) Nobel laureates, made marketing easy. Meriwether's roadshow to pitch the fund to prospective investors hooked in banks, pension funds, CEOs, McKinsey partners, university endowments, government-owned financial institutions, and more. When it was all done, LTCM opened with $1.25 billion under management, a larger pool of start-up investment than at any previous hedge fund, and perhaps the largest capital base of any start-up in history. "Never has this much academic talent been given this much money to bet with," gushed *Businessweek*.

To be sure, the professors would not be directly involved in the fund's daily trading activities. But their theories would guide the fund's approach. In broad terms, these theories suggested that financial markets would become increasingly efficient over time, reflecting with greater and greater accuracy all available information. Prices in efficient financial markets can be thought of as statements about underlying economic realities, and thus prices even in very different markets (markets in different parts of the world, markets for different types of financial instruments) should, over time, become increasingly consistent with each other. Or so the theory predicted.

Reportedly, most of LTCM's trading strategies involved identifying some kind of disparity in market prices and betting, heavily, that this disparity would vanish (such trading strategies are typically known as "arbitrage" or "relative value" strategies). An early target was thirty-year U.S. treasury bonds, which are issued every six months. Sometimes the bonds that have been issued most recently pay a little less interest than those issued six months before. This disparity probably exists because the most recent bonds are traded most actively — and hence have greater appeal to investors who think they might need a financial instrument they can dump quickly to raise some cash. Over time, as newer bonds come onto the market, the differential between the bonds issued six months apart should vanish. It sounds complicated, but this was perhaps the simplest trade LTCM got involved in (these were, after all, geniuses). In 1994, when LTCM got its start, the differential was wide: bonds issued in February 1993 were trading at a yield of 7.36 percent, while the more actively traded bonds from August 1994 were yielding "only" 7.24 percent.

A tenth of a percentage point of interest would be negligible to most people (would you move your savings account for that?), and yet for LTCM it was a big opportunity, because the differential was almost guaranteed to vanish over time. It was as close to a sure thing as financial markets get.

Yet actually executing a trade that would take advantage of the disparity on U.S. treasury bonds was quite a challenge, which is why the gap persisted. Arranging the necessary combination of long and short trades wasn't hard; the problem was LTCM would make only about $16 on each $1,000 it put into the trade. Earning serious money would mean buying and selling a lot of bonds—like, say, $1 billion worth, which is just what LTCM did. Few investors had that kind of money. Even LTCM didn't have that kind of money (or rather, it did, but if it had used it, this one trade would have tied up the firm's entire capital).

Overcoming this problem involved executing the trade using other people's money, and finding a way to borrow this money almost without cost. Because the gap LTCM was targeting was only about a tenth of a percentage point, even a small interest cost relating to borrowed money would have made it unprofitable. This magic trick of costless borrowing was accomplished via the careful balancing of collateral from various transactions. Thus the geniuses at LTCM were innovative in many ways. They had come up with a new approach to identifying opportunities; they had invented new mechanisms to act on these opportunities; and they had developed financial models that could assess the risk associated with the resulting billions of dollars of complex exposures and determine whether it was worth it.

Initially, LTCM was all but alone in taking on this kind of trade, with this kind of scale. Within a few months, its trades on the tenth of a percentage point differential in U.S. treasury bonds had yielded $15 million for the fund. Indeed, most of LTCM's early trading strategies were astoundingly lucrative. In 1995, the fund earned a return of 59 percent. Investors, after paying LTCM's rather generous management fees, received 43 percent, a fairly spectacular return. Compare this to the profitability of Circuit City (usually less than 5 percent), and one understands why, despite the high fees, investors were falling over themselves to get involved.

That year, LTCM added an additional billion dollars in funds from new investors, bringing its capital under management to $3.6 billion. And it was just getting started. In 1996, LTCM delivered returns of 57 percent, or 41 percent after fees. The partners had invested much of their own money in the fund (some even borrowed money and invested this as well). Thus, as the fund went up in value, the partners were becoming very, very rich. Some bought sports cars; others left their wives, dyed their hair, or bought mansions. LTCM's total profits in 1996 of $2.1 billion exceeded those of McDonald's, Merrill Lynch, Disney, Xerox, American Express, and Nike. And these corporate titans were bested by LTCM's staff of fewer than one hundred people.

And yet, as a hedge fund, LTCM had one crucial vulnerability. That is, it could not directly execute its own transactions. To carry out its trades—buying long, selling short, making derivatives deals—it had to rely on investment banks. This was a big change from Meriwether's days running his arbitrage group at Salomon Brothers, which could execute all of its trades internally.

This was a vulnerability because when LTCM asked investment banks to carry out its trades, it was, in effect, telling them what it was doing. This was risky because, in addition to their client businesses, investment banks had trading arms (like Meriwether's group at Salomon Brothers). There was nothing to stop the banks' trading arms from then copying LTCM's underlying strategies. Hence every trade LTCM executed was, in a sense, a deal with the devil.

Indeed, LTCM faced similar threats from all sides. One eager investor during Meriwether's initial roadshow was PaineWebber.

As a fund management company, PaineWebber was, in a sense, a competitor to LTCM. One objective of its $100 million investment in LTCM was to gain access to new trading ideas. A number of the fund's other investors probably had the same plan. Needless to say, Meriwether kept his letters to investors, in which he described the fund's strategy and performance, as abstract as possible.

Overall, LTCM attempted to share as little information as was legally permissible. To this end, the fund parceled out its trades piecemeal among several banks. Where a complex set of balancing trades were required, it would approach a different bank to carry out each part, hoping to maintain the bankers' ignorance of its overall strategy. Most junk bond trades went to Goldman Sachs; most government bond trades went to J.P. Morgan; most mortgage trades went to Lehman Brothers; and Merrill Lynch got a lot of work in derivatives. "Larry [Hilibrand] would never talk about the strategy. He would just tell you what he wanted to do," recalled Kevin Dunleavy, a Merrill Lynch salesman. The banks, of course, objected, complaining about LTCM's lack of "transparency." But they typically went along. In part, it was good business; and in part, they were probably capable of deducing much of what was happening anyway. If LTCM was tying up $1 billion in a single trade, it stood to reason there was an offsetting trade somewhere.

One junior trader, interviewed after the collapse, recalled being perpetually worried that if the press found out about any of his trades, he would lose his job. Even LTCM's own employees were, as much as possible, kept in the dark—just in case one might be poached by a rival. Some Connecticut-based employees of the fund resorted to calling their London counterparts in an effort to discover what the firm was actually doing. There was even a social separation. Traders were reportedly never invited to partners' homes and were also excluded from most of the meetings where key decisions were made. Some later complained that partners refused to engage the trading staff even in polite conversation.

But even this rather extreme effort at secrecy was not enough. LTCM was making so much money that it was going to attract the best of the best as competitors—the kind of people who were not intimidated by little things like Nobel Prizes. The elite investment banks quickly jumped on the bandwagon. Goldman Sachs and Credit Suisse First Boston started their own arbitrage units. By the late 1990s, nearly every investment bank on Wall Street had an arbitrage desk. LTCM's success also inspired more direct imitators. Hedge funds using arbitrage strategies (usually referred to as "relative value" strategies) were, by the end of the 1990s, being set up "every week" according to one analyst following the sector. Indeed, by this point, hedge funds using relative value strategies reportedly accounted for about a quarter of the trading volume on the London stock market.

By 1997, this competition had started to bite. LTCM's returns were plummeting. The fund earned "only" 25 percent that year— 17 percent after fees. Not bad compared with most businesses, but less than half of what the fund had been making. The partners simply couldn't find the kinds of opportunities they wanted. As competitors piled into arbitrage trades, the price disparities that LTCM thrived on vanished quickly. By the end of the year, LTCM had decided to return about half of the money that outside investors had put in, whether the investors wanted it or not. "Everyone else was catching up to us," said LTCM partner Rosenfeld. "We'd go to put on a trade, but when we started to nibble, the opportunity would vanish." The fund handed back $2.7 billion it couldn't use.

FROM GOOD TO AVERAGE

Perhaps Meriwether's team of math geniuses and Nobel laureates *were*, in the early days, doing something so clever that no one else could even understand what they had done. But if so, it didn't last.

There are, as we've already observed, a lot of clever people in the world, and until someone finds a way to get rid of them, competition will remain a problem even for geniuses.

That LTCM was able to stay ahead of its competitors as long as it did owes a great deal to two relatively unique aspects of the hedge fund business. The first is leverage—the ability to use other people's money to amplify one's bets. Indeed, LTCM's combined bets, totaling some $2 trillion, were not far shy of a hundred times the amount of money actually in the fund. Unlike regulated financial institutions such as banks, the main constraint on the use of leverage is a fund's ability to convince others to extend credit at a reasonable price. But LTCM, in part due to its sterling reputation, was able to leverage itself to the hilt.

As a hedge fund, LTCM also enjoyed another advantage that is relatively unique to the hedge fund sector: secrecy. The big investors that are allowed to get involved with hedge funds are presumed to be sophisticated enough to look out for themselves. Hence hedge funds are required to report very little of what they do. As a result, Meriwether was wholly within his rights in keeping his investors in the dark about what he was doing with their money. Most companies have extensive reporting obligations—especially to their investors, but also to the government and, increasingly, to society at large. This applies to publicly traded corporations, of course, as well as to mutual funds, and is an obvious obstacle to secrecy. It was much easier for LTCM to keep secrets, at least for a time.

The combination of leverage and secrecy makes it possible, even without wealth secrets, to make real money in hedge funds. Secrecy implies the possibility of retaining a unique advantage, at least for a little while; and leverage means you can make (or lose) huge amounts of money quickly, so in that little while you can become a billionaire. Some of LTCM's partners were, at their peak, worth about half a billion dollars. And four of the hundred richest people on earth—George Soros, Ray Dalio, John Paulson, and James Simons—are hedge fund executives. Of course, four out of one hundred is not all that many; the far more lucrative question of where the other ninety-six fortunes come from is something I'll explore in later chapters. But still, starting a hedge fund is not a bad way to make a fortune.

Indeed, that was probably how the story should have ended: with some modest fortunes, followed by a slow ride into the sunset as the credits rolled. The most likely scenario was that LTCM's performance, after its spectacular early years, would drift gently back to earth. Fans of Daniel Kahneman will recognize this phenomenon as "regression to the mean." The mean performance of the hedge fund sector is approximately equivalent to the broader market return (according to many academic studies). In 1998, the Dow Jones Industrial Average returned about 16 percent. In 1997, LTCM's returns had been roughly that amount. In 1998, one might have expected more of the same.

But LTCM's performance did not regress to the mean. Instead, the fund's value fell catastrophically. Indeed, it lost so much money that it threatened to cause a global financial collapse.

The proximate cause of LTCM's demise was financial market turbulence triggered by Russia's 1998 debt default. In August 1998 alone, LTCM lost 45 percent of its value. On one particularly bad day, August 21, it hemorrhaged nearly half a billion dollars. And LTCM had used so much of other people's money to make its bets that, when these bets went sour, it was a realistic prospect that one or more Wall Street investment banks (which had, in effect, extended LTCM the credit it used) might collapse. Fortunately for them, the U.S. Federal Reserve stepped in to broker a rescue deal. Wall Street's investment banks agreed to take over LTCM and jointly manage its unwinding. There would be a fire sale here too — but not of LTCM's physical assets. Rather, the banks would arrange the sale of LTCM's investments and derivatives contracts. By 1998, LTCM had some 60,000 swaps positions on its trading books, so it was one of the messier fire sales in history.

I should emphasize that LTCM's investors, including its founding partners Meriwether, Rosenfeld, and Hilibrand, as well as the Nobel laureates, were not rescued. Their vast fortunes were largely wiped out. The U.S. Federal Reserve, when it stepped in to broker a deal, was not trying to rescue LTCM; it was trying to rescue the investment banks (which was very interesting, and the basis for a wealth secret, as we shall discover in chapter 4).

Why did LTCM implode so spectacularly? One explanation for the fund's collapse involved the efforts of the partners to continue to produce extraordinary returns in the face of rising competition. With their favorite trades no longer profitable once the investment banks knew about them, LTCM was forced to seek out price disparities in ever more esoteric markets. For instance, it reportedly plunged so heavily into the tiny market for commercial mortgage-backed securities that it caused the size of the market to double. At that scale, LTCM's trades were driving market prices, not responding to them. The fund also began to make some bets where theory could not help them. One such bet involved the share prices of companies that were contemplating a merger. These prices can be expected to converge *if* the merger goes forward, which has nothing to do with market efficiency. "This [type of] trade was by far the most controversial in our partnership," said Rosenfeld. "A lot of people felt we shouldn't be in the risk arb[itrage] business because it's so information sensitive and we weren't trying to trade in an information-sensitive way." Because the fund's bets were so large — as noted above, constituting some $2 trillion in theoretical exposure to loss — a few unwise trades such as this might have been enough to lose everything LTCM had and more.

These kinds of explanations are, however, a little unsatisfying. For one thing, although its exposure was huge, most of LTCM's trades were balanced against each other, so that the fund was—or at least should have been—exposed only to a very few, carefully selected types of risk. Moreover, it wasn't a few unwise trades that went wrong. In the fall of 1998, just about every trade LTCM had on seemed to go against them.

The LTCM partners offered their own explanation for what happened. They contended that other financial institutions—possibly the investment banks that had carried out LTCM's trades—knew where the fund had bet heavily, and thus where LTCM, once it got into trouble, could be forced to sell assets at an exceptionally low price. According to this explanation, the investment banks (or perhaps other hedge funds) were trying to force a fire sale. "It was as if there was someone out there with our exact portfolio," said Victor Haghani, an LTCM partner, "only it was three times as large as ours, and they were liquidating all at once." Meriwether agreed: "The few things we had on that the markets didn't know about came back quickly," he said. "It was the trades the markets knew we had on that caused us trouble." This explanation should also be taken with a grain of salt. The banks were by this point overseeing the salvage of LTCM, so if they had been squeezing the math whizzes, they would have been shooting themselves in the foot. However, LTCM's implosion was indeed spectacular—so spectacular that such conspiracy theories are not entirely implausible.

The next time around, the result would be more in line with expectations. Meriwether gathered together a few of his LTCM colleagues and started another hedge fund. After losing 44 percent of its value between September 2007 and February 2009, it was quietly closed down. That is the harsh reality of life in the absence of wealth secrets. One enters with a team of geniuses, two Nobel laureates, and not one but several revolutionary ideas. And within a few years, one quietly exits stage left, having earned next to nothing and seeded an entire sector of copycats.

WINNING THE WEALTH SECRET WAY

There are things that make companies (like Circuit City) great, and people (like LTCM's partners) great. And then there are things that make companies and people very, very rich. These aren't really the same thing, so it's time now to turn to the latter.

I have already alluded to a few wealth secrets, albeit modest ones. Circuit City found itself in the possession of a wealth secret—its scale—once the U.S. government stopped enforcing antitrust law in retail. And so the company built cheerful, identical red buildings with plug-shaped entrance halls all across America, crushing its mom-and-pop competition in the process. But only temporarily. Once its approach was copied by other companies—which also went public and used the funds to build thousands of identical shops in cheerful primary colors—it was no longer a source of profitability. A better wealth secret was Circuit City's brand, which was, and remains, uncopyable (a discount online retailer bought the rights to the brand in the fire sale). But even this wasn't enough to save the company from its own strategic mistakes.

Similarly, Long-Term Capital Management had wealth secrets of a sort. Its brilliance—or good luck, if you are a cynic—enabled it to do something that others found it hard to replicate. Together with the secrecy and leverage that are the privileges of the hedge fund sector, this brilliance (or luck) was a foundation for temporary, but extraordinary, success. But it wasn't really a wealth secret, and once it was copied, the fund's ingenious strategies became a vulnerability.

True wealth secrets have far more staying power than LTCM's great ideas or Circuit City's scale. While they are fundamentally sustainable, exploiting them to their full potential may well require genius—I leave that for you to judge, after reading the character studies that follow. The next chapter takes us back to ancient Rome and, appropriately enough, the story of a man who for a long time was believed to have been the richest person who had ever lived.

2

Wealth Secrets of the Ancient Romans

ROMAN BLING

The ancient Greeks gave us philosophy. Ancient Rome gave us debauchery. Ancient Roman accounts of their own behavior are so extraordinary that modern celebrations pale by comparison. Take, for example, this excerpt from Tacitus, written in about AD 100: "[The emperor Nero] had a raft constructed on Agrippa's pond, put the guests on board and set it in motion by other vessels towing it. These vessels glittered with gold and ivory. The rowers were all perverts, arranged according to age and special sexual skills." To cap off the ensuing orgy, the already married emperor then conducted an exhibitionist wedding ceremony complete with "dowry, a marriage bed, and ceremonial torches" in which he married a male friend (the emperor donned the bridal veil) and "everything was on show which is normally covered by night."

That was a good party, but there were better. A party thrown by the emperor Domitian makes the masked ball in *Eyes Wide Shut* look like Mary Poppins's tea party: "[Domitian] had a room prepared that was black everywhere, on the ceiling, the walls and the floor, with plain couches of the same color on the bare floorboards. Then he invited the guests in singly, at night, and unattended. And first he put beside each guest a grave-tablet with the guest's own name, and a little lamp of the sort placed in tombs. Then in came some pretty boys, naked and painted black, like phantoms, who moved around in a frightening dance, and then one stood at the feet of each guest." This kind of thing went on for some time, with additional death-themed details such as "things that are normally offered at sacrifices for the dead" passed around on black plates. The fact that Domitian was known for killing people on a whim can only have heightened the excitement.

Upon reaching home after the party's apparent conclusion, the guests no doubt heaved a great sigh of relief. Until: "just as each guest reached his home and had begun to breathe again, he was told that there was a message from Domitian Augustus. This time, while they were again expecting to die, someone brought in the guest's grave-tablet (made of silver), and then gradually others brought in different things, including the dinner dishes, which were very expensively made. And at the end came the boy who had been the 'ghost' of each guest, now cleaned and adorned. So after having been terrified for an entire night, the guests now received their gifts." What fun!

Of course, it was not just theatrical parties that interested the Romans. There was also money. The historian Suetonius, one of Tacitus's contemporaries, records that the emperor known as Caligula "burned so with the desire to handle money that often he would walk up and down upon heaps of coins, and wallow with his whole body among huge piles of gold pieces, strewn here and everywhere in a great open place." Suetonius also tells of the goings-on at the emperor Tiberius's holiday home on Capri, the ruins of which still stand today: "On retiring to Capri he devised a place for his secret orgies: teams of wantons of both sexes, selected as experts in deviant intercourse . . . copulated before him in triple

Romans in the Decadence of the Empire, by Thomas Couture (1847). As in many modern representations of ancient Rome, the Romans appear to be partying in a ruin. Where is all the bling? (Musée d'Orsay / Google Art Project. Licensed under public domain via Wikimedia Commons)

unions to excite his flagging passions. Its bedrooms were furnished with the most salacious paintings and sculptures, as well as with an erotic library, in case a performer should need an illustration of what was required.... He trained young men (whom he termed 'little fishes') to swim between his thighs when he went swimming and tease him with their licks and nibbles." (Suetonius has much more to say on this, but in deference to good taste I will stop there.)

To be sure, some details of these parties were probably based on rumor or outright fabrication. The most outlandish descriptions were, very likely, political propaganda, written in an effort to discredit the emperors as deviants. That said, there are many credible accounts of Rome's opulence. For instance, Pliny the Elder—generally seen as a stand-up guy—reports that Caligula's wife Lollia Paulina once attended a wedding banquet wearing "emeralds and pearls, which shone in alternate layers upon her head, in her hair, in her wreaths, in her ears, upon her neck, in her bracelets, and on her fingers," valued at 200,000 sesterces (something like $4.4 million today), and "she was prepared at once to prove the fact, by showing the receipts."

All this bling is a little out of keeping with our modern view of Rome: plain columns, high ceilings, white statues. But bear in mind that every ancient Roman space on view today has been systematically looted. This is true even of Pompeii, from which—happily but inconveniently for the historical record—probably as many as eight out of every ten people succeeded in escaping before the eruption, taking with them everything worth carrying. Prior to the looting, the Romans lived in a world if not perhaps of baroque splendor, then at least of copious shiny knickknacks. Rome's temples and the parlors of its superrich glittered marvelously in the light of oil lamps. The emperor Augustus alone records melting down eighty silver statues of himself—"on foot, on horseback, and standing in a chariot"—that were no longer wanted. Even so, the sheer scale of Rome's wealth can produce some cognitive dissonance. When the U.K.'s Mildenhall Treasure first came to light in the 1940s, some thought it a hoax, refusing to believe that such finely wrought silver could have been used in the relative backwater of Roman Britain. But more recent discoveries of buried Roman treasure, like the Hoxne Hoard (now in the British Museum), with its 15,000 gold and silver coins, have underlined that the Romans were as rich as they claimed, and great quantities of bling reached the farthest corners of the empire.

Indeed, economic historians now believe the Romans to have been truly rich—not just by the standards of the time, but in world history. Scholars have estimated that by around AD 1, the wealth of Rome's ten richest citizens had risen to about 100 million sesterces each, or roughly $2.2 billion today. That kind of fortune is a rare achievement in any era—and it's even rarer to see such fortunes gained simultaneously by so many people in the same period.

This is part of what makes Rome's decadence special and indeed exceptional. There have been many rich emperors and kings and czars throughout history. But the assets of supreme rulers are difficult to disentangle from the assets of the states they rule, and by definition, there can be only one supreme ruler at any one time. By contrast, many of the richest Romans were not kings or emperors but private citizens, and they were in constant competition to outdo one another with their displays of wealth. (Pliny the Elder is at pains to inform us that the wealth of Caligula's wife came not from imperial bequest, but from her father.)

Estimates of the wealth of Rome are based on both ancient accounts (like that of Pliny the Elder) and the archaeological record. One charming piece of evidence came from the "bread and circuses" that delighted the masses in the Colosseum, which regularly included exotic animals such as rhinoceroses. After Rome's empire went into serious decline, there were no more such entertainments. The next rhinoceros to appear in Europe would not arrive until some 1,000 years later, in AD 1515. Broader evidence of Roman wealth comes from commercial remains: archaeological evidence of mining and shipping activities indicates that more of both went on during the Roman era than during the Middle Ages. In short, the wealth of ancient Rome was unmatched in Europe for at least a millennium.

Of course, in the modern day, when it comes to knowing how rich someone is or was, what we really want is a figure in dollars. Attempts to convert Roman sesterces—a currency of the time—into modern cash equivalents are little more than educated guesswork. The goods you could buy with an ancient Roman sesterce (more slaves, fewer iPods) are difficult to compare to modern products and services. But a fortune on that scale was enough to purchase luxuries such as a vacation villa on the coast near Naples, an army of slaves—the average Roman senator is believed to have had some four hundred household slaves—a private zoo, a grand theater to delight the public, or some serious bling. I'll present dollar equivalents for Roman wealth in this chapter, but these are rough approximations.

An alternate approach to comparing wealth across the years is to value it in terms of labor. The World Bank economist Branko Milanovic adopts this approach in *The Haves and the Have-Nots*, his book on global income inequality. At these rarefied heights, the question is no longer "How can I keep up with the Joneses?" but rather, "How many of the Joneses can I employ?" This metric puts the richest Romans in truly exceptional historical company. The highest estimated fortunes of ancient Rome were those of senator Gnaeus Cornelius Lentulus (around 50 BC), and Narcissus, a freed slave (around AD 50). Each of these two could have used their fortunes to employ some 64,000 of their countrymen annually. Taking these estimates, and using a labor-based yardstick of wealth, one might plausibly claim the largest Roman fortunes were on a par with that of Bill Gates—currently America's richest man—who could, if he so chose, personally employ 75,000 American workers of average salary annually. These Roman fortunes are also comparable to the fortunes of Gilded Age America, when Andrew Carnegie could have employed 48,000 American workers of the time.

This is all well and good, but how did these rich Romans reach a standard of wealth that matches up (by some measures) to the greatest in history? How did ancient Rome produce not one but multiple personal fortunes simultaneously? How did Rome do this, without an industrial revolution, without mass education, and all the while relying on some—by modern standards—primitive technology? (Although, as we will see, not so primitive as one might expect.)

In short, how did the rich Romans get to be *so* rich?

To answer this question, I call upon Marcus Crassus, a larger-than-life Roman citizen. Crassus is an ideal choice because, throughout much of history, he was believed to be the richest man who ever lived. This was probably overstated. Indeed, Crassus was apparently not even the richest man in ancient Rome. As well as the aforementioned Lentulus and Narcissus, there were Marcus Antonius Pallus, a freed slave, whose fortune was estimated at 300 million sesterces, or $6.6 billion, and the emperor Octavian Augustus, who had an estimated 250 million sesterces, or $5.5 billion. By contrast, the fortune of Marcus Crassus was recorded at "only" 170 million sesterces (about $3.7 billion) by the Greek historian Plutarch, and slightly higher by Pliny the Elder.

Still, Crassus was rich. Taking a standard list of Roman prices, he could have purchased the following with that fortune: about 25 million haircuts (probably fairly utilitarian haircuts at that price), 250,000 pounds of fattened goose meat (goose was expensive), 1.9 million pints of excellent wine, between 30,000 and 60,000 slaves, about 100,000 statues of himself, or around 500 luxury villas.

Despite his great wealth, Crassus's reputation could use some rehabilitation. In ancient times, the Roman orator and statesman Cicero did a very effective job of character assassination. Roman history buffs will probably know Crassus best as the awkward third wheel in the Caesar-Pompey-Crassus triumvirate that reigned amid much splendid intrigue. In modern times, Crassus is usually cast as a brute. Followers of the 2010–2013 television series *Spartacus* will remember Crassus for his well-defined pectorals, odd grammar, and ill-fated taste in mistresses, rather than his genius at moneymaking.

But though he was better known for his other sins, Crassus was first and foremost a financial genius. Not only did he gain one of the largest fortunes in Roman history, but he did it using a wealth secret that would produce a generation of rich Romans—on average, some 400,000 times richer than their countrymen (the ten richest Greeks, by contrast, are estimated to have been "only" about 2,500 times richer than the average citizen of the period).

Yes, the Greeks gave us philosophy; but it was the Romans who had wealth secrets worth studying.

FISH SAUCE AND OIL LAMPS

Marcus Crassus was born rich, in about 115 BC, but it didn't last. When he was in his twenties his father, who had been governor of Spain, ended up on the wrong side of a dispute with the Roman consul Cinna. It is not certain how Crassus senior died, but we know it was unpleasant. Some say that he and Crassus's elder brother were executed; others that he committed suicide when his eldest son was murdered by Cinna's followers. Or, perhaps he killed his own son to save him from falling into the hands of Cinna, and was then killed himself. Whichever story one believes, Marcus Crassus suddenly found himself very much alone. He inherited his brother's wife (as was the custom of the time), as well as a fortune much smaller than he might have expected, after Cinna's coconspirators seized the rest. Crassus then fled back to Spain, perhaps to friends of his father. According to one ancient historian, he was reduced at one point—for many months and possibly even years—to hiding in a cave. Not a good start.

To understand just how bad it was, we need a bit of context. Crassus was probably keen to regain his fortune. He may also have thirsted for a bit of revenge. So what paths were open to a young Roman eager for economic advancement?

From a modern perspective, Roman commercial life was a combination of the profoundly exotic and the eerily familiar. On the exotic side was slavery. Oddly enough, while slaves in ancient Rome were at the bottom of the social ladder, they were not necessarily at the bottom of the economic ladder. Roman slavery was very different from our modern idea of slavery—and quite unlike slavery in the antebellum American South, or in colonial Brazil, for instance. Just how different is perhaps most effectively evidenced by documents surviving in the ruins of Pompeii. Among the ashes, many records were found referring to the government of Pompeii, the administration of which was—somewhat astonishingly to our modern views—headed by a "public slave." In Roman times, slaves could be owned not only by private citizens, but by public institutions, like cities or temples. One of these public slaves (official title *"slave of the colonists of the colonia Verneria Cornelia"*) charged with administering Pompeii's accounts was named Privatus; another, in office a few years later, was named Secundus. Both men feature prominently in receipts regarding government-owned properties, inscribed upon the peculiar three-copy sandwich boards that were used for official documents, and then buried under volcanic ash for nearly two thousand years.

It was not only lofty government jobs to which slaves could aspire. A great many positions that would today be considered "professional" or highly skilled—such as administrators of estates, copyists, readers (most ancient Romans were illiterate), business managers, and silversmiths—were held by slaves, who were sometimes educated to a high level. Roman slaves could be called upon to do such skilled and technical jobs because they had a strong incentive to work hard: freedom, a reward Roman citizens presumably granted only to their most diligent and obedient slaves. Newly liberated slaves would then customarily take as their family name that of their former master. These former slaves could do very well: not only were two of the largest recorded fortunes in Roman history obtained by the freed slaves Narcissus and Pallus, but in the town of Herculaneum, which was buried under volcanic ash like Pompeii, roughly half of the citizens are believed to have been former slaves.

Of course, even in exile Crassus was no slave. Hence he could have applied himself to the pursuit of success in the business sector (at some social risk, as Roman nobles tended to regard such activities with disdain). The business sector was the segment of the

Roman economy that might seem most familiar to modern readers. As today, it was filled with people eagerly striving to get ahead, succeeding briefly, being copied by their competitors, and slinking back into obscurity.

Despite the challenges involved in attempting to earn a vast fortune through commerce, Romans were keen on trying (in Pompeii, in front of one of the larger private buildings, one finds the prominent inscription "Welcome, profit"). Archaeological evidence and ancient historical writings reveal all manner of Roman commercial ventures, from banks to consumer-goods businesses to construction companies. For instance, also in the ruins of Pompeii are the remains of an elaborate fish sauce operation belonging to one Aulus Umbricius Scaurus and his family. Fish sauce, or *garum*, was evidently the most popular condiment of the day. Like ketchup for Americans, it went with everything. This sauce was made, roughly speaking, by putting some seafood and some salt in a vat and leaving it in the sun for a few months to rot. Unfortunately, or perhaps fortunately, *garum* has not survived in the modern Italian diet, so no one knows exactly what it tasted like. It sounds unappetizing, but fermented—which is to say, rotted—foods were much more popular before the invention of reliable cold storage.

The thing that made this sauce promising as a business proposition, though, was that Romans were willing to pay more for "good" rotted-fish sauce. As with the balsamic vinegar manufacturers of modern-day Modena, the person who created a better fish sauce would find the Roman world beating a path to his door. One of the best varieties was evidently made with pure mackerel, which does sound kind of tasty. Pliny the Elder writes that Pompeii was known for its top-quality fish sauce. The shop of Aulus Umbricius Scaurus in Pompeii housed many vats of fish sauce, branded at varying levels of quality from "best fish sauce" to "premium best fish sauce" and "absolutely the best fish sauce" (taking roughly the same branding approach used for gasoline today).

But the most interesting thing about the surviving fish sauce containers is that they suggest a miniature fish sauce empire: while some are from the factory of Scaurus himself, others are from operations run by two individuals called Aulus Umbricius Abascantus and Aulus Umbricius Agathopus, whose names indicate that they were freed slaves who had once been owned by Scaurus. It appears that they carried on working for Scaurus, going on to manage new production facilities as the business expanded.

While Scaurus's fish sauce business did not reach the scale needed to produce the fortune that Marcus Crassus would eventually gain, the evidence suggests that some Roman businesses, including consumer-products ventures, could reach a truly extraordinary scale (as we shall see in a moment). To manage such a commercial empire in the Roman era would have been a considerable challenge. Business owners faced what economists call a "principal-agent problem." Simply put, in an age when communication and transport took a huge amount of time, there was no way to ensure that if you put your employee in charge of a distant factory, she would not simply steal the assets. By the time the news reached you, months might have elapsed; and by the time your agents reached the scene of the crime, additional weeks. (By which time the thief would be living under a new identity in the tropics.)

According to economic historians, one way this problem was overcome was by using slaves. Slave owners had the absolute right to torture their slaves or indeed seize all their personal property at a whim; and furthermore, slaves were often working diligently to gain their freedom. This system, combining the tasty carrot of freedom with the nail-studded stick of torture, created powerful incentives for slaves to play fair. As a result, educated slaves were, ironically enough, a business owner's most trustworthy agents, and business transactions in far-flung locations were frequently entrusted to slaves rather than to employees or colleagues. There are a number of surviving records of slaves acting as agents for

business or government entities in major financial transactions—
for instance, the slave Phosphorus Lepidianus, in his capacity as a
government administrator, lent 94,000 sesterces (over $2 million)
to the bank of the Supicii in AD 51. In many cases, the top-
performing slaves of a business owner were freed and then put in
charge of a significant operation—as appears to have happened
at the fish sauce factories of Scaurus in Pompeii. It was a bit like
receiving a promotion.

Perhaps one of the largest such businesses, for which extensive
physical evidence survives, was in the oil lamps that were used
throughout the Roman Empire. Roman oil lamps were covered
oval terra-cotta bowls, about three to six inches long and two to
three inches wide, with a handle on the back and a wick at the
front. Despite their small size, a great many of the hundreds of
thousands that have been dug up (almost 90 percent in some locations) have a "brand name" marked on the bottom. More than
2,100 distinct "brands" have been found. Most of these brands are
confined to small geographical areas. But some are not—and these
are the interesting ones. For instance, one brand, Fortis—meaning
"strong"—is found throughout Italian archaeological sites in
vast numbers, as well as in numerous sites in modern Switzerland,
Germany, Hungary, Romania, Bulgaria, Spain, and even a couple
in North Africa. There are a few other brands, such as Atimeti,
Cresces ("You will become visible"), and Strobili, distributed
almost as widely and concentrated in similar areas. Luni Alexi, by
contrast, predominates in the south of the empire.

What is even more intriguing about these brands is that their
distribution is localized within these vast territories. That is, they
are clustered around certain locations, presumably where their
manufacture took place. And indeed, while the Fortis brand is generally believed to have originated in Italy, the first surviving Fortis
production molds to be found were located in the Roman province
of Pannonia, which stretched over what is now eastern Austria/

western Hungary. Unfortunately, no Roman historian wrote in detail about the Fortis business, but it sounds a lot like Scaurus's fish sauce venture, only on a grand scale. Rather than being manufactured in a single location, the Fortis lamps were, it appears, manufactured in several locations, but under the same brand name.

It is perhaps not too great a leap to link this structure with the pattern of Roman businesses where single enterprises had "branch operations" managed across great distances by slaves and freedmen beholden to the owner. No one knows for sure, but if the Fortis operation was, as it appears, a single business (as opposed to a number of separate enterprises "borrowing"—in modern terms, franchising—this famous brand), then it was a business on a scale that could have produced a substantial income. Fortis was, in a manner of speaking, one of the world's first multinational enterprises.

The problem, of course, with trying to make a fortune from lamps or fish sauce was the same problem that plagues would-be giants of commerce in the modern era (as we saw in chapter 1). Steal away one former slave from Pompeii's *garum* maker, and the secrets of "absolutely the best fish sauce" are yours for the taking. The maker of Fortis lamps sold a great many lamps, but profit on these lamps would have been harder to come by, as there were well over 1,000 other lamp brands to choose from—not to mention (presumably cheaper) generic "unsigned" lamps. Nonetheless, scholars have estimated from records of business accounts that incomes in some sectors could have reached 66,000 sesterces (over $1 million) or higher. Not bad—but not at the "über rich, wealth secret" level where we want to be.

The Roman economy was exceptionally sophisticated compared to other preindustrial economies. But this very sophistication was an obstacle to making serious money. About thirty years ago, historians generally thought that Rome's economy was state controlled, driven by a form of central planning. Today, some scholars argue that the Mediterranean economy of ancient Rome operated more or less as a single market. In particular, Peter Temin contends that prices of goods were fairly consistent throughout the empire, but—and this is crucial—adjusted for transport costs, which suggests either an extraordinarily enlightened dictator or, more likely, the operation of a vast, possibly well-integrated free market. While such a sweeping assertion is hard to prove, there is good evidence that transport costs in certain provinces (notably Egypt) were low, fostering movement of goods and people, and thus market competition.

Romans hoping to make a fast sesterce would have been greatly dismayed if this was true. The existence of such a well-functioning market would have implied that if one started charging too much for wheat, someone else would start importing wheat from the

Fortis oil lamps like these were probably the Roman Empire's most popular "brand." Produced in multiple locations and exported widely, they illuminate the commercial sophistication of ancient Rome. Some, like the one in the lampholder, from the Museum of London's "Roman kitchen" display, had simple decorations. (Photographs by Frederique Rapier)

nearest alternate location, and people would buy that instead. Or if a Roman lamp merchant started charging too much for the Fortis brand, he or she might find some of the other thousand lamp brands suddenly for sale at lower prices in neighboring streets. Likewise, Romans taking up positions as skilled laborers might find themselves in competition with hardworking slaves. In essence, a Roman businessperson might have found himself facing the nightmarish world of "perfect" competition outlined in chapter 1.

The great expansion of Mediterranean trade fostered by well-developed financial and legal structures may have made the Roman Empire rich, but it was a thorn in the side of any merchant hoping to corner a local market. If Marcus Crassus was going to rise above this aggravatingly efficient economy, he would need to do something different.

Fortunately, Crassus knew what to do. Crassus knew about politics.

CHECKS AND BALANCES

Abuse of political power to make a personal fortune was an ancient tradition by the time of the Romans. Tyrants had taxed their subjects, and grabbed the wealth of other tyrants, for thousands of years. The problem for Crassus was that Rome was sophisticated, well ordered, well run, and well protected. If Crassus was going to get into the giant piggy bank that was Rome, he was going to have to find a fracture, place a chisel, and hit that chisel very hard — repeatedly. Happily, when it came to moneymaking, Crassus was himself just such a blunt instrument.

The Roman Republic had in place an elaborate system of what we would today call "checks and balances." That is to say, the structure of Roman government was such that its various parts were placed in opposition to each other, effectively obstructing any single individual's attempt to make a grab for absolute control. One way this was done, for instance, was through term limits. The most powerful executive offices typically had term limits of a single year. The office of "mayor" of Pompeii, held by the son of the fish sauce merchant Scaurus, was limited to one year, as was the powerful office of tribune in the Roman capital. For the office of consul, not only was there a term limit of one year, but two consuls served simultaneously, and they had to agree with each other in order for a policy to be implemented. While a leader was in office, he was immune to prosecution. But after leaving office, he could be put on trial—and the death penalty was an option. Such penalties made it very difficult for anyone to win political office and then use that position to build a vast fortune by looting the Roman treasury.

These elaborate checks and balances also had the effect of preventing any single Roman politician from gaining too much power. But, of course, driven by the overwhelming need for wealth and status that motivates us all, Roman politicians had been worrying away at these obstacles for many years. Ultimately, Crassus was able to exploit a weak spot in the Roman political order that had been created by generations of power-hungry Romans who had hurled themselves against the machinery of the Roman state in an effort to increase their personal wealth.

The first to make a serious crack in the walls was a tribune named Tiberius Sempronius Gracchus, in 133 BC. His innovation was to bring the masses into politics. The Roman Republic was, of course, a democracy of sorts, but an intricate system of constraints prevented anyone from having any real power outside of a few thousand knights and, especially, two hundred senators. Gracchus came up with the idea for a program of land reform whereby the estates of Roman senators that had been won by military conquest and were above a certain size would be redistributed to relatively impoverished Roman citizens. This so-called reform was, in fact, already on the statute book but had been ignored by the senators (some of whom had been discreetly redistributing the lands won by conquest to themselves). Historians disagree about Gracchus's motives, but whatever they were, he had found a flaw in the checks-and-balances system. If he could distribute landholdings to thousands of Roman citizens, that would enable him to build a power base among the people unmatched by any of his fellow senators.

Whether they understood the risk from this power play of Gracchus's or simply did not want to give up their ill-gotten lands, the senators resisted this measure by all procedural means possible. Marcus Octavius, the tribune who served with Gracchus, vetoed the proposal. Not once, but three times. All that achieved was to slow Gracchus down: Gracchus impeached Octavius and then forcibly passed his reform. After Gracchus rolled out a few more procedural measures of similarly dubious legality (including a blatant attempt to ignore the term limit of his office, supported by an armed band of his followers entering the election hall), the other senators had had enough: taking up clubs, they joined together, attacked the chambers where Gracchus was holding a meeting, bludgeoned him and many of his followers to death, and then dumped the bodies in the Tiber River.

Despite this morbid ending, Gracchus had shown that mass support—particularly if motivated by the promise of a redistribution of land—could overcome Rome's carefully constructed political procedures. It was not losing a vote that did him in, but brute force (the final deed was reportedly accomplished with a chair leg). His "success" would inspire imitators. His imitators would, in turn, end up on the wrong end of the proverbial chair leg themselves. Two further proponents of land reform, including Gracchus's younger brother, were killed by hired assassins. Another was pelted to death by a mob wielding roof tiles.

The man who finally broke the elaborate system of checks and balances that upheld Rome's political order probably did so unintentionally. He was a general by the name of Gaius Marius. His fateful step was to remove the property qualification for Roman soldiers, in 104 BC. Up to this point, would-be members of Rome's fabled legions were required to own property. The foot soldiers of Rome were, in a sense, knights in miniature — landed gentlemen-warriors serving the glory of Rome rather than any particular lord or general. (Indeed, one of the checks and balances of ancient Rome was that generals were frequently rotated from legion to legion, to prevent any legion from becoming too loyal to a particular commander.) Marius's reform launched a process that would eventually end this system. With the land qualification removed, soldiers could be drawn from the vast masses of the poor, and motivated to fight by the promise of the spoils of victory. Marius first offered to reward any surviving veterans of his campaign with some of his own land if they fought for him. But an army so rewarded might no longer be a Roman army. It might be, in practice, Marius's army.

It is difficult to know whether Marius initially understood the political implications of what he had done. At the time, he was struggling to raise troops to fight in North Africa, and perhaps he got tired of waiting for the senate to find a solution to his personnel problems. But once he had returned victorious, and indeed rewarded his veterans with land, he realized that their support gave him an unprecedented power base. He was elected to seven terms as consul — five times in a row between 104 and 100 BC. This was more or less legitimate; but it was the presence of masses of well-trained military veterans owing allegiance to Marius that made it hard for the senators to vote against him. And there was a clear next logical step — a step soon taken by a politician named Lucius Cornelius Sulla.

Sulla, who himself had once been poor, understood better than most the motivating lure of money. (He was able to escape impoverishment only after a wealthy courtesan, perhaps motivated by his blue eyes and golden hair, left him a fortune in her will.) Sulla ended up in a bruising political battle with Marius over the right to command a military campaign in Greece. Having neither Marius's guile nor his political support in the form of his veterans, Sulla lost this contest, and the right of command was awarded to Marius by the senate.

Sulla's enraged response was to promise "his" army, poised to march on Greece, the rewards of the spoils of an alternate victory. He turned around his legions and marched on Rome itself, in 88 BC. This was in direct contravention of perhaps the most sacred political check of the Roman Republic: no general was permitted to enter Rome in command of an armed legion. All of Sulla's officers save one resigned in protest. But his foot soldiers, motivated by spoils both provided and promised, were willing to march. As they entered Rome, outraged citizens pelted them with roof tiles, in the account of some historians, and the troops responded with fire arrows. Eventually they reached the senate, where Sulla demanded that Marius and his supporters be declared outlaws. No doubt with one eye on Sulla's heavily armed legionaries, the senate voted as suggested. To further enrich his veterans, Sulla created new Roman colonies from which his soldiers could receive land.

Once Sulla had marched his legions on Rome, a great boundary had been crossed: major internal political conflicts could take place not just in the senate but also outside, backed by personal armies. Procedures such as senate votes and approval by tribunes were reduced to fig leaves covering the naked exercise of power. The machinery of the Roman state that had prevented any single individual from gaining too much power was not yet broken, but it was badly cracked. And so, by implication, were the checks and balances that protected the property of Rome and its elite.

Enter Marcus Crassus, armed with ambition great and terrible.

CRASSUS MAKES HIS FORTUNE

Though Sulla had triumphed by marching his "personal army" on Rome, his victory was short-lived. After Sulla had left the capital to take up the military command in Greece he had wanted so badly, Marius returned, this time backed by his own loyal legion and a personal battalion of armed slaves as well. He also took the further precaution of killing a number of Sulla's supporters— among them Crassus's father and brother. This was the point at which Marcus Crassus fled to Spain, where we left him earlier in the chapter. But he was only biding his time. Ancient historians disagree on the timing and sequence of what followed. Crassus may have used the remnants of his inheritance to recruit a personal army while in exile, or perhaps some money lent by friends of his father; he may have contemplated leading an assault against his family's killers in Rome; and he may have sought and then rejected alliances with other anti-Marius factions around the Mediterranean. In any event, Crassus eventually joined Sulla in Greece, and Sulla welcomed him to the cause.

By now it was clear to everyone that the rules of the political game had changed. The top political offices in Rome would not be ceded without a fight—so if Sulla wanted to return to power, it was going to take a civil war. There is little sign that Sulla hesitated. Crassus became one of his generals, invading Italy from Greece. For the first time in hundreds of years, Rome's legions would fight each other. It was such a violation of Roman codes of behavior that one legion, under Cinna, mutinied and killed its commander rather than fight. Others, however, obeyed. By 83 BC, an all-out civil war had been raging for about a year, and Sulla's forces were nearing victory. But then—in a portent of things to come—the Samnites, a tribe from central Italy that had been defeated by Rome some two hundred years earlier, decided to rise up and seize the now unde-fended Roman capital. The vanguard of Sulla's army raced back to

Rome, where it met the Samnite army still outside the city walls, and entered a pitched battle in front of the Colline Gate. This battle raged from noon until the evening, when Crassus's troops arrived. Overwhelmed and pinned against the city wall, the Samnite army was crushed and its leader killed.

This was Marcus Crassus's big break. After destroying the Samnites and seeing off the remainder of Marius's forces, Sulla entered Rome unopposed. Crassus had backed the winning side. From obscurity and exile he had catapulted himself to the highest echelons of political power. Most importantly, he had accomplished this at a time when the already strong link between power and money in ancient Rome was about to become much, much stronger.

Immediately after taking office as Rome's new dictator (an office hitherto reserved for military emergencies), Sulla introduced a new political tool that was both cruel and innovative, in an effort to punish his enemies. This tool also inadvertently provided Marcus Crassus with the chisel he would need to crack open the Roman piggy bank: a list of "proscriptions" of the enemies of the regime, posted in the Forum. To be proscribed meant that one was outlawed, and not only one's life but also one's fortune could be immediately seized without trial. Squads of soldiers hunted down the victims. Slaves and even family members of those proscribed were offered rewards to lead the death squads to their quarry.

The proscriptions brutally, and arbitrarily, wiped out a sizable portion of the Roman elite. After hundreds of years of Republican peace, this must have been a shock. The ancient historian Appian writes: "[Sulla] proscribed about 40 Senators and 1,600 knights.... Shortly afterwards he added the names of other Senators to the proscription. Some of these, taken unawares, were killed wherever they were caught....Others were dragged through the city and trampled on."

In theory, the victim's lost fortune would then end up in the

An eighteenth-century engraving by the Polish artist Silvestre David Mirys of Sulla's proscription list: one of history's blunter, but more effective, wealth secrets. (The Getty Internet Archive. Licensed under public domain via Wikimedia Commons)

Roman treasury, but in practice much of it found its way into the hands of the proscribers. The mechanism by which this was accomplished is unknown, but presumably the threat of additional proscriptions kept anyone from complaining too much. Naturally, Sulla and his allies did well, the new dictator receiving several choice villas and estates, and his wife Metella and their son also received numerous "gifts." About 120,000 of the legionaries who had fought for Sulla in the civil war received plots of land. But perhaps Marcus Crassus did best of all.

Crassus had been placed in charge of drawing up the proscription lists on Sulla's behalf. While others in this position might have felt burdened by the responsibility of consigning some of Rome's most prominent citizens to death, it seemed to make Crassus a little giddy. (To be fair, having lost his family to Marius's regime, Crassus may have been high on long-awaited revenge.)

At some point, Crassus stumbled into an important insight: he realized that Rome's checks and balances preserved not only the distribution of power among the elite, but also the distribution of property. With these legal protections undone by the new dictator, the wealth of Rome's greatest citizens was ripe for the taking. The proscription list was a vehicle not simply for the destruction of one's enemies, but for the seizure of their fortunes.

Proscriptions soon became Crassus's tool for amassing matchless wealth. The proscription lists were intended to destroy Sulla's enemies but eventually grew to include supporters of those enemies; and then supporters of those supporters; and then simply any rich person whose wealth Marcus Crassus coveted. Through manipulation of the proscription lists, Crassus apparently acquired what Greek historian Plutarch termed "numberless" mining operations, mostly silver mines in Spain. He also obtained a huge amount of real estate. In time, he got a little carried away. The last straw came, allegedly, when he added to the list the name of a millionaire (a billionaire, in today's money) who was no particular enemy of Sulla's—probably for the sole purpose of obtaining his wealth. This caused such scandal that Crassus had to be removed from his post. Indeed, one might well wonder why Crassus wasn't punished more severely. Presumably, Sulla, who was newly in power, wanted to sweep the incident under the rug and get on with being dictator.

And thus Crassus's fortune had been made. Plutarch famously wrote that Crassus gained his wealth through "fire and plunder." Proscriptions—and the process by which the assets released by proscription found their way into Crassus's hands—were his wealth secret.

In itself this did not, perhaps, make Crassus so different from others who had profited from proscriptions. What Crassus did next, though, was a departure. As mentioned earlier, most of Rome's nobility, like extremely posh people everywhere, turned up their noses at business dealings. But Crassus's new fortune appeared only to whet his appetite. He sought to make a further quick sesterce from a strategy that today one might term insider trading. Sulla announced that he would appoint three hundred individuals to the senate to replace those killed in the civil war. Presumably, given his hitherto close links with Sulla, Crassus would have had advance notice of this policy. Because all senators were required to own property in the Roman capital, new appointees who did not already own such property would have been required to immediately purchase it. Crassus had a great portfolio of properties ready to offer them when this happened, and the price of real estate in Rome duly soared. Along with silver mining, property speculation would form a central plank of Crassus's business ventures for years to come. Among his clients appear a number of famous names— including Cicero, to whom Crassus sold a villa for 3.5 million sesterces (about $77 million). It must have been a pretty nice villa.

After the proscriptions scandal, Crassus kept a low political profile for many years. Perhaps putting all those names on the list made him powerful enemies. Perhaps he focused on nurturing his fortune, via real estate speculation and mining. Perhaps he simply spent hours each day luxuriating in a bed piled high with gold and jewels or commissioning large statues of himself on horseback, as I would have done in his situation. During this period he did play a part in world history, by guaranteeing the debts of a young politician on the rise by the name of Julius Caesar. Eventually, Caesar would pay Crassus back by making him the first line of distribution for slaves captured in military operations abroad—not entirely unlike the modern-day practice of U.S. presidents rewarding their most generous campaign contributors with ambassadorial appointments. And Crassus made very good use of the slaves he received from Caesar. While most rich Romans were slave owners, the twist in Crassus's approach was that he educated his slaves and then offered them for hire. Crassus trained up an army of slaves as stewards, stable servants, metalworkers, bookkeepers, and scribes and then marketed their services in the city of Rome. By investing in their education he of course made them more valuable; indeed, some sources suggest that Crassus would buy slaves, educate them, and then sell them at higher prices (one of history's more literal illustrations of the phrase "human capital").

Marcus Crassus also reportedly had another, more unusual method of earning money from his slaves. Buildings in ancient Rome were built close together, and since Rome has a hot and dry climate, devastating fires were common. It was difficult to get enough water onto the fires to put them out, and so the main method of firefighting was to knock down adjacent buildings and hope that this would stop the fire from spreading. It is said that when a fire broke out in Rome, Crassus would approach the owners of nearby buildings and offer to buy these properties on the spot. Landlords, fearing the worst, would sell cheap. Only then would Crassus send in slaves trained in firefighting to save as many structures as they could. (This accounts for the "fire" portion of Plutarch's description of the sources of Crassus's money.)

Some modern historians suggest that Crassus sought to add to his fortune solely as a means to expanding his political power. While that probably overstates the case, wealth certainly gave him political influence. In 76 BC the tribune Cicinius attacked virtually every leader in the senate except Marcus Crassus. When asked why Crassus had been spared, Cicinius responded that "Crassus has hay on my horn," apparently some kind of Latin double entendre that has been interpreted to mean that he, like Caesar, was in debt to Crassus. Similarly, when an informant in testimony before the senate alleged that Crassus had been a member of a conspiracy against the government — and there was at least some circumstantial evidence to support his claim — the senators immediately declared this to be perjury, so that Crassus's innocence could be voted upon and confirmed. Which was surprising, given that many powerful men were put to death following allegations of their participation in the conspiracy. According to the Roman historian Sallust, though, Crassus's escape was made possible by the fact that so many senators were "obligated to him through private dealings."

More colorfully, Crassus was accused of sleeping with the vestal virgin Licinia. According to witnesses he had been spending a lot of time at her villa. Such a serious religious violation was punishable by death. However, Crassus cleverly used his reputation for avarice to argue that he was simply interested in purchasing the villa, and had been visiting frequently to argue the price down. He was acquitted of the charges.

Whether he was interested in power or simply in money for its own sake, Crassus was quite likely the richest Roman up to that point. It was, to be sure, possible to build a modest fortune in Rome by competing in the market economy. One could deftly rot "absolutely the best fish sauce," like Scaurus in Pompeii, or even mass-produce oil lamps on the scale of the empire-spanning Fortis brand. But the fish sauce merchant had to compete with mass-produced fish sauce from Spain, and there were more than a thousand oil lamp brands to choose from, not to mention generic unmarked lamps. Marcus Crassus's proscription list faced no such constraints. The money he took was his, not tied up in some business that was soon to face rising competition.

MEET THE PARTHIANS

Marcus Crassus was not the first Roman politician to exploit his office to make money; he just did it better than anyone had before. The other rich Romans whose fortunes I have mentioned were likewise political operators: Gnaeus Cornelius Lentulus, like Crassus, oversaw a list of proscriptions, while the former slaves Narcissus and Pallus both worked for the Roman emperor Claudius, who effectively outsourced the running of the empire to them—from which they profited mightily. In ancient Rome it was, to some degree, expected that holders of political office would use their positions as a means to get rich—in contrast to the tiresome public service ethos of the modern era.

Indeed, Roman politicians were required, after a fashion, to "buy" their offices. To gain the position of "mayor" of Pompeii, held by the fish sauce merchant's son, required not only winning an election but also a one-time payment of about 10,000 sesterces ($240,000). Officeholders were also expected to give generously to the community out of their personal funds. It is difficult to avoid the impression of a quid pro quo: you, the officeholder, may use your power to make yourself rich(er); but then the drinks are on you. What Scaurus's son gave the people of Pompeii is not known, but another mayor's gifts are recorded in detail on his tombstone. The first time he was elected he presented games in the Forum, including bullfighters, boxers, and a cabaret; the second time he was elected, he presented more games in the Forum, as well as gladiators and wild beasts in the Amphitheater; by the third time he was elected, some donor fatigue may have set in—the stone just says "Games with a first-rate troop and extra music." Crassus, as befit a man of his stature, apparently held great public feasts to which all citizens in the Roman capital were invited.

Even better than being a politician in Rome was being a Roman politician abroad. The governorship of foreign provinces offered scope for serious self-enrichment. Marcus Crassus's father had been governor of Spain; Crassus himself, following a decade of modest political activity, had his eye on Syria. One reason for this was that the ancient trading route from China to Europe, the Silk Road, flowed through Syria. The import-export duties that could be collected there would be immense.

Governing foreign provinces was good, but conquering them

was even better. Indeed, Roman political leaders were heavily incentivized to engage in foreign conquests, as they were allowed to keep much of the loot. They were entrepreneurs of violence, and the scale of the takings from a major campaign could be vast. For instance, returning from campaigns in the East, Pompey paid into the treasury 200 million sesterces (about $4.4 billion), distributed 100 million sesterces (about $2.2 billion) among his officers, and then divided among his soldiers a further 300 million sesterces (about $3.3 billion). That is, about 600 million sesterces ($10 billion) in total (making this campaign more lucrative, if a little riskier, than founding Twitter). The spoils from a single campaign of Caesar's are estimated at 600 to 1,750 million sesterces, or between $13.2 and $38.5 billion today—a volume of loot so staggering, in fact, that the price of gold in Rome fell by 25 percent following this campaign.

Conquest, though, is a brutal way to earn a living. It requires a different skill set than the subtlety and backstabbing of politics. It requires physical courage, an understanding of one's enemy, and deft command of battlefield tactics. Reportedly, none of these were Crassus's strong suits. Nonetheless, the idea of trying his hand at a bit of conquest became increasingly appealing to him. Perhaps the fact that there were so many other rich men in Rome made his own success seem less special; perhaps it seemed like easy money. When he gained the provincial governorship of Syria in 55 BC, he had no intention of merely sitting around collecting taxes. He had his eye fixed on a larger prize.

Matthew Canepa, a historian at the University of Minnesota, notes that when Marcus Crassus became governor of Syria, the Romans and the Parthians did not know each other well. The two expanding empires were just beginning to clash over territory, and there had been minor border skirmishes. The Parthians were seizing territory to the west and had only just begun to feel the pressure of Roman resistance. Meanwhile the Romans were expanding to the east and had not yet met any threat they could not handle. But that was about to change.

Even today, little is known about the economy of the Parthian Empire—and Crassus was probably even more in the dark. It is clear, though, that Parthian politics was very different from the variety practiced in Republican Rome. When the Persian god-king roars in the movie *300* that he is "the King of Kings," he means it literally. The Parthians generally left political structures intact when they took new territories, simply demanding that sitting kings pay homage to their new overlords (and usually introducing, through subterfuge or marriage, the Parthian bloodline into the local royalty). The greatest cities of the Parthian Empire were city-states founded hundreds of years before by the Greek commander Alexander the Great. The largest of these cities was Seleucia on the Tigris, home to an estimated 500,000 people, which would eventually become modern Baghdad in Iraq. But the Parthian king did not live there: he was a nomad, touring his vast domain with his army, often spending the hot summers in the highlands of what is modern Iran.

In the forested and hilly terrain of Europe, the Roman legions with their interlocking shields and siege engines reigned supreme. But the plains of Asia, where battles ranged fluidly across vast distances, suited the Parthian style of warfare far better—the Parthians were horse-lords, deploying mounted archers in great numbers. And the Romans, probing eastward for new territory, were unaware of this.

MARCUS CRASSUS TAKES PART IN A PLAY

For Crassus, venturing into the unknown was worth the risk. The Parthian Empire was an exceptional prize. If Crassus could add the loot from a great campaign to his vast fortune, he would stand head and shoulders above the other leaders of Rome. In addition he would be all but guaranteed a triumph—a formal victory procession through the streets of Rome—and the political capital that attended it.

The early days of Crassus's governorship in Syria were extremely promising. If the available accounts of his looting are to be believed, Crassus amassed cash and gold worth more than 240 million sesterces (about $5.3 billion) in about a year. He also gathered a great army—lured, as by then was the custom, with promises of personal reward—composed of seven legions, four thousand light infantry, and four thousand horsemen. (Crassus once famously remarked that unless a man was able to fund six legions out of his own pocket he could not be considered truly rich.)

In 53 BC, Crassus and his army crossed the Euphrates and set out to attack the Parthians. The historical accounts of what followed are somewhat confusing. Crassus may have set out with the intention of sacking Seleucia, knowing that the nomadic king of the Parthians was elsewhere. Some say he ignored the advice of his officers and was led astray by guileful locals, tiring his legionaries with an endless desert trek. But the Romans eventually met the Parthians on the open plains, near the town of Carrhae in modern Armenia. There was some sort of surprise involving the Parthians' armor—in one historian's account, the Parthians covered themselves in animal hides to appear as simple tribesmen and then charged the Roman lines, throwing off their cloaks as they did to reveal their gleaming mail. What is clear is that the Parthians had a great force of mounted archers, and that they had somehow arranged for these archers to be provided with an apparently unlimited supply of arrows.

These mounted archers would charge the Roman lines, release their arrows, wheel around before the legions could reach them, and then turn in their saddles and fire yet more arrows as they galloped away. The Roman cavalry failed to react effectively. Perhaps they were exhausted from the desert march, or perhaps they were undone by a feint maneuver that led them to charge after the Parthians, away from their own forces—whereupon they were impaled upon Parthian lances.

Either way, Marcus Crassus was in for the shock of his life. Like Napoleon in Russia, when things started to go wrong, he was a long way from home. The Roman defeat was total. It is said some twenty thousand Romans were killed on the battlefield, including Crassus's son, and ten thousand more were taken prisoner. Only a few thousand managed to escape to Carrhae and then back to Rome. Crassus himself, presumably protected by his elite commanders, survived this initial, brutal assault, although he apparently witnessed the sight of his son's head being mounted on a Parthian spear.

Crassus agreed to meet the Parthian commanders, perhaps because of an offer of battlefield parley. But there was some kind of misunderstanding, or possibly a trick. A scuffle broke out between the Roman and Parthian envoys, and Crassus was struck down dead.

He had gambled everything and lost, having come agonizingly close to the greatest of all prizes. Overreaching had been his downfall. Although ancient historians mostly ridiculed him for this blunder, some modern scholars have argued that if Crassus had been successful, he and not Caesar could have been Rome's first emperor. Schoolchildren thousands of years in the future would have learned of Marcus, not Julius. There would have been innumerable jewels carved in Crassus's image; statues of Crassus on horseback erected throughout the empire; and a modern pizza chain called "Little Crassus's." But of course, this was not to be.

There are a number of stories about the fate of his remains. One is that the Parthians poured molten gold down his throat to punish him for his avarice. But it was the Romans who were always pouring molten metal on people's heads, so this could well be a story manufactured by one of their own historians. A more plausible tale is that Crassus's severed head was sent to the court of the Parthian king, arriving just as an actor by the name of Jason of Tralles was performing a scene from the Greek playwright Euripides's somewhat miserable tragedy, *The Bacchae* (when the Parthians took the Greek city-states, they also discovered Greek high culture). Thinking quickly, Jason seized Crassus's severed head and incorporated it as a prop in one of the final scenes. Thus did Marcus Crassus's dreams of unparalleled glory and power die.

It was also quite possibly the end of Rome's attempts to seize the Parthian Empire. Once the few surviving members of Crassus's army had limped home, Rome knew that a new power had risen in the east. In the years to come, Roman generals, particularly Trajan, would undertake a great many border raids—some quite deep into Parthian-controlled territory—but arguably none with the intent of directly overthrowing the King of Kings.

And Marcus Crassus, far from becoming Rome's first emperor, would be vilified by history. He is largely remembered as venal, grasping, corrupt, opportunistic, and an incompetent military commander—this last perhaps somewhat unfairly, as no Roman, not even Caesar, ever succeeded in conquering Parthia. Indeed, right up to the end, he probably stood a reasonable chance of achieving the greatest political office humankind had ever known. But history is cruel to also-rans.

THE END OF EMPIRE

I was curious to see Marcus Crassus in person. He left little physical evidence of his passing. The Parthians, of course, didn't build him a tomb. But in the Louvre there is a bust that is said to be of Crassus, and another at the Ny Carlsberg Glyptotek in Copenhagen. He is not, in either portrayal, a sympathetic character. In the Louvre he is younger, his features thickset, with the large outturned ears of a wrestler. He is not fat—not like the busts of his contemporary,

Bust believed to be of Marcus Crassus, in the Musée du Louvre, Paris. (Rome101.com)

Pompey—but he does have prominent cheekbones, a large nose, and a thick brow that leaves his eyes in shadow. He looks like he would have been a large man (the root of his family name, *crass*, means "thick" or "heavy"). A brawler. Not a person to bump into in a dark alley.

His statue in Copenhagen reveals an older man, probably in his fifties, and so, we can presume, only short years away from his death at Parthian hands. His Adam's apple is flanked by sagging folds of flesh, his cheeks now droop slightly, and his large forehead has been creased by wrinkles. Whether due to age or the sculptor's eye, he looks thinner, more fragile. But his expression is still hard, his countenance no less set and determined, his eyes glaring. This bust is not regal, in the manner of the busts of Caesar; nor aloof, like those of Pompey; nor patrician, like the busts of Marius. Marcus Crassus does not stare grandly into the middle distance. He

looks back at the viewer with intensity of purpose. It is very difficult to imagine that face smiling.

And appropriately so. Marcus Crassus's ambition was too great
even for Rome's republic. The use of political power to build personal fortunes changed Roman politics. Indeed, the overuse of
Crassus's wealth secret arguably contributed to the collapse of the
republican system of government—ushering in the age of des-
potic emperors—and in time the fall of Rome. After the victory of
Sulla and Crassus, contests for term-limited political offices of the
Roman Republic were replaced by desperate struggles to defend
one's life and property. In the decades and centuries that followed
Crassus's exploits, many a Roman political leader backed by a private army would seize power and loot the estates of Rome's richest.
Thus their gains from winning office would be astronomical. But
for the losers in these contests, the losses were total. They forfeited
not simply the chance to hold political office but also, in many
cases, their lives and their property, and with them almost any
chance that their heirs would ever recover their social standing.
Formerly civilized Roman political contests turned bloody.

According to the political scientist Jeffrey Winters, from the
moment of Marius's reform to enable landless Romans to serve as
soldiers, the collapse of the prevailing political order in Rome was
all but assured. The checks and balances that stabilized Roman
politics had been undone. Crassus's exploitation of proscriptions
can only have added fuel to the fire. Roman leaders now had, in
effect, private armies of loyal followers and the ability to run rough-
shod over the property rights of even the empire's richest citizens.
This created a generation of very, very rich Romans; it was also a
recipe for repeated civil war.

The end of the republic, after Julius Caesar famously crossed
the Rubicon, appears to have bought more than a hundred years of
stability, in part by limiting the frequency of political contests. But
then, from about AD 180 on, even the emperors-for-life began to

lose their grip. There was either a civil war or an attempted coup nearly every decade. When the Vandals came to sack Rome, they arguably found much of their job done for them. The capital was distracted by incessant internal conflict, and thus vulnerable. It was an event foreshadowed by the Samnite uprising during that first civil war hundreds of years before.

I suppose there was some compensation: the best parties were held in the years leading up to the sacking of Rome. The perverted pool parties of Tiberius; the terror-theater of Domitian; the multimillion-dollar jewels worn by Caligula's wife—all these came after Crassus made his mark. It was also, not coincidentally, the era of Rome's most barbaric leaders. The emperor Caligula, for instance, reportedly enjoyed sawing political rivals in half. (Of course, both the parties and the cruelty were likely exaggerated. Political opponents would embellish these tales in an effort to discredit bad leaders. Political leaders would add their own exaggerations in an effort to dissuade coup plotters.)

Roman leaders after AD 180 could enjoy lives of the most extraordinary decadence, but at a cost: they ruled under constant threat of violent overthrow. They were born onto a treadmill, and had to run or die. One is reminded of the North Korean leader Kim Jong-un, who, according to Chinese media reports, not long after taking power, fed a disagreeable uncle to a pack of wild dogs (a story later officially denied by North Korean diplomats). Kim must either retain his absolute grip on power or be killed if his government falls. Under such circumstances, a reputation for sadism is highly desirable.

WHO MOVED MY CRASSUS?

Crassus may not have been the greatest battlefield commander, but it is not military secrets we seek. Rather, the life of Marcus Crassus illustrates a principle inherent in most wealth secrets, past and present: in a competitive market economy—*especially* in a competitive market economy—the way to get rich is to change the rules.

If Crassus could address the would-be billionaires of the modern day, he might say something like the following: "Politics is the path to riches (and business is the path to modest fortune)." (Although, when I attempted to contact him via my Ouija board, he said only "WHERESMYHEA" before the connection was broken.)

There are many in the modern day who appear to be listening to Crassus. Indeed, the somewhat blunt strategy he used to get rich is still in wide application. When a warlord deposes a sitting government and seizes control of an oil-rich African country, thereby gaining access to its oil revenues, he is following in Crassus's footsteps. For these individuals, the invention of Swiss bank accounts has been a blessing: even if you lose the next war, you can still hang on to assets held overseas rather than having them vanish in the inevitable proscriptions (or modern equivalent). In the oil-rich Republic of Congo, Pascal Lissouba and Denis Sassou Nguesso served as alternating rulers of the country, engaging in a succession of civil wars and spending the off years equably in exile in London or Paris.

A more subtle approach was taken in Russia in the late 1990s. When the Soviet Union ceased to exist, it was decided that the assets of the communist state would be redistributed into private hands. The men who would become Russia's "oligarchs" saw their chance. They maneuvered to seize these assets—much as Crassus seized the assets that had been released by proscriptions (which were, in theory, assets of the Roman state). The oligarchs, no fools, understood that, as a result of the lack of legal protections in post–Soviet Russia, what they had done could in turn be done to them, and therefore shipped much of their wealth offshore for safekeeping—thus contributing to a near 50 percent contraction in the Russian economy in only a few years (we'll see more of the oligarchs in chapter 7).

Whether applied bluntly or with subtlety, Crassus's wealth secret is a risky one. Taking property, by legal proscriptions or by force of arms, inspires determined opposition. Not long ago, Mark Thatcher, the son of former U.K. prime minister Margaret, banded together with some friends and had a go at overthrowing the government of tiny, oil-rich Equatorial Guinea (at least according to the leader of the plot, Simon Mann). Thatcher was arrested, convicted of aiding the attempted coup, and spent some time in a South African jail for his trouble. Had he been extradited to Equatorial Guinea—which at one point appeared possible—his circumstances could have become decidedly unpleasant. The Russian oligarch Mikhail Khodorkovsky was not so lucky. Rather than fleeing with his assets into exile, he appears to have made an attempt to gain political office in Russia. Like Crassus's bid for Parthia, this was a risk too far. It could have paid off. Khodorkovsky could have been the next Russian premier, with all but unlimited control of Russia's still-vast wealth (not all of Russia's money has been relocated to Cyprus or Mayfair). Instead, Khodorkovsky spent many years in a Siberian prison until his recent release into exile. He was accused of corrupt dealings but seen by many to be, in effect, a political prisoner.

For would-be billionaires of the modern era, I am happy to report that there are better ways to fulfill your dreams. And there is no need to risk African jail time or the Russian gulag. In the next chapter, we will uncover a wealth secret that would have been recognizable even to Crassus, but which was applied most brilliantly in the turn-of-the-century United States. The underlying strategy employed is the basis of nearly all great fortunes of the modern era. Indeed, this wealth secret gave rise to the greatest fortune ever possessed by an American—a fortune that puts the opulence achieved by even Bill Gates firmly in the shade.

3

Wealth Secrets of the Robber Barons

THE SUPERYACHT

John Pierpont Morgan (hereafter Pierpont Morgan, to distinguish him from his bank, J.P. Morgan) cut a larger-than-life figure. He stood more than six feet tall, weighed over two hundred pounds, and suffered a permanent skin condition that so disfigured his nose that a Russian finance minister advised him to have it surgically corrected. England's Queen Alexandra recommended a treatment involving electric shocks (which Morgan did try, but to no effect). Today the condition would be treated with lasers. Morgan's portrait photographer Edward Steichen called the nose a "sick, bulbous mass in the center of his face," and retouched the photographs. A children's rhyme of the day included the line "Johnny Morgan's nasal organ has a purple hue." More charitably, a mistress said, "One forgets his nose entirely after a few minutes." Morgan also had a walrus mustache, wore a top hat, carried a mahogany cane, and chain-smoked Cuban cigars (when he was seventy years old, his doctor demanded that he *reduce* consumption to twenty per day).

Pierpont Morgan became, if not a head of state, the uncrowned king of American finance. The kaiser sent a life-size bust as a gift (this was wisely misplaced in 1914). England's King Edward VII stopped by Morgan's London pied-à-terre for iced coffee and was reportedly impressed, although he felt the setting too cramped to display Morgan's vast personal art collection (Rembrandt, Van Dyck, Gainsborough) to good effect. After meeting Morgan in 1905, Pope Pius X noted with regret: "What a pity I did not think of asking Mr. Morgan to give us some advice about our finances!" When, years later, Morgan's reputation was besmirched, Joseph Stalin took it upon himself to defend the man: "We Soviet people learn a great deal from the capitalists....Morgan, whom you characterize so unfavorably, was undoubtedly a good, capable organizer."

Morgan's first yacht was the *Corsair*. At the time of its construction in 1882, it was the largest and most advanced yacht in the United States, combining steam power with schooner rigging and a hull of iron (later models — there were two more in Morgan's lifetime — were made of steel). It was built for speed and looked the part, with a low profile, gleaming black hull, clipper bow, and raked-back smokestacks. The main saloon had black-and-gold silk upholstery and a tiled fireplace. Within nine years, Morgan had outgrown it. He commissioned a second, larger *Corsair* weighing 560 tons with eight staterooms, oak paneling, and dark green upholstery. Each room had a working fireplace, sponge hooks in the bathrooms, and a nook by the bed on which to place one's watch at night. Its length was limited to 241 feet by Morgan's requirement that it be able to turn around in the Hudson River below his weekend home, Cragston. Outfitted with cannon, it blockaded and destroyed a Spanish fleet at Santiago Harbor during the Spanish-American War (with the help of two other American ships), although a mast was damaged by a Spanish shell. Morgan promptly commissioned another *Corsair*, larger still. This one had maple paneling, a library the width of the hull, a player piano, leather portfolios filled with "Corsair" stationery, silver-backed hairbrushes, pearl-handled fruit knives, gold spoons, eighty-four linen tablecloths, forty-seven finger bowls, and one cocktail shaker marked "JPM." It also eventually saw service in the U.S. Navy, during both world wars. Meanwhile, Morgan's London getaway had been acquired by the U.S. government and pressed into service as the U.S. embassy in Great Britain.

Pierpont Morgan was, in all respects, a big man. Rumors of his ill health caused the U.S. stock market to slump. And yet, he is in a sense an odd choice as our "wealth secret" representative of the U.S. capitalists known today as the robber barons (Morgan, Carnegie, Rockefeller, Gould, Vanderbilt). Morgan's fortune was large: at his death, his estate was valued at roughly $80 million (about $1.9 billion today). But by the standards of the robber barons, who achieved levels of opulence hitherto unmatched in history—eclipsing even the ancient Romans—this was small potatoes. "And to think, he was not a rich man," said Andrew Carnegie, hearing of this figure upon Morgan's death. Carnegie's fortune was, at its peak, $240 million (about $6.8 billion today).

And yet, in another respect, Morgan was the quintessential robber baron. He despised competition, and worked relentlessly to prevent it from happening. "Ruinous competition," he called it, "wasteful rivalry," or "competitive skulduggery." Of course, most right-thinking businesspeople hate competition, as it is what prevents them from getting richer. John D. Rockefeller, the wealthiest of all the robber barons, wrote in his autobiography: "the one thing which...a business philosopher would be most careful to avoid... is the unnecessary duplication of existing industries. He would regard all money spent in increasing competition as wasted, and worse. The man who puts up a second factory when the factory in existence will supply the public demand...[is] unnecessarily introducing heartache and misery into the world."

Truer words were never spoken, but the question is *how* to prevent anyone from building a second factory, when the first factory is spectacularly lucrative and indeed its owner is well on his way to becoming the wealthiest person in history. This is the question that Morgan, more than any of the other robber barons, was able to answer, and as a result a few Americans became fabulously rich. Indeed, without Morgan's assistance, Andrew Carnegie may well have been unable to secure his fortune.

Moreover, Pierpont Morgan showed that, if one has a wealth secret, there is no need to work particularly hard. He seemed to spend about half of his life on holiday, and still made a billion dollars (in today's money). Indeed, he lingered so long vacationing in France that the town of Aix-les-Bains named one of its streets after him.

Now that is a wealth secret I can relate to.

AMERICA RISING

A modern executive, traveling back in time to study Rockefeller's wealth secrets at the great man's knee, would—assuming she could avoid the usual pitfalls of entering the wrong date in her time machine or being hunted by Bruce Willis—have found commercial life in the United States of the 1800s tremendously frustrating. While the robber barons would change the face of American commerce into something our executive might recognize, before their rise, American business, and the American rich, would have seemed a different breed.

There was, to be sure, a thriving market capitalism. But America was a long way from becoming an industrial powerhouse. Most manufacturing was concentrated in the North, while the economy of the South was driven by plantations and hence slave labor (the Civil War would erupt in 1861). Unlike Roman slavery, of course, there was almost no chance of upward economic mobility for

American slaves. There were railroads, but these local, point-to-point lines generally used different track sizes so that direct interconnection was impossible. Train engines and cars were routinely ferried across rivers because building bridges was too expensive. There were no motorcars, nor of course airplanes, so the rich traveled by rail (and the very rich, by private rail carriage or personal yacht). Wall Street was already the nation's center of finance, and traders there bought and sold bonds and shares. At first, they conducted their business standing out on the street itself, but eventually moved indoors.

Our time-traveling executive would have found the monetary system particularly jarring. In the early 1800s, the federal government issued gold and silver coins, but all paper money was issued by banks, only as reliable as the bank that issued it and generally usable only in the locality surrounding the bank. There were some seven thousand different kinds of banknotes in circulation, with no centralized regulation and, naturally, rampant counterfeiting. This would change during the Civil War, when the government of the North began to issue paper currency backed by a law that required debtors to accept it. As these notes were written in green ink, they came to be known as "greenbacks," a nickname for the U.S. dollar to this day. When the North eventually won the war, the system went national.

The development of a national paper currency was a distinct improvement. But there was little sign of progress on another horizon: hardly anyone in business was making any money. Taking time off from searching for a method to power a flux capacitor, our time traveler might have tried her hand at a little commerce, but conditions for most businesses were worse even than those described in chapter 1. Circuit City at least made a decent sum before being dragged back to earth. The same with LTCM. In the 1800s, by contrast, most businesses faced conditions approximating perfect competition, and had little leverage. As a result, individual proprietors had to work for decades just to pay themselves a living wage. U.S. industry and agriculture were dominated by what the trade unionist Samuel Gompers called "small, ruinously competitive companies." Really, it was horrible.

Indeed, the only large businesses to speak of were in infrastructure. As late as 1884, when the Dow Jones company first began to print its stock market average, nearly all of the stocks in the index were railroads. The few others were telegraph and steamship companies, and there was not much else worth including beyond that. In 1899, the ten largest railroads each had a market value of more than $100 million (about $2.9 billion today), but outside the rail sector even the biggest companies were comparative minnows. Indeed there were few industrial companies valued at more than $10 million. Manufacturing was apparently the wrong sector in which to hunt for wealth secrets.

That said, Britain had undergone its industrial revolution, and the United States was following, initially by stealing British technologies—most notably spinning and power loom designs, which spurred the growth of textile mills. By the mid-1800s, this young country was leading the world in some areas of innovation. In particular, it excelled at inventions that enabled the replacement of skilled manual labor with unskilled workers, which was politically difficult in Europe, with its long tradition of guilds.

Our time traveler, hoping to escape the plague of competition, would have been drawn to such developments. The patent laws that encouraged these innovations protected business inventors from imitation, so patent owners fared far better than most small proprietors of the day. Yet their earnings never matched those of the robber barons. The greatest of the inventors, Thomas Edison, created not only the first reliable electric lightbulb but also the telephone, record player, and motion picture projector—registering 1,093 patents, an average of one every two weeks, over a forty-year period. He did very well for himself, but never quite made the rich list, probably in part because he did not seem to care about money.

However, many of the companies that would later come to dominate the U.S. economy acquired patents from men such as Edison, and used them as tools to fend off competition. Indeed, some scholars have argued that these patent laws enabled the concentration of U.S. industry that took place during the last two decades of the 1800s. (And in recent years, patents have evolved into a crucial wealth secret, as we shall discover in chapter 6.)

But our executive from the future would be dismayed to find that, in the early 1800s, most rich individuals were not inventors or industrialists, but landowners (and, in the South, slaveholders). How dull! Fortunately, in a country whose borders were rapidly expanding at the expense of Native Americans, there was also a great deal of money to be made in the acquisition of "new" land. America's first president, George Washington, owned sixty-five thousand acres in thirty-seven different locations, and was thus at the time very likely the country's richest man (it seems appropriate that America's first political leader should also have been a master of wealth secrets). Even in bustling 1800s New York, elite society would have seemed, to a businessperson who had become unstuck in time, astonishingly feudal in character. The city's richest families—the Morrises, Bayards, Livingstons, Van Rensselaers, Beekmans—were landed gentry, owning large estates along the Hudson River that were worked by tenant farmers. (After 1862, the situation became rather more democratic, as the U.S. government distributed over a billion acres of "public" land—not to mention the associated oil and mineral rights—via the Homestead Act.)

America's early economic elite were not only estate owners; they also, in many cases, enjoyed government-granted monopolies (again, not so very different from the feudal Europe they had left behind). This system was partly a holdover from colonial times. But as far as wealth secrets went, it was probably the most exciting thing going, and our executive would have been very intrigued. In the early 1600s, for example, the English crown had awarded Sir Ferdinando Gorges a monopoly over fishing rights in New England, although protests from the colonists prevented it from being enforced. Efforts to enforce a monopoly covering the processing of salt, for the son of the governor of the Massachusetts Bay Colony, were more successful. In the early 1800s, the patriarch of the Livingston family (one of New York's semifeudal elites) obtained, via acquisition, a monopoly over all steamboat traffic in New York that was enshrined in state law. This was fabulously lucrative: in 1818, his profits from operating steamboats were $61,861 ($1.2 million today) on revenues of $153,694 ($2.9 million)—a 40 percent profit margin. This was on par with investing in LTCM, but without the market risk. The achievement was perhaps matched only by that of the Stevens family, who obtained a monopoly over rail travel in the state of New Jersey in the 1830s. In this instance, however, there was at least the pretense that this monopoly was something more than a gift to the well-connected Stevenses. The rail monopoly was held not by the Stevens family, but by a corporation—the Camden & Amboy Railroad—that had publicly traded shares. And the purpose of the monopoly was, in theory, to incentivize the development of desperately needed infrastructure (the monopoly rights attracted investors by all but guaranteeing a substantial financial reward). That said, the legislation was unambiguous in its generosity, establishing that "it shall not be lawful...to construct any other railroad or railroads in this State, without the consent of said companies"—the "said companies" being the Camden & Amboy.

The reason for this pretense was that the political climate in the United States was becoming increasingly hostile to the idea of government-awarded monopolies. In 1776, the laws of the newly independent state of Connecticut railed theatrically against "monopolizers, the great pest of society, who prefer their own private gain to the interest and safety of the country, and which if not prevented threaten the ruin and destruction of the state." The laws of Massachusetts included an "Act to Prevent Monopoly and Oppression."

Despite the rising hostility toward monopolies, there were a few individuals who soldiered on, using political connections and government-awarded monopolies to make their fortunes. Those who succeeded in these efforts have since come to be known as "political entrepreneurs." Like the patent holders, their fortunes would not really compare to those achieved by the robber barons. But one or two political entrepreneurs achieved a fame that persists in the modern day.

One example is Leland Stanford, founder of California's Stanford University. The young United States was eager to promote the development of infrastructure to connect the country's fast-expanding territory. To encourage the construction of transport networks crossing state lines, the federal government offered subsidies and land. For instance, hoping to foster the creation of a transcontinental railroad, Congress passed the Pacific Railroad Act, which offered railroad builders ten square miles of land—and loans—for each mile of track they constructed. The two groups that took up the offer were the Union Pacific, building west from Nebraska, and the Central Pacific, building east from California, and both had bribed Congress extensively to obtain the legislation (one railroad director had traveled east with some $100,000 in railroad stock to distribute to congressmen). The law's passage set off a desperate and famous race between the two groups. In a sense, the legislation achieved its objective. Never was there a more eager attempt to lay track miles, since whoever laid the greatest number would obtain the most land and the most loans.

In another sense, the legislation was a disaster. The railroads were, in effect, incentivized to take circuitous routes to increase the track miles laid and to use the cheapest materials possible (even after the lines were "completed," rebuilding them properly would take years). The railroad builders, flush with government support, also had a limited incentive to focus on financial stability. At the time, conflicts of interest were common, and the officers of the railroads created their own supply companies and bought materials from these companies at vastly inflated prices. For instance, six officers of the Union Pacific railroad created the Wyoming Coal and Mining Company, mined coal for between $1.10 and $2.00 per ton, and then had their railroad buy the coal at $6.00 per ton. Leland Stanford, leader of the Central Pacific Consortium, managed to win election to the governorship of California on the basis of his railroad and staunch anti-immigrant platform (his brother helped by handing out gold coins to voters). Stanford then set about obtaining an additional $15 million in loans from the California legislature, after which both consortia returned to Congress to demand yet more land.

When all was said and done, the two railroads had received forty-four million acres in free land and $61 million in loans from the U.S. government, and yet both were almost bankrupt. "I never saw so much needless waste in building railroads," admitted Union Pacific's chief engineer. This inefficiency made a number of individuals very wealthy, but perhaps the most farsighted was Leland Stanford. Eventually, the Union Pacific collapsed into scandal and was placed under close U.S. government supervision, but Stanford was able to turn his Central Pacific railroad around. The financial records of the railroad were "accidentally" lost, thus avoiding political complications, and Stanford used his control over California politics to prevent any competing railroads from entering the state. He was thus able to dominate rail traffic in California until 1900. It may not have been as good as a politically awarded monopoly, but it was close.

So there were some wealth secrets to be found, but mostly in landholding, slaveholding, or exploiting political connections. The latter were perhaps the most interesting, but rising antimonopoly sentiment was beginning to pose an obstacle to such methods. Worse yet, some of the government-awarded monopolies were about to come undone. This was, initially, a wealth secrets catastrophe. Our time-traveling executive, if she had not already been kidnapped by the Morlocks or shot by a hunter in the Michigan woods, might have given up in despair. But ultimately, these changes would set the stage for the rise of the robber barons.

THE EMANCIPATION OF COMMERCE

The wealth secrets catastrophe was, ironically enough, triggered by a struggle among the most conventional of early American elites — a slaveholder and a monopolist. On the one side was the Livingston family, with its steamboat monopoly in New York; on the other was Thomas Gibbons, owner of a large slave plantation in Georgia, who decided he would like to operate steamboats in New York as well. It was a war by proxy. Fighting for the Livingston side was Aaron Ogden, a governor of New Jersey and holder of a license from the Livingston family to operate a steamboat himself, running from Elizabethtown, New Jersey, to New York City. Fighting for the Gibbons side was Cornelius Vanderbilt, a physically immense, uneducated boat captain. The dispute itself was largely an accident. A minor business disagreement between Ogden and Gibbons had escalated into a matter of honor, and the aristocratic plantation owner Gibbons showed up at Ogden's door, whip in hand, demanding a duel. Ogden had no intention of dueling and escaped by a back window. He also charged Gibbons with trespassing. Denied satisfaction, Gibbons decided he would try to bankrupt Ogden's steamboat line — a style of combat more appropriate to the emerging postfeudal age. But it was still something that was just not *done*. Secure on their estates and in their monopoly privileges, America's semifeudal elites had no love of competition. As a member of the aristocratic Stevens family wrote plaintively: "Gibbons runs an elegant steamboat for half-price...purposely to ruin Ogden....Ogden has lowered his price and now Gibbons says he will go for nothing...did you ever hear of such malice?"

Since Ogden and the Livingstons held a legal monopoly, bankrupting the line would be no easy task. Fortunately, in Cornelius Vanderbilt, Gibbons had found a brave, willing, and sometimes violent champion. Over the course of his long career, Vanderbilt would reportedly beat into unconsciousness an army officer; a steamboat passenger who had sat in his seat; an unfortunate person named Hugh McLaughlin (the fact of the beating is recorded in a lawsuit, although not the circumstances); and a professional boxer who was running for political office (although this last tale may be apocryphal). In addition to relishing a fight, Vanderbilt was a superb captain. In his early days at the helm he would almost single-handedly rescue, through feats of deft piloting, a British vessel that had run aground; a U.S. vessel that had become trapped in ice; and a small steam ferry that was drifting out to sea in a storm.

Gibbons provided Vanderbilt with a steamboat to start a service that would compete (illegally) with Ogden's ferry. Vanderbilt would vary the piers and timing of his boat's arrival so that the New York authorities who showed up to arrest him for violating the monopoly were unable to catch him (presumably the annoyance to passengers was compensated for by lower prices). An attempt to seize Vanderbilt on the open water failed when he hid himself in a secret compartment on his vessel. To add insult to injury, Vanderbilt would often race directly beside Ogden's vessel. One passenger wrote that "it was quite an interesting sight to see such vast machines, in all their majesty, flying as it were, their decks covered with well-dressed people, face-to-face, so near to each other as to be able to converse." In 1821, the Ogden steamboat rammed Vanderbilt's vessel, but Vanderbilt's skillful sailing apparently enabled him to avoid serious damage.

In the meantime, Gibbons began a legal attack on the Livingston-Ogden monopoly as well. He lost at first, but appealed his case, challenging the monopoly's validity all the way up to the U.S. Supreme Court. In 1821, Vanderbilt, having at last been caught by the New York police while running his illegal steamboat service, added a case and appeal of his own. In 1824, the Supreme Court ruled on the case of *Gibbons v. Ogden*. It was the first-ever ruling regarding the U.S. Constitution's commerce clause, which gave the federal government sole authority to regulate commerce that crossed state lines. The Supreme Court ruled that attempts by the state of New York to enforce the Livingston-Ogden monopoly ran counter to the Constitution, because the route crossed state lines. According to the Constitution, only the federal government had such authority. Hence Gibson and Vanderbilt would be free to operate their line and compete as they wished.

This ruling opened a floodgate through which competition came surging. The surge reached far beyond the Hudson River, swamping many a political entrepreneur. Monopolies that lay entirely within a state—the Camden & Amboy Railroad of New Jersey, for instance—could continue to be upheld. But for interstate commerce, monopolies were abolished. Fares for steamboat travel on the Hudson immediately plummeted to less than half the monopoly rate. The number of steamboats registered in New York increased from six to forty-three in a single year. The impacts were felt nationwide. By the following year, steamboat traffic on the far-away Ohio River had doubled; the year after that, it had quadrupled. Legal historian Charles Warren called the court's decision "the emancipation proclamation of American commerce." A biographer of U.S. Supreme Court Chief Justice John Marshall claimed that the decision, by encouraging interstate transport and business, "has done more to unite the American people into an indivisible nation than any other force in our history, excepting only war." A newspaper of the time, the *Evening Post,* was even more extravagant in its praise, calling the decision "one of the most powerful efforts of the human mind that has ever been displayed from the bench in any court."

The ruling helped to unleash productivity and progress. From 1830 on, U.S. economic growth rates rose from the 3 percent average rates of the 1820s to between 5 and 6 percent per year on average (in inflation-adjusted terms) and remained there, with a few interruptions, until nearly the end of the century. In 1830, at the time of the ruling, average U.S. income was two-thirds the level of U.K. income. By 1860, Americans were, on average, as rich as the British. While the American Civil War (1861–1865) caused great loss of life, the forty years that followed it would witness the most rapid sustained economic growth achieved by any country in history, and probably not surpassed until the post–World War II rise of Japan. Between 1870 and 1900, the U.S. population rose from 40 million to 76 million while economic output increased by three times and per capita income doubled.

Onto this stage of cutthroat interstate competition and rising prosperity would stride the robber barons, and they would transform the U.S. economy. The boat captain Cornelius Vanderbilt, though initially only a pawn in the *Gibbons v. Ogden* battle, would pave the way. Pierpont Morgan, Andrew Carnegie, John D. Rockefeller, and Jay Gould would follow, launching their careers during the Civil War and after. Their efforts would produce industrial giants towering over the small-business landscape of the time: Standard Oil, International Harvester, U.S. Steel, General Electric, J.P. Morgan, and American Telecom and Telegraph, among others. Many of these famous corporate names continue to thrive today. The robber barons would build monuments to their wealth that a century later would continue to define the tourist map of

The robber barons (clockwise, from top left): Cornelius Vanderbilt; Pierpont Morgan (the famous nose has been retouched); Andrew Carnegie; John D. Rockefeller. (Vanderbilt: "Cornelius Vanderbilt Daguerreotype2," restored by Michel Vuijlsteke. Original image Mathew B. Brady / Library of Congress. Licensed under public domain via Wikimedia Commons. Morgan: Library of Congress. Carnegie: Library of Congress. Rockefeller: Harris & Ewing / Library of Congress.)

New York City: Carnegie Hall, the Metropolitan Museum of Art (the first board meetings were held in Pierpont Morgan's home), the Museum of Modern Art (developed by Rockefeller's wife), Rockefeller Center (developed by Rockefeller's son), and the Museum of Natural History (Pierpont Morgan was one of the founders), among others. Innovation flourished in this competitive economy, and by the 1890s a well-off American home might include electric lighting, an electric stove, an electric washing machine, and an electric doorbell. But the robber barons would bring this era of cutthroat competition to a close, while in the process making themselves spectacularly wealthy.

PIERPONT'S RETIREMENT

In contrast to the political entrepreneurs, the robber barons did not rely on politically awarded monopolies or subsidies to make their money. Nor were they particularly interested in innovation ("Pioneering don't pay," Andrew Carnegie famously said, after an attempt to use a new process for manufacturing steel rails went badly awry). They discovered a new wealth secret—one for a postfeudal age—and their fortunes would greatly eclipse those of political entrepreneurs like Stanford.

While the robber barons would end their lives luxuriating in gilded bathtubs and using large-denomination bills to wipe their bottoms just because they could (OK, I made that last bit up), most were not born rich. Vanderbilt lacked even a basic education. "You will reccolect the *Bellona* must be halled up weather you have hir 12 feet longer or no," he once wrote to Gibbons, pleading for an extension to his boat and demonstrating a creative approach to spelling and grammar. Jay Gould began his life in poverty, abandoned at age thirteen by his father with only his clothing and fifty cents (about fifteen dollars today) to make his start in the world. John D. Rockefeller's father was well-off enough to extend loans to his son at several crucial points, but was at the same time a con man who maintained a second family during long absences from the Rockefeller home. Andrew Carnegie's father, a Scottish weaver, had prospered initially but had fallen on hard times during Carnegie's early childhood.

Pierpont Morgan was the exception, as his father had established a thriving banking business. In 1837 young Pierpont was sent abroad to Göttingen University in Germany to study, noting proudly that he furnished his student rooms in "royal splendor and Eastern magnificence." After his younger brother died, Morgan became heir apparent for the family's London-based bank. His first memorable commercial venture, however, came when he took a starter job at another bank and boldly but somewhat randomly bought a boatload of Brazilian coffee that had arrived in New Orleans without a buyer (Morgan happened to be visiting the city at the time). He flipped it for a quick profit, but this terrified his superiors, who had given him no authorization to buy anything. Morgan was clearly better suited to being his own boss, and at the age of twenty-four he and a cousin set up a banking partnership in New York. In 1861, Morgan took part in another controversial deal, financing a scheme to buy guns from a U.S. government warehouse at $12.50 each, upgrade them slightly, and then resell them to a U.S. general in the field at $22 apiece. Because the Civil War had by then broken out and the U.S. Army was desperate for weapons, this looked a lot like war profiteering. For one reason or another, Morgan pulled out of the deal early, but not before making a commission of more than 25 percent.

Morgan soon found himself involved in another questionable wartime venture. As noted previously, during the war, the North had issued the first public paper currency, the so-called greenback. This was a new phenomenon (and the survival of the issuing government was by no means assured), so no one knew quite how far to trust these paper notes. Hence the exchange rate between greenbacks and gold fluctuated depending on the progress of the war (there was always a chance that the only thing of value in the northern treasury would turn out to be its gold holdings). Pierpont Morgan and a colleague stealthily accumulated gold worth over $2 million, financing further accumulation by borrowing against their initial hoardings. They then shipped $1.15 million in gold to London and announced publicly that they had done so. This created a temporary shortage, driving gold prices up. Morgan earned $66,000 ($1.8 million today). It was something of a speculative gamble, and it enraged his father. It also was seen by critics as an unpatriotic attempt to profit from the northern government's wartime monetary troubles.

Morgan at this time suffered a personal tragedy. He had married Amelia Sturges, nicknamed "Memie," in 1861. His father disapproved, in part due to Amelia's obvious ill health, but conceded that romance was blossoming: "she of all others possesses those qualities of heart and mind best calculated to make his life happy." Shortly after the wedding, Amelia was diagnosed with tuberculosis, and she died within six months. Morgan's father, upon learning the news, mixed sympathy with the need to reestablish that father knows best: "I have, as you know, taken a gloomy view of our dear Memie's case, but was wholly unprepared for the sudden termination of it," he wrote. Four years later, Pierpont Morgan married Frances Louisa Tracy (nicknamed "Fanny"), this time with his father's approval. She was perhaps a more sensible choice, both in terms of her health and family background. But she did not like either travel or city life, two things that Morgan adored.

This personal turmoil notwithstanding, and despite embarking on two long honeymoons in a five-year period, Pierpont Morgan's income had by the mid-1860s risen to about $60,000 per year ($885,000 today). Respectable, although still far from robber baron territory. Vanderbilt, who had an earlier start, had reached an annual income of $680,728 ($10 million) by 1863. Still, as the son of a rich man, Morgan was already very well-off. In 1871, at the age of thirty-three, he decided to retire, but was talked out of it by his business partners. He chose instead to leave the banking partnership with his cousin and found a new company, Drexel, Morgan, based out of New York and Philadelphia.

Exhausted by these labors, he then set off on holiday for fifteen months, traveling to Rome and Vienna, and sailing up the Nile.

THE BANKRUPTCY PROBLEM

Any feeling of well-being and relaxation Morgan may have gained from his holiday travels evaporated upon his return—all thanks to the railroads. Railroads, as noted, were America's largest commercial enterprises at the time. Investment bankers like Morgan, who made a living by arranging large-scale financing, could not stay away. There was, however, a serious problem: railroads went bankrupt with great frequency.

The economics of infrastructure could be blamed for these insolvencies. Not only railroads but also steamboat lines operated with very high fixed costs (costs of buying train engines, cars, or steamboats). By contrast, variable costs (the cost of seating an additional passenger on a train or boat that was already going to run) were very low. This meant that a steamboat or railway that was trying to lure a passenger away from a rival would benefit from winning the additional passenger even if that passenger paid next to nothing. Hence rival steamboats or railroads would, when in competition, reduce their prices almost to zero. (When competing against Ogden, Vanderbilt would sometimes charge nothing, hoping to make money via onboard drinks sales, like an early Ryanair.)

Most types of businesses would not do this. A hamburger shop that reduced its prices to next to nothing would lose more money the more hamburgers it sold—so it would stop selling so many hamburgers. In the transport business, however, by cramming more passengers onto a steamboat that was already going to sail, or a train that was already going to run, the owners would make more money, even if these passengers were paying only for drinks. This was great for passengers, but bad for the steamboat lines. Because of the high fixed costs associated with buying steamboats in the first place, steamboat companies tended to have a lot of debt. The situation was even more extreme for railroads, which not only had to buy the engines but also the track. Given their high debt burdens, if steamboat lines or railroads charged too little for too long, they would be unable to meet their interest payments and thus go bankrupt. The result of such competitive dynamics was that, unlike hamburger stands, it was very difficult for either railroads or steamboat lines to divide a market. Eventually, all competitors on a particular route except one would usually go bankrupt. It was a winner-takes-all struggle. (And it's the same reason why airlines tend to bankrupt themselves with such frequency in the modern day.)

People like Vanderbilt thrived on such contests. For them, the reward was worth the risk. Once they had bankrupted their competitors, they would enjoy a monopoly — at least, as long as another steamboat or railroad did not enter the market. And, while they were enjoying this monopoly, they could charge exorbitant fees. Potential competitors might be attracted by the resulting profits but would think twice before entering: not only would they face a long period of low earnings while the two steamboat companies battled it out, but there was a risk that the new entrant would be the one to go bankrupt. Hence a steamboat owner could reap a fair amount of profit — real profit, economic profit — without worrying about competition.

Within a year after the *Gibbons v. Ogden* ruling, Vanderbilt had bankrupted Aaron Ogden — the former New Jersey governor and U.S. senator — sending him to debtor's prison (briefly, until his political connections got him out). Vanderbilt then moved from steamboats into railroads, where he once again attempted to bank-rupt all comers or—better yet—threaten competitors with bank-ruptcy and then acquire them at knockdown prices. By the end of the 1860s, Vanderbilt had by such means gained control of all the railway lines leading into New York City. This monopoly on New York rail traffic was fabulously lucrative and by 1870 was paying the largest dividend of any company in U.S. history. Vanderbilt built the Grand Central Depot, the forerunner to today's Grand Central Station, located at Forty-Second Street in Manhattan (because that was as far south as noisy, polluting steam trains were allowed to travel). He then linked his two New York lines together, via the Spuyten Duyvil railroad, adding more flexibility to his network. The New York & Hudson Railroad soon stretched to over 740 miles, with another 300 miles of network branches. A *New York Times* article compared Vanderbilt to the German barons who had extracted tolls from traffic on the Rhine—a comparison that gave rise to the term "robber baron."

But if Vanderbilt was worried about the criticism, he didn't show it. To blow off steam, he would race his horse-drawn wagon against all comers down the streets of New York, sometimes acci-dentally running down pedestrians. At the age of sixty-nine, he crashed into his rival during one of these races and was thrown from the wagon, landing on his head. From such a trivial accident he recovered quickly. By this time, to the public, Cornelius Vander-bilt was known simply as "the Commodore." His rapidly expanding rail network was so lucrative that, according to some estimates, he was by that point the richest American who had ever lived. The press of the day estimated his fortune at between $85 million ($2 billion today) and $150 million ($3.4 billion). But these were only guesses, as Vanderbilt, seeking to retain an edge over market manipulators, tended to keep his books in his head, and hid his holdings under other names.

Regardless of exactly how much Vanderbilt was worth, the

winner-takes-all contests in the railroad business were clearly delightful for the victors. Vanderbilt was one of these winners. Jay Gould, another railway tycoon, was another. The problem, from Pierpont Morgan's perspective, was that there were also losers. One of them was a political entrepreneur, Jay Cooke, who had enjoyed a lock on the financing of U.S. government debt. In 1873, Cooke used his vast fortune to diversify into railroads. Here his political connections were of less value, and he miscalculated badly, eventually bankrupting not only his railroads but himself. This bankruptcy touched off a financial panic, and by 1876 one half of the country's railroads were insolvent.

Pierpont Morgan observed this growing financial turmoil with dismay. To drastically oversimplify a complex business, the incentives of a banker who finances steamships or railroads are very different from the incentives of the owners of those businesses. Vanderbilt might have been willing to risk everything on winner-takes-all contests, knowing that if he won, the profits would more than justify the risks. A banker, by contrast, makes loans or underwrites bonds. No matter how well a borrower does, the value of the loan never rises. The same amount is always paid back. Hence the banker does not want winner-take-all contests. Instead, a banker wants all the competitors to stay in business and to reliably pay back their loans. "The kind of Bonds which I want to be connected with are those which can be recommended without a shadow of doubt, and without the least subsequent anxiety, as to payment of interest, as it matures," wrote Pierpont Morgan.

With the nation's railroads lurching into bankruptcy, Pierpont Morgan again considered retiring—who needed such aggravation?—but consoled himself by taking his family on holiday to Europe for the summer of 1876. He also began to devise a scheme to control railroad competition, a scheme that had first begun to bear fruit in the early 1870s. Drawn into a contest between Vanderbilt and the rising tycoon Jay Gould, Morgan came to Vanderbilt's aid with a huge financing package. He then took payment in power, becoming a board member of the newly merged railroad.

This maneuver gave Morgan significant control. As a board member, Morgan could oversee the actions of management and stand up for the bankers' interests. Because Morgan was also the main agent arranging financing for the railroad, his influence was significant. "*Your* roads belong to *my* clients [the bondholders]," Morgan once lectured a recalcitrant railroad president who did not wish to follow orders. And what Morgan wanted was for railroads to avoid competing with each other, and thus to reliably pay their debts. When, in the early 1870s, the directors of the Chicago & Alton Railroad wanted to add an extension to Kansas City, Morgan objected strongly: "we have had for several years past a fever for building and extending competitive lines, and nearly every company that has undertaken it has suffered accordingly," he explained. Nothing good ever comes of competition, he admonished. At least, not from the banker's perspective.

When Cornelius Vanderbilt died, Morgan attempted to broker an alliance between the railroad tycoon Jay Gould and Vanderbilt's son. In 1880, Morgan's bank underwrote the public offering for Vanderbilt's railway, the New York Central. In the process, Morgan put himself on the railroad's board of directors. He also brokered a meeting between the heads of the railroads competing with the New York Central "with a view of making permanent running arrangements" to divide up traffic (this was not at the time illegal). It did not work. Jay Gould, who preferred winner-takes-all contests, quickly went back to competing. But it was a start.

In 1884, Morgan's father attempted to broker a truce between the two largest railroads in the United States, the Pennsylvania and the New York Central (the latter then run by Vanderbilt's son). Morgan senior implored the two networks to give up their "absurd struggle for preeminence" but was unsuccessful. In 1885, Pierpont Morgan would succeed where his father had failed. He invited the heads of the railroads onto his yacht and sailed up and down the Hudson while negotiations continued—the implicit threat being, presumably, that they would continue to sail, imprisoned in luxury, until a deal was reached. The head of the New York Central was singing from Morgan's hymn sheet: we need a "community of interest" to avoid "ruinous" competition, he urged. Still, it was not until 7 p.m., when the yacht finally docked at the Jersey City pier, that a deal was agreed upon to divide the market and avoid competing on shipping rates. There was nothing illegal about such cartel agreements at the time, and some of the press of the day celebrated the agreement. "To railroads, least of all, would our people like to see applied the principle of the survival of the fittest," wrote the *Commercial and Financial Chronicle* (championing the banker's doctrine of the survival of everyone).

Shortly thereafter, Morgan rescued the bankrupt Philadelphia & Reading Railroad. Rearranging the company's financing, he created a "voting trust" that would represent the interests of the shareholders and oversee the actions of managers. This arrangement gave Morgan even greater control than serving on the board, and would become a key mechanism for him to exert his influence over the companies he financed. Morgan used his new powers to replace the management and oversee the restoration of the financial health of the railroad.

With these deals, Pierpont Morgan was on his way to becoming a rich man and climbing out of his father's shadow. He bought his first yacht, the *Corsair Mark I*, in 1880. But as far as preventing the nasty business of competition goes, Morgan had only just begun. Perhaps to celebrate his early victories, he vacationed in Europe, visiting Rome with his father. He left his wife, who had had enough of traveling, at home.

SIZE MATTERS

The freeing up of competition occasioned by the *Gibbons v. Ogden* ruling meant that politically awarded monopolies were becoming increasingly scarce. But the rise of the railroad tycoons hinted at a new possibility. By 1887, this possibility had been given a name: a "natural monopoly." The political economist who coined the phrase in a lecture to the inaugural meeting of the American Economic Association did not go into much detail, applying the term to businesses with average costs that declined as the business grew. But soon, the term was being used to explain why one company, Western Union, had come to dominate the U.S. telegraph business nationwide. Both Vanderbilt and Gould were involved with Western Union's rise to dominance, and had made a good deal of money in the process. Only about 3 percent of the U.S. population were telegraph users at the time, so it was not *that* lucrative (most of Vanderbilt's money came from the railroad business). But Western Union's natural monopoly made for some excellent profitability. The day when someone might achieve a similar feat of nationwide dominance with the railroads did not appear that far off. Under men like Vanderbilt and Gould, the railroads were rapidly consolidating into interlinked networks that controlled large geographic regions of the country. Indeed, by the late 1890s, the national network would be dominated by six major systems.

Having a natural monopoly was not quite so good as having a legislated monopoly. As with the operator of a steamboat line, one still had to worry about potential competition. (Indeed, some economists prefer not to use the word "monopoly" to describe such businesses, because they still face competitive pressure. For more on this debate, see this volume's endnotes.) I have said, for instance, that Vanderbilt enjoyed a "monopoly" on New York rail traffic. But if he squeezed New Yorkers too hard, or ran his business inefficiently, someone else might build a new rail line into the city. Of course, given the risks of competing with Vanderbilt, the railroad could comfortably earn a lot of profit before there was any likelihood of that happening.

And thus these new natural monopolies, even if they faced competitive pressure, were attractive business propositions. Indeed, these natural monopolies were in some ways *more* attractive than legislated monopolies, because the *Gibbons v. Ogden* ruling did not apply. There might be some limit to the prices that could be charged. But, crucially, there was no limit to the scale. It was theoretically possible to grow a natural monopoly business that would dominate an industry across the entire United States. And indeed, after Western Union achieved this very feat, it was no longer just theory.

The problem was, this wasn't easy. Businesses like Western Union, the railroads, and later the telephone networks enjoyed a wealth secret advantage now known as "network effects," as we shall discover in chapter 6. Most businesses in most industries didn't have such advantages.

The advantage most of the robber barons had to work with was a more general principle known as "economies of scale." Turning scale economies into a wealth secret required some ingenuity. But first, the basics: a business is said to enjoy economies of scale if average costs fall as size increases — in other words, if the business's activities become more cost-effective when larger quantities of labor or capital are employed. For instance, while some extremely high-end automobiles are even today made by small teams of people, such handcrafted supercars are only bought by people for whom money is no object. It is much cheaper to manufacture automobiles using assembly lines involving hundreds of workers (or, more recently, hundreds of robots) performing specialized, repetitive tasks.

Economies of scale mean that even if a car manufacturing business is obviously profitable, it is still hard to copy, because one needs a lot of labor and capital to do it efficiently. This fact limits the number of competitors that will enter the automobile market, enabling some profitability for those in the market (the profits on offer must be large enough to justify a substantial up-front investment by new entrants). If the economies of scale are extreme, the number of competitors could be very small and profits potentially very large. For instance, there are only two jumbo jet manufacturers in the world (Airbus and Boeing) because building a jumbo jet requires a tremendous mobilization of people, equipment, and technology. For a third player to get involved, the profits of these two companies would have to be extraordinarily high. The new entrant would enter with the intention of bankrupting one of them, and would need to factor in not only the huge costs of establishing a manufacturing operation on the necessary scale, but also a long period of low profits necessary to drive one player into bankruptcy, and furthermore the very real risk that Boeing or Airbus would in response raise their game and the new entrant would be the one bankrupted. Hence Boeing and Airbus can earn a decent return, or make a lot of commercial mistakes, without worrying about attracting competition.

But jumbo jets are unusually large and complex items. For most industries, economies of scale are not really a wealth secret of a magnitude that would interest us. Even in the automobile industry, the profits of U.S. auto manufacturers have been eroded to the point that the industry frequently requires government bailouts. The troubles of the auto sector stem partly from the fact that economies of scale are generally offset by "diseconomies" of scale. Larger firms tend to be more complex, more bureaucratic, and more difficult to manage efficiently (a case in point being railroads like the Union Pacific, the business affairs of which were so complex that managers were able to steal money from right under the noses of investors). Hence turning economies of scale into wealth secrets was no simple task, especially in a large national market such as the

United States. This was doubly true in the 1800s, because management, accountancy, and other crucial business control techniques were still in their infancy. Diseconomies of scale in most industries probably set in fairly quickly. As a result, anyone who wanted to turn their business into a natural monopoly in the 1800s was probably going to have to find a way to change the fundamental economics of that industry.

The man who without question was most successful in doing so was John D. Rockefeller.

ROCKEFELLER RIDES THE RAILS

John D. Rockefeller's early family life defied conventional norms of morality. Rockefeller's father, a con man generally known as "Big Bill," made his living selling fake medicine. Big Bill was tall, handsome, a superb marksman, a natural athlete, and a capable ventriloquist. He also spent several years posing as a deaf-mute, communicating via a small slate and chalk, apparently because he felt it made his sales pitch more credible. Big Bill seduced Eliza Davison, a pious farmer's daughter from Richford, in western New York. He married her, but failed to rid himself of his girlfriend, Nancy Brown. Big Bill lived with the two women in a small homestead near Richford. Officially, Nancy was the housekeeper. Big Bill had four children, two by each woman, in the space of two years. One of these children was John D. Rockefeller.

His was a schizophrenic childhood. On the one hand, Rockefeller seemed in awe of his father. "I come of a strong family, men of unusual strength, a family of giants," he would later say. Yet Big Bill would vanish unexpectedly from the home, for weeks at a time, leaving his family to survive on only a line of credit from the local grocer. When he returned, he would appear in fine clothes, riding a new horse, sometimes driving a new carriage, sometimes with diamonds on his shirtfront. He would pay off the grocer theatrically, drawing large-denomination bills from a thick wad. "He made a practice of never carrying less than $1,000 [about $32,000 today], and he kept it in his pocket," Rockefeller remembered. Big Bill was then the life of the party, frolicking with his young sons, until he vanished again, throwing his family back into uncertainty, dependent on the generosity of the grocer. Young John D. Rockefeller, as the eldest son, was forced to shoulder adult responsibilities from an early age. He also began to take on his mother's piety.

When Rockefeller was a child, the family (sans Nancy) moved to Moravia, a few miles away. Big Bill used money from his sales of fake medicine (there were also rumors of horse theft) to start a lumber business. This period of near respectability ended when Big Bill was accused of raping his new housekeeper, a woman by the name of Anne Vanderbeak. For some reason, the case never went to trial. But as a result of the scandal, the family moved again, this time to Owego, on the Pennsylvania border. Big Bill soon wanted to move farther away. He chose the Cleveland area, where he deposited his family with some of his relatives, paying his sister $300 annually (about $10,000 today) to board his wife and children. He then began a secret second life, marrying a seventeen-year-old Canadian girl and settling with her in Nichols, New York. About three to four times a year, he would reappear unexpectedly in Cleveland, still the charmer, usually brandishing money. Thanks to these irregular infusions of cash, John D. Rockefeller was able to attend good high schools (which were scarce in rural America at that time) and even had visions of attending college. In the end, though, he was forced to drop out suddenly, and never finished high school. The historian Ron Chernow speculates that Big Bill, stretched thin by the expense of maintaining a second family, had arbitrarily cut his son off.

Young Rockefeller frequently declared to his school friends that he would one day be rich. Friends from New York and Ohio recall him vowing to attain a net worth of $100,000 (more than $3 million today), although Rockefeller, in later years, would deny having said any such thing. Perhaps this youthful desire reflected a wish to emulate his father's charismatic habit of carelessly revealing a roll of large-denomination bills. Or perhaps he was traumatized by the uncertainty of not knowing whether the next grocery bill would be paid. Quite possibly both. In any event, cast out of high school, Rockefeller engaged in a now-legendary job hunt, visiting every potential employer in Cleveland to ask for work as a bookkeeper. When this failed, he started at the top of the list and began again, making applications in person from early morning until late afternoon, six days a week for six consecutive weeks. Big Bill suggested that if the job hunt didn't work out, John D. could come back home. Rockefeller later said he felt a "cold chill" at hearing these words. He was finally hired as a bookkeeper at a trading company on September 26—a day he continued to celebrate as "Job Day" for the rest of his life. He was sixteen years old.

Through this position Rockefeller came into contact with the first large sum of money he had ever seen in his life, a banknote for $4,000 (about $111,000 today). He reported opening the office safe and gazing open-mouthed at the bill several times over the course of the day. But this love of money was perhaps the only thing he had in common with his father. Young Rockefeller was hardworking and disciplined, arriving at the office at 6:30 a.m. and rarely leaving before 10:00 p.m. (although he took a break for dinner). From his modest salary as a bookkeeper, he gave to charity, at first 5 percent and then 10 percent of his wages. With his father absent, Rockefeller had been raised mainly by his mother, a strict disciplinarian and a pious Baptist. He took to the faith and was from his early days in Cleveland an active member of the church there. He soon became a trustee of the church, a Sunday school teacher, and an unpaid clerk, attending Friday evening prayer meetings and services twice on Sunday.

And yet it was his father who proved crucial to young Rockefeller's start in business. As a sort of a going-away present, Big Bill, before absconding to live with his younger family, built his Cleve-land family a house. He charged John D. Rockefeller with oversee-ing the construction. When Rockefeller mentioned that he needed $1,000 to start up a trading company with his friend, Big Bill gave it to him. With less than three years of experience in the working world, Rockefeller became his own boss.

Soon the trading company launched a side venture in oil refin-ing that would come to define Rockefeller's career. Oil refining was a booming sector. The lamps of the day were powered by whale oil. This was an improvement on the Roman olive oil lamp, but prohibitively expensive for all but the rich. Whales generally did not wish to become lamp fuel, so catching them was costly. When large deposits of petroleum were found in Pennsylvania—and, unlike the whales, made no effort to swim away—this discovery offered a potential source of cheap lighting for the masses. But first, the oil needed to be refined into kerosene.

It was a rough-and-tumble, unregulated business. Traveling to the Oil Region of Pennsylvania to secure supplies for his refinery, Rockefeller found that oil barrels were carted from the drills to the railroads by teamsters in wagons. The unpaved, rutted road over which they traveled was covered in a black muck of spilled oil bar-rels. The roadside was dotted with the corpses of horses that had died on the job, their hair and hides eaten away by petrochemicals. The situation on the rivers was perhaps even worse. "Lots of oil was lost by the capsizing of barges and smashing of barrels in the con-fusion and crush of the rafts," Rockefeller later explained. Indeed, there was so much oil in the water that in 1863, the Allegheny River caught fire. At the refineries, things were not much better. If you have seen a modern refinery, you may have noted that each tank is surrounded by an earthen bank to catch spilled oil. At the time, this safety feature had not been developed, and a fire in one oil tank would quickly spread to others, developing into an uncontrolled blaze. Refinery fires became so common that these operations were banned from inside the Cleveland city limits. Eventually, desperate oil producers began posting signs that read "Smokers will be shot." Meanwhile, gasoline, at the time a useless by-product of crude oil, was burned or simply dumped on the ground. "The ground was saturated with it, and the constant effort to get rid of it," said Rockefeller.

One reason refining was such a slipshod affair was that it was lucrative, and thus drew in new refiners by the droves. "In came the tinkers and the tailors and the boys who followed the plow, all eager for this large profit," said Rockefeller. Many of these rookie refiners possessed little more than a single trough, a tank, a still to boil the oil, and barrels to put it in. Some of these operations handled no more than five barrels a day. Demand for kerosene was so great at first that even such inefficient small producers could make some money. But soon so many small refineries had piled into the business—not only in Cleveland but also in New York, Pittsburgh, and Philadelphia—that competition was fierce. Rockefeller needed to stand out. After he added another business partner, Henry M. Flagler, who brought to the venture a loan of $100,000, he was beginning to make progress. He was gaining a size advantage over rivals.

Whether or not Rockefeller initially understood that larger operations would be more efficient, his mind-set was ideally suited to the exploitation of cost advantages. His discipline and his fascination with money were evident in his relentless focus on cost control. Rockefeller famously managed, to his obvious satisfaction, to reduce by a single drop the amount of solder used in sealing kerosene cans. He constantly double-checked the work of his accountants, once discovering that 750 barrel stoppers had been lost, for which he demanded an explanation. He devised schemes for using the waste products of the refining process. And on one occasion, when he heard that a buyer had secured a delivery of oil at below market price, he "bounded from his chair with a shout of joy, hugged me, threw up his hat, acted so like a madman that I have never forgotten it," recalled one acquaintance.

The problem was, Rockefeller was far from the only go-getter in the oil business. Many of his competitors were, like him, adding scale. With larger operations, they began to refine the business of refining, making improvements such as mechanization, better production processes and still designs, and the use of acids and other chemicals to improve the final product. Rockefeller needed an edge—and he found it not in technological advancement but in innovative contractual arrangements. Rockefeller—or perhaps his business partner, Flagler—came up with the idea of making volume-shipping agreements with the railroads. For instance, Rockefeller signed an agreement with a Vanderbilt railroad that gave his refinery a 30 percent discount in exchange for a guarantee to ship at least sixty tank-car loads of oil each day. Another agreement, this time with Jay Gould's Erie railway, offered rate concessions in return for volume guarantees and was sealed with an exchange of stock. Such deals would be illegal today—and indeed caused an outcry when eventually made public—but were wholly permissible at the time. These deals "leveraged" Rockefeller's existing size advantages, giving his refinery an advantage in shipping costs to augment its lower production costs. By this point, he clearly understood that bigger was better. "The larger the volume the better the opportunities for the economies," Rockefeller explained, "and consequently the better the opportunities for giving the public a cheaper product without... the dreadful competition of the late '60s ruining the business."

The agreement with the Vanderbilt railroad, involving the promise of sixty tank cars loaded with oil each day, proved to be a breakthrough. Because Rockefeller's refinery did not have the capacity to fill sixty tank cars with oil each day, he was evidently agreeing to coordinate shipments from other refineries. This arrangement was a huge advantage for the railroads, which could then dispatch trains composed solely of oil tankers, rather than a mix of cars for a mix of cargoes. Working with Rockefeller, the railroads were thus able to reduce their active fleet of railcars from 1,800 to 600. The associated cost savings probably more than justified the discount they gave Rockefeller's refinery. Perhaps even more importantly, this innovative deal probably got the railroads thinking, What if Rockefeller could guarantee even larger shipments of oil? Wouldn't that be even better for us?

It's unclear who first came up with this idea. The answer is quite literally lost to history: the Rockefeller Foundation has made Rockefeller's personal papers available to historians, but one year is missing: 1872. That was the year Rockefeller succeeded in changing the economics of the oil refining industry. The mechanism by which Rockefeller rose to dominance was, on the face of it, straightforward: he suddenly acquired twenty-one of the twenty-six oil refineries in Cleveland, gaining a near monopoly on oil refining in the region and control of one-quarter of the refining capacity of the entire United States (some historians say twenty-two of twenty-six, but that is really the only disputed point). The question is *how* he accomplished it.

Rockefeller had reorganized his business as Standard Oil Company in 1870, and it was one of the first joint-stock corporations outside the railroad sector. The great advantage of such a corporate structure, for Rockefeller, was that it enabled acquisitions at a low upfront cost. To be specific, Rockefeller could buy small, inefficient refiners by offering them stock in Standard Oil as compensation.

"Well," you might think, "that doesn't sound so hard—he achieved monopoly by acquisition." But in point of fact, this strategy almost never works (if it did, there would be many more monopolies). The reason it almost never works is that once one company is obviously on the path toward industry dominance, the owners of other companies in the industry will tend to turn down acquisition offers because they expect the removal of competition to result in higher prices, which will benefit every firm in the industry that remains standing. So they will try to hang on, even operating at a loss, in the expectation that better times are to come. (This kind of behavior deeply annoyed Rockefeller: "oftentimes the most difficult competition comes, not from the strong, intelligent, the conservative competitor, but from the man who is holding on by the eyelids and is ignorant of his costs, and anyway he's got to keep running or bust!") In sum, unless a company can actually bankrupt its rivals (like the steamboats and railroads Vanderbilt owned), these rivals, especially the last of the rivals, are unlikely to sell out.

So the question was, how had Rockefeller managed to make these acquisitions happen? In "natural monopoly" businesses, weaker competitors that are headed for bankruptcy will sometimes sell out to the industry leader. But oil refining was not obviously a "natural monopoly" type of business. Rockefeller needed a way to change this. He did so with a scheme that came to be known as the South Improvement Company: essentially, a cartel. Yet unlike most cartels of the day, which revolved around gentlemen's agreements not to compete (like the railroad agreement brokered by Pierpont Morgan on his yacht), this cartel would include a number of innovations. One was that all the cartel members would invest in a holding company, called the South Improvement Company, which would in turn invest in all of the members, thus giving all participants a financial incentive to uphold the agreement. Second, the cartel would not only involve three railroads (the Pennsylvania, the New York Central, and the Erie) that among them controlled all rail traffic in Cleveland, but also several oil refiners, of which Standard Oil would be the largest. Third, the railroad members of the cartel would raise their shipping rates — which is, of course, the point of any cartel. But at the same time, the oil refinery members of the cartel would receive rebates. Hence, while their shipping rates might go up, their cost advantage over rival refineries would increase (the rebates were as much as 50 percent in some cases).

But the most extraordinary element of the cartel agreement was the following: oil refiners that were not cartel members, and shipped oil over the railroads, would also be assigned rebates. But these rebates would go, oddly, to the cartel members. This agreement would transform the economics of oil refining. For nonmember refineries, economies of scale would be erased: the more oil they shipped, the more rebates they would hand to their competitors. It was a murderously anticompetitive arrangement.

The advantage to the railroads was that Standard Oil agreed to act as an "evener." Railroad cartel deals often broke down because one member, eager to get business, would secretly reduce its prices below what the cartel had agreed. Standard Oil would police such behavior, by allocating its shipments among the railroads so that the Pennsylvania Railroad would get 45 percent of all the oil shipped from Cleveland, and the Erie and New York Central would get 27.5 percent each. If one railroad lowered its prices and raised its share, Standard Oil would reallocate its shipments to the other railroads to make up the difference. Hence none of the railroad members of the cartel would have any incentive to cheat. For this to work, of course, Standard Oil had to be by far the largest refiner in Cleveland, which is why the railroads were willing to go along with the anticompetitive rebate scheme.

Oddly, however, the South Improvement Company deal never went into effect. It was not illegal, and yet when the deal was made public, the backlash was tremendous. Oil producers responded with an embargo, knowing that it would be bad news for them if one company came to dominate oil refining. Lobbying by the intended victims in the refining sector was also overwhelming, and the Pennsylvania legislature soon revoked the South Improvement Company's charter. The proposed cartel was never put into practice.

So how did Rockefeller achieve his buyout of nearly all the refineries in Cleveland? Apparently, by using the prospect of the deal to threaten these companies with bankruptcy. The brilliance of the South Improvement Company deal was that, had it come into force, any small refineries that held out in the face of Standard Oil's rising dominance would not have expected to see their profits rise in the future. Instead, they would have expected to see their shipping costs surge and their rebates go to pay Standard Oil. Rather than resisting acquisition, they would therefore rush to be acquired before they were bankrupted. One Cleveland refinery owner later testified that "after having had an interview...with Mr. Watson, who was president of a company called 'The South Improvement Company,'" he came to believe that "no arrangement whatever could be effected...that would enable [his] firm to compete with the Standard Oil Company." Another refiner, John Alexander, recalled "a pressure brought to bear upon my mind, and upon almost all citizens of Cleveland engaged in the oil business, to the effect that unless we went into the South Improvement Company we were virtually killed as refiners; that if we did not sell out should be crushed out."

Credence is given to such tales by the fact that all of Rockefeller's acquisitions happened during a crucial three-month period: the three months between the creation of the South Improvement Company and the revoking of its charter—in other words, during that brief period when the refineries knew of the deal and still believed that it was going to go into effect. An owner of the second-largest refinery in Cleveland "stated positively that...[he] *never* considered selling out to the Standard before the SIC [South Improvement Company] was formed," a journalist later reported. Indeed, in one extraordinary forty-eight-hour period, Rockefeller managed to acquire six refineries, several of which were apparently purchased at large discounts. The Cleveland owner quoted above claimed he had sold a refinery worth $100,000 for only $45,000 as a result of his certainty that he would be unable to compete. Many other refineries were sold for a quarter of their original construction cost—essentially, what the plants might have been worth at a bankruptcy auction. These were, for Rockefeller, fire sale prices.

There were, nonetheless, a few brave attempts at profiteering: once word got out that Standard Oil was buying everything in Cleveland, some refineries were started up purely in an effort to be acquired. To put a stop to such tactics, Rockefeller required the owners of refineries he was buying to sign agreements never to reenter the refining industry. Today, such anticompetition contracts would also be illegal, but there was nothing criminal about it at the time.

While there is a great deal of circumstantial evidence that the South Improvement Company deal was the driver of Rockefeller's success, Rockefeller himself would, as long as he lived, vigorously deny these charges. When he was in his late seventies, the journalist William Inglis conducted an extended interview with the great man over the course of three years. In all those hours of interviewing, which produced some 1,700 pages of transcripts, Rockefeller lost his composure only twice. The first was in reference to his father. The second was in reference to the events of 1872, and accusations of coercion using the South Improvement Company. "That is absolutely false!" Rockefeller exclaimed, jumping from his chair. He stood over Inglis, his face flushed with anger, his fists clenched. "That statement is an absolute lie!" One could imagine that the rage was provoked by righteous indignation. Or by accusations that were close to the mark.

What happened after the rollup of Cleveland refineries was no less astonishing. Rockefeller consolidated his new holdings into six large, state-of-the-art refineries with scale production advantages (in the process shutting down many of the operations he had acquired, as their small size made them irredeemably inefficient). He then went on a nationwide buying spree. Some other refineries slated to be invited into the cartel had also made acquisitions—a company in Pittsburgh, for instance, had snapped up more than half of that city's refining capacity. None, however, had moved so far in those three crucial months as Rockefeller had, and he was clearly the industry leader. By 1874, only two years after the South Improvement Company scheme was dismantled, Standard Oil had merged with the dominant refiners in New York, Philadelphia, and Pittsburgh. Rockefeller thus controlled 40 percent of U.S. refining capacity. He then, in each of these cities, repeated the tactics of Cleveland by buying the small refineries.

How he achieved this is something of a mystery, as no hard evidence has ever been produced of any other scheme along the lines of the South Improvement Company. Yet modern academics have uncovered evidence for a sort of "South Improvement Lite." The railroads were charging Standard Oil much less than any of its competitors (enough to make the difference between profit and loss in the refining sector), possibly in exchange for a tacit agreement by Standard Oil not to pit the railroads against one another. Indeed, in a court case from the late 1870s, a vice president from the Pennsylvania Railroad testified that Standard Oil was by this point serving as an "evener" for a national railroad cartel. He stated that the agreed shares of oil shipping were 52 percent for the Pennsylvania, about 20 percent for both the New York Central and the Erie, and 9 percent for the Baltimore and Ohio, all enforced by Standard Oil. Did Standard Oil obtain rebates in exchange for this service? No one knows, although a comparison of published railroad shipping rates with Standard Oil's (significantly lower) transport costs suggests something unusual was going on. By 1877, Rockefeller controlled 90 percent of the U.S. oil refining industry, and had for all intents and purposes a "natural" monopoly position and the profits that went with it. Between 1883 and 1896, average earnings at Standard Oil were a healthy 14.9 percent; from 1900 to 1906, earnings jumped to an impressive 24.5 percent.

If Rockefeller felt any moral qualms about his wealth secret, which turned oil refining into a natural monopoly business via the clever use of cartels, he did not show them. "The Standard was an angel of mercy" for these other refineries, he said, "reaching down from the sky, saying, 'get into the Ark. Put in your old junk.'" While the language was grandiose, it was not delusional. Those Cleveland refiners who accepted Standard Oil shares when they sold out to Rockefeller were indeed made very rich, as the company of which they had thus become part owners went on to reap monopoly profits. They put their refineries into the Ark, as it were, and it bore them to financial security (although Rockefeller neglected to mention that he was the source of the Flood).

Rockefeller continued: "Our efforts [were] most heroic, well meant — and I would almost say, reverently, Godlike — to pull this broken-down industry out of the Slough of Despond." As to why this process should have made one man unbelievably rich, Rockefeller considered that he had performed a great service to the nation by bringing an end to competition. Competition, in his view, had done no one any good. "It was the battle of the new idea of cooperation against competition, and perhaps in no department of business was there a greater necessity for this cooperation than in the oil business," he said.

Rockefeller remained throughout his life, as you may by now have surmised, a devout Baptist. He conducted his home life accordingly, generally staying in at night with his family, avoiding the theater because it was proscribed by his religion. He perhaps remembered some tricks of his father's, entertaining his children by balancing plates on the tip of his nose. His children became accomplished musicians, entertaining their parents by forming a household quartet.

The charitable giving of Rockefeller's early years in business expanded exponentially. He donated the funds that turned the University of Chicago into a world-class institution, founded

Rockefeller University, and created the Rockefeller Foundation. He also constructed a family estate in upstate New York that the American playwright George S. Kaufman memorably described as "what God would have done if He'd had the money." And Rockefeller, perhaps more than any other robber baron, founded a dynasty. Eminent Rockefellers remained part of the U.S. political scene until the retirement of Senator Jay Rockefeller in 2013.

"I believe the power to make money is a gift from God—just as are the instincts for art, music, literature..." said John D. Rockefeller. "Having been endowed with the gift I possess, I believe it is my duty to make money and still more money, and to use the money I make for the good of my fellow man."

CARNEGIE SCALES UP

Andrew Carnegie was born in Dunfermline, Scotland, in 1835. The town was notable for a castle and an abbey, the tomb of Robert the Bruce, and its prosperous population of handloom weavers. The problem facing the Carnegie family was the rise of the power loom: in 1813, there had been only 1,500 power looms in Scotland; by 1829, there were 10,000; and by 1845, there would be 22,300. This problem was made more serious by the brutal competition even among handloom weavers, as weaving had briefly been lucrative as a result of an export boom driven by U.S. demand, leading to an influx of new weavers in Dunfermline's population.

Nonetheless, handwoven linen remained a desirable luxury even following the rise of power looms, so a hardworking, determined weaver might have continued to find work. But Will Carnegie, Andrew's father, was not determined, nor, in the accounts of neighbors and relatives, particularly hardworking. Andrew's mother, Margaret, soon took over as the family's main breadwinner, binding shoes and selling the contents of pigs' heads rolled into little balls (a Scottish delicacy called potted meat) out of the front of the family home. These heroic efforts fell short when Will Carnegie's work ceased completely. When Andrew was twelve, his desperately poor family set out for America, borrowing money for the journey from a friend.

Carnegie would later claim he had enjoyed the trip—which may have been true, as it was only the second time he had left Dunfermline—and it was certainly an adventure. The first stage was by rail, although the rail carriage was pulled by horses. A rowboat then took the family across the Firth of Forth to a steamer that deposited them at Glasgow's port. From there they boarded the *Wiscasset*, a transatlantic passenger liner that was in fact a converted whaling ship, for forty-two uncomfortable days at sea. Arriving in New York, the family then traveled up the Hudson River to Albany by passenger steamboat (perhaps one of Vanderbilt's), and then by canal boat to Buffalo via the Erie Canal. They reached Cleveland in another steamboat, this one following the shoreline of Lake Erie, and then by several other canal boats and riverboats they attained their final destination of Allegheny City, Pennsylvania, where Carnegie's mother's sister had already established herself. Rail travel would have been faster, but it was too expensive.

It was fortunate that the Carnegies had relatives to fall back on, because Carnegie's father again showed little interest in finding work. His mother was once more pressed into service as the family's main breadwinner, again by cobbling (Clevelanders were presumably less keen on potted meat). As the situation grew increasingly desperate, young Andrew was sent to work as a bobbin boy at a cotton mill, where his job was to run from machine to machine, exchanging worn bobbins for fresh ones for twelve hours a day. He was thirteen years old. His next two jobs were possibly worse, involving the operation of a boiler in a bobbin factory and dipping newly made bobbins in oil. After that his luck turned when, with the help of another Scottish immigrant, he secured a position in a telegraph company. During the job interview, he evidently claimed that his father was dead. This was to become something of a pattern. Years later, in his *Autobiography*, Carnegie would claim that his father had died three years before he actually had. In his apparent desire to kill off his father he had something in common with Rockefeller, who in high school solemnly informed a school administrator that his mother was a widow.

That was just about the only personal quality Carnegie shared with Rockefeller. While Rockefeller was tall and lanky, Carnegie was short, standing just over five feet tall. In contrast to the pious and disciplined Rockefeller, Carnegie was nonreligious, and through most of his career worked only a few hours each day. He also had a lifelong tendency to embellish. A recent biography of Carnegie by David Nasaw identifies several examples. Carnegie fabricated or at least exaggerated a story about sustaining an injury in the Civil War (all of the robber barons, by one means or another, sat out the conflict); he erroneously claimed never to have engaged in stock speculation; and he lied to investors regarding the legal status of a bridge for which he was trying to sell bonds.

Despite his lack of schooling, Carnegie had a love of learning and sought to educate himself. He soon developed a supply of quotes from Shakespeare and Robert Burns that he would deploy at the slightest provocation. In his teens, he exchanged letters with an uncle in which he extolled with some eloquence the virtues of American democracy: "Government is founded upon justice and our creed is that the will of the people is the source, their happiness, the end of all legitimate government."

Carnegie's big break came when he was hired as a telegraph operator for the Pennsylvania Railroad. He quickly stood out, as he had developed the ability to decode a telegraph by listening to the machine operate rather than working from the printed transcription as nearly everyone else did. But his humble position first became a path to riches when Carnegie's supervisor and mentor,

Tom Scott (a railroad executive who would later become, together with Rockefeller, an architect of the South Improvement Company), wanted to hide some of his shares under Carnegie's name. The reason for the subterfuge was a conflict-of-interest scheme. Scott and Carnegie would first invest in a sleeping car; Scott would then instruct the railroad to engage the company as a key supplier, dramatically boosting the sleeping car company's value. The share prices would soar, and the result would be a tidy profit. A few years later, Carnegie's original $450 investment (equivalent to about $12,500 today) was paying the young man dividends of $5,000 each year (about $139,000 today)—a princely sum equivalent to between two and three times his annual salary. At the time, such conflict-of-interest schemes were commonplace, but evidently Carnegie's boss thought it best to keep the whole thing under wraps—hence his interest in using Carnegie's name.

Carnegie had stumbled onto a small wealth secret. By the time he was twenty-five, he had been promoted to superintendent of the western division of the Pennsylvania Railroad. He also had made several more investments, mostly in apparent connection to railroad suppliers. Naturally, these were paying off handsomely. These deals, together with a lucky investment in the Pennsylvania oil fields, soon made him a rich man by the standards of the day. Carnegie, however, was dissatisfied. He contemplated taking up a career in politics, but instead decided to take some time off. Just short of his twenty-ninth birthday, Carnegie and some friends embarked on a grand yearlong tour of Europe.

Fresh from his travels, Carnegie then attempted some further investments, in areas such as iron manufacturing and coal mining. He had the right idea, focusing his investments on patents that could have been used to ward off competition (which can be a wealth secret, as we shall discover in chapter 6). But making money on untried technologies was not as easy as making money from conflict-of-interest deals (for which the railroad's purchasing policy all but guaranteed the success of the target company). Outside the friendly confines of railroad suppliers, Carnegie chose badly, and between 1865 and 1866, his income fell by half.

Fortunately, he had more tricks up his sleeve, notably yet another rather bold conflict-of-interest scheme involving telegraph companies. He created a company, Keystone Telegraph, with a single asset: a contract from the Pennsylvania Railroad to string telegraph wires along railroad routes, with shares allocated to himself and his colleagues at the railroad. They then sold Keystone to an actual telegraph company, making more than $150,000 (over $2.6 million today) in the process. It was such good—and, let us be honest, easy—money that he repeated this scheme with another route and telegraph contract.

But Carnegie's greatest early success was an infrastructure project, the St. Louis Bridge (in part financed by Pierpont Morgan's father). The bridge was something of an engineering marvel, pioneering techniques that would later be used to build the Brooklyn Bridge. It was also completed years late and well over budget. Blowing the budget did not, however, matter to Carnegie, because the bridge was a conflict-of-interest masterpiece. Carnegie's St. Louis Bridge Company secured the bridge deal via a long-term lease with the Pennsylvania Railroad, of which Carnegie was a director; the construction was carried out by the Keystone Bridge Company, of which Carnegie was the primary partner; Keystone purchased its iron from the Union Iron Mills, of which Carnegie was the primary owner; and the financing for the bridge was also arranged by Carnegie. He was earning commission on the project bonds as well as 10 percent, on a cost-plus basis, from the contract between his bridge company and the railroad, and also from the contract between his bridge construction company and his bridge company. The more it cost, the more he made. It was not just Carnegie who was in on the deal: the Pennsylvania Railroad's president, Edgar Thomson, was another partner in Keystone. Of course, as noted before, there was nothing illegal about these transactions at the time, and conflict-of-interest deals were common in the railroad sector—albeit perhaps not on such an ambitious scale. Only a few years after Carnegie finished the bridge it was insolvent, although by then he had taken his money and run.

Then, in the mid-1870s, Andrew Carnegie abruptly changed tack. It is unclear why he did so; possibly he felt the end was nigh for conflict-of-interest dealings. Along with a business partner, he had been thrown out of the long-suffering Union Pacific railroad (by this time under close U.S. government supervision) after they engaged in what appeared to be some insider trading (again, not illegal at the time, but increasingly seen as unacceptable). Furthermore, by 1874, the Pennsylvania Railroad, where Carnegie worked, had started to actively investigate conflict-of-interest deals among its directors.

Another possible explanation for Carnegie's change of direction was that he had some kind of crisis of conscience. In 1868, alone in a hotel room on a business trip to New York City, he had written himself a memo: "Beyond this never earn—make no effort to increase fortune, but spend the surplus each year for benevolent purposes." He continued: "The amassing of wealth...[is] one of the worst species of idolatry. No idol more debasing than the worship of money." He resolved to "settle in Oxford & get a thorough education making the acquaintance of literary men." Carnegie apparently never showed the memo to anyone, hiding it away in his personal files. And he did not, to be sure, do as he had resolved.

He did, however, abruptly change his vocation. During a holiday in England, Carnegie had seen large-scale steel mills in action, which had captured his imagination. Steel was a good choice. Even more than oil refining, steelmaking was characterized by economies of scale, so there was less need for ingenious schemes to change the economics of the industry. In the early, rough-and-tumble days of U.S. oil refining, tiny one-man-and-a-still oil refining operations were—at least for a time—able to make money. But even in Carnegie's day, the production processes in steelmaking required large factories. Hence competition in the steel sector would be inherently limited. Carnegie was therefore, at least at the beginning, in a stronger position than was Rockefeller.

To operate at scale, Carnegie needed a lot of money; fortunately, thanks in large part to his conflict-of-interest deals, he had a lot of money. And Carnegie's first investment in steel was tremendous: he built the largest manufacturing plant the nation had yet seen in any industry, covering 106 acres. It was constructed from scratch for maximum efficiency. Even "the buildings were made to fit the transportation," explained Alexander Holley, the plant's designer. Wherever possible, skilled labor was replaced by mechanization. Stacking the deck further in his favor, Carnegie all but locked in a major customer, the Pennsylvania Railroad, which was rapidly replacing its iron rails with steel.

Conveniently, the president of the Pennsylvania Railroad was Carnegie's old business partner in the St. Louis Bridge deal, Edgar Thomson. Just to make sure there was no doubt about the intended first customer, Carnegie named the vast steelworks the Edgar Thomson Works. And the first order, for two thousand steel rails, duly arrived from the Pennsylvania. It was not a conflict-of-interest deal, but nor was it entirely out of keeping with what had gone before. Indeed, Carnegie had apparently tried to interest Thomson in making a large investment in the steelworks, although Thomson had politely refused.

Carnegie rarely sought to push the technological frontier. Rather, he adopted production processes that had been worked out by others and then scaled them up spectacularly. This gave him an edge over the competition—although a temporary one. Like Rockefeller, Carnegie's genius as a business manager related to cost control. (The difficult family circumstances and associated psychological scars of their youths probably helped, giving both men a relentless focus on penny-pinching.) "If I use a dozen more bricks than I did last month, he knows it and comes round to ask why," complained a foreman at one of Carnegie's factories. "Show me your cost sheets," Carnegie himself explained. "It is more interesting to know how well and cheaply you have done this thing than how much money you have made, because the one is...due possibly to special conditions of trade, but the other means a permanency that will go on with the works as long as they last." This overstates the case—in steelmaking, costs of labor, energy, and iron ore can fluctuate dramatically—but it does capture the mindset of the man. The economies of scale in steelmaking were just beginning to be felt in these early days of the industry, and he would seek out these economies with a miser's fervor.

Carnegie would need all these advantages, especially at the start. The Edgar Thomson Works took so long to build, and the financing requirements were so vast, that the plant nearly went bankrupt before production began. But Carnegie hung on, with a little help from Pierpont Morgan's father, who arranged a crucial bond issue. Carnegie also sold off his previous investments and poured the funds into the steelworks. Once production began, his efforts to achieve scale were vindicated. Within its second full year of operation, the plant was producing a 20 percent return on investment.

Indeed, Carnegie's obsession with costs and therefore scale probably paid off more than he had expected. It turned out that competition in steel had more than a little in common with the cutthroat competition in steamboats or railroads. Steel plants are most efficient when operating at maximum output. Hence even when demand is low, companies will tend to run at full capacity and dump the excess on the market, which leads to plummeting steel prices (in contrast to most businesses, which would naturally cut production when the price for which additional products can be sold falls below the cost of producing them). "For my part,"

Carnegie once said, "I would run the works full for the next year even if we made but two dollars per ton." This tendency meant that when demand fell, the higher-cost producers in the industry were rapidly driven into bankruptcy. Carnegie would then acquire his insolvent competitors, and the Edgar Thomson Works became the centerpiece of a growing empire. In 1883, Carnegie acquired the money-losing Homestead Works, which had also been suffering labor problems (problems that, following an exceptionally heavy-handed crackdown on striking workers, resulted in some very bad publicity for Carnegie). In 1890, Carnegie acquired Allegheny Steel, which was facing bankruptcy. Eventually, through acquisitions and upgrading of plants, Carnegie Steel had expanded so much that it accounted for about a quarter of U.S. steel production.

There were some accusations—understandably, given his early career—that Carnegie had some sort of sweetheart deal with the railroads. And the Edgar Thomson Works did enjoy some attractive volume-shipping discounts. But mostly, Carnegie just had a head start, and scale did the rest. For a while, at least, scale was a wealth secret in steel. At the time, U.S. capital markets were underdeveloped, and it was very difficult to fund factories of the size that Carnegie relied upon. Even Rockefeller, who rarely seemed short of money, had complained: "The hardest problem all through my business career was to obtain enough capital to do all the business I wanted to do and could do, given the necessary amount of money." Such constraints probably served to prevent the rise of competitors who could have challenged Carnegie—at least at first. Furthermore, he was sheltered from foreign competition by high tariff barriers.

In his late forties and unmarried, the Scottish magnate had become a very eligible bachelor. One reporter claimed to have been "denied the pleasure of an interview with Mr. Carnegie, not because he is not approachable...but for the fact that he is, I am told, almost continually SURROUNDED BY LADIES." This was something of a change for Carnegie, who up to that point had shown little interest in the opposite sex, preferring the company of his mother, with whom he lived and whom he adored. "She is the center from which radiates, in small as in great things, the clear rays of unimpeachable truth and honor," Carnegie once wrote of his mother.

Although he never carried out his ambition of moving to Oxford, he pursued his scholarly aspirations relentlessly, aided by his short workday. His first breakthrough was a travelogue reporting on a lengthy holiday he took in Asia, published by Charles Scribner. In it, he offered progressive views regarding racism and feminism, although he did note that Chinese women "are as like as peas, and one may as well marry one as another." American women less so, and perhaps as a result it was not until 1886, at the age of fifty-one, that he at last married thirty-year-old Louise Whitfield after a lengthy courtship. Carnegie's mother had died earlier that year. Louise signed a prenuptial agreement forsaking her rights to the Carnegie fortune, the reason being that her betrothed had already decided he would give most of his fortune away during his lifetime. Carnegie's next book, *Triumphant Democracy*, received some negative reviews but was largely taken seriously in its arguments regarding the sources of American advantage. He had achieved his ambition of becoming a public intellectual.

PIERPONT SAVES THE DAY

Despite the great size of his steelworks and his large share of American steel output, Carnegie was by no means in an unassailable position. Indeed, Carnegie found himself facing off against Rockefeller, after Rockefeller began buying up iron mines (a key input of steel production). After intense negotiations, the two men stepped back from the brink, signing an agreement not to compete with one another.

But that was only the beginning of Carnegie's problems. Carnegie Steel achieved a record $7 million in profits in 1897 ($203 million today), and then tripled that number over the next two years. But by 1900, achieving profitability had become a challenge. In part this was due to an ill-judged shift in corporate structure that resulted in a crippling burden of interest and dividend payments. Indeed, Carnegie soon realized that the company would be unable to pay its dividends. Doubling down, he advocated halting dividends and delaying interest payments as well, but his business partners, not wishing to panic the bondholders, talked him out of it. The reason he was so desperate to conserve cash was that he wanted to invest. The scale economies he had achieved were becoming less of an advantage over time, and Carnegie was afraid a competitor would catch up with him. In 1896, the Dow Jones company inaugurated an industrial average for the stock market (supplementing the earlier average, which was composed almost entirely of railroads). Companies in electricity, refining, tobacco, and agricultural products led the index. This was a sign of the times: investors were increasingly willing to invest in industry, and the days of Carnegie Steel being the only company able to marshal enough investment to achieve economies of scale were rapidly coming to an end.

Enter Pierpont Morgan. In 1895, Morgan had reorganized his U.S. banking interests, creating the financial institution, J.P. Morgan, that today bears his name. By this point his father had passed away, leaving him banks in New York, Philadelphia, and Paris, and also a banking partnership in London. The lock on government finance that Jay Cooke had once enjoyed was now Morgan's. In 1895, he almost single-handedly arranged a financing syndicate to bail out the U.S. government. The bailout was a success but the taxpayers were ungrateful, noting the size of Morgan's profits. So the next round of U.S. government financing was raised via a public bond issue rather than a private deal with Morgan. Morgan consoled himself by winning the America's Cup yacht race and holding an elaborate wedding for his daughter against the wishes of the young couple, who wanted a smaller ceremony. There were two thousand guests. President William McKinley, the Rockefellers, and several Vanderbilt children attended both the wedding and the reception. Andrew Carnegie was invited only to the wedding.

This slight snub may have been because Morgan had by this point become the agent of the competition that would rise to challenge Carnegie. Morgan had agreed to fund mergers among the companies in the steel industry that Carnegie did not control, leading to the creation of Federal Steel in 1898. The new president of Federal Steel, Elbert Gary, then set about arranging mergers in steel products, creating companies called American Tube (which brought together 85 percent of the steel tube and pipe makers in the country) and American Bridge. When Gary began to integrate these companies and source their raw materials internally rather than from Carnegie, Carnegie did not hesitate to respond, creating a steel tube factory of his own. The stage was set for a showdown to determine market dominance. With Morgan on one side and Carnegie on the other, it promised to be an epic battle. "The situation is grave and interesting," wrote Carnegie to a business partner. "A struggle is inevitable, and it is a question of the survival of the fittest."

The showdown never happened. Morgan met with Charles Schwab, the president of Carnegie Steel, first at a dinner in 1900 and then at Morgan's home in 1901. He devised an extraordinary plan for consolidation of the steel industry. Perhaps because Carnegie understood that his scale advantages were no longer unassailable, or perhaps because he wished to turn more of his attention to the charitable activities that would define his legacy, he agreed to sell out. After deliberating overnight, he wrote the price he wanted—$480 million—on a single sheet of paper and handed it to Schwab, who delivered it to Morgan. Morgan took one look at the paper and said, "I accept this price." Carnegie had made $240 million overnight ($6.8 billion today). Shaking Carnegie's hand, Morgan said: "Mr. Carnegie, I want to congratulate you on being the richest man in the world." A few weeks later, Morgan announced the creation of U.S. Steel, the world's largest company at the time, eclipsing even the railroads.

Carnegie understood exactly what Morgan had done. "It is a marvel," he said. "The new company will make such enormous profits it can afford to pay...what it has [for Carnegie Steel]." In other words, part of the reason Morgan was willing to pay so much for Carnegie Steel was that the company itself was valuable. But dampening price competition in the steel industry was what really justified the price, and was the wealth secret that secured Carnegie's place in the pantheon of business greats. Carnegie's vast fortune, the fortune of the richest man on earth, was in part a payoff. A congressional investigation into the matter summed it up: "in buying the Carnegie Company, [U.S. Steel] paid not only for tangible assets, but also—and very liberally—for earning power, and, perhaps more important still, for the elimination of Mr. Carnegie." The new conglomerate controlled half of U.S. steelmaking capacity. In 1901 it controlled two-thirds of the steel market in the United States. "Pierpont Morgan is apparently trying to swallow the sun," wrote the historian Henry Adams. More prosaically, Elbert Gary, the president of U.S. Steel, explained that the deal was necessary to "prevent utter demoralization and destructive competition such as used to prevail."

After its creation, the managers of U.S. Steel made little effort to achieve further scale economies. Because the behemoth faced no immediate threat of new entrants of a similar size, there was no need for such expense. Indeed, U.S. Steel made little effort to innovate, introducing no major technological advances over the next thirty years (an inconvenience for many clients: the Pennsylvania Railroad eventually set up its own steel innovation center and then passed on new product specifications to U.S. Steel). U.S. Steel was nonetheless spectacularly profitable, earning $90 million in profits in 1902 and over the next twenty-five years turning in the best performance of any stock in the industry save one. With its industry dominance, it was able to set and maintain steel prices for the nation. Prior to the creation of Morgan's new company, between 1880 and 1900, the cost of making steel rails had fallen from $20 to $11.50 per ton, as competing steelworks scaled up and bid prices down. After U.S. Steel, the game changed. The price of steel rails stayed at a constant $28 per ton for the next thirty years.

This was not, to be sure, Pierpont Morgan's first monopolistic merger. His first major consolidation outside the railroad sector had been General Electric, which was created by combining Edison General, which owned power stations, and Thompson-Houston, which produced electrical products as well as owning power stations. Initially, Morgan did not see the value of combining the two companies, but the economics of electric power are a bit like those of railroads, characterized by high fixed costs and winner-takes-all competition. Henry Villard, a financer of Edison General, proposed ending the "ruinous" competition via a cartel agreement, but the two competing firms would not go along with it. As the two companies squared off, preparing to battle to the death, Morgan changed his mind: "I entirely agree with you that it is desirable to bring about closer management between the two companies," he wrote to a business associate.

After General Electric proved to be a success, Morgan never looked back. He created U.S. Steel and then returned to the problem of the railroads. In this latter case he was given a sharp push. While he was on holiday in the south of France, a budding railroad tycoon by the name of Edward Harriman attempted to take control of one of Morgan's railroads by stealthily buying up stock.

Disaster was averted only thanks to a stroke of good fortune, when a broker carrying out Harriman's orders inexplicably delayed a crucial stock purchase by one day, giving Morgan's business partners time to respond. Although his partners had overcome the immediate danger, Morgan returned to the States via London with uncharacteristic haste. He called upon the king of England at Windsor Castle but required the king of Belgium to come to England, as he had no time to visit Brussels. Upon returning home, Morgan was determined to end the problem of railroad competition once and for all. He created the Northern Securities Company, which brought together the Northern Pacific, the Chicago, the Burlington & Quincy, and the Great Northern. It did not merge the companies, but because all were invested in Northern Securities, each had a financial interest in the success of the other. This arrangement created, in effect, a natural monopoly on rail traffic west of the Mississippi River. The railroads "wanted peace in their time," explained Morgan with uncharacteristic eloquence.

J. P. Morgan striking at photographers with his cane. Self-conscious about his nose, Morgan abhorred paparazzi. (Library of Congress)

And he was only getting started. In 1902, Morgan backed the creation of a shipping trust, bringing together more than 120 steamships in an effort to create a "community of interest" in transatlantic shipping. Crucial to the deal was a pooling agreement signed with the kaiser aboard Morgan's yacht. Morgan also supported the creation of International Harvester, a conglomerate of businesses that, once merged, had an 85 percent share of the U.S. farm equipment market (although this was mostly devised by Morgan's partner, George Perkins). While not all of these combinations were Pierpont Morgan's ideas, his support was crucial. But not all of them were successes. His shipping trust soon stumbled into a debilitating rate war with Britain's Cunard Line. (As the *Wall Street Journal* opined, "the ocean was too big for the old man.") Although Morgan was by no means the only person arranging such consolidations—similar mergers occurred in plate glass, lead, smelting, and coal—a great many of his conglomerates were especially successful. International Harvester dominated the U.S. farm machinery market until the 1970s. U.S. Steel remains to this day the largest steel company in the United States. And General Electric today ranks among the five largest companies in the world. While there have been a great many twists and turns since Morgan's day, achieving near-monopoly positions—at least for a time—was a great foundation for success.

Morgan did have one consolidation effort that was almost immediately unsuccessful: the Northern Securities Company. And the reasons for its failure were entirely unexpected.

When Morgan imagined his downfall, if he ever entertained such morbid thoughts, he probably pictured some calamity in keeping with his elevated station: a spectacular yachting accident; an assassination carried out by an elite team of Hessian mercenaries; or perhaps the devil arriving in person to collect him. Instead, the problem was some angry farmers. They did not come with pitchforks, precisely. And if they had hoped to wrest away Morgan's fortune, they were to be disappointed. But the political movement they supported would give rise to the greatest challenge Morgan had yet faced.

THE TROUBLE WITH FARMERS

The figures below list the proportion of farm incomes that come from government subsidies, compared to the portion of the workforce that are farmers, for several countries in 2012. Looking at the data, it immediately becomes obvious that in many countries, farmers receive a great deal of government money. Indeed, there are several countries where government subsidies account for more than 50 percent of the income of farmers:

Country	Government subsidies as a proportion of farmer income (percent)	Employment in agriculture as a proportion of total employment (percent)
China	16.8	34.8
Indonesia	20.9	35.1
Japan	55.9	3.7
Kazakhstan	14.6	25.5
Norway	63.1	2.2
Switzerland	56.6	3.5

You will also notice a more surprising pattern. Generally speaking, the more people who are employed as farmers, the less money these farmers receive. Conversely, the fewer farmers there are, the more money they get. This seems counterintuitive. Countries where many people are farmers (China, Indonesia, Kazakhstan) tend to have lower rates of subsidies. Countries where only 5 percent or so of laborers are farmers (Japan, Norway, Switzerland) are extraordinarily generous. If government subsidies reflect the lobbying power of farmers, wouldn't countries where there are more farmers subsidize more?

This pattern was explained in the 1960s by the American economist Mancur Olson, and his theories are still widely used today. His explanation revolved around what he called "collective action problems." Consider a mass of people with a common problem — say, for instance, Indonesian farmers who want more subsidies. With numbers on their side, one might think they could get anything they wanted. But they face what Olson called a "free rider" problem. Those who travel to the Indonesian capital to lobby parliament to increase subsidies will bear all of the costs of getting more subsidies, in terms of time and effort and risk. Yet they will enjoy only a small portion of the benefits. After all, every Indonesian farmer's subsidies, including their own, will be slightly increased. At the same time, people who decide not to travel to the capital and instead stay at home — the free riders — will enjoy the same benefits. So the rational choice is to stay home and be a free rider.

Small groups have crucial advantages in this regard. First, small groups are easier to police. They can identify any free riders, and force them to take action or exclude them from any benefits the rest of the group receives. Second, small groups often have advantages of cohesion: very clear common interests. Third, and perhaps most important, consider the sharing of benefits. For a large group, the collective benefits are great but individual benefits are small. If farm subsidies in Indonesia are increased, the total bill for the Indonesian government is huge, but each individual farmer gains only a small boost in income. This situation is reversed for a small group. If subsidies for Japanese farmers increase, the cost to the government is relatively small, and the share of the benefit for each farmer is large. The size of this benefit may justify a Japanese farmer's lobbying effort, even if some other Japanese farmers are free riders.

Once a group is large enough, the benefits of collective action, while great, are too thinly distributed. In this case, rational members of the group tend to become free riders and fail to act together. As a result, large groups, which superficially seem to have great power by virtue of their superior numbers, are rarely effective in organizing politically. In democracies, the result is a constant balancing act. In a vote, the majority will win out. In relatively technical areas such as agricultural policy, where concerted lobbying can pay large dividends, small groups have an advantage. This pattern is reflected in the history of agriculture. When farmers are the overwhelming majority of the labor force, government policy tends to work against them (peasants in feudal Europe were in many cases exploited ruthlessly and generally appeared to have little sense of themselves as a group with common interests). In the United States of Morgan's day, the government placed large tariffs on the import of manufactured goods, which benefited the small number of emerging manufacturers and was costly for American farmers. As countries begin to develop and the number of farmers falls, they begin to organize more successfully. Eventually, in most countries, the policy focus switches, and the government begins to subsidize farmers. Farmers move from exploited majority to coddled minority.

To be sure, in the United States of the 1800s, farmers were still a long way from becoming subsidy recipients. Here, the switch to subsidies did not begin until 1933, long after the era of the robber barons had ended. On the other hand, by the early 1900s, farmers' days as exploited peasants were coming to an end. In 1800, farmers made up 90 percent of the U.S. labor force; by 1840, about 70 percent; by 1870, 50 percent; and by 1900, farmers were a minority at 38 percent. With falling numbers came more effective political organization. The momentum built slowly. In 1867, a movement called the Grangers sprang up, based around social clubs for farmers in the Mississippi Valley. In 1873, the Grangers began to organize grassroots actions to protest high rates charged to farmers by the railroads for the shipping of their produce. Initially, the Grangers did not have much political impact. ("The Granger movement?" Vanderbilt asked, when interviewed by a reporter in 1875. "What the devil is that?") But the power of agriculture was rising. Small-scale agriculture was by the 1870s being replaced by "bonanza farms"—farms of several thousand acres, with factory-style management and bookkeeping. The owners of these large operations were more willing to engage in political lobbying. These businessman-farmers were also gaining powerful allies in other sectors. Rockefeller, for one, was far from delighted by Pierpont Morgan's efforts at railway consolidation, as he needed to transport his oil by rail.

Unfortunately, the farmers had a tendency to fall at the last hurdle. Granger groups agitated powerfully for change but were relatively ineffective in shaping new laws to control railroad rates. Those laws that did exist—in Illinois, Iowa, Minnesota, and Wisconsin, for instance—tended to be the product of lobbying by business groups, with farmers relegated to a supporting role. At the national level, by the end of the 1880s, the rising power of the Grangers had made some sort of legislation to rein in the pricing power of the railroads almost inevitable. And indeed, in 1887, the U.S. Congress passed the Interstate Commerce Act, which was duly signed into law by President Grover Cleveland. That said, things had not gone precisely as the Grangers had intended. Rather than a law making price discrimination illegal, which is what the Grangers wanted—and was reflected in a bill introduced by Democratic senator John Reagan of Texas—the act as passed established a five-member commission to determine "just and reasonable" rates to be charged by the railroads on a case-by-case basis. The act did provide some guidelines: railway fares would need to be published in publicly available schedules, rebates were to be avoided, and price-fixing pools were prohibited. The kind of discounts that Rockefeller and Carnegie had used to leverage their scale advantages would, at least in theory, no longer be permitted.

Morgan's father was deeply upset, calling the act "a disturbing cause...imposed by the National Will, a case of *force majeure*." But Pierpont Morgan was more sanguine. He realized the act was relatively toothless. The commission mechanism left a lot of leeway in how it would be enforced. Morgan and his colleagues were quick to capitalize on this leeway. Morgan arranged a meeting of a dozen officers of the country's largest railroad lines in his house on Madison Avenue. Even though price-fixing pools were forbidden by the act, Morgan harangued the attendees to avoid competing with each other: "this [competition] is not elsewhere customary in civilized communities and no good reason exists why such a practice could continue in railroads." One of the attendees suggested that, if they could bring the commissioners (who were supposed to be enforcing the measure's provisions) over to their side, the Interstate Commerce Act could actually become the basis of a railway cartel. After all, to the railroad presidents, a "just and reasonable" railroad rate would be a very high rate. They approached the five commissioners, and three of them agreed to play a role in the proposed cartel, monitoring railway rates to make sure no one railway cheated on the agreement. One of the commissioners even became the head of the industry's new association. Twenty-two railroad presidents agreed to join the new "Interstate Commerce Railway Association," a cartel that would set rates nationwide.

It was ingenious, but only partly successful, because Jay Gould still had his eye on a few weak railroads he thought he might be able to bankrupt or take over. Intending to win a few more rate wars, Gould refused to obey the terms and hoped the association would suffer a quick death. "Is it worthwhile for [my railroad] to be represented at the [next] meeting of the...Association in Chicago," he asked, "or shall [I] simply send flowers for the corpse?"

The Grangers, however, had a more radical agenda. Corporations had evolved from charters issued by states (usually, as I have noted, involving infrastructure projects); charters in turn had evolved from semifeudal grants of monopolies. The Grangers tended to see every corporation as inherently monopolistic. They wanted a return to the world of individual proprietors, in which everyone competed with everyone else and no one made much money. In particular, the Grangers wanted "free and unrestricted competition" in the area of interstate commerce. Why should a corporation from one state be able to merge with a corporation from another state? Why shouldn't corporations from different states be forced to compete with one another?

The first business organization that officially crossed state lines was founded in 1882 by Rockefeller, as a new corporate structure that could sidestep the limitation that U.S. businesses at the time could only be incorporated in one state. He called it a "trust." Eventually, all large businesses, regardless of their corporate structure, came to be referred to as trusts. Thus the movement against their existence came to be called antitrust.

The initial impetus for a national antitrust law came from the Grangers. They were mainly hoping to break up the railroads, but by the 1880s, labor unions and small business lobbies had joined the movement. In 1888, Texas senator John Reagan struck again, introducing a radical antitrust bill for Senate debate. But the lobbying skills of the Grangers once again proved wanting. The Sherman Act that emerged from Congress two years later, in 1890, was marvelously vague, passing both congressional houses almost unanimously. Modern scholars debate the reasons for its easy passage—surely the robber barons would have opposed a bill that condemned "every contract, combination...or conspiracy in restraint of trade or commerce." (At the time of its passage, Morgan was on holiday in the U.K.'s Lake District with one of his mistresses.) It appears that the rhetorical flourishes of the bill were intended to cover up its weakness. The watered-down bill was probably signed into law partly in an effort to disguise the passage of tariff legislation that, in effect, further taxed America's long-suffering farmers.

The first antitrust action taken under the Sherman Act was against a monopoly that controlled more than 95 percent of U.S. sugar production. And yet somehow, it was ruled that this monopoly did not need to be broken up, as it had not acted illegally. Indeed, four of the first six cases prosecuted by the Justice Department under the Sherman Act were, ironically enough, against labor unions (which had joined with the Grangers in promoting the antitrust cause). For the antitrust campaigners, it appeared that the act was backfiring. Big business, meanwhile, kept on getting bigger. After the act's passage, some two hundred trusts were created. Between 1898 and 1901 alone, forty-four new major trusts were formed, many—like the conglomerates backed by Morgan— controlling major shares of industries.

But that was about to change. Eventually, the ambiguity of the Sherman Act would become its strength. In 1901, President McKinley was assassinated, and Theodore Roosevelt took office. He calculated that appealing to the Grangers and their allies (populists, opponents of the gold standard, labor unions) was now a winning political strategy. He was proved right a few years later, when he won reelection in a landslide.

In 1902, shortly after taking office, Roosevelt announced that he would use the Sherman Act to prosecute the Northern Securities Company. He planned the move in secret, consulting only one other member of his cabinet, and announced the prosecution suddenly. Shocked, Morgan hurried to the White House to meet the president. He did not quite understand that the political game had changed. Morgan said to Roosevelt: "If we have done anything wrong, send your man to my man and they can fix it up." "That can't be done," Roosevelt replied. The U.S. attorney general cut in, explaining to the uncomprehending Morgan: "We don't want to fix it up, we want to stop it."

In 1904, the U.S. Supreme Court ruled that Morgan's conglomerate, the Northern Securities Company, had operated illegally in restraint of trade and should be broken up. It was the beginning of a wave of antitrust actions. Initially, it was a very small wave. Railroad rates were a key concern of the Grangers, and so breaking up Northern Securities was good political theater. After that, the White House seemed reluctant to take strong action. The government began to look at U.S. Steel and International Harvester. But rather than taking the cases to court, it negotiated agreements directly with Morgan's men to give the White House secret oversight of the companies' books. When U.S. Steel sought to buy the next bankrupt steelworks, TC&I, in 1907, Morgan's men quietly sought White House approval first. Approval was granted, but these cozy arrangements could not survive the imperatives of politics. In 1911 a new president, William Taft, brought antitrust action against U.S. Steel (ironically, focusing on the TC&I acquisition that Roosevelt had tacitly approved). The tempo of antitrust action rose dramatically from there. Roosevelt had launched fifty-seven antitrust prosecutions; Taft would launch ninety. In 1911, Rockefeller's Standard Oil was broken up on orders of the U.S. Supreme Court, although Morgan's U.S. Steel and International Harvester survived their court challenges. In 1914, Congress passed the Clayton Antitrust Act, which arguably had more teeth than the Sherman Act, especially against price-fixing cartels.

Despite such antitrust actions, there was no return to the era of unrestricted competition in which steel mills and railroads regularly bankrupted one another. Instead, the federal government tended to accept the existence of big business and even natural monopolies, but it exercised far greater oversight. The government monitored the prices that railroads, telegraph companies, and electric power utilities could charge, even if it rarely forced breakups. With such price regulation in place, the profits were not so large as they had been in the robber barons' heyday. Moreover, the conflict-of-interest dealings, insider trading, and in particular cartels and other agreements in restraint of trade that had been crucial to the robber barons' fortunes were also, over time, made illegal (rest assured that the central principle of the robber barons' success, the use of ingenious schemes to turn economies of scale into a wealth secret, remains as important today as ever).

Ironically, these actions of government probably had the effect of securing the robber barons' fortunes, because they prevented anyone from following directly in their footsteps, thus limiting the competition they faced in their twilight years. And oddly, the robber barons were not entirely uncomfortable with this regulated world. "What is the difference between the U.S. Steel Corporation, as it was organized by Mr. Morgan, and the Department of Steel as it might be organized by the government?" asked George Perkins, one of Morgan's partners. Well-regulated monopoly capitalism would be "socialism of the highest, best, and most ideal sort," he contended. Elbert Gary, Morgan's man at the helm of U.S. Steel, also embraced such a vision: "I would be very glad if we had some place where we could go, to a responsible governmental authority, and say to them, 'here are our facts and figures, here is our property, here our cost of production; now you tell us what we have the right to do and what prices we have the right to charge,'" he said. The inconvenience of government oversight was evidently a small price to pay for an end to competition.

If Morgan was upset about the breakup of his trusts, he consoled himself with some good parties. He had a series of glamorous mistresses, and was famous for buying them jewels. A popular joke in the early 1900s ran this way: "One chorus girl says to another,

'I got a pearl out of a fresh oyster at Shankley's,' and her friend says, 'That's nothing, I got a whole diamond necklace out of an old lobster'"—a reference to Morgan's age and reddish-purple nose. At one party in Cairo, Morgan tossed a handful of gold jewelry onto a hotel table and cried to the ladies: "Now, help yourselves!"

Morgan was asked yet again about the possibility of medical procedures to address the disfigurement of his nose. There was no need, he explained. His nose had become "part of the American business structure."

THE MONEY TRUST

But there is a further mystery. We now know the wealth secrets of Vanderbilt, Carnegie, and Rockefeller—men who, by hook or by crook, sought to establish monopolies, albeit "natural" monopolies, without benefit of government license or charter.

But what about Morgan? Banking is not usually seen as a natural monopoly business, and indeed Morgan never had a monopoly. So why was Morgan able to earn such huge profits over decades? Why did no other bank displace him? Even if Morgan's fortune never matched those of Vanderbilt, Carnegie, or Rockefeller, he was doing very well for himself.

This is a surprisingly difficult question to answer. Morgan himself was unhelpful. He was a man of few words, given to staring at people in silence, with intimidating effect. On the mantel in his study he kept a sign that read *Pense moult, parle peu, écris rien* [think a lot, say little, write nothing]. When he did speak on the record, it was in many cases either a transparent effort to serve his interests or so incoherent it was incomprehensible. Morgan was "more reserved than any man I ever knew," said the rector of St. George's Church, William Rainsford.

To be sure, the banking business in Morgan's day tended to be cozily profitable. Commercial and investment bankers at the time operated under a sort of informal code by which they did not seek out new clients, but waited for clients to arrive. There was no advertising, and price competition was restrained by the tradition that, if a new client came through the door, he would be taken on only if his former banker agreed. The idea was to make it difficult for new banks to enter the business. Banks that violated these rules were generally ostracized by other bankers, who would refuse to partner with them on deals. And in a world of little financial regulation, companies tended to assume that any bank that *did* aggressively solicit business had either been driven to desperate acts by approaching insolvency or was scamming.

But even in this cozy world, Morgan was extraordinarily dominant. From about 1900 until the beginning of World War I, every American financing in excess of $10 million was handled by either J.P. Morgan or one of three other firms. Eventually, the politicians came after Morgan, accusing him of having formed a "money trust." While Morgan was on holiday in Egypt, a congressional subcommittee headed by Louisiana representative Arsène Pujo was formed to investigate Morgan's supposed banking monopoly. The subcommittee commenced its hearings; meanwhile, the accused continued his holiday, vacationing in Europe and helping the kaiser win a boat race. In November 1912, at the age of seventy-five, Morgan was hauled before the committee to testify. Despite this, the Pujo Committee did not achieve its objective, which was to prove that Morgan had formed a banking cartel to exploit his clients. It did, however, reveal the extraordinary degree of his influence. Partners at J.P. Morgan sat on the boards of directors of 112 companies, in industries ranging from railroads to mining to transportation. Via directorships, Morgan himself controlled four of the six large rail networks that dominated the nation's transport. Morgan had a majority stake in one of the country's largest insurance companies, Equitable Life. He owned a large block of stock in National City Bank, the nation's second-largest bank, and his son, Jack Morgan, was on the board. Through voting trusts, Morgan controlled numerous other financial institutions, including Guaranty Trust. Among its seventy-eight clients, J.P. Morgan counted many of the conglomerates that dominated the nation's industries, ranging from General Electric to AT&T. One modern estimate is that, if one aggregates the expenditures of the companies Morgan financed, controlled via voting trusts, or controlled via directorships, Pierpont Morgan (or more accurately his bank) oversaw approximately 40 percent of all the capital invested in the U.S. economy at that time.

At the Pujo Committee hearings, Morgan evidently tried to explain something, although no one knew quite what. "Without you have control, you cannot do anything," he said.

The committee's investigator, Samuel Untermeyer, asked, not unreasonably: "Unless you have got control, you cannot do what?"

Morgan: "Unless you have got actual control, you cannot control anything."

Untermeyer: "Well, I guess that is right. Is that the reason you want to control everything?"

Morgan: "I want to control nothing."

Untermeyer: "What is the point, Mr. Morgan, you want to make, because I do not quite gather it."

The Pujo Committee was unable to show that Morgan's "money trust" was exploiting its clients, in part because client after client of J.P. Morgan testified that even though the bank charged high fees, the fees were well worth it. They did not say this merely because they feared reprisals. Recent analysis has shown that Morgan's clients did indeed receive extraordinary value. In fact, when Morgan was at the height of his powers, nearly everything he touched turned to gold. Having a J.P. Morgan partner on a company's board of directors tended to increase the value of that company's equities by some 30 percent, almost entirely because these companies became more profitable. If not for Morgan's one major failure (the attempt to create a shipping monopoly), the figure would have been much higher, perhaps as high as 70 percent. Having a Morgan partner on the board also made it much easier for a company to obtain funding, at a time when most U.S. companies were (as I have mentioned) seriously credit constrained.

These facts alone may explain some of Morgan's dominance. The companies on whose boards J.P. Morgan bankers sat were well run, at a time when conflict-of-interest dealings were common. Morgan would thus have obtained a reputation that would have been difficult for other bankers to match — potentially, an important barrier to competition. A company that is well thought of can generally be trusted to continue to behave with probity, because sharp dealing will undermine the confidence of its clients. By contrast, it is difficult to build a good reputation from scratch. In the early stages, when one's reputation is not yet worth much, there is a very strong temptation to go for short-term profit because, after all, the value of the reputation is still low.

My own pet theory, however, is that Morgan had created a kind of banking network. Louis Brandeis, an antitrust campaigner and U.S. Supreme Court justice, offered this memorable description of a Morgan network operation: "J.P. Morgan (or a partner), a director of the New York, New Haven, and Hartford Railroad, causes that company to sell to J.P. Morgan and Company an issue of bonds. J.P. Morgan and Company borrow the money with which to pay the bonds from the Guarantee Trust Company, of which Mr. Morgan (or a partner) is a director. J.P. Morgan and Company sell the bonds to the Penn Mutual Life Insurance Company of which Mr. Morgan (or a partner) is a director. The New Haven spends the proceeds of the bonds in purchasing steel rails from the United States Steel Corporation, of which Mr. Morgan (or a partner) is a director. United States Steel Corporation spends the proceeds of the rails in purchasing electrical supplies from the General Electric Company, of which Mr. Morgan (or partner) is a director... [and so on]."

How could such transactions fail to be profitable for all parties involved? It is the banker's dream realized. While in the "real world" one company might dominate the others—a dominant railroad forcing the steelworks to compete on price with rivals, for instance—in the Morgan network one presumes each firm made a profit. Not an excessive profit, but a reliable and consistent profit. There was no "ruinous" competition here. As the network spread, it grew more valuable, offering more and more stability to the next company that joined. And one presumes that Morgan did not welcome these companies doing business with rival bankers—although, testifying to the Pujo Committee, Morgan did say, charitably, that he liked "a little competition."

Although Pierpont Morgan's family, and many of the nation's newspapers, celebrated the man's performance before the Pujo Committee, the political inquest appeared to take a toll. The end of the Morgan era was coming soon, and Pierpont probably saw the storm approaching. In 1914, J.P. Morgan partners startled Wall Street by resigning en masse from the boards of thirty companies, shortly before the Clayton Antitrust Act of that same year forbade cross-memberships among the boards of competing companies. Other banks would soon rise to challenge the dominance of J.P. Morgan.

Following his testimony to the Pujo Committee, Pierpont Morgan, naturally, went on holiday, once again traveling to Egypt. His health, however, quickly worsened. The pope and the kaiser cabled their concern. Within about four months of his testimony, Morgan was dead, passing away in his sleep in Rome. Many J.P. Morgan partners attributed his death to the strain imposed by the Pujo Committee's persecution of their master, but Morgan was a heavy drinker, chain-smoker of cigars, and opponent of exercise. Hence seventy-five years might be considered a reasonable span.

When he died, it was found that his estate was worth about $80 million ($1.9 billion today). This put him in robber baron ter-

Pierpont Morgan's funeral procession. "And to think, he was not a rich man," observed Andrew Carnegie, hearing upon Morgan's death that he was worth "just" $80 million ($1.9 billion today). (Bain News Service / Library of Congress)

ritory, though nowhere near the top. But there were some mysteries surrounding this estimate. The *Corsair* was valued at $135,000, even though Jack Morgan had, in earlier conversations with the government, said the value of the hull alone was $850,000. The value of Morgan's art collection was less than Morgan himself claimed to have spent on it, which was even more implausible, as many of the works had even by that point appreciated significantly. Quite possibly the existence of a New York estate tax had something to do with these apparent undervaluations. Pierpont Morgan may well have been worth somewhat more than is recorded by history.

But as Sereno S. Pratt, an editor of the *Wall Street Journal*, observed: "[Morgan's] power is not to be found in the number of his own millions, but in the billions of which he was the trustee."

Why didn't Morgan exploit this power to expand his own fortune? Why was he content, for instance, to make Carnegie the world's richest man, rather than saving the honor for himself? We will never know. But I wonder if having been born rich—uniquely among the robber barons profiled here—Morgan was simply less obsessed with money. Big man that he was, he never seemed to need to prove anything to anyone.

FOLLOW MY NOSE

Most of the robber barons burst uninvited onto the national economic scene, dominating new industries through unorthodox business methods. Vanderbilt, eager to fight all comers; Gould, seizing what he wanted; Rockefeller, strangling his competitors via cartels; and Carnegie, plowing capital obtained by dubious means into an all-out effort to achieve scale. Morgan, by contrast, *arrived*, serene and unhurried, on the national stage, his establishment connections unrivaled, his ambition not easy to discern. In the company of the robber barons, Morgan at times seemed an anachronism, given his posh habits, royal cronies, and clubby ways of doing business.

Yet the robber barons had a great deal in common. Most notably, they all spoke out against competition, that oppressive force that prevents great men from achieving fortunes commensurate with their greatness. They all succeeded, to varying degrees, in blunting the force of competition in their industries. And Morgan, watching over them, sought to banish competition from every industry.

These men pursued, and in most cases achieved, new kinds of monopolies. The old, semifeudal monopolies had been based on political connections and government-awarded privileges, and were awarded primarily by state governments. The Supreme Court ruling, *Gibbons v. Ogden*, emancipated American commerce, unleashing a flood of competition. That could have been very bad for wealth secrets. And indeed, for the political entrepreneurs whom the robber barons swept aside, *Gibbons v. Ogden* was very bad indeed (Vanderbilt bankrupted a great many political entrepreneurs beyond the few stories I've told here). Lesser men might have stopped there, content to divide up the market with rivals. But the robber barons surged ahead, railing against the curse of competition, racing to find wealth secrets that would enable them to reestablish monopolies at the national level — "natural" monopolies, based on the economics of their industries, on cartels, and on Pierpont Morgan's assistance.

Broadly speaking, the race to establish national monopolies had two types of winners. The first were network businesses: railroad lines, telegraph networks, and ultimately — although I have not covered them here — telephone networks (we will meet the modern counterparts of these "network effect" businesses, and explain how their wealth secrets work, in chapter 6). At first, the monopolies involved were localized and were based on the economics of infrastructure (in effect, one party tended to bankrupt the others). Vanderbilt was the master of these contests, establishing numerous local monopolies, and this became his first wealth secret. He was also partly successful in taking the next step, to build a national railroad network (as we'll see in our final chapter). But the railroad system he struggled to create in the later part of his life was only partially completed, and was soon given up (in part to Gould) by his heirs. The same fate, ironically enough, befell Gould, whose heirs lost key railroad properties to Edward Harriman. Only when Morgan at last brought the railways together, creating the Northern Securities Company, was the dream of a network monopoly covering a large area of the United States truly realized (until the federal government spoiled the fun by breaking it up).

The second group of winners in the race to establish national monopolies was composed of businesses enjoying economies of scale in production. In this chapter I have focused on Rockefeller and Carnegie, in oil and steel, respectively. Economies of scale—which exist in many industries—are rarely, as I have noted, a wealth secret, in part because these are offset by diseconomies of scale once factories or companies become too unwieldy to manage well. For that reason, the industrial robber barons needed a little help to become national monopolists. While many of the specific methods used by these men were subsequently made illegal, schemes to turn economies of scale into wealth secrets remain a staple of modern fortunes (as we shall discover in chapter 5).

For Rockefeller, the boost to scale economies came in the form of the marvelously anticompetitive South Improvement Company scheme, probably followed by similar schemes on a national level. These were his wealth secrets. For Carnegie, the assistance was provided by Morgan. The $480 million Morgan was willing to pay to buy Carnegie Steel reflected not the value of its assets or future revenues, but the value of reduced competition in the country's steel market. It reflected, in short, the value of monopoly (or more accurately, the value of market concentration, as U.S. Steel controlled "only" two-thirds of the nation's steel production). While attaining monopoly by acquisition is hard, Morgan, with his ubiquitous control and overwhelming desire to end competition, was able to do it—although it mostly made other people rich. Carnegie was only the most famous beneficiary. The monopolistic consolidations Morgan supported added to many other great fortunes of the robber baron era that I have not discussed, including those of Charles Albert Coffin (who had a large stake in one of the companies that were merged to become General Electric) and Cyrus McCormick, Jr. (who owned one of the companies that was merged to become International Harvester).

Such monopoly fortunes were the greatest fortunes of the age, and, by most measures, the greatest fortunes to that point in history. Indeed, Rockefeller, the richest of the robber barons, may well have been the richest American who ever lived, depending on which measure one uses. Rockefeller's fortune was estimated at $1.4 billion in 1937, the time of his death, which is about $22.7 billion today. In terms of sheer purchasing power, that doesn't compare to today's billionaires, but if we use World Bank economist Branko Milanovic's labor-based yardstick of value, then Rockefeller's wealth approximates that of the richest American of our time, Bill Gates. The fortunes of Carnegie and Vanderbilt are slightly lower (roughly on a par with that of Crassus); Morgan falls further below these lofty heights. But by another standard—comparing personal wealth to the nation's economic output—Rockefeller is in a class by himself. Rockefeller's net worth at his peak was not far off 2 percent of U.S. economic output at the time. Bill Gates's wealth in 2014, by contrast, amounted to less than 1 percent of U.S. output.

Despite the backlash against the robber barons, America would ultimately follow Morgan's shiny red nose into a new economic era. While Carnegie and Rockefeller wanted to bankrupt everyone and reap the fabulous profits that resulted, Morgan was different. He wanted stability. He didn't seem too obsessed with earning money. He just wanted everyone to be able to pay their debts. And to accomplish that, what he needed was oversight; what he needed was regulation. Morgan used his influence to prevent the railroads from lurching headlong into competitive battles with each other. He used his influence to merge companies until industries were stabilized. Morgan, of course, thought that he ought to provide this regulation of the U.S. economy personally, via his extensive network of directorships. The rest of America ultimately disagreed, but only on this last point. Morgan's vision of giant enterprises facing limited competition ultimately came to pass in many industries. But it was the federal government, rather than J.P. Morgan, that would serve as the regulator and guarantor of stability.

This era of corporate stability may have come at a cost. Following Morgan's consolidations and the transition to regulated competition, the pace of U.S. economic growth began to slow. From the *Gibbons v. Ogden* decision of the mid-1820s until roughly the turn of the century, estimates by modern scholars suggest that inflation-adjusted economic growth in the United States generally averaged between 4 and 6 percent per year—an extraordinary, and indeed at the time unprecedented, pace of economic progress. From the 1890s onward, however, U.S. economic growth averaged between 2 and 4 percent per year, a less remarkable achievement. Indeed, the U.S. economy appears to have muddled along at roughly this rate until a second major growth spurt began following World War II (turning the country into an economic superpower). It would be too much to lay the blame for this slowdown at Morgan's feet. Economic growth rates are influenced by a huge number of factors. But the replacement of cutthroat competition with regulated monopolies in many industries was hardly a spur to economic progress. For example, the lack of innovation by U.S. Steel, the dominant company in this crucial industry, was one result of Morgan's consolidations.

More importantly for our purposes, the onset of regulated competition was not advantageous for wealth secrets. There would in future be few fortunes on the scale of those amassed by the robber barons. Antitrust law and limits on cartels made it harder to achieve true monopolies (although cozy oligopolies, involving a few large firms, were very common). Moreover, with the government keeping a close eye on their profits, the next generation of corporate titans would rarely approach the wealth of Vanderbilt, Gould, Carnegie, or Rockefeller (although Henry Ford, in automobiles, came close).

But do not despair. There are still wealth secrets out there. Indeed, in the next chapter we will discover not a few great individuals, but an *entire industrial sector* that outperformed, producing a veritable legion of millionaires—the rising stars of today's one percent.

4

Wealth Secrets of Today's One Percent

THE MONEYED HERD

I was recently in Singapore, after not having visited for several years, and went to lunch with an acquaintance. His company specializes in corporate investigations and the provision of what have come to be known as "private contractors"—generally, former military personnel who perform security roles in places like Iraq, Afghanistan, and Nigeria. Indeed, when I met him, security work in Iraq accounted for a majority of his company's revenues. I asked his advice on places to visit while I was in town; I liked the look of a new casino with an infinity pool on the roof some fifty stories above the ground. "Oh, don't go there," he said. "It has a high dick quotient." I was a little taken aback. How annoying would people have to be, I thought, in order to get under the skin of a man who spends his professional life working with mercenaries?

But to be fair, the moneyed herd could be annoying at times. These were the young men of finance, hopped up on bonuses, who could be found in the high-end bars, restaurants, and strip clubs of

Manhattan, London, Hong Kong, and of course Singapore. "You had people in their 30s, through hedge funds and Goldman Sachs partner jobs, people making $20, $30, $40 million a year," explained Holly Peterson, a socialite and chronicler of the lives of the rich, "and there were a lot of them doing it. They started hanging out with each other. They became a pack. They started roaming the globe together as global high rollers and the difference between them and the rest of the world became exponential." Peterson's figures are a little high—a ballpark estimate for average Goldman Sachs partner compensation is $1.5 million. And not all those high-earning bankers were men in their thirties. That said, on nights out it was the young men who made a big impression, and $1.5 million buys a lot of tailored suits, Rolexes, and Ferraris. "Everyone's always measuring their dicks," one told the journalist and author Kevin Roose. "If I'm a Goldman banker, I go up to a McKinsey consultant and I'm like, 'My dick's bigger than yours.'"

It looks like a great view from the bar atop the Marina Bay Sands, Singapore, but I was warned about the "high dick quotient." (© Guy Keating [ozgfk@flickr.com])

What made the moneyed herd so unusual was that there were so many of them. In 2007, employees of the five largest investment banks shared a bonus pool of more than $36 billion. In 2008, a bad year for banks, more than 1,500 JPMorgan Chase bankers nonetheless received bonuses of more than $1 million, and more than 200 of their Goldman Sachs counterparts received $3 million or more. This meant a lot of wealth one-upmanship, a lot of bankers who made $1 million as a bonus and felt the need to compensate somehow. "There is the desire to possess quality things," explained an investment banker turned real estate agent interviewed by the New York Times. "The desire to show off; the difference between men and boys being the size of their toys."

In Andrew Ross Sorkin's account of the global financial crisis, Too Big to Fail, there is a moment when, in the midst of orchestrating the Wall Street bailout, Timothy Geithner of the U.S. Federal Reserve pauses for a moment to reflect: "This is what it is all about, he thought to himself, the people who rise at dawn to get in to their jobs, all of whom rely to some extent on the financial industry to help power the economy. . . . This is what saving the financial industry is really about, he reminded himself, ordinary people with ordinary jobs." And indeed, Geithner was right — more right than he knew. He was talking about ordinary people who had jobs beyond the financial sector; but the moneyed herd was itself made up of ordinary people, and he was saving them. These were not the reclusive billionaires you meet once and then have a cocktail party story to tell for the rest of your life. These were the people you went to school with, worked with, or saw on the streets every day, particularly if you lived in Manhattan or London. The only difference was that they were all relatively rich.

When you were young your parents probably told you to become a doctor or lawyer. You should have listened to them. Doctors and lawyers together make up more than 20 percent of the so-called one percent of the highest income earners in the United

States. The relative financial success of people in these professions is partly attributable to the fact that the government requires that you have a license in order to practice medicine or law. And for good reason — if every person on the street was a potential heart surgeon, the cost of heart surgery would fall dramatically, but so would your chances of surviving an operation. Doctors are licensed partly in order to protect the public. But the license requirement is, on a very small scale, a wealth secret. It means that even though people can see how much money doctors are making, and would like to be doctors, they cannot, because they do not have a license. As the license is not an insurmountable obstacle, doctors rarely rise to the ranks of the superrich, but in the grand scheme of things they do pretty well. What makes doctoring lucrative is the limit on competition.

If your parents told you to become a banker, however, it was even better advice, and if you did not take it, you are now probably very sorry. As is well known, in many countries, average incomes for "one percenters" have grown in recent years while incomes for the majority have grown more slowly or stagnated (more on this toward the end of this chapter). But average incomes in the financial sector (including commercial banking, investment banking, asset management, real estate, and insurance) have grown extraordinarily — indeed, financial incomes have grown at the expense of the rest of the one percent. In the United States, for instance, financial sector employees have very nearly doubled their representation among the nation's top income earners between the 1970s and today — forcing some well-off doctors, executives from other industries, farmers, entrepreneurs, and pilots out of the one percent. Indeed, over this period, the financial sector is the *only* profession that materially increased its representation among the nation's top incomes. The rise of finance is arguably the phenomenon that makes everyone else feel, in this case accurately, that they are very rapidly falling behind.

Perhaps the most visible representatives of this success are bankers (including investment bankers). But what was it that allowed an entire sector to outshine the rest of the economy? There is, after all, no license requirement to become a banker. So far in this book we have followed the fortunes of remarkable individuals and corporations. But what kind of wealth secret empowers an entire *industry*? To answer that question, we must follow the moneyed herd back to its rather humble origins.

THE DEPOSITOR'S GUARANTEE

Following the 1929 stock market crash and wave of bank failures that ushered in the Great Depression, the U.S. government decided to put an end to banking crises once and for all. In June 1933, Congress created a new government institution: the Federal Deposit Insurance Corporation, or FDIC, to insure U.S. bank deposits. The idea was to eradicate bank runs. Depositors would know that even if their bank went bust, the funds in their accounts were insured by the FDIC (which was in turn funded by fees paid by banks).

There were some obvious problems with this, of course. Deposit insurance "may reduce the incentive for good management because...the public may become indiscriminate in selecting the association with which it wishes to deal," worried one banking executive in the 1940s. If deposits are insured, does it matter if I stash my money in a good bank or a bad bank? Probably not. In response to such concerns, the FDIC demanded, and was granted, the right to terminate the insurance of banks guilty of unsafe or unsound practices. Unfortunately, this power was almost unusable in practice, as termination would provoke the very bank run the FDIC was created to prevent.

But it did not really matter. The Banking Act of 1933, better known as the Glass-Steagall Act, made it all but impossible for

U.S. banks to get up to anything too risky. Banks insured by the FDIC were forbidden from engaging in investment banking or expanding across state lines, and faced limits on the number of branches they could open. The federal government even established a maximum ceiling on savings account interest rates to prevent banks from competing with each other to attract funds. This intrusive regulation limited competition and produced tidy profits for bankers, but also meant they had little chance of achieving great wealth. Banking was boring, although it was not a bad life. Bankers were said to live by the "3-6-3 rule:" pay 3 percent interest on deposits, charge 6 percent interest on loans, and at 3 p.m. head to the golf course.

During this time, when bankers were out golfing, a number of regulatory changes were made that would transform the industry. And yet banking was so boring that it took a long time for anyone to notice what had happened. The first crucial change came in 1935, when the FDIC was granted the option to facilitate the merger of weak banks instead of liquidating them and paying off insured depositors. If a bank was about to fail, the FDIC could try to induce another bank to buy it, if necessary by subsidizing the purchase using deposit insurance funds. This had a very interesting implication, in case anyone was paying attention (no one was). The FDIC was supposed to be insuring only small depositors. But when it arranged a government-assisted merger—called a "purchase and assumption" transaction—the result was that *all* depositors were protected, because all deposits, whether insured or not, were taken on by the purchasing bank, with the help of an FDIC subsidy.

By the 1940s, purchase and assumption transactions had become the default option for the FDIC. This meant that the FDIC was, in practice, guaranteeing all U.S. bank deposits. In the 1950s, there was a political backlash against this policy, and for a time banks were once again left to collapse. But it didn't last. By the 1960s the

FDIC was up to its old tricks. A mid-1980s review of the fifty largest bank failures to that point found that in forty-six of the fifty cases—including every one of the twenty largest—the FDIC had either bailed out the bank or arranged a subsidized merger, thus providing, in practice, 100 percent deposit insurance to every depositor, large or small. Another study discovered that between 1979 and 1989, 99.7 percent of *all* deposits (not just the small deposits the FDIC was supposed to be insuring) had been protected from loss by FDIC actions. Moreover, from the 1960s on, the FDIC's deposit insurance fund was taken into the national budget, suggesting that U.S. bank deposits might well be backed by the full faith and credit of the government.

This was very interesting. It is a popular misconception that the banking industry is unique in attracting risk-crazed maniacs who seek, largely successfully, to bankrupt their own companies in pursuit of a quick profit. In actual fact, *all* right-thinking corporate executives in all industries should behave in this manner, if they are allowed to do so. If someone has entrusted you with his money, you should immediately gamble it on ultra-high-risk ventures that may get you a quick return—it's not your money, after all. Or you should use the money to add to your fortune at the shareholders' expense, as with the endemic conflict-of-interest deals of Pierpont Morgan's day. But for most executives, such strategies are frustratingly difficult to execute. If you start stealing money, or losing money, people stop giving it to you. Rating agencies, accountancies, and boards of directors all monitor this kind of thing, albeit imperfectly. You may get away with it for a little while (think Enron, or Bernie Madoff). But if they catch you, you will go to jail.

But what if, for some reason, the government decided to guarantee all the money invested in your company, so that no investor who gave you money could ever lose? Would anyone care what you did with the cash?

The answer, of course, is no.

After a brief hiatus in the 1950s, this magical scenario had come to pass in the banking sector, at least as far as depositor funds were concerned. All funds in insured banks had, in effect, an FDIC guarantee. Hence nobody cared what bankers did with their money. Not small depositors (who might have had limited ability to police a bank's actions anyway). Nor, more crucially, wealthy depositors, or other banks, which might have been expected to provide effective oversight. Perhaps the most important constraint on executive behavior in the U.S. banking sector was thus removed. Bankers could do whatever they liked with other people's money. People who had previously admitted to insider trading could start taking deposits—and depositors, knowing the safety of their money was all but guaranteed, would not care.

And that is exactly what happened.

THE S&L MELTDOWN

The warm-up act to the global financial crisis was a crisis in the United States savings and loan (S&L) sector during the 1980s. This was a thoroughly American crisis, involving Texans, suburban sprawl, obesity, the U.S. Congress, a woman known as "Joy Love," and yet more Texans. Yet this somewhat comical small-time fiasco very precisely foreshadowed the global financial catastrophe that would occur roughly two decades later.

It was the fact that the S&L sector was considered to be so unexciting that enabled the crisis to take place (and the marvelous profits leading up to it). S&Ls took deposits from people and were allowed to use these deposits for one thing only: to make home loans. This was the sector that gave the world *It's a Wonderful Life*—the sleepy small-town banker with the forgetful uncle who is loved by all and gives everyone their mortgages. As long as government controls on interest rates remained in place, it was hard to lose much money in the business (if someone defaulted on their mortgage, you would get her house in exchange). It was also a hard business to make much money in. But the S&L sector had one very important thing going for it: it was considered such a backwater that no one really bothered to regulate it.

In 1980, as overall deregulation of the financial sector was under way, the S&Ls (also called "thrifts") led a push to increase the limit on federal deposit insurance to $100,000 per account. In light of what transpired later, the various politicians and regulators present at the meeting cannot now recall who agreed to this measure. But one senator's aide claims, probably accurately, that "we kind of regarded it as a cookie, a crumb for the dumb thrift lobby." The S&Ls were seen as unsophisticated, but what they were asking for was no mere crumb. This increase in limit helped give the thrifts access to a vast new source of funds. The average individual deposit in an S&L at the time was less than $10,000. But Wall Street investment banks managed what were called "brokered deposits" for wealthy individuals or corporations. These were essentially roving bank accounts, transferred from institution to institution in search of the highest interest rate. Raising the deposit insurance limit to $100,000 (from only $25,000 a few years earlier) meant that these deposits could be managed in $100,000 chunks, which made the business a lot more worthwhile (as did subsequent decisions to remove limits on the fees that could be charged by the brokers). Brokered deposits totaled $3 billion industry-wide in January 1982, but had exploded to $30 billion by January 1984.

In exchange for their fees, the Wall Street investment banks hunted for the financial institutions paying the highest interest rates and parked their clients' funds there. They were also, at least initially, supposed to monitor these institutions closely to make sure there was no risk of insolvency. Once the deposit insurance limit was raised, the business suddenly became much more attractive, and amid all these new efforts to find the highest rates, monitoring was all but abandoned (because the funds were insured). The CEO of

Merrill Lynch, a bank that offered brokered deposits, told Martin Mayer, a business writer, that his bank only put depositors' money in "investment grade" S&Ls. This might have been the literal truth, but was rather misleading, as Merrill Lynch had parked several hundred million dollars in Gibraltar Savings, Lincoln Savings, and Imperial Savings, three S&Ls that were at the time technically insolvent. But of course it did not matter. Any deposit of less than $100,000 was fully insured and thus risk-free. Deposits larger than this amount were very likely to be protected as well. If Merrill Lynch's CEO *had* been engaging in extensive monitoring of the S&Ls where his clients' funds were stashed, he would have been wasting his time. The only thing that mattered was where the interest rate was highest.

One S&L that offered an exceptionally high interest rate—the highest of any S&L in the country, in fact—was the American Diversified Savings Bank of Lodi, California. The capital requirement for an S&L was 3 percent, meaning that if an S&L owner had $3 million to his name, he was legally allowed to take in $100 million in savings accounts. Ranbir Sahni, the owner of American Diversified, obtained the necessary start-up funds via a government-subsidized inner-city rehabilitation project that was probably appraised at well above its actual value. The S&L he founded had no obvious banking apparatus: no teller windows, no street-front bank, no mortgage loans. Rather, American Diversified specialized in brokered accounts, attracting funds by offering (literally) the highest interest rate in the nation. Sahni then invested this money in such random projects as attracted his fancy: shopping centers, condominiums, a nationwide wireless paging system, a plant for processing chicken guano, wind farms, junk bonds. Most of these ventures failed to make money, so Sahni was soon using depositors' funds to pay interest. By the time the California S&L regulator shut him down in December 1985, American Diversified had grown to $1.1 billion in deposits, and had lost nearly all of it. Perhaps as much as $800 million had to be paid off using U.S. government funds (by this point, losses in the industry were so large that the insurance fund had been overwhelmed, and the federal government had—as expected—stepped in to make up the difference). Indeed, American Diversified's ratio of losses (about $800 million) to assets (about $11 million) was so impressive that it attracted admiration at the highest levels. "This anecdote is tantamount to a news report that a drunken motorist has wiped out the entire city of Pittsburgh," wrote an analyst with the investment bank Sanford Bernstein.

The most egregious examples of S&L mismanagement and fraud tended to be concentrated in California, where American Diversified was located, as well as Maryland and Texas. S&Ls in these jurisdictions had the option of being overseen by state-level, rather than national, regulators. In general, state S&L regulatory agencies made little effort to regulate anything, operating as de facto industry associations (some were funded by the S&Ls they regulated) or providers of cozy retirement jobs for S&L executives. This was not really an issue when the industry was so sleepy but became a serious problem once the thrifts began to attract huge quantities of brokered deposits on a no-questions-asked basis. As the California S&L industry was melting down in 1988, five members of the regulatory staff flew to Italy to pick out granite for their new headquarters, which was not atypical behavior. A new staffer arrived at the Texas S&L regulator in 1986 to find that the employees there did not have typewriters, much less computers—they were penciling in the results of S&L examinations on paper forms. An accountant hired to clean up the mess in Maryland found that one S&L was storing all of its individual retirement accounts in a paper bag in the office refrigerator, because no one knew how to process them. She wondered how this institution had passed even the most cursory regulatory inspection.

This unprofessional approach to regulation was exacerbated by the fact that, once the brokered funds started flowing, small-time state regulators found themselves receiving big-time favors. The California S&Ls donated $154,000 to the campaigns of California assemblyman Patrick Nolan in the 1980s—a lot of money for state. government. In 1982, Nolan sponsored a bill that permitted S&Ls regulated by the state of California to invest their money in anything, from wind farms to junk bonds (which is just what American Diversified then set about doing). California S&Ls had been the most regulated of all financial institutions, permitted only to make home loans; soon they were becoming the least regulated. The global banking giant Citicorp, envious of these freedoms, briefly considered converting its entire banking operation into an S&L.

The Texas regulator went one better: in addition to investing in anything they wanted, Texas S&Ls were allowed to make loans to other businesses owned by their owners. This ushered in an age of conflict-of-interest dealings unknown since the time of Carnegie. In 1983 a visiting national regulator was somewhat alarmed to find himself in the backseat of a Rolls-Royce owned by Spencer H. Blain, Jr., a former vice-chairman of an S&L industry regulatory body and now chairman of Empire Savings and Loan. "I don't know any thrift executive who drives a Rolls-Royce," said the man from Washington, perhaps a little nervously. "We're just very profitable down here in Texas," said Blain. In 1982, Empire had deposits of just $17.3 million. Two years later this had exploded to $308.9 million—85 percent of it brokered funds from Wall Street investment banks.

Shortly after that, a suspicious federal regulator chartered a private plane and shot a video of the vast Empire-sponsored developments stretching along Interstate 30 east of Dallas. The video unrolled for more than twenty minutes, its voice-over narration describing "hundreds and hundreds of units that are under construction, none occupied." At least 50 percent of the condominiums were empty, including many buildings that appeared to have been abandoned. Many of the completed and "virtually totally vacant" units showed signs of freeze damage, vandalism, and arson, and across the street the video revealed yet more units under construction. These newly built ghost towns were used for "flipping" — quick purchasing and reselling of real estate, often between related companies, producing large paper profits. But the last party in the chain of transactions (and the S&L that had lent the money for the project) would then be left with a nearly worthless asset. After federal regulators finally closed Empire in 1984, the government paid out $279 million in losses to depositors.

Empire Savings and Loan was by no means the only Texas S&L to have a close relationship with its regulators. Lamar Savings

The U.S. government became a condo owner after the collapse of Empire Savings and Loan. About two hundred condos were simply bulldozed, as they were judged to be worth less than nothing. (David Woo / *Dallas Morning News*)

Association had the chairman of one government banking institution on its board of directors and counted the head of S&L supervision in Texas among its shareholders. Lamar had big ambitions — Texas-size ambitions. At one point it attempted to get involved in a deal to fund the construction of what would have been the tallest building in China. When Lamar eventually failed, in 1988, bailing out the S&L's depositors cost the U.S. government $805 million. Another Texas thrift, Vernon Savings and Loan, was notorious for hiring prostitutes (most famously a Ms. "Joy Love" of Dallas) to entertain regulators. When Vernon failed, with an astonishing 96 percent of its loans having gone bad, the S&L's president testified during the ensuing trial that since the regulator who had received the prostitutes was impotent, he had not in fact been bribed. The jury, evidently unconvinced, found for the prosecution.

In Maryland, the situation was quite possibly even worse (or better, if you were running an S&L). A special investigator's report for the state governor noted the "total absence of regulation of savings and loan associations; individuals in the industry who took advantage of that absence of regulation to expropriate depositors' money for their own use; and a hopelessly flawed system which permitted the industry to make and enforce its own rules." Maryland's Old Court S&L became infamous after its morbidly obese proprietor, Jeffrey Levitt, used depositors' money to buy $400,000 worth of jewelry, seventeen automobiles, a Rolls-Royce golf cart, and three thoroughbred racehorses. The public thrilled to the smallest details of Levitt's decadence. At a Baltimore restaurant, he and his wife were spotted after a meal consuming six desserts *each*, or so the papers said.

By the mid-1980s, S&Ls across the country had lost so much money that the deposit insurance fund was overwhelmed. The industry as a whole would require a government bailout. But there was a problem. The S&Ls had gained political clout at the national

level. There were allegations regarding the provision of prosti-
tutes here as well, but mostly the favors S&Ls provided to national
politicians and regulators were wholly legal. The S&Ls funded
all-expense-paid trips for congressmen and their staffers; offered
jobs to retiring regulators; and made large campaign contributions.
When Congress and federal regulatory authorities began to discuss
bailout packages for the beleaguered S&Ls, they found the industry had sufficient political clout to (rather ungratefully) dictate
the terms of its own bailout. Lawrence Taggart, a California S&L
regulator turned Texas S&L lobbyist, wrote a letter to the U.S.
secretary of the treasury claiming that any bailout that imposed
onerous conditions on the thrifts (such as shutting them down,
merging them, or allowing them to be acquired by banks) was
"likely to have a very adverse impact on the ability of our Party to
raise needed campaign funds in the upcoming elections." Taggart
continued: "Many who have been very supportive of the Administration are involved with savings and loan associations which are
either being closed by the [national S&L regulator] or threatened
with closure."

And thus, much to the annoyance of national regulators,
throughout the 1980s the industry received a series of bailout packages that above all else endeavored to keep S&Ls in business
(which had the effect of giving them more time to lose, or steal,
money). One early 1980s bailout scheme was a series of S&L-specific
changes to accounting regulations that, in effect, incentivized
S&Ls to lose even more money by paying out illusory profits as
dividends. The changes also failed to solve the problem of thrifts
going bust. By 1985, a federal investigation found that 434 S&Ls
across the country were technically insolvent and 850 more were
on the verge of bankruptcy. The spectacular cases of S&L mismanagement emerging from Texas, California, and Maryland
offered an alarming insight into the scale of the fraud that was one
cause of these difficulties. The S&L industry nonetheless managed

to wangle yet another bailout, this one involving the creation of a quasi-public organization to dispose of bad assets, which would be managed almost entirely by leading figures in the S&L industry.

This did not, of course, resolve their problems. When, in 1986, the federal government had to top up the deposit insurance fund, the industry wanted to dictate the terms of this bailout as well. The highest-ranking members of the Senate Banking Committee had received large campaign contributions from the S&Ls, and the chairman of the House Banking Committee, Fernand St. Germain, was under an ethics investigation for allegedly receiving extensive financial favors from banks and S&Ls. All told, the S&L industry contributed about $4.5 million to the campaigns of members of Congress between 1983 and 1988. In the end, the thrifts didn't get the no-questions-asked taxpayer-funded gift they wanted, but did manage, with spectacular chutzpah, to include an $800 million government subsidy for "healthy" S&Ls on top of the $10 billion bailout package for their failing counterparts.

It was still not enough. By 1987, the S&L industry as a whole was making a $6.8 billion loss. A report in April 1988 found that Texas S&Ls alone were losing $27 million each day and thus were on track to lose up to $10 billion within a year.

By 1991, the game was up. Lots of commercial mismanagement, political influence peddling, cozy relations with local regulators, and a fair amount of outright fraud had added up to a massive sum: a taxpayer-funded bailout of the S&L industry that would cost $153 billion, or about 2 percent of total U.S. economic output. Some estimates put the cost over the long term as high as $1 trillion, after various other guarantees and interest payments were included. The scale of the sums involved attracted national attention, and for once the industry's lobbying power was overwhelmed. This time the bailout would be accompanied by the merger, acquisition, or shutdown of hundreds of badly run S&Ls. Within a year, the federal government had taken over 402 S&Ls in forty states with total assets exceeding $220 billion. The 1989 Financial Institutions Reform, Recovery and Enforcement Act cleaned up the S&Ls' cozy regulatory relations, and the Federal Deposit Insurance Corporation Improvement Act of 1991 mandated that banks (and S&Ls) be closed when they reached a certain capital-to-assets ratio.

The days of an S&L with political connections using its clout to stay in business were therefore over. Failures soared between 1991 and 1993 as the FDIC sorted out the mess.

Even more importantly, the 1991 act essentially ended the universal deposit insurance promise. After 1991, the subsidized purchase and assumption transactions that had hitherto characterized bank failures came to a halt. From 1991 on, depositors of less than $100,000 would be protected, but the rest would lose their money when a bank failed. At least in theory: between 1992 and 1994, only 65 percent of uninsured depositors actually lost money. Still, that was a sizable majority. The days of throwing money at banks, no matter how badly managed, and knowing that an insurance fund — and, if necessary, the U.S. government — would pick up the tab, were over.

For a brief time in the 1980s, opening an S&L was the ultimate wealth secret. West Coast regulatory authorities calculated that with a $2 million start-up investment and an S&L charter, it was possible to create a $1.3 billion institution within five years, if one attracted enough deposits. Indeed, with highly mobile and undiscriminating brokered deposits seeking a home, this was not only possible but feasible. You could, in sum, gain access to $99.85 of depositors' money for every $0.15 in start-up capital you had, and then use the depositors' money more or less however you wanted.

And yet this money was, in a manner of speaking, fool's gold. Those charged with sorting out the aftermath of the S&L crisis tended to have poorly disguised contempt for the small-time perpetrators involved. "I remember we called American Diversified [the California S&L whose losses were compared to a drunk driver wiping out Pittsburgh] once and wanted a balance sheet figure," said a West Coast regulator. "Sahni didn't know what we were talking about. None of these people were brilliant." Most of the moneymaking schemes deployed during the S&L crisis were both simple and illegal. Many S&L owners, including the obese, dessert-loving Levitt and the Rolls-Royce-owning Blain, faced civil or criminal trials. During sentencing, Levitt pleaded for leniency on the grounds that he was a first-time offender. "The biggest first offender the state has ever seen," said the judge, rather cruelly.

These schemes were nonetheless extraordinarily pervasive. A General Accounting Office study of large S&Ls failing between January 1985 and September 1987 found that conflicts of interest played a role in twenty of the twenty-six failures. One rough estimate is that fraud or insider abuse was a contributing factor in about 40 percent of S&L closures. And there were many who lost huge sums but stayed on the right side of the law. Charles Knapp, for instance, created the nation's largest S&L, Financial Corporation of America, in California. He came to the attention of national regulators after he bought large equity stakes in Walt Disney Company and American Express, apparently as a prelude to a takeover attempt. By the time his S&L failed, the bill to taxpayers was $6 billion. Knapp was investigated but never charged, appearing on *Lifestyles of the Rich and Famous*, cruising the high seas on a 120-foot yacht with a movie actress fifteen years his junior. "I have not, to my knowledge, done anything illegal," Knapp said, and given the laxity of S&L regulation in California, he was probably right.

What the tawdry story of the S&L meltdown proves above all else is that all you really need in order to make money in finance is a financial guarantee. It was not only ignorant small depositors hurling money at the S&Ls; it was Wall Street. The most sophisticated financial institutions in the world poured not just millions, but tens of billions of dollars, in brokered deposits into the worst-managed S&Ls—some of them run, it eventually turned out, by petty criminals. Imagine what those geniuses at LTCM could have done with this kind of wealth secret.

But the largest and most profitable banks of the modern day are not S&Ls. Indeed, until recently, many were investment banks, and depositor funds in these types of banks were not insured.

So how on earth did they end up with a government guarantee?

TOO BIG TO FAIL

Blanket protection for bank deposits had been removed and regulatory loopholes had been closed, meaning that the days when crooks with S&L charters could attract floods of depositor funds and do anything they liked with them were over. This was a blow to those seeking wealth secrets in the financial sector. And yet, also in the 1980s, ignored amid the barrage of headlines regarding the political scandals and lowbrow spending habits of S&L millionaires, another extraordinary change in banking regulation had taken place. Though obscure, it would usher in a new era in banking and a phrase that would come to be seared into the public consciousness: "too big to fail."

Like the S&L disaster, this regulatory change had its roots in the exceptionally uninteresting *It's a Wonderful Life* world of U.S. banking that persisted from the passage of Glass-Steagall until the 1970s. Specifically, in 1950, Congress passed a piece of legislation that gave the FDIC, the U.S. bank regulator, the power to provide Open Bank Assistance. That is to say, the FDIC could, at its discretion, use deposit insurance funds to bail out a failing bank. The bank would not be closed, nor would it be merged; it would just be bailed out and go on its merry way. It was unclear why the FDIC was given this rather extraordinary power. The language in the bill suggested that Congress had in mind an alternate ending to *It's a Wonderful Life*, in which the government steps in and saves the day (rather than, as in the movie, the bank's depositors). The 1950 law envisioned bailing out a bank that was "essential" to a community — a phrase perhaps intended to describe a small town in rural America that had only one bank. But banking was so boring in the 1950s that no one thought much about the possible implications, and for two decades the FDIC's new power went largely unused.

Then, in the 1970s, the FDIC faced a wholly unexpected challenge. Race relations in the United States were tense, and one of the very few minority-owned banks in the country was about to go bust. Unity Bank of Boston was teetering, and more than 90 percent of its depositors were black. The FDIC decided to bail it out. "In 1971 no one could be sure that the failure of a black bank in a rundown urban center would not touch off a new round of 1960s-style rioting," explained Irvine Sprague, one of the three men who made the decision, in his memoirs. "The Watts; Washington, DC; and Detroit race riots were not long behind us," he wrote. It was a very political decision, an odd one to place in the hands of a banking regulator, and one that appears, with the benefit of hindsight, to have been unintentionally based on racist assumptions (when a white-owned bank fails, the depositors meekly accept their payoffs, but when a black-owned bank fails, they riot?).

And then, almost immediately, in 1972 the FDIC found itself facing another, remarkably similar situation. In this case a Detroit bank, the Bank of the Commonwealth, was struggling. While not minority owned, it was a large bank — with $1 billion in assets, ten times the size of the next-largest previous bank failure in the U.S. — and it had a dominant position in economically troubled Detroit. Because of this, and because of the bank's "service to the black community," Sprague and his colleagues decided to bail it out as well.

After this unusual episode, the genie might conceivably have been put back in the bottle. Indeed, the bailout option was not used again for the rest of the decade. The FDIC dealt with failing banks either by closing them and paying off depositors or via government-subsidized merger. But then, in 1980, the First Pennsylvania Bank, the nation's twenty-third largest at the time, with assets of more than $9 billion, started to fail, and there was no one to buy it. Banks were not, at that point, allowed to branch across state lines, so the only possible buyers were Pennsylvania banks. But only one of these was large enough to make such a purchase, and if these two behemoths were merged, the resulting institution would have enjoyed a near monopoly in the state. The alternative, closing First Pennsylvania, was seen as too disruptive. "The domino theory dominated discussion [among the FDIC regulators]," wrote Sprague. The argument was this: "If First Pennsylvania went down, its business connections with other banks would entangle them also and touch off a crisis in confidence [that] would culminate in an international financial crisis."

Somewhat reluctantly, Sprague and his colleagues authorized yet another bailout. With a sense of theater, Sprague insisted on delivering it in the form of a single paper check from the U.S. Treasury Department for $325 million (which caused a problem, as the Treasury's check-writing machines had no way of cutting a check that large). Surprisingly, the government's generosity did not appear to be appreciated. Some weeks later, visiting the First Pennsylvania, Sprague found his portrait hanging in the entryway to the office toilet.

Then, in 1982, something even more surprising happened. Congress decided to *expand* the FDIC's bailout powers, enabling the FDIC to come to the rescue if that was the least-cost option (compared to a failure or subsidized merger). On the face of it, this was odd. Both Unity Bank of Boston and Detroit's Bank of the Commonwealth had, despite the bailouts, failed to recover and were on their way to collapsing again. But recall that at the time the S&L crisis was still in its infancy; instead, legislators and regulators saw a track record of unprecedented government-administered financial stability. Struggling banks were merged, depositors didn't lose money, race riots were avoided, financial panic was averted. The bailout option had been successful in preventing economic disruption. More of that, please.

And yet, immediately after receiving its expanded bailout power, the FDIC decided not to use it. In 1982, Penn Square Bank, located in Oklahoma City, was on the brink. The bank had been making loans to energy companies, hoping to make a killing on large oil and gas discoveries. At the time, banks were both closely regulated and relatively restricted in the riskiness of the activities they could get up to, and by 1981, the Office of the Comptroller of the Currency, a national regulator, had started to take steps to rein in Penn Square's risky behavior. But then, unexpectedly, oil prices plunged and Penn Square was headed for immediate collapse. Nobody wanted to buy it. The FDIC decided to teach the banking industry a lesson and let Penn Square fail. The FDIC's chief of bank supervision, Jim Sexton, argued the case: "If we don't [let the bank fail and] do a payoff [of depositors] in this case...then this will mean 100 percent insurance for the entire system—forever." So Penn Square was allowed to collapse, and only its insured depositors were paid. "The myth that a large bank would never be paid off is gone forever," wrote Sprague, with evident satisfaction.

Unfortunately, letting Penn Square fail had very nearly the opposite of its intended effect. Penn Square had been selling its energy loans to other banks. When it went down, banks that had bought a lot of these loans almost immediately failed as well. Seattle First Bank collapsed first, and was dealt with through a subsidized merger. Chase Manhattan and Michigan National suffered large losses but appeared likely to survive. And then Continental Illinois National Bank, which had a $1 billion exposure to Penn Square, started to fail. Continental Illinois was huge. It had assets of $34 billion in 1982. Regulators were concerned about the risk of touching off a national, or even global, banking collapse; there were estimates that some 2,100 small banks had $6 billion in deposits with Continental, some 90 percent of which were too large to be insured (or were owned by foreigners). If the bank failed, a lot of people would lose a lot of money. So in 1984 the FDIC decided to use its bailout power once again. There were, to be sure, onerous conditions attached to it. But there was no denying that all depositors were protected from loss, and indeed that even "the stockholders received an outright gift from the FDIC," as Sprague later wrote.

In 1984, in testimony before Congress, Comptroller of the Currency C. Todd Conover explained the situation more fully: "Had Continental failed and been treated in a way in which depositors and creditors were not made whole, we could very well have seen a national, if not an international, financial crisis, the dimensions of which were difficult to imagine." He testified that the eleven largest banks in the country, including Continental Illinois, had grown so large that there was no way they could ever be allowed to collapse. Congressman Stewart McKinney had this sarcastic response: "Mr. Chairman, let us not bandy words. We have a new kind of bank. It is called too big to fail. TBTF, and it is a wonderful bank."

The *Wall Street Journal* listed the eleven too-big-to-fail banks in an article the next day.

This was very, *very* interesting.

At the time, not many people noticed. After all, the FDIC was still providing protection for nearly all depositors in nearly all banks. The poorly regulated S&L sector was at the forefront in exploiting the resulting opportunity; banks, and especially large banks, were heavily scrutinized by regulatory authorities. Still, the guaranteed protection was a bonus. Even in the 1980s, there was at least the chance that your funds might fall among the 0.3 percent that did not receive protection from the FDIC. Moreover, in light of what had happened to Continental Illinois, it was possible that shareholders would be at least partly protected by an FDIC bailout as well. If nothing else, the markets were paying attention. Academic research later showed that the eleven too-big-to-fail banks had received a share price boost the day the *Wall Street Journal* listed them.

The cat was out of the bag: no matter what one of these eleven banks did, the FDIC would either arrange a bailout or a subsidized merger (and if the deposit insurance fund ran out of money, the taxpayer would very likely be on hand to top it up). And so, predictably, the banks wanted to ramp up their risk taking. Because the FDIC would make good any losses, they would have no trouble attracting funds to play with. But these banks were not S&Ls. They would face off against the country's most sophisticated regulatory agencies (including not only the FDIC, but also the Office of the Comptroller of the Currency and the Federal Reserve), which would endeavor to prevent them from taking unwise risks. These regulators were generally impervious to simple bribery or the charms of women such as Joy Love.

And yet, with full protection from failure, regulatory constraints would be the only limit on how much money these banks could earn. There was no downside, because the federal government would pay much of the losses. For these eleven banks, the U.S. financial system had become a casino, in which the house would always lose and the gamblers would always win.

This touched off what was probably the greatest and most sophisticated effort to game the system that the world has ever seen.

MEET THE SYSTEM

Bankers in the modern era have always operated in an environment that is slightly disconnected from economic reality. There is no bankruptcy law for banks (although, in the wake of the global financial crisis, authorities have attempted to create one). Unlike other companies, a bank does not go bankrupt when it can no longer pay its creditors. A bank goes out of business when a government regulator—specifically, in the United States, the Office of the Comptroller of the Currency—says it should.

In 2012, I was interviewing the chief risk officer of a global insurance company regarding his firm's risk management practices. He explained that the company used two financial measures to assess its business performance under hypothetical worst-case scenarios. The first, economic capital, determined whether the company was likely to be solvent; and the second, regulatory capital, looked at whether the business would be allowed by regulators to continue to operate. Even if the economic capital model showed a high likelihood of insolvency, "if it doesn't impact my regulatory capital, I may still be in business, even though maybe I shouldn't be," he said.

It's a slightly schizophrenic worldview. But in contrast to most S&L regulators, the national banking regulators in the United States were both sophisticated and professional. They were also well aware of the potential problems posed by a government guarantee for banks. "It is time to face up to the reality: despite our best efforts to find other alternatives, certain banks are too big to let fail," wrote Sprague, the former FDIC regulator, in 1986. Sprague argued that regulators should at least keep the banks guessing, rather than announcing which banks were too big to fail. Otherwise the government would be issuing "an open invitation to investors who, having nothing to lose, could dump money into them for use in freewheeling lending and other speculative endeavors. The slight degree of uncertainty we have now preserves at least a modest amount of market discipline."

Of course, once the Comptroller of the Currency had listed eleven banks that could not fail (i.e., in which depositors could not lose money), there was little uncertainty remaining. If anything, the main question was whether too big to fail extended beyond the privileged eleven. After Continental Illinois, there were several further bailouts: First National Bank and Trust of Oklahoma City in 1986, First Republic Bank of Dallas in 1988, MCorp of Houston in 1989, and Bank of New England Corporation in 1991. All were large banks, but none were actually on the 1984 list, which suggested that too big to fail might in fact be a very large category. Presumably, the disaster that had resulted when Penn Square was allowed to collapse had convinced regulators that almost *any* major bank was too big to fail.

At the beginning of the 1990s, though, there was another major twist. The S&L crisis focused regulators' attention on the risks associated with financial guarantees for banks. And so the laws that were passed in the wake of the S&L fiasco attempted not only to put a halt to the bailouts of small banks, but also to end too big to fail. A 1991 law sharply limited the FDIC's ability to provide bailouts. A 1993 law specifically forbade the FDIC to provide bailouts that protected shareholders.

There was, however, one important exception: cases where the failing bank posed a "systemic risk." This stipulation seemed like a step forward, suggesting that only highly interconnected banks were in the sacred category (hence the issue wasn't really too big to fail—it was too *connected* to fail). But the new law was also a step back, because now too big to fail was not just something a regulator had said—it was enshrined in U.S. law. Moreover, the law contained an amendment that enabled the Federal Reserve to extend emergency financial assistance not only to deposit-taking banks but to investment banks and even insurance companies, bringing the Federal Reserve into the bank rescue business alongside the FDIC. This suggested that not only deposit-taking banks but *any* financial institution—including investment banks and insurance companies—could potentially qualify for some kind of government assistance. Not only that, but in the wake of the S&L bailout, any ambiguity about whether the U.S. government would step in and top up the insurance fund if it ran out of cash was effectively removed. Too big to fail was not just a financial guarantee; it was a *government* guarantee.

Walker F. Todd, a lawyer and researcher at the Federal Reserve, was alarmed by the prospect that companies like AIG, Merrill Lynch, and Lehman Brothers would begin to gamble at the too-big-to-fail casino. "Managers now have potential access to another funding source during financial crises," he wrote in a 1993 article. "Whether this potential access alters nonbanks' business decisions—so as to make their calling upon that funding source more likely—remains to be seen." Todd's language was circumspect, a lawyer's language. He was saying that the prospect of government assistance might encourage financial institutions to take more risks. In other words, the availability of protection during a crisis could make a crisis more likely. His reward for this prescient concern was a reprimand in his personnel file.

Despite their flaws, these laws—especially the 1993 law that forbade bailouts of shareholders—may have created some genuine uncertainty about too big to fail. In the early 1990s, the share price boost that the eleven largest banks enjoyed appeared, at some points, to vanish. Some academic studies find the boost; some don't.

But then, in 1998, as you will recall from chapter 1, Long-Term Capital Management collapsed, rather spectacularly. The Federal Reserve stepped in to broker a rescue deal, in which Wall Street's investment banks cooperated on the orderly disposal of LTCM's vast trading portfolio. But the rescue was not for LTCM. The math geniuses lost all of their assets in the fund; so did the fund's external investors. Rather, the rescue was for the nation's investment banks, which the Federal Reserve was concerned might be damaged by an uncontrolled collapse. The geniuses at LTCM did not have a wealth secret. But from that point on, it was obvious that the bankers did. No longer was there any doubt about too big to fail and whether it applied to investment banks. In the markets, the share price boost for the largest banks was back. Indeed, they began to enjoy not only a share price bonus, but also better solvency ratings and lower costs of funds than their peers.

More-modest-size banks were deeply annoyed. In 2001, the small bank trade association testified to Congress that "it is harder to keep up with loan demand as community banks lose deposits to…too big to fail banks." The Federal Reserve assured them that too big to fail was only in their imagination. The small bank lobbyists were unimpressed. "Federal Reserve spokesmen reject the notion that any bank is too big to fail," said the small banks' representative in congressional testimony. "The historical record, however, is to the contrary."

Also in 2001, the Federal Reserve published a list of "large complex banking organizations." The publication indicated that these institutions would come in for additional regulatory scrutiny, a tacit acknowledgment of the too-big-to-fail problem—but at least the government would have its eye on these institutions. And indeed, this was the main mechanism by which too big to fail could be managed. In order to monitor bank behavior and limit risk taking, regulators would look not only at a bank's financial accounts, but also at its internal processes, systems, and procedures, in an effort to discover whether or not the bank was making an effective effort to manage its own risks. This approach came into effect for U.S. banks in 1991, roughly matching a 1987 global banking regulation agreement called Basel I. U.S. regulation specified that banks would pay *risk-adjusted* premiums for their federal deposit insurance—so banks that ran higher risks would pay more for insurance protection. This mirrored the approach taken by Basel I, which required that globally active banks hold more capital if they took more risks. With luck, these measures would remove the incentives for risk taking. Unfortunately, the Basel I rules were fairly simplistic. The riskiness of assets was measured crudely, and concentrations of assets were not considered. A bank that put all its eggs in one basket, by lending to a particular geography or sector — as Penn Square bank had done with the energy sector — was not considered more risky.

In June 2004, many of these deficiencies were remedied by Basel II, although the new rules were only partially implemented. Risk-adjusted capital standards were improved so that a bank's portfolio was considered. Regulators were given more discretion, enabling them to evaluate factors such as a bank's business processes and culture via more intrusive inspections. And an effort to introduce market discipline was imposed, as banks were required to conduct stress tests — essentially, to evaluate the impact of worst-case scenarios on their potential performance — and release these results to the public. "Market discipline" did not, of course, mean that banks were directly exposed to commercial reality. It would still be regulators who decided whether or not to shut a bank down, and these regulators had intimated that there were several banks (and possibly insurance companies) that would never be shut down, no matter what. That said, it was a very sophisticated system, which *simulated,* through various compliance requirements and risk-adjusted capital levies, what might happen if markets actually cared how much risk banks and insurers were running. The 1991 law had also made U.S. capital requirements — the amount of money a bank must hold in reserve as a hedge against unforeseen losses — among the most stringent in the world.

If bankers were going to game this system, they were going to have to work very, very hard.

But the days of 3-6-3 were over. The bankers were young, hungry, had something to prove about the size of their paychecks, and were working eighty- or ninety-hour weeks.

The system didn't stand a chance.

THE RISK-SWAPPING GAME

At times, though, those who chose to work alongside the hard-charging, gung-ho, testosterone-fueled young men who dominated banking's moneyed herd must have wondered whether it was all worth it. One team of bankers from J.P. Morgan, on an all-expenses-paid trip to Boca Raton in Florida, threw their team leader into the swimming pool with his clothes on, then broke the nose of their second-in-command and threw him into the pool as well. The next day the team created the idea of credit derivatives. Or at least, they think they might have. Many of the participants were so hungover during the meeting that they cannot now recall what was discussed.

Regardless of who invented it, it was a breakthrough. Derivatives — financial assets whose value is *derived* from that of another, underlying asset — had been around for hundreds of years. But the underlying asset in a *credit* derivative — a loan — related to the most fundamental business activity in banking. A credit derivative was a contract between two parties. One party agreed to make a stream of payments; the other agreed to make a large, lump-sum payment if and only if the underlying loan went into default. Usually this payment would be equal to the value of the loan. A credit derivative thus, in effect, allowed a bank to take out insurance on the risk that a loan would go bad. The risk that borrowers will default on their loans is, of course, the main type of risk faced by most banks. Credit derivatives therefore offered, at least in theory, a way for banks to eliminate the main risk they faced (for a fee, of course). Since the primary obstacle to banks making more money was government-imposed limits on risk taking, this idea was potentially dynamite. Depending, of course, on how much it cost to get rid of the risk.

The first major application of credit derivatives came in 1994. The *Exxon Valdez* oil tanker had inadvertently delivered a large volume of oil to a lot of Alaskan seabirds and marine mammals that did not want it. Exxon expected to be fined up to $5 billion for the oil spill, and asked J.P. Morgan for a line of credit to cover the potential fine. Exxon was a long-standing J.P. Morgan client, so J.P. Morgan both wanted to make the loan and to keep the loan on its books rather than selling the loan to another bank. But $5 billion was a lot of money, and since this money was at least in theory at risk, banking regulators would require J.P. Morgan to hold a significant amount of capital in reserve against the possibility that Exxon would, for whatever reason, require the funds and then go into default. What some of the drunks in Boca Raton had come up with, though, was a way around this problem. Their innovation was called a credit default swap because, in effect, it allowed J.P. Morgan to *swap* the credit default risk with another party. Another bank would sign a contract agreeing that, in the unlikely event that Exxon did not pay back its loan, that bank would pay instead. In return for this insurance-like protection, J.P. Morgan would pay fees to the other bank every quarter. The risk was low and the fees were generous, so it was an attractive deal. What J.P. Morgan got out of the deal was the ability to take the risk off its books. What the bank on the other end of the swap got out of it was a steady stream of fee payments. J.P. Morgan would still make the loan; but since another bank was taking on all the associated risk, from a risk management perspective the loan would disappear. At least in theory, J.P. Morgan should not have to hold capital in reserve against it.

Of course, the deal was not *that* magical. J.P. Morgan was still paying a substantial fee to remove the risk. But there was more innovation to come. J.P. Morgan's bankers borrowed an idea from the world of securitization. Securitization involved the transformation of loans into *securities*—financial assets that could be traded. This process allowed a bank to make a loan, repackage it as a tradable asset, and then sell the payments stream from the loan on the open market. At the time, the cutting edge of securitization involved packaging numerous loans or bonds into complex structures known as collateralized debt obligations. A collateralized debt obligation (CDO) was more than a simple package of loans or bonds; it was an independent legal entity (usually a special-purpose vehicle, domiciled in an offshore jurisdiction such as the Cayman Islands). In effect, the CDO itself owned the loans or bonds that had been packaged within it, and would issue notes (somewhat analogous to when a company issues shares or bonds). Investors would buy the notes, and the funds thus raised would form part of the structure's *collateral*. The collateralized debt obligation would then use the interest and principal payments coming in on the loans or bonds packaged within it to make payments to the investors who had bought these notes (the payments promised to investors were the entity's *debt obligation*). The notes were grouped into tranches (a French word meaning "slice"). The CDO would funnel the payments it was receiving into the different tranches, and thus out to the investors who had purchased notes, in order of seniority. Investors who had bought notes from the first tranche, the most "senior" tranche, would be paid first. Hence, even if the CDO got into trouble (that is, some of the loans or bonds it owned went into default), investors in the most senior tranche would be very likely to continue to receive their payments nonetheless (from the remaining good loans or, if necessary, using some of the entity's collateral). As a result, notes from the most senior tranche were the most expensive.

Essentially, a collateralized debt obligation was a way of taking a very complicated mix of loans and bonds, packaging them together, and selling parts of the package such that each part had a specific risk level associated with it. This was especially appealing to investors that were restricted to low-risk assets (such as pension funds), enabling them to get involved in an area of economic activity (loans to companies and individuals) from which they had been more or less excluded. Furthermore, as long as the loans or bonds in the package reflected debts of unrelated businesses or individuals across a variety of industries or regions, it was very unlikely that they would all go into default at the same time. This meant that even if a CDO owned lots of assets that were individually risky, it was still able to sell some low-risk senior notes. Indeed, according to modern financial theory, the low-risk tranche was often very large. This was not completely crazy. Most people would accept that a large bank, such as Citigroup, makes some high-risk loans (for instance, Citigroup once unwisely gave me a credit card) but is itself a very stable financial institution unlikely to go bust. In a similar manner, a CDO was created in such a way that it was able to, in effect, manage the risks to which it was exposed. In the case of the CDO, the risk was "managed" based on the law of large numbers—that is to say, the more loans packaged within it, the less likely they would all go bad at the same time, generally speaking.

The J.P. Morgan bankers were about to add a further layer of complexity. Rather than creating a CDO that packaged up loans or bonds, they would create a CDO that packaged up credit default swaps. The first of these deals packaged the risks relating to $9.7 billion in underlying loans that J.P. Morgan had made to 307 companies. J.P. Morgan would enter into credit default swap contracts with the CDO. Thus J.P. Morgan agreed to make a quarterly stream of payments, and in exchange, the CDO agreed to compensate J.P. Morgan if any of these companies defaulted. As with an ordinary CDO, this new instrument would in turn issue notes to investors. Payments on these notes would be made as long as the CDO could afford to make them. The money invested in these notes would become the entity's collateral, and, as before, investors in the most senior tranche of notes would be paid first.

And thus, J.P. Morgan had found a way to market its new credit default swap product. Investors did not have to know about all

307 companies, the default risk of which determined the value of the package; they could simply buy notes from tranches at risk levels with which they were comfortable. Eventually, structures of this type came to be called *synthetic* CDOs, because they in effect owned credit derivatives that referenced underlying loans or bonds, rather than directly owning the loans or bonds themselves.

There was a further, crucial payoff for J.P. Morgan. With an ordinary CDO, as noted above, even if the packaged-up assets were individually risky, the likelihood that they would all go into default at the same time was extremely low. A CDO therefore created a low-risk tranche from a pool of risky assets. Indeed, usually, because unrelated assets were grouped together, the low-risk tranche was the largest tranche. A synthetic CDO used the same law-of-large-numbers trick, and therefore necessarily involved not just one credit default swap (like the Exxon loan) but a huge number of swaps referencing a huge number of loans. Hence there was a tranche, usually a very large tranche, that was profoundly unlikely to suffer losses and earned the title "super senior." J.P. Morgan calculated that for the synthetic CDO it had created, this tranche, exposed to almost no risk, constituted a whopping $9 billion out of the total $9.7 billion in loan-default exposure. That might seem a little rich: the bank had made $9.7 billion in loans, and there was no risk associated with 93 percent of the exposure? But to be fair, for this first deal, J.P. Morgan had selected a set of loans that were relatively unlikely to default. So J.P. Morgan decided not to put any capital behind this super senior tranche. That is to say, while the special-purpose vehicle would be the counterparty on credit default swaps referencing $9.7 billion in underlying loans, it would need to raise only $700 million in collateral by issuing notes to investors. The $9 billion super senior tranche would thus be "unfunded"— in effect, backed by nothing except the bank's calculations that losses would never get this high.

The real magic of the deal lay in the decision not to fund this super senior tranche. *Poof!* Fully $9 billion in credit risk had vanished from the books, at a relatively negligible cost to J.P. Morgan. While the bank would, of course, pay the premiums on $9.7 billion in credit default swaps to the synthetic CDO, which would in turn make payments to investors on the $700 million worth of notes it had issued, the premiums on the remaining "unfunded" $9 billion would, in a manner of speaking, be returned to J.P. Morgan.

Again, it was not completely mad. J.P. Morgan had, in a sense, created an insurance company to insure itself. Of course, the insurance company, the synthetic CDO, didn't have any offices, or managers, or even employees; but based on J.P. Morgan's clever math, it had been carefully structured so that the law of large numbers—the low probability that many hundreds of diversified loans and bonds would go bad simultaneously—implied that the "insurance company" would, without further intervention, carry on operation in all possible market conditions, with a negligible risk of going bust.

Regulators—particularly European regulators—were initially skeptical. It looked an awful lot like J.P. Morgan was entering into credit default swaps with itself, even if there was an independent investment vehicle sandwiched in the middle. The synthetic CDO agreed to compensate J.P. Morgan if the loans went bad, and J.P. Morgan would be required to fund the synthetic CDO in the unlikely event that it used up all its premiums and collateral.

But the Morgan bankers had a solution. They got a *real* insurance company involved, AIG, which was willing to insure them against the risk that the special-purpose vehicle's losses would reach the super senior tranche. Because this risk was, at least in theory, remote, AIG was willing to offer this insurance for about two cents on each dollar of exposure.

By this point, U.S. regulators had convinced themselves that J.P. Morgan's calculations were plausible. While Morgan's relationship with the newly created independent entity was rather intimate, under any realistic scenario, the CDO's finances were sound. The credit default swaps it owned were no longer on J.P. Morgan's books. And so the risk associated with potential defaults on the loans to which the swaps applied was gone. Or mostly gone: U.S. regulators stated that J.P. Morgan could reduce by four-fifths the amount of capital it was required to hold against these risk exposures. But the fees AIG was charging were so low that J.P. Morgan, although it initially had been inquiring about insurance mostly to satisfy the regulators, decided to be doubly sure and buy the insurance from AIG anyway.

Despite the double layer of protection, there was some sniping at the vanishing-risk magic trick achieved by J.P. Morgan. "They thought they were the smartest guys on the planet," said a journalist from Dow Jones to Gillian Tett, who authored a book on J.P. Morgan's creation of the credit derivatives business. "They had found this brilliant way to get around the [Basel] rules, to play around with all this risk. And they were just so proud of what they had done." According to Tett, Wall Street traders joked among themselves that BISTRO, as J.P. Morgan dubbed this first deal, stood for "Bank for International Settlements Total Rip Off" (the Bank for International Settlements was the international institution that oversaw the Basel banking regulations).

These comments were probably somewhat unfair. Assuming the underlying data that had been fed into the models were accurate and that the deal was structured correctly, the odds that losses would reach BISTRO's super senior tranche were indeed vanishingly small. While the structure pushed the system's rules regarding risk to the limit, to say that an independent entity holding $0.7 billion in collateral would be able to manage $9.7 billion of risk exposure was not ridiculous: $0.7 billion is a bit more than 7 percent of the total exposure. Many major banks don't hold much more than that in reserve (as tier one capital) against losses.

The problem was the assumptions regarding correct data and structuring. The first shortcut banks started to take involved the structure of the deals. Rather than special-purpose vehicles, which were relatively independent from the banks that had created them, banks began to create synthetic CDOs using structured investment vehicles, which were partly funded by the banks. Structured investment vehicles should not have made possible the vanishing-risk magic trick, but hidden within the Basel II banking regulations was a simple loophole: banks did not need to hold capital against credit lines that were less than a year in duration. If funding for the structured investment vehicles was arranged via short-term credit lines, and these were rolled over every year, then from the perspective of the Basel II banking regulations, the associated risk exposure vanished from the balance sheet. It vanished into a gap between market reality and what banking regulations said was reality.

Not only banks but insurers piled into the credit default swap business, and it went global. AIG, in a case of truth in advertising, called its business in this area "regulatory capital" because it allowed banks, primarily in Europe, to evade capital requirements imposed by Basel II regulations. (Whether it reduced economic capital, i.e., the actual risk of insolvency, was an open question.) The members of the J.P. Morgan team that had come up with this innovation were paid well, although not exorbitantly. Most received annual salaries of between $500,000 and a bit more than $1 million. It wasn't yacht money or private jet money. But the team was able to celebrate by gambling in Atlantic City and holding beach parties at their new houses on Long Island. Blythe Masters, who became the public face of the business, on one occasion declared that it was bow-tie day, and her entire team showed up to work wearing colorful ties. Other J.P. Morgan employees started to find the team's hijinks annoying. Bill Demchak, who led

Bankers may be rich, but it's the rare financier who achieves the status of cultural icon. Blythe Masters, immortalized here by graffiti artists, played a key role in the development of the complicated, controversial "synthetic collateralized debt obligation." (Courtesy Organ Museum [Thierry Ehrmann] / Abode of Chaos / Demeure du Chaos © 2014, www.AbodeofChaos.org)

the team, offered a qualified apology. "Yes, it was a bit like a frat culture at times," he said. "But we had an amazing team spirit, it was just an amazing time. And we assumed it would last forever."

Anyway, it wasn't really Masters or Demchak or even J.P. Morgan that was making a lot of money off this deal. It was the whole banking industry. The synthetic CDO gave the industry a way to make risk vanish, almost cost-free. And that meant the banks could take more risk—and enjoy the high returns associated with some exceptionally risky behavior.

At least, the risk vanished from the point of view of banking regulators. The lenders and depositors handing money to banks might have been more skeptical, but frankly, they had no reason to care, because after all the banks were too big to fail.

THE RATINGS GAME

There was another problem with the activities described above. These schemes all involved ways of repackaging risks from underlying loans, whether loans to companies or loans to consumers. The reason that regulators looked favorably upon these schemes is that they combined the risk of multiple loans in such a way that all the individual loans were unlikely to go bad at the same time. Presumably, though, in order to make such a judgment, one would need to know a great deal about each of the underlying loans.

That was easily achieved for the first credit default swap, which dealt with the risk from one loan, to a well-known company (Exxon). It was also not too difficult when the first synthetic collateralized debt obligation took $9.7 billion in loan risks off J.P. Morgan's books—at least, not from J.P. Morgan's perspective, as presumably the bank knew its customers fairly well. But what about from the regulator's perspective? How would the regulator know about what to expect from the behavior of these loans?

The financial sector had a way to deal with this problem: rating agencies. The rating agencies were charged with collecting and analyzing detailed information about entities that issued debt, whether these were companies, banks, governments, special-purpose vehicles, or anything else, and rating their ability to repay those debts on a simple 20-point scale, where AAA was best. As the federal Office of the Comptroller of the Currency put it, "Ratings are important because investors generally accept ratings...in lieu of conducting their due diligence investigation of the underlying assets." This overstates the case: many sophisticated investors were well aware that the system had flaws. But the ratings did offer a convenient shorthand, especially from a regulatory point of view. It is a lot easier to look at a single score than to examine a company's credit situation in detail. Roles for ratings were over time written into literally hundreds of U.S. and global regulations.

For the rating agencies themselves, this prominent role as a tool of regulators was a double-edged sword. In 1975, the Securities and Exchange Commission had designated three, and only three, rating agencies—Moody's, S&P, and Fitch—as Nationally Recognized Statistical Rating Organizations. This decision had the effect of limiting competition in the industry to these three companies, more or less. As a result, profits were reliable. (Warren Buffett, liking what he saw, bought a 15 percent stake in Moody's.) But working at a rating agency was probably a bit like being an American banker in the 1950s: comfortable, but not exciting. In such a regulated world, how could anyone make real money? Revenues at Moody's in 1999 were $564 million, and while profits were high thanks to the company's privileged status, revenues at that level wouldn't even put the company in the Fortune 2000.

And then, in the late 1990s, things started to change. The rating agencies had long suffered from an obvious conflict of interest: since the 1970s, they had received their revenues from the entities they assessed. Obviously, one way to attract more clients would have been to assign whatever rating the client wanted. For some reason—perhaps because the industry was so closely regulated—this never seemed to cause a problem. But then, in the late 1990s, Moody's in particular started monitoring its market share and passing this information to its analysts, presumably in an effort to motivate them to be more responsive to client needs. At the time, what the banks needed was high ratings for the special-purpose vehicles that were taking risks off their balance sheets. Officials from the Office of the Comptroller of the Currency and the Federal Reserve stated that synthetic CDOs could be used to remove risks from banks' balance sheets if and only if these were assigned AAA ratings.

There was just one small problem. Once Wall Street started packaging lots of loan risks, especially mortgage-related risks, information about the individual loans that underlay these structures was very hard to come by. The team at J.P. Morgan, which had created credit default swaps, had decided *not* to offer credit default swaps involving mortgages, because information about individual borrowers was generally not available and there was almost no data on what might happen to mortgages during a downturn. The rating agencies were unable to be so high-minded. Banks began to ask them to assign ratings based on extremely limited information. The banks needed a rating from only two of the three agencies, so they could threaten to exclude an agency that did not play along. "Heard your rating could be five notches back of moddy's [sic] equivalent," wrote one UBS banker, in an e-mail to S&P that later became public. "Gonna kill your resi[dential mortgage] biz. May force us to do moodyfitch only…"

When Moody's went along with what the bankers wanted, it was very good for business. By 2005, Moody's had more than tripled its revenues to $1.6 billion. Its profitability figure, at 50 percent, was even more spectacular—a testimony to the benefits of limited competition. Unfortunately the rating agencies were doing some things that were more than a little odd. Banks had started to assemble packages of debt obligations based on so-called subprime mortgages. These were mortgages from risky borrowers who had limited ability to repay their loans. The rating agencies were assigning AAA ratings to some of these packages, indicating that lots of risky mortgages, when packaged together, contained almost no risk at all. This defied common sense. In 2007, there were only six companies in the United States that had AAA ratings. But literally tens of thousands of collateralized debt obligations, including many that packaged only high-risk loans, were rated AAA.

The models, which indicated an infinitesimal chance that all of these risky borrowers would go bankrupt at the same time, suggested that everything was on the level. But the rating agencies actually had no usable data that were analogous to the loans in the packages. "The purest information to use is data on [historic] defaults, but the sample is just too small," explained one Moody's analyst. "So we look at correlations on ratings movements." That is to say, the rating agencies had little data on what had caused borrowers to default on their mortgages in the past, and in particular on the crucial question of what had caused multiple borrowers to default at the same time—mainly because there had not been a serious housing market downturn in the country in a very long time.

As an alternative, Moody's started looking at data on ratings the company had itself assigned to mortgage loans. There were two problems with this approach. The first was that assigning ratings to packages of mortgages based on data on its own mortgage ratings was, well, rather circular. The second was that Moody's was, in effect, enabling both banks and banking regulators to paper over the fact that no one knew what would happen to portfolios of mortgages in the event of a housing market downturn.

Or rather, they probably did know, but were trying very hard not to think about it.

THE RISK MANAGEMENT GAME

Ever since I was young I have felt that the parable of the emperor's new clothes was being misinterpreted. In my version of the story, the emperor is well aware that he is naked. He is an exhibitionist and a pervert. The weavers who pretend to create his "invisible" clothes are like the rating agencies. They are paid well and they keep their mouths shut. The child who shouts out that the emperor is naked is a whistle-blower. In my version, the kid ends up in a ditch somewhere and the emperor carries on exposing himself to his subjects, happily ever after.

Like the rating agencies, bankers relied heavily on financial models to assess risk. Indeed, Basel II regulations allowed banks to use their own internal risk management models instead of relying on rating agency assessments of risk. J.P. Morgan had just the model for the job. It was based on an approach called value at risk, a sophisticated statistical technique that represented risk exposures using a single, easily understood number. The genius of the value at risk approach was that it could compare apples and oranges — it could evaluate the risk of loans, of investments, of derivatives, even operational risks such as fraud. Value at risk not only compared these things, it combined them, and given accurate data could provide an instantaneous readout on a bank's total risk exposure. Specifically, value at risk models were often used to assess, with a 95 percent probability, the maximum amount of money a bank might expect to lose on a given day.

From the perspective of gaming the system, the value at risk approach had a crucial advantage. Like the rating agency models, value at risk was only as good as the data fed into it. Oversimplifying somewhat, if you fed in data from the Great Depression (nobody had data going back that far), a value at risk model would show that it was possible to lose very large sums of money in mortgage lending. If you fed in data from the post-2000 financial markets boom (which most people did), it would show that your risks were minimal. The J.P. Morgan bankers who created the value at risk approach were well aware of its limitations. One Morgan banker, Peter Hancock, later said that "we were all taught to think that models are useful, but that they also have limits. It is an obvious point, but it is also something people so often forgot." A Goldman Sachs executive later testified that, from December 2006 on, the bank's risk models had "decoupled" from the reality of what was happening in the markets. A risk manager at Merrill Lynch put it this way: "if the VaR [value at risk] is small it means we are taking risks on things we can't measure." This is not universally true, of course; but for any bank making a lot of money, it's probably true.

J.P. Morgan then did something a little odd. After inventing this industry-leading methodology, they gave it away. By the end of 1999, Morgan had handed out fifteen thousand copies of the value at risk models to clients at no charge. The details of the value at risk approach were also published in a book called *The J.P. Morgan Guide to Credit Derivatives*, which was handed out freely. It is unclear why they did this. Partly, it may have been because banks did not consider risk management to be an aspect of competition. (I myself have produced two edited volumes regarding aspects of bank risk management and have found bankers eager to share their knowledge with the world.) Another reason may be that doing so helped value at risk become an industry standard. As early as 1993, the G30, an influential group of economists and academics established to promote international cooperation in the field of finance, endorsed the use of value at risk models. By the new millennium, most global banks were using them, and many regulators had endorsed them.

But for banks, the most difficult aspect of gaming the system probably related not to the Basel II rules or value at risk models, but to their own internal risk management staff. I recall on one occasion being asked to give a presentation to the "senior" risk management staff of a European bank and turning up to find an audience of several hundred people. If these are only the *senior* members of staff, just how many risk managers are there at this bank? I wondered. (The answer, it turned out, was several thousand.) Because risk management staff were so numerous, and were often intelligent and sometimes proud, when it became increasingly apparent that many banks were not actually interested in managing risk, this created some very human problems.

Of course, even bankers who saw the inherent shortcomings in the models had a strong incentive to keep their mouths shut. Traders at banks were usually compensated based on their trading results, adjusted to account for the risks they were running. Managers at banks were, in turn, compensated in part based on the aggregate performance of the traders. Such risk-adjusted compensation was considered in the industry to be the height of sophistication. But the risks the traders were taking were estimated using the value at risk models. This meant that the more risk the model ignored, the more money the traders and their managers would make. The models were ignoring a lot of risk, and the traders were making a lot of money. It likely wasn't going to be a trader who cried out that the emperor was naked.

There were a few bankers who spoke out nonetheless. At Deutsche Bank, for instance, a statistics expert by the name of Ron den Braber expressed concerns that the company's risk models did not reflect reality. He was encouraged to leave the bank. Some of these whistle-blowers were probably motivated by conscience; others by the tendency, common among semiautistic math geniuses, to always want to be right no matter what the cost.

One way to avoid the whistle-blowing problem was to underfund the culprits. If, like the Texas S&L regulators, the risk management department was chronically understaffed, they might not realize that the emperor was naked—and certainly would not be able to prove it. AIG took this approach. "So far as I can tell, AIG had no formal risk function," said a former consultant who had worked with the company. Another agreed: "Even though it had gotten huge, there was no big-company infrastructure. The systems were completely antiquated. It still gathered its earnings data every quarter by hand." In 2005, AIG gained a new CEO, who started to upgrade the company's systems. What he did not do was revitalize risk management. Indeed, he canceled the hitherto regular risk management meetings.

The part of AIG that was showing awkwardly through the company's transparent underpants was their underwriting of risks associated with the super senior tranches of synthetic CDOs (like the original J.P. Morgan BISTRO deal). In 2005, AIG stopped doing this, but by this time it was heavily, well, *exposed*: the insurance it had offered totaled some $60 billion. Worse yet, AIG's insurance contracts specified that if the value of the derivatives products declined, AIG might be forced to post collateral so that its counterparties could be assured of protection from loss. The understaffed risk management department noticed this exposure only in the summer of 2007, once markets were already crashing.

Indeed, even as the financial crisis unfolded and AIG executives probably began to wish they had paid more attention to risk management in the past, the company continued to make elementary mistakes. The unit that had insured risks on credit derivatives started making payments to counterparties without informing the rest of the company what was going on. One part of AIG increased its exposure to mortgage securities even as the rest of the company was desperately trying to reduce exposures. In the fall of 2007, AIG's accountants warned that they would have to report a "material weakness" regarding "control concerns around risk management."

AIG wasn't the only company trying to avoid the whistle-blowing problem by defunding the whistle-blowers. The rating agency Moody's maintained a compliance department to monitor the company's adherence to an internal code of conduct. As the money from rating Wall Street's exotic creations poured in, Moody's started firing its compliance officers and replacing them with employees from the department that was producing the AAA ratings of derivatives products (or so a lawsuit from the state of Connecticut alleged). The head of the Moody's compliance department himself later complained that "my guidance was routinely ignored if that guidance meant making less money."

In banking it was the same story. As the mortgage lender Countrywide expanded its operations, the bank's chief risk officer wrote an e-mail warning of "higher-than-expected default rates and losses." He was ignored. In 2005, he cautioned that default risks for the company's home equity loans had more than doubled compared to the previous year. In 2006, a new president, Dave Sambol, took over at Countrywide. The executive risk committee, which had met about six times per year under his predecessor, met only once between 2006 and 2008. A similar phenomenon was taking place at Merrill Lynch. Initially, Merrill's head of market risk, John Breit, reported directly to the CFO. In the early 2000s, after a reshuffle, he lost his direct line of access to the company's board of directors; in 2005, following a further reshuffle, he began to report to the head of credit risk, who in turn reported to the chief administrative officer, who in turn discussed risk issues with the board. Breit resigned in protest. He was eventually convinced to return, only to find that Merrill Lynch was facing some $6 billion in losses. To calculate the figure, he had to go around the models, which had been calibrated so they did not detect the exposures. Indeed, Breit discovered that Merrill's internal risk models had been updated recently in a way that hid the risks relating to credit derivatives, although he believed this to have been a genuine mistake.

THE GLOBAL GAME

The United States was by no means the only country whose banks had become too big to fail. In many parts of the world, banks were state owned and therefore backed by government guarantees. In March 1994, for instance, the French government bailed out Crédit Lyonnais, a bank for which it was the major shareholder. During its 1998 banking crisis, Norway bailed out not only state-owned institutions but also large private banks. In the U.K., government intervention to prevent bank failures was a long-standing tradition, including for the investment banks of the City of London. There was a secret 1974 bailout of London and County Securities (among others) but also a more public, and more controversial, 1984 rescue of the prestigious trading house Johnson Matthey, which had made some very unwise loans. To be sure, the United Kingdom, like the United States, did make some exceptions, allowing a few major casualties—Barings Bank in 1995, for instance, which was undone by a Singapore-based rogue trader. Yet even this was a mixed signal: the Bank of England initially attempted to arrange a bailout, and allowed Barings to collapse only after making an explicit decision that the failure would not pose a systemic risk. This sequence of events implied that larger and more integrated banks would almost certainly be too big to fail. Rating agencies duly began to include an explicit "public support uplift" in their ratings of the U.K.'s largest banks. The U.K.'s banks eagerly joined their U.S. counterparts in issuing complex financial products. By 2005, the Royal Bank of Scotland had issued eleven CDOs with a total value of $3.3 billion. In 2006 and 2007, it issued at least fifteen more, worth more than $11.7 billion.

Meanwhile Japan was providing an object lesson in the inevitable outcome of too-big-to-fail policies, if anyone had been paying attention. Generally speaking, Japan never allowed banks to collapse. Rather than provide bailouts, though, the powerful Ministry of Finance forced failing banks to merge with healthy ones. As in the United States of the 1950s, the government's blanket guarantee initially did not cause too many problems, because banking in Japan was a fairly straightforward business. Despite the huge changes brought about in the 1980s with financial sector deregulation, the Japanese government attempted to stick to its no-failure policy—saving the Heiwa Sogo bank in 1985, for instance, by arranging a merger with Sumitomo Bank coupled with an injection of about ¥200 billion from the Bank of Japan and other banks.

This had unfortunate, if predictable, consequences. Japanese banks started looking for risk in a big way, and depositors who were certain of a bailout were willing to give them money, no questions asked. Lending to real estate and construction companies soared, helping to inflate the mother of all property bubbles. At one point, famously, the land under the Imperial Palace in Tokyo was worth more than all the land in the state of California. Eventually, in 1989, the bubble burst and the Japanese banking system collapsed. From 1990 on, Japan attempted to introduce the concept of bank failure. It first allowed small banks to go under, and then regional banks, and finally major city banks, all the while contending that the country's twenty largest banks were too big to fail. The series of bank bailouts that accompanied this decade-long process produced one of the largest public debt burdens of any country in the world and contributed to more than a decade of zero economic growth.

In the United States and Europe, no one heeded the warning. The moneyed herd lived the high life. In August 2005, a U.K. banker famously spent £40,000 on champagne at a club near Oxford Street. It was not fun and games for everyone, though. A secretary in one City of London bank complained to the *Sunday Times* that she had received her Christmas bonus in £25 Spearmint Rhino tokens. Spearmint Rhino is, of course, a strip club. Surely not *everyone* in banking wanted to spend their bonuses on lap dances.

THE WINNINGS

From 1980 on, and in particular from 1990, the U.S. financial sector boomed, riding a wave of deregulation. A sizable portion of the financial sector's growth was related to the ability of financial institutions to remove risks from their books and therefore extend more and more risky loans. The first credit default swap was issued in 1993, and it became a popular tool. By 2005, there were some $12 trillion in credit default swap contracts in the market. Banks also turned high-risk loans into low-risk assets via securitization, issuing $1.4 trillion in CDOs between 2004 and 2007. Perhaps unsurprisingly, the peak came right at the end. In the final three months of 2006 alone, banks issued $130 billion of CDOs, of which about 40 percent were based on "subprime"—which is to say, high-risk—mortgages.

This securitization of mortgages, combined with the risk-swapping game, and the risk management and rating games that enabled both, made possible a spectacular boom in lending to risky borrowers. In 2005 and 2006, roughly $1.2 trillion worth of subprime mortgage loans were extended. This was up from less than $100 billion annually in the 1990s. In 2006, the peak year, more than 20 percent of mortgages issued in the United States were subprime loans, nearly four times what it had been only four years earlier. And it was not only subprime that was booming. Between 2000 and 2007, household debt in the country doubled from $7 trillion to $14 trillion, and housing-related debt accounted for 80 percent of the increase.

The associated profits were also extraordinary. Frankly, anyone who did at this point speak up and say that the emperor had no clothes was either a saint or a fool. In 2006, revenues at investment banks rose by 33 percent over the previous year, and profits were up 38 percent. It was an exceptional year but also the continuation of a long-standing trend. Between the end of World War II and 1980, the financial sector's (including banks') share of U.S. corporate profits had been relatively stable, at about 15 percent. After 1980, financial sector profitability exploded. Indeed, by the early 2000s, financial firms were earning about 45 percent of *all* corporate profits in the U.S. economy.

Employee compensation in the financial sector also soared. Prior to 1980, financial sector employees earned, on average, roughly what the average U.S. employee earned. By 2000, the average financial sector employee was earning about 60 percent more than the average American worker. By 2007 the gap had widened extraordinarily, especially in investment banking. The average

U.S. worker made about $46,000 that year, while the average investment banker was making about $358,000 nationwide, and in Manhattan, $880,000. If you suspected that all your friends in investment banking were millionaires, you were probably right.

Despite the strength of this trend, investment bankers did not dominate the one percent of the highest-income earners in the United States. There were simply too many doctors and lawyers with licenses—about 1 million each in 2012, with each individual earning roughly $200,000 on average. But the number of people employed in investment banking did rise dramatically, from 0.3 percent of the U.S. workforce in 1978 to 0.8 percent in 2008. Switzerland saw an extraordinary increase, with a near doubling of employment in the sector between 1998 and 2008. The United Kingdom and France also experienced a boom, with a roughly 60 percent increase in investment and securities employment over the same period.

Still, given the relatively small executive-level employment in the financial sector, the job categories that dominate the top one percent of income earners tend to be more prosaic. In the United States, doctors make up about 16 percent of the nation's top income earners. But the financial sector is not far behind, at 14 percent. And, as noted above, it is the financial sector that has grown, nearly doubling its representation among the nation's top income earners between 1979 and 2005, the latest year for which data are available. By contrast, the representation of all other professions recorded in the data has either stayed roughly constant or declined slightly at the expense of finance. Among an even more elite group—the top tenth of one percent of all income earners—financial sector representation is even higher. Financial sector employees make up nearly one-fifth of this group, against only about 5 percent each for doctors and lawyers. And hence it is fair to say that the rise of the financial sector has played a large role in making everyone else (including doctors and lawyers) feel relatively poor.

Statistically speaking, as is now well known, the top one percent of income earners have broken away from the rest, in both the United States and many other countries. In the 1970s, the top one percent of income earners accounted for about 10 percent of overall U.S. national income, but by the new millennium their share had risen to 20 percent.

There is, of course, a caveat: investment banking didn't catapult many people into the ranks of the world's richest. If you wanted that, you were better off selling textiles in India (discussed in chapter 5) or building a technology monopoly (discussed in chapter 6). As noted previously, only ten of the world's billionaires—less than one percent of them—are bankers from the global financial centers of London or Wall Street.

The reason that banking made many people rich but very few superrich is that within the industry there are relatively few restraints on competition. Unlike doctors or lawyers, one does not need a government license to be a banker (although one does need a license to open a bank). There are (or rather were, until the global financial crisis) a lot of too-big-to-fail banks—not just one. Financial products cannot be patented, and so when a bank comes up with something new and innovative, another bank almost immediately copies it. After Salomon Brothers did the first derivatives transaction, J.P. Morgan copied it; after J.P. Morgan did the first credit default swap deal, other banks almost immediately piled on with their own versions. CDOs and their synthetic counterparts were quickly copied as well. Indeed, by the mid-2000s, a J.P. Morgan banker was complaining that "there doesn't seem to be a way to make money on the structures." So many banks had piled into the credit derivatives market that the fees associated with the deals had been cut roughly in half.

Hence, while the too-big-to-fail banks were making money, they were all making, basically, about the same amount of money. In 2006, profits at JPMorganChase were about 10 percent, profits at

Citigroup were about 10 percent, profits at UBS were about 10 percent, profits at Morgan Stanley were about 10 percent, and profits at Goldman Sachs were about 13 percent. It was an oddly egalitarian boom. While the rise of finance separated a large mass of rich people — the moneyed herd — from the rest of society, they had to work hard to stand out from each other. Large banks were a lot more profitable than small banks, but among the big banks there was no clear winner (except possibly Goldman Sachs).

When the global financial crisis finally arrived, of course, all the hidden risks suddenly took center stage, with one in particular triggering an avalanche of losses: the risk that U.S. house prices would decline nationwide, in most locations, at the same time. Similar concerns materialized in other countries, notably Ireland and Spain. Nearly all of the AAA risk ratings assigned by the agencies to the special-purpose vehicles and special-investment vehicles turned out to be wrong, as all the underlying loans went bad at the same time. All of the value at risk models used by the banks turned out to be wrong as well, largely for the same reason. By early 2009, banks and insurance companies had written down more than $1 trillion in losses, and estimates of potential losses had risen to almost $3 trillion.

These losses should probably have resulted in the breakdown of the U.S. financial sector — a banking collapse on a scale of that which preceded the Great Depression. As of 2007, U.S. banks were holding less than $50 billion in reserves against losses. But of course this collapse didn't happen, because the banks were too big to fail.

In an uncanny echo of earlier bailouts, the U.S. government initially attempted to draw a line in the sand, allowing Lehman Brothers to fail (after bailing out Bear Stearns via a taxpayer-subsidized merger). The Lehman collapse was an extraordinarily bold but ultimately doomed attempt by regulators to pretend that what they had claimed all along was true: that too big to fail did not really exist. Everyone was shocked, but most particularly Richard S. Fuld, Jr., the CEO of Lehman Brothers. In testimony to Congress, he said he could not understand why Lehman was allowed to collapse. "Until the day they put me in the ground I will wonder," he said.

Fuld's puzzlement was not without justification. Allowing Lehman to go under caused an almost immediate change in the fundamental patterns of global finance. Previously, no one cared what risks the banks were running because they were assumed to have government support. After Lehman Brothers failed, suddenly everyone started to care, and refused to give big banks any more money. In particular, banks became almost totally unwilling to lend to one another, causing the interbank lending market to collapse. Without access to short-term funds the global financial system was on a path to implosion. If depositors decided to withdraw funds, banks, unable to access short-term finance, would be unable to pay their depositors, thus triggering a panic. That week I happened to be interviewing the chief economist of a large U.K. bank. "This is the endgame for the global financial system," he told me.

And so the governments stepped in with bailouts. The United Kingdom led the charge, announcing plans to hand £65 billion (about $87 billion) to eight large banks. In the United States, banks and insurance companies eventually received several hundred billion dollars from taxpayers in bailout funds, coupled with government guarantees amounting to somewhere between $12 trillion and $24 trillion in value. Switzerland handed CHF6 billion ($6.3 billion) to UBS. Several European countries joined together to inject €6 billion ($7.6 billion) into Dexia, and another set of countries gave €11 billion ($14 billion) to Fortis in a part nationalization. These actions had the intended effect of restoring confidence. Too big to fail was back — thank goodness. The global economy fell into recession, but financial markets quickly rebounded. The bailouts also took government protection to another level, by making it clear in each of these countries who was too big to fail and who wasn't (in the States, Washington Mutual, the nation's largest savings and loan, didn't quite make the cut).

The handouts were also, at least in the United States, rather generous (in Europe they tended to involve nationalizations). Shareholders in many cases benefited, and managers often kept their jobs. Of course, even for those thrown out of work, crashing the banks was still good business. Despite losing most of his paper net worth, Richard Fuld, the CEO of Lehman Brothers, walked away with at least $260 million in compensation. A study by three Harvard professors has estimated that the total retained income of the top executive teams at Bear Stearns and Lehman Brothers was close to $2.5 billion, even after the failures.

In the wake of the financial crisis, the question of just how much banks had benefited from the too-big-to-fail guarantee became a matter of significant political interest. At least in the States, most of the bailout money was paid back and most of the emergency guarantees were never called upon. So the real question revolved around the value of government guarantees in banking. Academics, think tanks, and government bodies found a variety of answers: investors tended to overlook risks taken by too-big-to-fail banks; the largest banks could raise bond market funding more cheaply than smaller banks; credit ratings for the largest banks were three to four notches higher than for smaller banks; larger banks paid lower interest rates on deposits than smaller banks; larger banks tended to take on far more risk than smaller banks. Attempting to put a number on such benefits, a study of U.S. commercial banks estimated the annual value of the too-big-to-fail subsidy as about $4.71 billion per bank. A U.K. study estimated the total value of the implicit government guarantee to the country's four largest banks at as much as £125 billion (about $210 billion) annually. A study of European banks estimated the value at more than 1 percent of total annual economic output for countries including Germany, France, and the Netherlands. While these numbers should be taken with a grain of salt—banks that are too big to fail are exceptional in many other ways, making accurate statistical estimates a challenge—figures of this magnitude would suggest that implicit government guarantees, which resulted in lower funding costs, accounted for at least a third, and perhaps all, of profits for many of the world's largest banks.

GAME ON!

In the wake of the global financial crisis, Wall Street expressed some contrition (while attempting, awkwardly, to cover up its naughty bits). JPMorgan Chase rebranded its investment banking arm as "J.P. Morgan" partly in an effort to emphasize its long history. The invitations to the bank's rather subdued annual party at the World Economic Forum meetings in Davos included a reproduction of Pierpont Morgan's signature. I am not sure, however, that Pierpont Morgan would have approved of his bank's modern wealth secret, which involved playing a game that was fundamentally out of control. This was dramatized by Chuck Prince, the CEO of Citigroup, who in the summer of 2007 famously proclaimed: "As long as the music is playing, you've got to get up and dance." As long as the good times were rolling, Prince felt obligated to play along. I doubt Pierpont Morgan would have shared this sentiment. At such a dance, he likely would have been found conducting the orchestra, not waltzing to someone else's tune. Moreover, all that scheming and innovating and risk taking probably involved too much hard work for Morgan's taste.

J.P. Morgan (the modern bank) also took the precaution of adding Al Gore and Tony Blair to the payroll as advisors, perhaps with one eye on the rising political backlash against banks. Other than that, not much changed in the years immediately following the crisis. The moneyed herd in 2014 could still be found whiling away the hours in pop-up strip clubs in midtown Manhattan. U.S. banks in 2013 had, after all, enjoyed their best year for profitability since before the financial crisis. The 2013 banking bonus pool of $26.7 billion for New York banks—an average of $164,000 per employee—was the largest the city had seen since 2007. Too big to fail was still very much in evidence, and it was still paying the gamblers over the odds.

Indeed, during the global financial crisis, smaller banks had engaged in a frenetic wave of mergers, apparently in an effort to achieve too-big-to-fail status. The most dramatic such attempt was the acquisition of Wachovia by Wells Fargo. At the time, Wachovia was collapsing. Hence the Federal Reserve arranged for Citigroup to take it over with some taxpayer support. This deal was announced on October 29. Only a few days later, however, Wells Fargo had swooped in and managed, in effect, to outbid the U.S. government, offering a better deal to Wachovia's owners, apparently in a brilliant (and successful) effort to become too big to fail. This was the first time anyone had outbid the FDIC, but the basic strategy was by no means unprecedented. Even before the crisis, banks were eager to become too big to fail. One study calculated that between 1991 and 2004, U.S. banks had paid an aggregate premium of $15 billion for acquisitions that would take them above the too-big-to-fail threshold.

Of course, there has been a regulatory backlash in the wake of the crisis. The Dodd-Frank Wall Street Reform and Consumer Protection Act of 2010 included an orderly liquidation process for failing banks. This was, in theory, supposed to end too big to fail. Barack Obama, signing the bill into law, observed that "the American people will never again be asked to foot the bill for Wall Street's mistakes. There will be no more taxpayer-funded bailouts, period." He may have had difficulty saying this with a straight face.

After the crisis, which involved numerous mergers of failing banks (Bank of America acquired Merrill Lynch; J.P. Morgan acquired Bear Stearns), the country's largest banks had become larger than ever. Indeed, by 2011, the four biggest accounted for roughly 50 percent of all outstanding loans on U.S. bank balance sheets. That one of these megabanks could be allowed to fail in an "orderly" fashion during a crisis defies belief. The same regulatory agencies that ordered the bailouts in 2007 and 2008 are still in charge. The tools and procedures these regulators bring to bear in a crisis have been tinkered with but not fundamentally changed. If anything, the likelihood that these regulators will do anything *except* bail out banks has diminished. Some of these megabanks are so large they may not only be too big to fail, they may be too big to merge.

A slightly more realistic approach has been taken at the global level. The Financial Stability Board, a multilateral institution based in Basel, Switzerland, which brings together twenty major developed and emerging economies and the European Commission, has released a list of Globally Systemically Important Financial Institutions. The downside of announcing who is too big to fail is that everyone knows who is too big to fail. The upside is that the banks appearing on the list can expect no end of harassment from both domestic and international financial regulatory authorities. In particular, the named companies are generally required to hold higher levels of capital in reserve against losses. Recently, U.S. regulators have been talking up a similar approach, perhaps involving capital charges so high that banks might be incentivized to shrink. That sounds rather serious, although still potentially gameable. A new regulatory approach in Europe involves the creation of "bailinable" debt, which would be converted to equity in a crisis. This approach takes direct aim at the benefits of too big to fail by threatening bondholders with losses. Still, it is a little hard to imagine regulators responding to a really severe crisis by imposing a lot of losses on already panicky investors.

More fundamentally, banking has always been highly regulated, and most banking rules continue to rely on spectacularly complex and eminently gameable risk-weighted approaches to reserve requirements. Indeed, via a new global set of rules called Solvency II, this approach has now been extended in many countries to the insurance sector. If banking has become too hot for you, and you're looking for a similar game elsewhere, you might try there. Or you might head to another country: in China, the government has in most cases refused to allow failures amid an increasingly exotic array of financial schemes, suggesting that there is some good money to be made there before the eventual crash.

Or you might just stay where you are. While too-big-to-fail banks have always had a competitive advantage over smaller ones (thanks to their lower funding costs), their position has actually been improving. Some are now nearing monopoly positions in certain markets. In the United States, for instance, antitrust guidelines forbid any one bank from holding more than 10 percent of all U.S. bank deposits. These guidelines had to be waived for Bank of America, J.P. Morgan, and Wells Fargo, all of which blew through that ceiling some time ago. These banks, together with Citigroup, now control about half the U.S. market for new mortgages and two-thirds of the market for new credit cards. A mere five banks together control 95 percent of the U.S. market for derivatives contracts.

And thus, in sum, there are new (and mounting) challenges to be surmounted, but life in the financial sector still has much to recommend it. No matter what happens, you cannot fail. This means that no matter how reckless you are and how much risk you take, people will still give you their money — which has been the financial sector's wealth secret since the days of the S&L crisis. This in turn means that the only constraint on how much money you can make is the regulatory system. Your mission, should you choose to accept it, is to game this system. The rules have been tightened, but not so much, one hopes, that a creative and motivated person could not figure out how to get around them.

And so: game on.

A BETTER SORT OF BILLIONAIRE

But let's say you want more. One percent of the population is, after all, a lot of people. Let's say you prefer company that is a little more exclusive. Let's say you want to be richer than your garden-variety banker.

In that case, you'll want to go where the superrich can truly be found in abundance, which is, oddly enough, in poor countries. In the emerging world, we'll find individuals who not only outearn the bankers, but have at last exceeded the accomplishments of the Romans and U.S. robber barons—becoming, by most relative measures, the richest people who have ever lived. In their countries—today's emerging markets, such as Mexico, China, Russia, and India—the combination of lax government regulation and rapid economic progress that fostered the fortunes of the robber barons can still be found. Whether they've been able to surpass the likes of Morgan, Rockefeller, and Carnegie because their circumstances are more favorable or because they have even greater drive and ambition, I leave for you to decide. These emerging market fortunes, and that of one remarkable family in particular, are the subject of the next chapter.

5

Wealth Secrets of the *Forbes* Global Rich List

THE SOCIETY WEDDING

Dhirajlal Hirachand Ambani, known to his many admirers as Dhirubhai, and to his family simply as Dhiru, did not approve of the bride that his son Anil had selected—or so the gossip columns claimed. Dhirubhai hailed from a small village in Gujarat. He was a lifelong vegetarian by religious conviction. He insisted on holding a *puja*, a traditional Hindu blessing ceremony, for each new item of equipment installed at his first factory.

But his children had a rather different upbringing. Raised in cosmopolitan Mumbai, as a result of their father's success they had been part of the city's wealthy elite since at least their teenage years. And Anil, as billionaire bachelors are wont to do, had selected as his prospective bride a Bollywood starlet, a beauty pageant winner, a glamorous, independent woman whose previous relationship with a Bollywood leading man had been covered in salacious detail in the tabloids. There were rumors, probably untrue, that Dhirubhai used his political connections to have his son's love interest investigated on the off chance that she might have violated India's restrictive foreign exchange laws.

Dhirubhai may also have thought that falling head over heels for someone was a poor foundation for a marriage. His own wedding had been an arranged union. The wedding of his eldest son, Mukesh, was also arranged. But Anil Ambani's wedding to Tina Munim was not going to be that kind of wedding. It was going to be a love marriage—and a society wedding.

The wedding started relatively slowly, with a "simple" engagement ceremony at Dhirubhai's home, reported the *Times of India*. Assuming that it followed the tradition of most Gujarati weddings, the event gathered steam over several days in a series of ceremonies. These would have included a ceremony in which the hands and legs of the bride and the female members of her family were covered in henna decorations; another in which the two families would get to know each other by singing traditional wedding songs and dancing a whirling dance called the *dandiya raas*; another in which an uncle presented gifts of clothes and jewelry to the bride; and yet another in which the bride (and sometimes the groom) were anointed with a paste of sandalwood and perfumes.

The main ceremony, held on February 2, 1991, was kicked off by Anil, who appeared suddenly amid the wedding guests—there were some 5,000 guests in total—dressed in white astride a white horse and wearing a sequined turban. He led the guests in procession to the wedding venue, a fairy-tale palace of flowers constructed on a football field in the center of Mumbai. A brass band struck up a march and joined the procession while guests danced the *dandiya raas*. The ceremony itself lasted several hours, led by a bare-chested Hindu priest on a small stage. In traditional Gujarati practice, the bride and groom are first separated by a cloth screen, and later their clothes are stitched together to symbolize their union. (It is not all so serious: traditionally, the bride's mother attempts to pinch the groom's nose, and the bride's sisters attempt to steal the groom's shoes.) Anil and Tina then walked seven times around the holy fire of sandalwood, exchanging promises that made them man and wife. Even at this point, Anil's wedding was still gathering steam. By the next day, at a postwedding reception banquet, there were some 22,000 guests (possibly even outdoing Marcus Crassus's public feasts). Anil laid on an elaborate buffet of samosas, curries, fruits, and sweets for the assembled masses while police with sniffer dogs attempted to maintain a semblance of order.

Still, as Hamish McDonald, a journalist and author of a biography of Dhirubhai, noted, "by the standards of Bombay weddings a few years later, it looks a modest and traditional affair." McDonald had a point. The weddings of India's industrialists in the present day often include events in several cities, private performances by Cirque du Soleil, and extraordinary prizes for guests (at one 2012 wedding, an Audi, a BMW, and a Mercedes were handed out to winners of party games). Many wedding venues include purpose-built meeting rooms where guests, perhaps moved by the celebration of human union, can consummate commercial deals of their own during the lengthy ceremonies.

And indeed, the 2013 wedding of the first of Dhirubhai's grandchildren to be married, Nayantara Kothari, would cement his family's place among the nation's commercial royalty. One of the guests was Narendra Modi, today India's prime minister. The ceremony in Chennai lasted four days, and a prewedding party featured a performance by Yanni. There was reason to celebrate: Dhirubhai's granddaughter wed Shamit Bhartia, the grandson of K. K. Birla, a member of what is arguably the first family of Indian industry. The commercial dynasty of the Birlas stretches back to India's days as a British colony.

This was all rather remarkable, considering that Dhirubhai was born in obscurity and relative poverty in a tiny village in rural India.

There was little about his birth or even his upbringing to suggest that his children would be marrying movie stars and his grand-children the stars of the Indian business and social firmament.

So what was his secret?

THE LICENSE RAJ

Dhirubhai was born on December 28, 1932, in Chorwad village in Gujarat, on India's northwest coast. It is an out-of-the-way spot notable mostly as a waypoint on a pilgrimage road that runs between the Hindu holy sites of Somnath and Dwarka. Even today, it is the kind of place where, if you have some things you want to move from point A to point B, hitching a camel to a cart is a fairly common way to go about it (another popular option is a three-wheeled contraption that looks like a motorcycle mating with a pickup truck). An overly ambitious attempt at a holiday camp now stands derelict on the town's quiet beach. Most of the villagers reportedly live below India's national poverty line, and a main occupation is subsistence fishing.

To be sure, Dhirubhai was well placed among this group, hav-ing been born into a merchant caste, the Modh Bania, a subcaste of the Vaisya, who traditionally took jobs as merchants or bankers. His father was a village schoolteacher. His home — today a museum-cum-shrine — was one of the finest in the village, although the Ambanis shared it with several other families. But Dhirubhai was one of five children and progressed only as far as high school, since his family lacked the money to send him to college. Even this was an achievement, as at the time few residents of Chorwad would have been high school graduates. At school, Dhirubhai had only two sets of clothes, so he would sleep with one under the mattress so that by the next morning it would appear to have been ironed. It was an unlikely beginning for a man who would become one of history's richest people.

Dhirubhai's success was even more unlikely considering that in the 1960s, when he went into business, the regulatory environment in India was spectacularly hostile to the growth of private enterprise. India had adopted five-year planning, following the model of the USSR and many other developing countries. There were many reasons for this. One was that, when India gained its independence in 1947, the country's history of exploitation at the hands of the British East India Company was still very much in the minds of the nation's new leaders. State control of the economy was seen as one way to guard against risks posed by the avarice of foreign capitalists. Additionally, the first prime minister of India, Jawaharlal Nehru, leaned markedly to the left.

The Industrial Policy Resolution of 1948, the government's first major economic policy law, propelled the government into a leading economic role. Several industries were made state monopolies, including atomic energy and railways, and the government gave itself the exclusive right to make investments—inviting private cooperation only when it saw fit—in a further six industries, including steel, shipbuilding, and telecommunications. In a further eighteen industries the government would regulate and license the activity of private enterprises. The rest of the economy was open to the private sector—although "open" was perhaps being a bit generous.

Initially, any company employing more than one hundred workers and operating in one of the eighteen regulated industries was required to have a government license to produce anything. This license would specify how much could be produced, where it could be produced, and in what size factory. In practice, these strict guidelines were applied to all companies in these industries, whether they employed more than one hundred workers or not. The licensing regime was the unwieldy tool by which the Indian government attempted to fit the square peg of private enterprise into the round hole of five-year planning. Eventually, in some sectors, up to eighty government agencies had to be satisfied before a new business could be started; some seventy regulatory approvals were required each year for firms to carry on operations; and compliance with labor laws entailed the submission of some sixteen separate types of worker registries.

The resulting system, a bureaucratic nightmare, came to be known as "the license raj"—a reference to the British Imperial government in India, which had been dubbed the British Raj (raj means "rule" in Hindi). From the point of view of private companies, life under industrial licensing had more than a little in common with the arbitrary oppression of the colonial era. And as far as oppression of business was concerned, the Indian government was just getting started. In 1956, the schedule of industries in which the state would play a key role was, in effect, expanded, with the objective of giving the government a majority share of all investment undertaken in India. At first, the bureaucrats who ran the license raj tended to be relatively permissive, handing out licenses for the asking (perhaps because production was below targets in most areas). But by the 1960s, gaining a license to produce goods or import production equipment had become more of a challenge for many companies. And then, in the late 1960s and early 1970s, a new series of laws tightened restrictions further. Industries that had previously been exempted from licensing restrictions were placed under bureaucratic supervision. Large businesses would require specific regulatory approvals if they wished to expand further. Certain products were reserved exclusively for small companies. By the end of the 1970s, the list of products that large companies were not allowed to produce had expanded to include everything from clothing, to shoes, to sporting goods, to toys, to stationery.

The idea here was to encourage small entrepreneurs, but in effect the result was a budding tycoon's worst nightmare. If Dhirubhai wanted to start a business in one of the sectors reserved for small companies, he would be welcomed. Of course, so would anyone else, and thus it was all but guaranteed that any new product or production process that proved successful would quickly be copied. It seemed that India's leaders *wanted* to inflict on their people the horror of perfect competition. How cruel! And what if, by miraculous luck or gift of exceptional ability, Dhirubhai somehow did manage to make his business grow? In that case, the law set an upper limit on his expansion. These sectors were reserved for small businesses *only*. So if Dhirubhai did find some scale economies, the government wasn't going to let him have them.

It was perhaps a bit like being a rat stuck in a maze designed by sadistic research scientists. If, against the odds, you ran the maze and reached the cheese, there was no cheese. Or maybe there was cheese, a marvelous cheese, but it was on the other side of a glass wall. And sitting there on the other side of the wall, watching you and probably nibbling your cheese, were a bunch of Indian bureaucrats, giggling.

It seemed there was no way to make a decent profit in India. Or was there? One reason India's government had tightened licensing restrictions in the 1970s was that, contrary to expectation, a few of the country's largest businesses were both thriving and expanding rapidly under the license raj. In an economy that seemed designed to prevent anyone from amassing any wealth at all, a handful of people were somehow raking it in. Some people were reaching the cheese. But how?

THE BIRLAS

G. D. Birla was born into the Maheshwari subcaste of Marwari traders, and quickly assumed the occupation that was by tradition his birthright. Apprenticed in 1906 at the age of twelve to the family business in Mumbai, he apparently dabbled briefly in violent opposition to British rule while rising rapidly in a fast-expanding commercial enterprise, trading cotton, opium (neither unusual nor illegal at the time), and especially jute, a fibrous plant that, in the absence of plastics, served as packaging for just about everything in India, from rice to tea. Birla's family had broken the European monopoly on jute trading and used the resulting windfall to become leading philanthropists in Calcutta, where they had expanded their business after fleeing home to avoid the bubonic plague.

It was in Calcutta that Birla first met Mahatma Gandhi, the future leader of India's independence movement. Gandhi was at the time just beginning to attract a political following, and Birla was entranced by the man. As Gandhi was pulled in a horse-drawn cart through the market in Calcutta, Birla and another man unhooked the horses and, in a sign of devotion, pulled Gandhi's cart themselves. Birla attended all five of Gandhi's public appearances in Calcutta.

By the mid-1920s, Birla and Gandhi had struck up an improbable friendship. How the relationship began is unclear. Birla did make a generous contribution to the Tilak Swaraj Fund, which supported Gandhi's independence campaign against British rule. In 1924 Birla wrote a letter to Gandhi saying that "if any financial or personal service is required by Mahatmaji I shall be happy to render it." By 1925 Gandhi, an avid correspondent, was sending Birla letters approximately once a fortnight. Meanwhile, Birla's star was rising. The family trading company had prospered mightily during World War I, and Birla was becoming something of a spokesman for Indian businesses in the colonial era. By World War II, the house of Birla had become one of the leading non-European companies in India, and G. D. Birla himself was something of a public figure, taking, for example, a leading role in efforts to prevent famine in Calcutta. He traveled frequently to Europe on business and had also become an unofficial ambassador to the United Kingdom for India's independence movement. Gandhi stayed often at Birla House, the family's estate in New Delhi, when he visited the capital. After India gained its independence from Britain in

1947, Gandhi and his entourage moved into Birla House permanently, if briefly. Birla moved his family to the second floor and threw open the gates so that Gandhi could receive visitors below. While Gandhi was conducting an evening prayer at Birla House in 1948, he was assassinated.

Birla was by no means as close to Jawaharlal Nehru, who took office as India's first prime minister following Gandhi's assassination. But despite their differences, the two struck up a correspondence, their letters covering everything from the relative merits of communism and capitalism, to India's foreign policy, to tax policy, to the idea of turning Birla House into a memorial for Gandhi (an idea Birla politely opposed). But Birla did still have close ties to other members of Gandhi's Congress Party — and very quickly, the party found itself desperately in need of campaign funds. In 1952, the first election after independence, Congress realized that it would need to field about four thousand candidates, given the number of political offices up for grabs. Birla contributed 50,000 rupees (equivalent, in terms of purchasing power, to about $128,000 today) to the cause. It turned out that, having delivered India's independence only a few years before, the Congress Party was almost guaranteed to win, and did not really need the money. By 1957, however, at India's second general election, the contest was more open. The Congress Party was sorely in need of cash, and Birla took charge of fund-raising. He estimated that about 1 crore 92 lakh rupees (about $48 million today) could be raised from sympathetic donors (large figures in India are presented in units of lakh [100,000] and crore [10 million], a convention I'll use for rupee amounts). The Birla family business provided almost 70 percent of the funding that launched the campaign. By the time the campaign was complete, the Birlas and the Tatas — another major business house of the colonial era — were the largest contributors, providing 20 lakh rupees (about $5 million) each.

Although he would never quite equal the role he played in this first campaign, Birla would continue to be a major funder of the Congress Party. And his financial support for the party—including his brave backing of Gandhi in the preindependence era—paid off handsomely. Jawaharlal Nehru's leftist rhetoric regarding central planning sounded ominous for the future of private business, and Birla was distinctly uncomfortable with the idea of licensing, calling it a "Damocles' sword permanently hanging on you." But together with the Tatas and a few other members of India's precolonial business elite, Birla lobbied hard for favorable treatment of private businesses under the new regime. At some point, he realized that his financing of the Congress Party gave him a great deal of influence.

Indeed, Birla may have been slightly shocked by the extent of his success. The bureaucracy had a great deal of influence over Indian private business; politicians had a great deal of influence over the bureaucracy; and Birla, as a result of his campaign finance generosity and early backing of Gandhi, had a great deal of influence over the politicians. In the immediate postindependence years, numerous businesses that had been owned by Europeans came up for sale. The Birla family picked up many of these, at rock-bottom prices, including several jute companies, numerous tea estates (until then, reserved for European owners), and companies in sectors including milling, paper, and asbestos. Partly this was because the Birla group was one of the few organizations with money to spend. Partly it was because the government exercised extensive control over bank lending, and thus Birla was one of the few with ready access to finance.

It seemed that Birla had somehow ended up on the other side of the glass wall, with the bureaucrats and the cheese. It would doubtless be an exaggeration to claim that he influenced the shaping of the maze through which other Indian businesses were forced to run. But sometimes, it seemed like it.

A later government investigation found that in the decade

following independence, some 56 percent of bank lending in India had gone to the twenty largest business houses, and fully a quarter of this amount had gone to Birla alone. And this was just the beginning. On licenses, Birla did even better. To be sure, Birla was denied a license to enter steel production (that was reserved for the Tata family who, in effect, carried on the steel monopoly that had been awarded to them by India's colonial government). But Birla and the other major business houses quickly realized that licenses could be a tool for eliminating competition. A common tactic was to make multiple applications for licenses, via different companies controlled by the same business group. Only one or a few of the licenses would then be used—the rest would be held in reserve. Since the government had, at least on paper, allocated all the licenses needed to meet the plan targets, would-be competitors would then be denied the licenses they needed to enter the market. The Indian government soon figured out what was going on but could not prevent it from occurring. "Influential parties and large houses were permitted [to use licenses] to preempt capacities," a policy inquiry committee reported in 1969.

Perhaps because Birla had the most influence, the system seemed to work best for him. Between 1957 and 1966, the Birla group of companies received licenses amounting to approximately a fifth of all investment permitted in India during those years. This gave Birla room to grow while denying would-be competitors—especially smaller businesses, but probably even some of his fellow industrial titans—the same advantage. The result was only logical: by 1958, Birla and Tata had expanded so rapidly that between them they accounted for one-fifth of the assets in India's corporate sector. The four largest business houses together accounted for a quarter. The Birla family company had nearly tripled in size over the decade following independence, measured in terms of capitalization. During the 1960s, the Birla group's capitalization would double again.

There was bound to be a backlash in a nation pledged to socialism. This came when Indira Gandhi—the daughter of Nehru, and no relation to Mahatma Gandhi—took power as the nation's new prime minister in the mid-1960s. Birla sent her a silver tea set as a personal gift. It was returned. Just as they came for Pierpont Morgan, they would come for G. D. Birla. Hearings were held on the monopolistic practices of large businesses (ironically, since it was government action that had created these monopolies). G. D. Birla took on a new role, as public enemy number one. A junior member of the ruling Congress Party weighed in with rhetorical flourish: "a vigorous onslaught on their [the Birla group's] infinite crimes is essential." An investigation into the Birla group's "infinite crimes" was duly launched. It was known as the Sarkar Commission. Investigators labored for eight years, but—as with the Pujo Committee that investigated Pierpont Morgan—the results were inconclusive. The political witch hunt nonetheless continued. A portion of Birla House in New Delhi was nationalized and turned into a Gandhi Memorial in 1971. The Birla group also lost its bank, one of the five largest in India, to nationalization. Intensive restrictions on large business expansion, mentioned above, were put into place. G. D. Birla withdrew from public life. From 1969 to 1972, he went on pilgrimages to four of the holiest sites of Hinduism.

But the titans of the license raj would not fall so easily. While some large business houses, particularly those focused on textiles, suffered greatly during the crackdown, larger restrictions on private business meant, counterintuitively but inevitably, an even better life for any survivors. Greater powers for government bureaucrats meant that political influence would, following the crackdown, be an even more valuable commodity. For the most influential firms, competition was dulled even further—or, more accurately, there was competition for political influence rather than competition on price. The winners in such competitions would enjoy huge profits year after year while making little commercial effort.

To take just one example: Hindustan Motors, a Birla group company, began producing an Indian version of the U.K.'s Morris Oxford in the 1960s. The car was called the Hindustan Ambassador and remained essentially unchanged for decades. By the 1970s, it was outdated; by the 1980s, it was positively archaic. Yet it was still earning profits for Birla as recently as 1995. I had the distinct pleasure of riding in one in the late 1990s, for a 130-mile journey that, on traffic-clogged highways, lasted more than eight hours. The car had a certain retro charm. But frankly, it was a comically poor automobile, with appalling suspension, weak acceleration, and a dashboard that became too hot to touch, apparently due to the absence of a functioning radiator.

The Birla group did survive the crackdown on G. D. Birla, in part because the head of the family had taken the fall on the group's behalf. The group still faced almost no competition, and thus had no need to waste money improving their cars. By the 1960s, there was already a waiting list of between five and eight years for an automobile, and no way to grow capacity because all the licenses were taken up. Everyone wanted an Ambassador, primarily because they had no other choice. In this strange world "the job of marketing was one of allocation, not selling," noted Madhur Bajaj, a senior executive at Bajaj Auto, a scooter manufacturer. It was easy money—provided you had the influence to get the licenses, and the financing.

Nearly all the major business houses maintained a permanent embassy in New Delhi to liaise with government on key policy decisions. Outright corruption, initially limited, began to flourish. Bureaucrats realized that their gatekeeper roles could be a lucrative source of petty bribes from long-suffering businesspeople. Politicians realized that their influence with bureaucrats could command an even higher premium, because a few well-placed licenses could deliver, to a friendly businessperson, a captive market producing spectacular returns. In an effort to crack down on the exercise of influence via campaign finance, Indira Gandhi banned campaign contributions by companies in the late 1960s. This decision had the unintended consequence of driving the money underground, because Indian elections were no less expensive to fight. Black money became the main source of electoral funds. This resulted in what was dubbed "briefcase politics." Prices of regulatory decisions were measured in units of "briefcases," where each briefcase was presumed to contain approximately ten lakh rupees (about $2 million today). Allegedly, some particularly sophisticated political operators began to demand compensation as a percentage of returns, rather than simply stating a fixed bribe.

Although some major companies did suffer losses from nationalizations, for many of India's most influential businesses, the crackdown was, oddly enough, a golden age. Between 1951 and 1977, the Tata group's assets increased by roughly twenty-six times. The Birla group grew its assets by roughly forty-three times. Top enterprises occasionally lost political battles but managed to win the war. Despite new restrictions, a few reforms, and the occasional crackdown, this system persisted from the 1950s into the 1990s. Indeed, in 1990, the 210 largest companies in India earned some 72 percent of the profits of the entire corporate sector (composed of more than 200,000 companies). More than 70 percent of these profits were earned by companies that, like Tata and Birla, dated from the preindependence period. While the other rats were running and running and getting nowhere, for the politically connected it was all cheese all the time.

And thus, for seekers of wealth secrets, India's bureaucratic maze was both a Kafkaesque nightmare and, just possibly, a path to industry dominance. But how was Dhirubhai going to get involved? After all, the reason why Tata and Birla were growing so quickly was precisely because the licensing system and government control of finance prevented young, ambitious, intelligent men like Dhirubhai from doing what Tata and Birla were doing.

And so Dhirubhai did what young, ambitious Indians had been doing for decades and would continue to do for many decades to come: he left.

DHIRUBHAI'S DREAMS

In 1951, at the age of sixteen, Dhirubhai moved to Yemen. This was not an unusual route for a man of his caste, and he was following his older brother, already established in the Gulf port of Aden. In Yemen, there was a more liberalized economy (virtually tax-free) and a demand for English-speaking labor (Yemen was, unlike India, still a British colony at the time), so a young Indian man might command a high wage. After a short interview consisting essentially of an English-language proficiency test, Dhirubhai was hired by A. Besse & Co., a French trading company. Following his arrival in Aden, he engaged in some youthful hijinks demonstrating his bravery, determination, and love of sweets. In one famous incident, he swam from a boat to the shore at night through waters reputed to be shark-infested in exchange for a bowl of ice cream (some sources say the prize was an "ice cream party," in which case it was well worth it). But mostly, Dhirubhai worked and saved. He traveled from Aden to ports around the African coast, selling Shell and Burmah lubricants, and learning to speak some Arabic. He was promoted, eventually managing a Shell refueling station on a military base in Aden.

Working for Shell, Dhirubhai's eyes were opened to the possibility of commerce on a scale far beyond anything he was familiar with in India. While he and his colleagues, fanatical about saving money, would think long and hard before spending 10 rupees ($24 today), his employer, Shell, would willingly spend 5,000 rupees ($12,000) to send multipage reports via telegram, Dhirubhai later recalled. In Aden, Dhirubhai observed the construction of a new oil refinery, the most grandiose industrial plant he had ever seen.

Instinctively, he knew that this gleaming, stinking vision of a factory offered an alternative to the rat-eat-rat hypercompetitive world of Indian small businesses that he was familiar with from home. More than anything, Dhirubhai wanted one for himself. He thus conceived what would become his lifelong dream: to build an oil refinery.

By the mid-1950s, Dhirubhai had a little money in his pocket and was ready to marry. Back in Gujarat, a little money went a long way. Dhirubhai journeyed home, where, through family connections, a match was arranged with Kokila, a young woman from a port town about one hundred miles away from Chorwad, of the same caste as Dhirubhai. Dhirubhai was immediately taken with his prospective bride. But he worried: "I am so dark and she is so fair! She might not like me." This remark, whispered to Dhirubhai's sister, was overheard by his prospective bride, to her great amusement, because she was already eager to marry him. There was one hurdle to clear, however. Dhirubhai took Kokila (generally known as "Kokilaben"—the suffix is a term of endearment meaning "sister") on a long and strenuous walk as a fitness test, as he was worried that the delicate young woman would not survive the rigors of life in Aden. Evidently she passed the test and soon joined Dhirubhai in Yemen. The couple remained there for about four years, until 1958, by which time Dhirubhai had saved enough money to return to India and start a trading company.

Dhirubhai had already honed his trading skills in Aden, where he would often join the market traders after work, buying and selling rice and sugar on his own account. Upon returning to India, he traveled to Mumbai and in 1958 started Reliance Commercial Corporation, together with a friend and with the financial backing of his friend's father. The funds involved were tiny. The start-up company had four employees, including the two founding partners, and an office so small that if all four were present one would need to stand. Disappointingly, Dhirubhai could not later recall the origins

Present-day market stalls in Pydhonie, the Mumbai district where Dhirubhai traded yarn. (Sam Wilkin)

of the name Reliance—now one of the most famous appellations in India. He said that he had seen it written somewhere, and it stuck in his mind.

Dhirubhai had already celebrated the birth of his first son, Mukesh, while in Yemen. His second son, Anil, and two daughters, Nina and Dipti, followed within roughly the next four years. His family, together with his mother, younger brother, nephew, and nephew's family crammed themselves into a tiny two-bedroom flat in Jai Hind Estate, a type of Mumbai building known as a *chawl*, which set numerous small apartments around a central courtyard, generally with shared toilet and washing facilities. Sometimes as many as eight members of the extended family would sleep in a single room. It was far from luxurious, but it was not a bad standard compared to the shantytown slums that many new migrants to Mumbai experienced. Dhirubhai and his business partners initially traded in spices, relying on contacts in Aden. A business associate of the time remembered him as a "small time, paan-chewing trader, with a persuasive manner and a razor-sharp brain for finance." Each day at about 1:30 p.m. Dhirubhai would join the traders gathering in a square near Mumba Devi Temple known as the *Khada Bazaar,* the "standing market," to conduct his key trades of the day.

Soon, Dhirubhai was drawn from the spice trade into something more lucrative: synthetic fabrics. Given the presence of a huge domestic cotton spinning and weaving industry, the Indian government considered synthetic fabrics like rayon, nylon, and polyester unnecessary luxuries, and restricted their import. This had the effect of turning polyester and nylon into improbable status symbols. "Do you remember bri-nylon?" Dhirubhai asked an interviewer many years later. "When it first came, anyone who came in wearing a bri-nylon shirt would be walking two inches above the ground!" As a result, there was a large differential between the international price of synthetic fabric and the price buyers were willing to pay in India, and anyone who could somehow manage to import synthetic fabrics would make a killing.

Many chancers—not Dhirubhai—resorted to smuggling, a lucrative but risky alternative, and hardly a sustainable growth model if one had great ambitions. But there was another way. The Indian government began to offer licenses to import synthetic yarn to businesses that exported Indian textiles (in theory, to enable these firms to replenish their stocks of raw materials). Each license allowed the legal import of synthetic yarn up to a certain value. Whether the licenses themselves could be exchanged from one company to another was something of a gray area, and yet a market sprang up in which these licenses were traded. Dhirubhai focused on this market, reportedly becoming by the mid-1960s the largest trader in replenishment licenses. Trading in a gray market for government licenses was not for the fainthearted. At one point the bureaucrats cracked down, claiming the trading was illegal, and about a dozen traders were arrested. According to a former yarn merchant interviewed by Dhirubhai biographer McDonald, rather than backing down, Dhirubhai launched a charming offensive, charging into the police station, ostentatiously greeting senior officers, and handing out sweets to all comers. The traders were quickly released. When the bureaucrats struck again, impounding yarn shipments, Dhirubhai led the traders in a counterattack, retaining lawyers and arranging meetings with senior ministers, until after six months of courtroom battles the regulators' decision was repealed. "Whenever [Dhirubhai] fights an enemy he goes in the open," explained the merchant. Dhirubhai, it was clear, had guts.

He also had brains. At some point Dhirubhai made the intellectual leap to realize that, by laying down roadblocks to business, the government's licensing scheme opened a pathway to profitability. While most of the rats continued to run, Dhirubhai saw the walls of the maze. And he realized that he knew how to get to the cheese.

In 1966, Reliance — by this point wholly controlled by Dhirubhai — started a power loom operation at Naroda, a site on the outskirts of the Gujarat city of Ahmedabad, a bit more than three hundred miles from Mumbai (the land there was cheaper). He had about seventy workers and four knitting machines. The plant wove synthetic yarn into synthetic fabric, and was export-oriented. This entailed hard graft, because no one really wanted to buy synthetic fabric from India, as it usually fell well below international standards of value. But Dhirubhai, by this point 34 years old, was willing to work hard. Office hours were from 10:30 a.m. to 9:30 p.m. The staff at the Naroda plant would frequently work a full shift during the day and then a second shift selling in the evenings. Eventually, Dhirubhai would organize fashion shows in Russia and Poland, and export fabric to Zambia, Uganda, and Saudi Arabia. He also labored mightily to make his operations more efficient. This focus on performance was exceptional in the Indian power loom business, which was dominated by tiny operators. As late as 1975, a World Bank team reviewing textile mills in India found that only Reliance's operations even came close to an international standard.

It is questionable, however, whether even these Herculean efforts could have made Dhirubhai internationally competitive. India's exchange rate tended to be overvalued; the country's transport infrastructure was appalling, even by the standards of other developing countries; petty bureaucratic bottlenecks dogged every business decision or transaction; power was unreliable; labor laws were unwieldy; the local ecosystem of suppliers and distributors tended to consist of inefficient small businesses. The odds were against Reliance succeeding as an exporter. But global competitiveness was not Dhirubhai's objective. Rather, Dhirubhai understood that the license raj could be made to work for him.

As a result of government restrictions on imports, the local price of synthetic fabric was many multiples of the international price. This meant that Dhirubhai was willing to sell synthetic fabric internationally at a loss. These exports would give him access to replenishment licenses, and thus the synthetic yarn he needed to produce more fabric. And while some of this fabric would also be exported, much of it would be sold domestically, where the extraordinarily high prices would more than compensate for the losses on international sales. "There were occasions when we exported rayon at a loss, because the entire purpose was to get an import license for nylon," Dhirubhai later explained. Because the licensing scheme had artificially inflated the price of nylon, the markup on imported nylon was typically about 300 percent, and on occasion reached as high as 700 percent. "In this country, it is considered fashionable to complain about government restrictions," said Dhirubhai. "We took the restrictions as an opportunity. If the rules against nylon imports had not been there, I could not have made the money!" In 1967, the new power loom factory made profits of 13 lakh rupees (about $2.2 million today) on sales of 9 crore rupees ($152 million). Not bad for a first year in operation.

Most of the titans of the license raj affected a weary disdain for the system that maintained their dominance. The retired Indian industrialist and respected author Gurcharan Das recalled a meeting he once had with J. R. D. Tata, patriarch of the Tata clan. Das called on Tata at his home, The Cairn, an island of green in Mumbai's concrete jungle. To reach Tata's personal office, Das walked down a long and winding corridor past a number of public rooms, each filled with flowers. "I am powerless," Tata said during their interview. "I cannot decide how much to borrow, what shares to issue, at what price, what wages or bonus to pay, and what dividend to give." It was the late 1960s, and parliament was about to pass a law restricting the actions of the largest business houses. "Henceforth, I will not be allowed to start a new business or even expand an older one. What do they expect me to do? Sit here and wait till I die, I suppose," said Tata, his face filled with sadness.

It is difficult to take such comments at face value, given the success that the Tatas and the Birlas had enjoyed and would continue to enjoy long after the antimonopoly law was passed. While the public political attacks must have been tiring, and dealing with haughty Indian bureaucrats on a daily basis was surely a hassle (even if one's political contacts could eventually overcome most obstacles), didn't the Tatas and Birlas feel the system was ultimately working in their favor? Perhaps not. When I met Das in Delhi recently, he explained that "if not for the license raj, the dominant industrial houses would have done even better."

Frankly, it is hard to conceive what "even better" might have looked like for the Tatas and Birlas, given the extraordinary success enjoyed by their businesses. That said, it is not inconceivable that a man like J. R. D. Tata would have thought this way. The Tatas and Birlas may well have perceived only the frustration of having their plans rejected (more than one hundred expansion requests by the Tatas alone were turned down). They may not have realized that their superb commercial performance was in part the product of this same system acting even more brutally to prevent the growth of would-be competitors.

Dhirubhai, by contrast, saw things as they were. If you could understand the maze and work with it, he realized, it could make you rich. When Dhirubhai made his pronouncements crediting the license raj with producing his profits, he sounded like a man telling the truth as he saw it. Perhaps his willingness to embrace things as they were gave Dhirubhai a sort of power.

And he would need this power, because his success would soon bring him to the attention of those who had ruled Indian industry since the country's independence.

After a decade of hard work, Dhirubhai was, by the end of the 1960s, finally making good money. Like the ancient Romans before him, he used his newfound wealth to celebrate in inventive ways. At eleven one winter night, Dhirubhai abruptly announced to family and friends that they were having a picnic. About a dozen people piled into cars and drove to Rajeswari, some thirty-five miles from Mumbai. At around three o'clock in the morning, the group arrived at a pilgrims' lodge meant for ascetic Hindu holy men known as sadhus. The group spent a short time sitting in silence in the freezing cold. Then Dhirubhai lit a fire and they camped in relative comfort until dawn, when they cooked kedgeree (a dish of fish, rice, and curry powder) on the fire, told jokes, sang songs, and bathed in the hot springs, returning to Mumbai late the next afternoon.

After ten years in a cramped Mumbai *chawl*, Dhirubhai moved his family to comfortable accommodations at Altamount Road, on a hill overlooking the Arabian Sea. He arranged a private tutor for his children. He bought a Fiat, then a Cadillac. Dining out at a restaurant with a friend, he ordered an espresso. "What is an espresso?" asked his friend. "I don't know, but everyone else seems to be ordering it, so I did too," said Dhirubhai.

POLYESTER

The video from the DuPont company that Dhirubhai saw was not, by most accounts, a thriller. It involved lots of smelly factories, industrial processes, and serious technicians. But for Dhirubhai, it was more inspirational than *Field of Dreams*, *Dead Poets Society*, or even *The Wolf of Wall Street*.

The video showed, more or less, how to produce polyester, and it turned out that polyester fabric was made by weaving polyester filament yarn, which was in turn made from chemicals — which, after a long process, were made from natural gas. Seeing the video, Dhirubhai recalled his dream from his days in Yemen of one day owning an oil refinery and realized he was in exactly the right line of business.

What if he could expand his polyester business backward along the production process all the way to natural gas, so that he did not have to import anything or deal with any other Indian businesses? This approach, called "backward integration," could be a fabulously lucrative proposition in the Indian context. These were economy-of-scale businesses: "the more you make, the less it costs," explained Dhirubhai, echoing Rockefeller. And, in contrast to Rockefeller and Carnegie, who over time began to face imitators, if Dhirubhai could somehow start a large-scale operation, the license raj would render him all but impervious to competition. Anyone who wanted to match Dhirubhai would either need to import from large manufacturers abroad (which required import licenses, which were strictly limited) or set up a large-scale operation in India (which required production licenses, which were also strictly limited, as well as imports of expensive production machinery, likewise limited, and on top of that, financing from state-owned banks, which was perhaps hardest of all to come by). Moreover, the larger Dhirubhai's scale, the less likely it would be that anyone would be able to do something similar, since restrictions on imports and production were set at a national level. If Dhirubhai could set up an operation on a scale that dominated the nationally licensed limits, the result would be the most coveted license of all: a license to print money.

In 1971, Dhirubhai took a crucial next step on his path to large-scale production. Characteristically, he exploited India's restrictive regulations to find an oasis of profitability in what should by rights have been a desert scoured clean by the forces of competition. To do this, he exploited an incentive program called the Higher Unit Value Scheme, which for those who could not see the maze must have seemed a singularly dull piece of regulation. Previously, nylon exporters had been permitted to "replenish" their stocks of nylon yarn via imports. Under the new program, exporters of synthetic fabrics could import polyester filament yarn for any purpose they wished, provided they could sell their products internationally at a high price. There was still a huge demand for polyester in India, and import licenses were still nearly impossible to obtain. As a result, polyester filament yarn was selling in India for more than seven times the prevailing international price. With access to cheap yarn, Dhirubhai's mills would have a spectacular cost advantage.

The Higher Unit Value Scheme became hugely controversial in later years, and so the facts are difficult to establish. Some said it had been developed specifically for Dhirubhai, although there was no evidence for this claim. Dhirubhai later mocked such speculation, noting, accurately, that the scheme was at least in theory open to anyone. "When an elephant walks, dogs tend to bark," said Dhirubhai of his critics. Dhirubhai had reportedly cultivated good relations with Indira Gandhi (unlike G. D. Birla, whose tea set was returned). He also, it was speculated, had a close relationship with the minister for industries, T. A. Pai, whose Syndicate Bank had been an early backer of Reliance. Whether Dhirubhai had input into the creation of the new regulation or not, he was clearly the most forward-thinking in his exploitation of the opportunity. It took at least a year for any other business to join the Higher Unit Value Scheme. Almost a decade later, in 1980, Reliance was estimated to have accounted for some 60 percent of all the goods exported under the scheme nationwide.

Moreover, a number of other companies that attempted to use the scheme ran into a variety of obstacles. One exporter, called, improbably, Fancy Corporation, ratcheted up international nylon sales to 1 crore 50 lakh rupees (about $14 million today) per year, but found that the commerce ministry would not release the import licenses for which they qualified. On another occasion, in 1974, the Mumbai customs authority seized polyester filament yarn shipments from a number of importers on suspicion that their value was underdeclared. It finally released the shipments about a year later. Adding injury to inconvenience, it released all the shipments at the same time, causing a temporary glut in the market and a plunge in prices.

Reliance quickly became the dominant importer of polyester yarn into India. With the Higher Unit Value Scheme in place, the company achieved an exponential growth rate, doubling its revenues nearly every two years. Sales were 4 crore 90 lakh rupees in 1970 (about $72 million today), 30 crore 20 lakh ($274 million) rupees in 1974, and 209 crore 70 lakh rupees ($1.3 billion) in 1980. The company was soon the largest textile producer in India. Dhirubhai started a chain of retail stores and leveraged his scale advantages by—almost uniquely in an industry dominated by tiny businesses—spending heavily on marketing. While small competitors found that advertising added greatly to average costs, Reliance, by spreading marketing expenses across multiple retail operations in a given region, could increase its appeal to status-conscious Indian consumers with a manageable impact on costs. Dhirubhai's first brand was Vimal, named for a nephew. An early, memorable advertising slogan, which doesn't make sense and yet somehow does: "A woman expresses herself in many languages. Vimal is one of them." Reliance's synthetic fabrics were marketed as high-end luxuries, but most buyers came from the middle income bracket, reaching for something that would make them stand out from the crowd.

Dhirubhai on many occasions suffered political attacks, but in general he was able to avoid the bureaucratic obstructions that snagged his competitors. Perhaps this was because he saw the system for what it was. While most businesses might tend to focus on their customers, or perhaps their commercial rivals, Dhirubhai claimed that "the most important external environment [for business] is the Government of India."

Indeed, Dhirubhai and his business partners traveled so frequently to New Delhi, the seat of national government, that they made special arrangements to leave their briefcases and materials in storage at the Ashok Hotel. Eventually Reliance joined Birla and the other great business houses in establishing a permanent mission in New Delhi. India's bureaucrats were often petty tyrants—the kind of people who would deny you what you wanted if you failed to append a respectful "sir" to the end of every sentence. The older business houses, maintaining their disdain for the license raj, sought to remain above the bureaucracy, appealing to their friends in politics when the bureaucrats put up obstacles. Dhirubhai had no problem doing whatever the license raj required of him. "Selling the idea is the most important thing, and for that I'll meet anybody in government," he said. "I am willing to salaam [bow down to] anyone."

While the Tatas and the Birlas maintained a love-hate relationship with the license raj, for Reliance, it was love-love. As one Reliance executive vice president later explained, when one of the company's founder-directors "went on his usual rounds to the textile minister's office, he would sit with the peons on *their* bench and inquire about their families." It was a matter of humility; it was a matter of the human touch. The cultivation of such relationships was crucial not just for influence, but for information. As one Reliance executive put it, "they know what is happening in every single corridor of the government ministries."

At times, Reliance's reading of the Indian government's intentions seemed almost clairvoyant. For instance, in August 1977 the Higher Unit Value Scheme was abruptly canceled, enabling any business with a license to import polyester. But Dhirubhai showed a steely nerve. As the value of licenses crashed, rather than retreating, Reliance acquired more licenses at the knockdown prices. Then, only days later, the policy was changed again, so that any business that was not an exporter had to make use of the State Trading Corporation to obtain polyester imports, while exporters could continue to import as they liked. The State Trading Corporation took its time about setting up operations, and for nearly nine months Reliance, which had acquired a huge number of licenses during the crash, was importing and selling to a nearly captive market. In 1970, Dhirubhai had said to a colleague: "Do you know who the Tatas and the Birlas are? We have to get past them one day." But if Reliance was going to outdo the Tatas and the Birlas, the company would need to build factories on an industrial scale. And for that it would need money. A lot of money. And Dhirubhai did not have that kind of money. In India, even for successful businesses, finding capital was a challenge. Dhirubhai had obtained some financing from state-owned banks, but it wasn't going to be enough to enable him to get big quickly. Dhirubhai's solution to this challenge was characteristically unorthodox. Reliance went public, and Dhirubhai began to make appeals for shareholder investment.

It was an unusual strategy, because at the time it was especially hard to raise a sizable amount of money in the stock market. Most well-connected businesses, including Reliance, tended to rely on state-owned banks for funding. And businesses that were not well connected generally could not raise money at all.

The Bombay Stock Exchange, established in 1875, was one of the world's oldest, but volatility, fraud, insider trading, and market manipulation schemes remained serious risks until the 1990s. Those company managers that did list tended to be far more interested in enriching themselves than in enriching their investors (like Carnegie in his days at the Pennsylvania Railroad), and these problems kept investors away. So Dhirubhai decided to try something different. "The performance orientation started with Reliance," as a financial markets analyst I met in Mumbai put it. That is to say, Reliance was the first company in India to focus on the way in which its equities performed, particularly for small investors. Earnings were remarkably consistent, delighting investors by providing reliable dividend payments. When the company's profits did suffer, the company paid dividends regardless. Reliance also arranged numerous bonus share issues to reward loyal shareholders. Annual general meetings for stockholders took on the atmosphere of festivals, with Dhirubhai firing up the crowd by promising he would make them all rich. One meeting, famously held on the Bombay Cooperage Football Ground in Mumbai (the same football field on which a few years later his son would be married), attracted some twelve thousand shareholders, a world record.

The number of Indians owning shares exploded from less than a million in 1980 to about four million by 1985. Many were drawn specifically because of Reliance: by the middle of the 1980s, an astonishing one in four Indian share investors held Reliance shares. The company had by this point raised 940 crore rupees ($4.2 billion) from the investing public, a record for any Indian company. Perhaps because of his own rags-to-riches background, Dhirubhai knew how to appeal to middle-class dreams. Like Rockefeller but without the sanctimony, he offered his early backers an ark that would float them to financial security.

In 1980, Dhirubhai took his next big step toward large-scale production, winning a license to manufacture polyester filament yarn. Reliance already dominated import licenses for polyester yarn and operated power looms that wove yarn into fabric, but domestic production of this coveted material — in keeping with his backward-integration vision — would prove to be a lucrative next step. This was an industrial production process, turning chemicals into thread, and thus required substantial factories. Some four hundred companies applied for government licenses to produce polyester filament yarn. Forty-three were waitlisted. Only two companies won. Reliance was awarded a license for production of 10,000 tons per year; Orkay Mills was awarded a license for 6,000 tons per year. One of the unsuccessful suitors for licenses was Birla. It was a spectacular coup. From the beginning, by government fiat, Reliance would be the dominant player in domestic polyester production. But demand was estimated at 50,000 tons, at that point primarily satisfied by imports, so he had not yet sewn up the market.

The plant, at Patalganga, began production in November 1982. The technology involved was licensed from DuPont. Construction was supervised by Dhirubhai's eldest son, Mukesh, aged twenty-four, fresh from graduate study at California's Stanford University. Many said he was too young to take on such a critical job. "I delegate, I do not abdicate," Dhirubhai reassured them. Mukesh demonstrated his youthful stamina and devotion to the cause by camping out at the worksite for several months during construction.

In 1984, Dhirubhai added a license to produce 45,000 tons of his lucrative yarn's slightly less showy sibling, polyester staple fiber, which produced a less glossy fabric than polyester yarn. At the time, domestic production of polyester staple fiber was about 37,000 tons per year, mostly in small facilities. Imports were about 10,000 tons per year. Hence Dhirubhai had obtained a license that would enable Reliance to produce, in this niche market, everything the country needed. At last he was operating at scale. Perhaps the plant's outsized capacity reflected Dhirubhai's irrepressible optimism that demand would grow over time. But it was also a classic strategy of the period—applying for licenses so large that competitors would be shut out.

Yet Dhirubhai executed this strategy with a twist. Unlike those business groups that had used dummy licenses to "preempt capacities," Dhirubhai intended to produce everything his licenses allowed and more. So why would this be a wealth secret? you might ask. The answer is that, in industries characterized by economies of scale, having the largest production license would guarantee that Dhirubhai would be the lowest-cost producer (provided he could manage his operations with a reasonable degree of efficiency). Dhirubhai, in effect, blended the economics of natural monopolies and government-awarded monopolies to make a deliciously profitable concoction. And just in time: by this point the Higher Unit Value Scheme had been abolished.

Most of Dhirubhai's competitors in India were tiny, producing no more than 10,000 tons of polyester staple fiber per year. International producers typically had a scale of some 100,000 to 150,000 tons, but this did not concern Dhirubhai, given the existence of high import duties. Hence, with his new license, Dhirubhai would be operating at about four times the scale of his main competitors, which a World Bank study suggested could have saved the company roughly 25 percent in production costs. Twenty-five percent is a healthy profit margin. Reliance's sales increased by 458 percent between 1979 and 1985. Its profitability increased much faster, rising from 8 crore 21 lakh rupees in 1979 ($57 million today) to 71 crore 30 lakh rupees ($299 million) in 1985, an 869 *percent* increase in rupee terms. Before 1980, Reliance, despite its dominance in textiles, was not among the fifty largest companies in India. By 1984, it had sprung into the top five. Indeed, its domestic production of polyester filament yarn had by this point become the largest earner for the company, exceeding earnings from woven fabric.

In 1984, Dhirubhai sketched out a plan to grow Reliance's revenues by a factor of nine over the next ten years—which would make the company the largest in India. His colleagues, it must be said, were deeply skeptical.

THE FALL

One could understand their skepticism. Even if Dhirubhai owned one of India's largest companies, the Ambani family was still a minnow compared to the Tatas or the Birlas. Each of these industrial houses owned tens of major companies and enjoyed dominant positions in several industries. Moreover, Reliance's rapid growth was bound to be noticed by someone. And when that happened, the question of whether Dhirubhai was by now shaping the maze, or was just another rat, was going to be put to the test.

The inevitable conflict came to pass in the mid-1980s. Dhirubhai's opposition was the Wadia group—not so mighty as the Tatas or the Birlas, perhaps, but unquestionably a titan of the license raj. The group was founded in 1736 by Sir Lovji Nusserwanjee Wadia. Today it owns an airline (Go Air), Britannia Industries (which has roughly 40 percent of the Indian biscuit market), and Bombay Dyeing, a major textile producer—which was itself founded in 1879.

In the 1980s, Bombay Dyeing—which, as the name suggests, focused on the dyeing, spinning, and weaving of cotton yarn—was the group's flagship firm. The textile sector was highly politicized; as mentioned earlier, some parts of the sector were reserved solely for small businesses. Running a major operation in this sector therefore required constant political battles. Indeed, in 1971, the Wadias had contemplated giving up and relocating to Switzerland. But Nusli Wadia had, at the tender age of twenty-six, wrested control of the firm from his father (with some help from the Tatas) and kept it in India. It was worth doing: the crackdown on textiles, which the Wadias narrowly survived, had the effect of all but wiping out much of their competition. By the 1980s, Nusli Wadia was well established as the group's patriarch and had a formidable reputation. He was also hungrily eyeing the synthetic fabrics sector. Because production processes for polyester were factory dominated, there was no risk of the government attempting to reserve the sector for small firms.

Wadia knew how to play the license game. The Wadia group made a great success of National Peroxide Limited, which manufactured another chemical precursor to synthetic fabrics. Industry demand for this chemical was about 6,000 tons per year; Wadia's company had a license to make 4,800 tons per annum. He did have one major competitor, but since Wadia had a license to produce just about everything Indian industry needed, the other company was forced by the government to export all but a quarter of its production. Hence Wadia, in addition to being the lowest-cost provider, held a near monopoly by virtue of his licenses.

In 1978, he applied for a license to set up a plant to manufacture dimethyl terephthalate, a main component of polyester. Had he received his license promptly, the battle with Reliance might have been over before it started. But it was not until 1981 that Wadia was at last able to wrest the license from the hands of the bureaucrats. Wadia then had a great deal of difficulty setting up the plant, and it was not until 1985 that he was ready to begin production. By this time, Dhirubhai had chemical production licenses of his own. In 1984, Dhirubhai had received letters of intent stating that he would be awarded licenses to produce 75,000 tons per year of terephthalic acid and 40,000 tons per year of monoethylene glycol.

Wadia and Dhirubhai were, of course, producing different chemicals. But dimethyl terephthalate and terephthalic acid are both precursor chemicals to polyester. The two men were after the same market: to supply not only their own polyester factories, but all the polyester producers in India. And thus there would be trouble. The resulting battle would be astonishing in its ferocity and stretch to the highest levels of power.

Dimethyl terephthalate and terephthalic acid are close substitutes, but not perfect. To convert a polyester factory from using one chemical as an input to using the other usually takes a few months. Hence Reliance and Bombay Dyeing could have — and, in most countries, would have — comfortably divided the market. There would have been some competition between the two, but since converting a plant from one feedstock chemical to the other was expensive, there was room for profitability on both sides.

But when masters of wealth secrets compete, they do not compete in the market. From the beginning, it appeared that Dhirubhai and Wadia were out to destroy each other. Estimated demand for the precursor chemicals across all of Indian industry, including Wadia's polyester plants, Dhirubhai's plants, state-owned plants, and others was 80,000 tons in 1984. Wadia had a license for 60,000 tons of chemicals; Dhirubhai wanted a license for 75,000 tons. Perhaps both expected demand to grow very rapidly. More likely, they thought that if the majority of the synthetic fiber factories in India converted to "their" chemical, their opponent would be forced into bankruptcy.

Meanwhile, someone began rearranging the maze. On May 29, 1985, the Indian government placed terephthalic acid, the chemical Dhirubhai intended to produce, on the controlled import list. Since Dhirubhai's polyester factories ran on supplies of terephthalic acid, an inability to obtain imports would mean either shutting down his operations or switching to Wadia's chemical. Dhirubhai, said to know what was happening in "every single corridor of the government ministries," outplayed this opening gambit easily. There was a loophole in the law — a ninety-day grace period — and during that period imports previously arranged would be allowed to land. It soon emerged that Dhirubhai had presciently arranged for the import of 114,000 tons of terephthalic acid just before the restrictions went into effect, enough to supply his factories until his own licensed chemical plants came online.

The Indian authorities then struck again, claiming that all 114,000 tons would need to arrive during the ninety-day grace period. Dhirubhai fought back directly, taking the government to court. The government raised import duties on all precursor chemicals to polyester, which had the effect of helping Wadia, whose own factory had already gone online. On the counterattack, Dhirubhai managed to land a blow of his own. On November 26, after tense negotiations, a compromise with the government was reached, allowing users of terephthalic acid to import sufficient feedstock for their own needs. Dhirubhai's imports then flooded the market, forcing Wadia to shut his chemicals factory temporarily.

The battle had only just begun. Ramnath Goenka, a personal friend of Wadia and editor of the *India Express*, India's largest-circulation newspaper, entered the fray on Wadia's side. He hired a young chartered accountant to investigate the business activities of Reliance and publish a series of exposés on the company. With a titan of the license raj and India's largest newspaper joining forces against him, Dhirubhai's position now looked dire. Meanwhile, India's Central Bureau of Investigation began an inquiry into the possibility that the planned change in import policy had been leaked to Dhirubhai in advance. The finance ministry weighed in with claims that Reliance had avoided more than 27 crore 20 lakh rupees ($114 million) in excise taxes by underreporting production. This was the largest excise tax evasion charge in India's history. India waited on Dhirubhai's next move.

Suddenly, it appeared there was not to be one. In February 1986, Dhirubhai, until then in good health, suffered a stroke that left him partially paralyzed on his right side. He was fifty-three years old. His family denied that the stroke was stress related, attributing it to a hereditary condition. Even if you know it's just a maze, it can still kill you.

The day-to-day operations of Reliance were immediately taken on by Dhirubhai's sons, Mukesh, by then age twenty-nine, and Anil, age twenty-seven.

THE MURDER PLOT

Despite an initially poor prognosis, Dhirubhai began to recover, regaining his mental capabilities although physically he remained weak. He spoke to his sons from his bed, and they rushed to carry out their father's wishes.

There was no mercy from Dhirubhai's opponents. The exposé articles in the *India Express* were published. They were lengthy and typically opened with vitriolic editorials denouncing Reliance. The first and second articles focused on the company's capital-raising activities. On June 10, 1986, perhaps in response to these articles, the government announced a ban on a key financing technique used by Reliance. The third article argued that Dhirubhai's plans to open chemical factories violated India's antimonopoly laws. The fourth article focused again on Reliance's financing arrangements, and especially on its use of offshore vehicles based in tax havens.

Soon, Reliance's opponents appeared to be closing in for the kill. On June 17, the finance ministry reduced the import duties on polyester yarn, causing a 20 percent drop in yarn prices and pummeling Reliance's profitability. Even more worryingly, responding in part to the political furor unleashed by the exposé articles, the Reserve Bank of India announced that it was investigating Reliance's capital-raising activities. And the *India Express* had another exposé to publish. It would be the most damaging yet. This alleged that the reason Reliance had exceeded its licensed production capacity was that, interspersed among its permitted imports, the company had smuggled in additional production equipment. The relevant government ministries launched an investigation of these allegations on August 20, 1986. The Bombay customs authorities joined in, alleging that Reliance could owe customs duties of a staggering 120 crore rupees ($471 million), and possibly a large fine in addition, on undeclared production equipment. Meanwhile, the director of enforcement at the ministry of finance launched a detailed investigation into the offshore vehicles identified by the *India Express*, engaging a U.S. investigations firm, the Fairfax Group, to assist.

At this point, just when it appeared that Reliance's position was hopeless, something changed. Precisely what changed, or how this change was accomplished, is unclear. Whether effected by Dhirubhai, his loyal sons, or someone else entirely, is also unknown.

Rajiv Gandhi, the prime minister of India, apparently received two letters printed on the letterhead of the Fairfax Group. These suggested that the firm had been commissioned to investigate not only Reliance but the personal dealings of the prime minister himself, and that Wadia and the *India Express* were guiding the investigation. Admittedly, this seemed profoundly implausible, and the letters were considered by many to be forgeries. Meanwhile, the *India Express* published a letter from India's president reprimanding the prime minister. Bizarrely, the draft that the paper published differed from the letter the prime minister actually received, suggesting that the paper had received a copy of the letter in advance.

At about this time, and possibly in relation to the above developments, the relationship between Rajiv Gandhi and V. P. Singh, his finance minister, soured. Singh's troubles were probably good for Reliance, as the finance ministry had been driving the investigations of the company's financial arrangements. Perhaps the letters from the Fairfax Group convinced the prime minister that Wadia and the *India Express* were targeting him. Perhaps the publication of what appeared to be an early draft of a confidential letter further soured the prime minister on the role of the *Express*.

Whatever the case, the maze again began to change, and this time in Dhirubhai's favor. The finance ministry's investigation quickly cleared Reliance of wrongdoing. The Indian government began to investigate charges that government reports on Reliance had been leaked to the *India Express*. The author of the exposés on Reliance was arrested and questioned. It was now the turn of Dhirubhai's opponents to face charges of tax evasion. The finance ministry accused the *India Express* of evading customs duty and owing 2 crore 75 lakh rupees ($10 million) in back taxes.

On May 7, 1987, the restrictions on imports of polyester staple fiber were put back in place and import duties were returned to their original levels, restoring the profitability of Reliance's domestic polyester production. The higher output at Reliance's plant was retroactively approved. In July 1989, Wadia was detained following an overseas trip and threatened with deportation on the basis of questions regarding his citizenship status (he had been a British citizen).

And then, on August 1, 1989, the story took a bizarre turn. Detectives arrested Kirti Vrijlal Ambani, a general manager at Reliance, on charges of a conspiracy to murder Wadia. The details of the authorities' case served only to mystify the public. It turned out that Kirti Ambani's name was originally Kirti Shah, but that he had changed his name to "Ambani" in a slightly unnerving effort to honor Dhirubhai (an act of hero worship that did not stop him from retaining his position in the company). The coconspirator in the claimed murder plot, Arjun Waghji Babaria, was revealed to be a bandleader who played under the name Prince Babaria and His Orchestra. These unlikely conspirators had allegedly engaged the services of a Mumbai hit man, Ivan Leo Sequeira, nicknamed Shanoo, to carry out the deed, but their efforts had descended into farce, and no assassination attempt was ever made. It then emerged that the bandmaster Babaria lived in housing provided by the Mumbai police. Babaria's parents and grandparents—indeed some six generations of the family—had been police informants.

This alleged underworld conspiracy between a descendant of police informants and Dhirubhai's frighteningly devoted employee mystified everyone. Had some member of the Ambani family, at the moment when all hope appeared lost, attempted to arrange a corporate hit? Or had a devoted employee made an ill-judged attempt to please his leader and personal hero? Or was the entire murder scheme a bizarre effort to frame Dhirubhai?

After decades of delay—admittedly not unusual in India's creaking justice system—the trial has yet to be heard.

Following the involvement of India's prime minister, the revelation of the murder scheme, and Dhirubhai's return to relative good health, the political battle between the polyester titans eased. Perhaps the stakes were too high. Very likely they had fought to a standstill. In India the saga came to be known as "the Mahabharata in polyester," a reference to a Sanskrit epic poem telling of an ancient war among gods and kings.

PLASTICS

In that bizarre summer of 1989, Reliance was struck by another unexpected blow: monsoon rains poured down on the polyester plants at Patalganga. Some twenty inches of rain fell in only eight hours, flooding the facility and the region. There were 304 dead and 264 missing in the surrounding area. None of them were Reliance workers, but the plant was buried in debris—some 50,000 tons of it, from mud and machinery to dead animals. The company had no flood insurance. DuPont, after inspecting the damage, said it would take at least four months to restart production.

It took three weeks. "We lived inside the plant for days thereafter," said a senior Reliance executive. It was not only an astonishing work ethic that made the recovery possible. Some six thousand workers were mobilized for the effort. This ability to hire a vast, temporary labor force, apply them to a complex task, and somehow prevent them from tripping over each other became something of a Reliance hallmark. It would have been possible only in India, of course. The country's official labor force statistics hid vast under-employment. Even at the end of the 1980s, almost a third of India's labor force — rural and urban combined — operated in the unregulated informal sector without legal employment, like the subsistence fishermen in the village of Dhirubhai's birth.

As a result, when Reliance suddenly, unexpectedly, needed to call on six thousand workers for a Herculean task, it was entirely possible. The underemployed masses poured in, cleared the debris in record time, and then returned to the subsistence jobs from whence they had come.

This does beg the question: why didn't Reliance and the other leading firms of the license raj go into labor-intensive industries, in which India, with its abundant underemployed, unskilled labor force, might have been globally competitive? With something of a tin ear for the needs of India's legions of underemployed workers, Reliance executives would often boast that their plants were among the most automated in the world. And it wasn't just Reliance: the titans of the license raj tended to flock to capital-intensive sectors, like Birla in automobiles and Tata in trucks and steel.

Over the years, many reasons have been put forward to explain this puzzle. One of these reasons directly involves wealth secrets. Capital-intensive industries like steel, cars, and chemicals tend to be characterized by large economies of scale, unlike labor-intensive industries, which don't require expensive production machinery. For steel or chemicals, the bigger the factory, within reason, the more efficient it is. This means that, even without bribery or politi-cal influence, one could make a strong and credible case to the government bureaucracy that a production license for a single enormous operation that satisfied most of the country's demand was the most efficient way to hit plan targets. "Bureaucrats need to be convinced by numbers and details," explained one Reliance executive. "[Dhirubhai] Ambani and his team never went to Delhi without these." The bureaucrats would be happy, knowing that they had picked, at least in theory, the most efficient operation. The winner of the megalicense would be happy, knowing that its large-scale operation would face little competition. And thus rake in the profits.

Of course, even with such advantages, Reliance's commercial progress was not wholly without setbacks. The struggle with Wadia had taken a financial toll. Worse yet, following the inconclusive political battle, both companies were still in business. Demand for polyester and its production inputs was expanding fast. But competition on price put limits on profitability. In 1988, Reliance switched its calendar year for accounting purposes to end in April, enabling it to report results over a period of fifteen months. It then extended the calendar year for a further three months. This allowed Reliance to report a "record" result, but only by comparing an eighteen-month accounting year with prior twelve-month years. On an annualized basis, Reliance's profits were below what it had earned in 1985.

But the setback was temporary. Reliance had obtained permission and financing for its next great leap forward, a petrochemicals plant at Hazira, located on the coast of Gujarat, not too far from the village of Dhirubhai's birth. The huge site, on 280 hectares of land, would produce high-density polyethylene and polyvinyl chloride (often known as PVC), among other chemicals. In other words, it would produce plastics. India, where people shipped everything from sugar to cement in jute sacks (a basis for the fortune of the Birlas), was now ripe for the plastics revolution. The second phase of the plant would be even more ambitious. This would be a gas cracker, a major industrial plant that would produce ethylene,

Dhirubhai Ambani with his sons Mukesh and Anil. In the midst of the polyester war, the sons were suddenly forced to take charge of the day-to-day running of Reliance. (Raghu Rai / Magnum Photos)

propylene, and butadiene — key chemical components of plastics — from natural gas.

Reliance tackled the task of construction with characteristic speed and the application of mass labor. When monsoon rains put a stop to welding work, laborers swarmed the site and within three days had installed a temporary roof of nearly three thousand square meters. Executives from ICI, the foreign chemicals company providing its production technology to Reliance, arrived at the plant with a checklist of issues to be verified. Its executives expected results within a few months. According to the president of the Hazira Works, "1,000 fellows got down to work," nearly the entire staff pulled an all-nighter, and about 50 percent of the requirements were met by the following morning. The first phase of the plant, plastics production, went online during 1991 and 1992. Executives from Shell, the company providing technology for the gas cracker, estimated it would take four months to complete the piping and instrumentation for the plant. It took seven weeks.

Within two years, Reliance had a 73 percent market share in propylene. Indeed, it was well placed in nearly all the markets in which it operated. As of 1993, the company had a 26 percent market share in polyfilament yarn, a 30 percent share in polyester staple fiber, a 100 percent market share of terephthalic acid (the precursor chemical for polyester), and a 39 percent market share in polyvinyl chloride (a plastic). Considering that Indian antitrust law had at one point set a benchmark of a 24 percent share as indicating a dominant undertaking requiring investigation by antimonopoly authorities, Reliance was doing pretty well. Perhaps unsurprisingly, by the 1993–1994 financial year, Reliance Industries had eclipsed Tata Iron and Steel to become India's largest private sector company in terms of both sales and profits. Dhirubhai had achieved his objective of surpassing even the titans of the license raj.

The Reliance corporate headquarters at Maker Chambers IV, on Nariman Point in Mumbai, had become one of India's most famed corporate addresses. Dhirubhai, wholly in keeping with his love of scale, bought a gleaming white seventeen-story apartment building called Sea Wind to serve as the family home. The first five floors housed parking lots; the sixth and seventh a gymnasium; and the rest were devoted to quarters for the extended family and guests. The food and beverage manager from the famed Taj Mahal hotel was brought in to deal with catering for the village-size home. In this happy, extended household, there was no doubt who was the top dog. Not only the children but the grandchildren and great-grandchildren called Dhirubhai "papa." One father recalled being rebranded as "kukumummy" as a result. The extended family's arrival resulted in some *Beverly Hillbillies* moments, as when neighbors complained about buffaloes, goats, and a horse being kept in the backyard.

Sea Wind, Dhirubhai's seventeen-story skyscraper home, today. The helipad was added as Mumbai traffic worsened. (Sam Wilkin)

Dhirubhai, meanwhile, retained a certain humility. He empathized with the dreams of the small investors who put their life savings into Reliance stock. At one annual general meeting, an investor hearing Dhirubhai speak about "greenfield" or "grassroots" investments—a term meaning a new investment as opposed to an upgrading of an existing plant—stepped to the microphone and asked whether Reliance was therefore getting into agriculture. The assembled shareholders broke into laughter; Dhirubhai remained straight-faced. The laughter quickly died away. Dhirubhai answered the question thoughtfully.

By the 1990s, Dhirubhai was slowing down. Still weakened from his stroke, he would arrive at the office at about noon and leave at 3 p.m. Despite this, he still had one winning card left to play. He would need it. The license raj, the system that had at first oppressed him and then enabled his spectacular ascent, was about to be swept away.

THE REFINERY

When American captains of industry gather in their undersea lair just off Manhattan—a secret society that is *way* more secret than Skull and Bones—their meetings are attended by the embalmed corpse of their hero, Ronald Reagan (or so the story goes). When British bankers, the Trilateral Commission, and the Knights Templar assemble to arrange the bankruptcy of yet another southern European country, they open the dark proceedings with a toast to Margaret Thatcher, even before they salute the queen.

After Reaganomics swept the United States and Thatcherism the United Kingdom, a capitalist revolution of deregulation and privatization would eventually reach India as well. In 1991, India suffered an economic crisis and turned, cap in hand, to the International Monetary Fund for a bailout. The IMF demanded that India undertake extensive economic reforms, and a technocratic, reformist government under Prime Minister P. Narasimha Rao duly took charge. While the grip of the license raj had been loosening for at least a decade, under Rao the guiding hand of government all but vanished. Production licenses would be required in only eighteen sectors. Import licenses on production machinery were completely abolished. Restrictions on foreign investment were reduced. Import duties were cut drastically.

And yet, if there is a secret society of Indian industrialists, I am not sure Rao is toasted before each meeting. For the aristocracy of the license raj, Rao's capitalist revolution was a mixed blessing. On the one hand, there was more money to chase. Between 1993 and 1997, the Indian economy grew at an annual rate of 7.1 percent. An Indian middle class was on the rise. On the other hand, there were suddenly many more Indian companies chasing this money. Foreign competitors poured like the monsoon rains into previously closed industries, quickly soaking up any patches of profit. Many aristocrats of the license raj were struggling to keep their heads above water as new sectors (notably IT services) rose around them.

A comparison of the companies among India's top 100 firms in 1991 — when the license raj was dismantled — with those still standing in 1999, less than a decade later, gives a sense of the deluge. In 1991, six families, each of whose business groups dated from the preindependence era, controlled 37 of the top 100 firms. These were titans of the license raj: Tata, Birla, Thapar, Singhania, Mafatlal, and Modi. By 1999, all the businesses owned by Mafatlal and Modi had dropped out of the top 100. One Thapar business clung to its spot (down from four businesses). Singhania saw two of its four high-ranked businesses plummet from the top slots. Even the Tatas, known for their good management, struggled — despite some hard graft that turned their uncompetitive flagship steel enterprise into the lowest-cost steel producer in the world. The Birlas suffered perhaps worst of all. Birla Jute, in the top 100 in 1991, had fallen out of the top 250 by 1999 (thanks in part to Dhirubhai's rising plastics businesses). The same fate befell Mysore Cements, also owned by Birla. Century Enka, another Birla enterprise, dropped fifty places. Orient Paper, Century Text, Kesoram, and Hindustan Motors (makers of the Hindustan Ambassador), all Birla-owned firms, all fell from the top 100. Some Birla companies, especially those belonging to the Aditya Birla Group, managed to stay in the game. But an economic order that had persisted for more than four decades was falling.

Reliance was not going down without a fight. The company's financial reports tell the story. Prior to liberalization, Reliance spent little on research and development. It had no need to. Foreign companies like DuPont, ICI, and Shell were all but excluded from the Indian market and therefore eager to hand Reliance whatever technologies it wanted, in exchange for modest license payments. After liberalization, Reliance would need to develop its own technologies. Its former partners could now become its competitors. By the 1992–1993 financial year, Reliance's research and development spending was 2 crore 40 lakh rupees ($5.4 million). By the 1998–1999 financial year this spending had grown to 75 crore 10 lakh rupees ($104.5 million)—an increase of some 3,100 percent in only six years, in rupee terms. The 1998–1999 figure was not a large expenditure by international standards, but it was the largest proportionate increase of any Indian firm over the period and put Reliance among the top three Indian firms in terms of aggregate research and development spending.

Reliance was fighting back, but the very fact of having to fight in the marketplace was a costly and altogether unwelcome development. It was not the wealth secrets way. There were even some worrying signs that Reliance might crash like Circuit City rather than simply descend quietly into mediocrity. As competitors poured into the weaving industry, Reliance announced a comprehensive restructuring of its textiles business—the business that had launched the company into the world of licensed production more than two decades before. Beginning in April 2001, more than four thousand Reliance workers were laid off.

But Dhirubhai had one last visionary move to make, one that would satisfy the dream he had kept alive from the earliest days of his career in Yemen: to build an oil refinery. And what a refinery it would be. It was built a few miles away from Jamnagar, a dusty town on the Gujarat coast. A giant billboard stands out front, on which a beatific Dhirubhai proclaims it to be "the world's largest refinery." And indeed, if moved from its present location the refinery would cover an area half the size of London or Mumbai. When built, it accounted for more than 25 percent of India's refining capacity. At 24,000 crore rupees (about $32 billion today), it was the largest corporate investment ever undertaken in India. The refinery alone accounted for 5 percent of the Indian corporate sector's gross assets, 4 percent of its turnover, and 7 percent of the nation's tax revenues. It leveraged everything that Reliance had built into one massive throw of the dice, aiming for a scale that, even in liberalized India, no other private company would be able to replicate.

To be honest, though, it wasn't that much of a gamble. Even after further rounds of liberalization, production in the refining sector was still governed by licenses. And even if these licenses were swept away by further liberalization, Reliance had not only India's but the world's largest refinery in hand, so the likelihood of anyone entering the market on a larger, more efficient scale was essentially negligible.

Reliance employees set about their task with characteristic resolve. A jetty was needed to land equipment, and this threatened to hold up construction. "We worked twenty-four hours for the next four months," explained the president of Reliance Petroleum. And thus the jetty was completed on time, which the foreign company providing the technology (in this case Bechtel, a willing participant since the industry was still licensed) had said was "impossible." Once again, Reliance drew on the vast, under-employed Indian workforce. Some eighty-five thousand temporary workers took part in the construction. "It might be worth checking whether more workers were present at the site of the pyramids," one Reliance executive said with pride. And yet, also typically, the Reliance refinery was said to be the most automated in the world, needing only two thousand employees on an ongoing basis.

Dhirubhai had put his company in a very good place to survive the downfall of the license raj. Even after scaling back in textiles, in the early 2000s Reliance still had a 51 percent share of the polyester fiber market, an 80 percent share of the markets for key chemical intermediates used to make polyester, and about 52 percent of India's plastics (polymers) market. And these were not even the company's main line of business: by 2000, oil refining had replaced polyester fiber as Reliance's largest source of revenues. Reliance's profits grew by 29 percent per year on average during the 1990s, following the dismantling of the license raj. In March 2001,

Reliance earned 30 percent of the total profits of the *entire Indian private sector.* And it accounted for about 12 percent of the total market capitalization of Indian companies.

And then, on July 6, 2002, shortly after his youthful dreams had at last been realized, Dhirubhai had a second stroke. He fell into a coma. Twelve days later he died.

After lying in repose in the lobby of Sea Wind, his body, covered in lilies and white roses, was taken via open truck and then cane stretcher to the funeral site. Family, admirers, employees, and the curious thronged to the funeral. The attendees included a former prime minister, the serving deputy prime minister, numerous business leaders, and some of Bollywood's leading stars. The massing crowds surged forward, nearly throwing the pallbearers off balance. To the sound of Vedic chants, Dhirubhai's sons lit the funeral pyre of sandalwood and ghee, and the flames consumed their father's body. Born a pauper, he died a titan of Indian business. "We are all born into an orbit," Dhirubhai had said. "Very few of us ever break out of our orbit. My life has gone from one orbit to another. As I have gone higher, changing orbit, people have resented me....But it does not matter. I am no longer part of their orbit. There is nothing they can do to me now."

Dhirubhai's approach to business was unorthodox. He did not read business books or management journals, his son Anil explained. "He won't read the *Harvard Business Review.* He will say, 'Let my management chaps read that!'" The books Dhirubhai did recall reading were the books on world history by Jawaharlal Nehru, India's first prime minister. Liking these books was, of course, patriotic, but also practical. "They taught me that nothing could ever be achieved without money, influence and power," Dhirubhai said. Dhirubhai had also, his wife later recalled, frequently borrowed impressive-sounding phrases from the books when he wrote letters to bureaucrats appealing for those very first licenses he needed.

However much of an iconoclast he was, though, India was changing. Would Dhirubhai's way still be relevant in a new India, and would it provide a path to success for his sons?

NO MOAT

The equity research group at Morningstar, a U.S. investment research company, takes an unorthodox approach to evaluating the commercial prospects of the companies it covers. Morningstar assigns each company a "moat rating" that reflects the degree to which the company has succeeded in erecting barriers against competitors. The moat concept comes from the great investor Warren Buffett (we'll hear more about Buffett in chapter 7). Since many of the wealth secrets covered so far in this book involve erecting barriers to competition, you might think of the moat rating as a wealth secrets rating of sorts. The best possible moat rating is "wide moat," reflecting competitive barriers Morningstar expects to persist for at least fifteen years.

In 2014, Reliance Industries was rated "no moat," the worst possible rating. A few years after Dhirubhai's death, his wealth secrets had come undone. But how? Had his sons failed to heed their father's lessons?

Over the course of the 1990s, the eighteen sectors still subject to licensing were reduced to fourteen and then to nine. By the new millennium, the only major Reliance operation still sheltered from competition by a licensing regime was the oil refinery. But even as the maze was progressively dismantled, Dhirubhai's sons, Mukesh and Anil, tried to cling to the old ways. They had perhaps learned their father's lessons too well. They invested heavily in the few industries that were still highly regulated. And they were not alone. Most of the elite business houses that had survived the 1990s adopted the same approach, pouring money into telecoms, power generation, oil and gas, and finance. As India's *Economic Times* put it, in the 1990s "the corridors of Udyog Bhavan [referring to the ministry responsible for industrial licenses] may be empty after the dismantling of the 'license raj'...but the crowd of industrialists, touts, and agents has merely shifted to other ministries—power, telecoms, surface transport, civil aviation and petroleum."

At first, seeking shelter from the rising competitive tide in the last redoubts of the maze seemed like a good strategy. In 2001, Reliance pulled off a maneuver with Dhirubhai-like panache. The Indian government was auctioning off licenses for "local-loop" telephone services, as an alternative to fixed-line telephones. Local-loop telephones, like fixed-line telephones, operated via trunk lines that ran to villages or neighborhoods, but in the case of local-loop telephones the so-called last mile of the service was then provided by a radio transmitter. Such a network cost much less to construct than a fixed-line network. Reliance joined 131 other companies in bidding for local-loop licenses (in deregulated India, licenses would be allocated via auction rather than bureaucratic fiat). Reliance won the largest share, covering eighteen of India's twenty regional "circles."

But why had Reliance (or more accurately its new subsidiary, which came to be called Reliance Communications) put such an effort into winning in the fairly obscure and unexciting market for local-loop telephony? The name Reliance gave to the venture, IndiaMobile, was a crucial hint. Reliance had no intention of competing with fixed-line services. It was going mobile. Reliance had taken advantage of the fact that the end user on a local-loop service had, in effect, a type of mobile telephone (linked by radio to the transmitter). Typically, a local-loop telephone worked only with a particular local transmitter. But because Reliance had won licenses covering nearly all of India, it could build a network of compatible transmitters enabling it to offer, in effect, a nationwide mobile telephone network. To be sure, the service was not entirely "mobile"—the call would drop if the user moved from one transmitter to another. But while the fees other companies had paid for mobile telephone licenses were expensive, Reliance had paid relatively little for its local-loop licenses. It could therefore offer a mobile service on the cheap.

There were howls of outrage. The local-loop services were supposed to offer an alternative to fixed-line telephones, not serve as a Trojan horse for launching a national mobile network. Eventually the government issued new rules on pricing and interconnections, and in October 2003 penalized Reliance for violating its licenses, as well as requiring it to buy a new "unified" license covering all telecoms services — a total expense of 1,096 crore rupees ($1.3 billion). Reliance's cost advantage was wiped out, but by then it had already taken the lead. By the end of 2003 Reliance claimed to have six million subscribers, thus leapfrogging the previous market leader.

It was a great start, but by the mid-2000s, the brothers were stumbling. The obvious problem — the problem that made headlines — was that Dhirubhai had died without leaving a will. Eventually, Mukesh and Anil began a public battle over who would control Reliance. At first it seemed the war between the brothers was going to be over before it started. A relatively equable split of the business was agreed upon in a deal announced by their mother. Mukesh took charge of Reliance Industries, and thus the core businesses in polyester yarn, petrochemicals, and oil refining. Anil took charge of Reliance businesses reflecting new investments in telecoms, electric power, and financial services. But following the split the battle continued to rage, involving a nasty legal contest over gas prices that eventually reached India's Supreme Court.

The battle between the brothers also produced some amusing revelations. In 2008, Mukesh gave an interview to the *New York Times* in which he in effect acknowledged that Reliance maintained an "intelligence agency" in New Delhi to gather information on bureaucrats, competitors' lobbying efforts, and the interests of political leaders. It was, of course, common knowledge that India's dominant firms had maintained permanent political offices in New Delhi to liaise with the government. But to see the rumors regarding Reliance's extensive political operations confirmed as hard facts in a foreign newspaper was a little shocking. Mukesh's objective appeared to be to discredit his brother, whom he claimed had managed the "intelligence agency" and taken it with him when the group split. "We de-merged all of that," Mukesh told the *New York Times*. Anil sued for defamation.

But behind the scenes, Dhirubhai's empire faced a far more profound problem than sibling rivalry. This problem was that the maze no longer mattered. By the late 2000s, the telecoms venture, now in Anil's hands, had lost its cleverly won early lead in the face of rising market competition. By 2012, Reliance Communications had dropped to third place in the Indian mobile phone market. Anil's investments in toll roads and electric power had also stumbled. The company's stock price plummeted.

Mukesh's operations, anchored by the refinery, at first appeared more robustly insulated from competitive pressure. From its listing in 1977 to 2007, a thirty-year period, Reliance Industries was consistently one of the nation's best-performing equities. Indeed, in 2007, Mukesh briefly became the world's richest man, as stock markets in Western countries plunged following the global financial crisis. The world's largest refinery became even larger, adding a facility licensed for export production.

Mukesh also achieved a degree of global fame, or perhaps infamy, for his construction of a new home. This twenty-seven-story luxury residence took Dhirubhai's Sea Wind concept to new heights. Dubbed Antilia, Mukesh's tower has three helipads (Mumbai traffic is miserable) and room for more than 150 cars in six stories of parking lots. It reportedly houses a health club, a dance studio, hanging gardens, a ballroom, and a fifty-seat movie theater, and when seen in the right light is capped by the unblinking eye of Sauron (sorry: it's a *Lord of the Rings* reference). Even without a lidless eye of flame on top, it is an impressive sight. "All

Mukesh Ambani's twenty-seven-story skyscraper home, Antilia, in Mumbai (center tower). It has three helipads. (Sam Wilkin)

that for five people," said an Indian oil industry analyst I interviewed, pointing from his office window to Mukesh's skyscraper, visible in the distance.

But even atop his mighty tower, Mukesh could not escape the onrush of market competition. The refinery now faces global challengers. As Piyush Jain, an equity research analyst in Morningstar's office in Navi Mumbai explained, "The 'no moat' rating applies to refining and petrochemicals, which is now the core business [for Reliance Industries]." Following the global financial crisis and a slowdown in China, global petrochemicals demand has softened, even as new refineries across Asia and the Middle East continue to come online, producing a global capacity glut. "Operating margins that were reliably at 12 to 13 percent have fallen to 6 to 7 percent," Jain said. "Right now Reliance's return on invested capital, which drives investor return, is less than the cost of capital." That is to say, while the company may be profitable on paper, from an economist's perspective it is not profitable at all.

To his credit, rather than retreating deeper into the tattered remnants of the maze, Mukesh has come out fighting, attempting to use his company's vast wealth to buy other wealth secrets—wealth secrets you may recognize from elsewhere in this book. "They [Reliance] go with huge capacity. They seek to enter the market, and define the market," as Chirag Dhaifule, a research analyst at LKP Securities in Mumbai, put it. In 2009 and 2010, Mukesh made huge investments in two areas: telecoms and retail. Mukesh's new megainvestment in telecoms will produce a nationwide 4G (fourth-generation) mobile network, India's first. Not only will this leapfrog India's existing 3G networks (including his brother's) in terms of data speed, it will also be more extensive. India's largest 3G network currently reaches 500,000 of India's roughly 650,000 villages. Mukesh's next-generation network will reach 600,000 villages in two to three years. Characteristically, Reliance managed to gain the required licenses at a good price, via a maneuver that involved turning data-only 4G licenses acquired in 2010 into unified licenses by 2012. But to win in the long run will require advantages that regulatory maneuvering cannot provide. Mukesh is going for scale: "they are spending eleven billion dollars in telecoms, which is a quarter of their overall market capitalization," notes Jain. "A launch [on that scale] has no track record anywhere in the world." But will it be enough? "Reliance will be competing with the likes of Airtel, Idea, and Vodafone, with the latter having significant cash on its balance sheet," says Dhaifule. "We believe Vodafone will ramp up its investments in India once the tax issue [the company is embroiled in a tax dispute with the government] gets resolved."

In retail, Mukesh has been equally ambitious—replicating Circuit City's gambit, as deregulation enables corporate retailers to use scale to crush India's legions of mom-and-pop stores. Reliance is now India's number one retailer, with some 1,700 stores operating today (mostly Reliance Fresh, a grocery store), and more than 1,000 more expected within three to four years, on the back of billions of dollars in investment. Here again, the remnants of the maze help a little: foreign chains face obstacles to their entry, which has allowed Reliance a head start. Even after foreign chains eventually enter the country, it will take years for them to identify sites, negotiate leases, and establish a product mix that appeals to Indian consumers. By that time Reliance could have a thoroughly dominant position (and, as Circuit City CEO Richard Sharp noted, dominance in retailing can be a very exciting thing). Still, if this was a sure win, it would be reflected in Reliance's valuation, which it isn't. As another senior industry analyst I interviewed in Mumbai pointed out, Flipkart.com (an Indian competitor to Amazon) has achieved a valuation that is better than that of Reliance's retail arm, at a fraction of the investment cost and development time. The stock market, at least, seems skeptical that Reliance is the retailer of the future. Overall, I will grant that Mukesh, who seems undaunted by the prospect of gambling on high-risk ventures with everything he has, is clearly his father's son. But on Mukesh's bold efforts to find wealth secrets outside the maze, the jury has yet to deliver a verdict.

That said, there is at least some reason to think Reliance might survive. According to Surajit Mazumdar at Delhi's Jawaharlal Nehru University, the end of the license raj has by no means swept away the advantages of established firms in India. According to Mazumdar, outside of new industries (notably information technology services) and a few sectors where international firms have entered consequent to easing of restrictions (for instance, cement or automobiles), the rate of entry of new competitors since the end of the license raj has actually fallen.

DHIRUBHAI'S WAY

Mukesh's brief stop at the top of the Global Rich List during 2007 did not last. Microsoft's Bill Gates (see chapter 6) and a Mexican telecoms magnate, Carlos Slim Helú, have dominated the top slot for the past decade. Prior to 2010, Gates usually held the top position. Between 2010 and 2013, Slim was dominant. In 2014, the two swapped places at least twice.

Slim's wealth secret was almost comically simple: he secured a legislated monopoly on fixed-line telephone services in Mexico. To be fair to Slim, he won this monopoly fair and square, via an open and transparent privatization process. Furthermore, Slim, together with two foreign partners (France Télécom and Southwestern Bell Corporation), paid $1.76 billion to acquire their controlling stake in Telmex, the state-owned telephone monopoly. The total amount raised in the privatization was unprecedented and widely seen as a good deal for the Mexican treasury. Prior to the takeover by Slim, Telmex had been poorly run, and it sometimes took years for Mexicans to receive telephone connections. Slim quickly changed that, bringing down the waiting time for a new telephone from months to days.

It was an amazing deal for Slim as well, though. He had won the sole right to operate fixed-line telephone services in Mexico — an exclusive monopoly — for six years, with few restrictions on pricing. Facing little competition, he could charge whatever he wanted for telephone services. And so he did. By 1994, Slim was the richest man in Mexico, with a $6.6 billion fortune.

By the time the six-year monopoly expired, his position was untouchable. He had turned his government-awarded monopoly into a natural monopoly. Indeed, as of 2012, Slim still had 80 percent of the nation's fixed-line business, and had added a 70 percent share of the country's mobile phone market as well as a large share of the Internet market (estimated, by some sources, at nearly 90 percent). Facing little obvious competition, Slim did what any right-thinking businessperson would do: he charged a lot. A 2012 study by the Organisation for Economic Co-operation and Development found that Mexican telecommunications costs were among the highest in the OECD (the OECD is composed primarily of countries much richer than Mexico). Compared with countries at a similar level of income, Mexican telephone rates tend to be multiples of the rates charged elsewhere. For instance, Telmex's business rates were, in the mid-2000s, roughly three times the fees charged in Argentina and four times those charged in Brazil. The average Mexican was estimated to be paying Slim $1.50 per day (add all Mexicans together and that amounts to $67 million in total, every day of the year).

This made Carlos Slim the world's richest man, but at a cost. The 2012 OECD report does not mince words, concluding that, over five years, the "welfare loss attributed to the dysfunctional Mexican telecommunication sector is estimated at…1.8% GDP [1.8 percent of the country's entire economic output] per annum." According to the OECD's calculations, the majority of this loss (about $130 billion in aggregate) reflected the high costs of communication services paid by Mexican consumers and businesses. And yet, if you are searching this book for moral lessons, it is not entirely fair to blame Slim. The Mexican government was almost certainly well aware what was going to happen when it handed Slim a monopoly; it auctioned off the right to, in effect, overcharge the Mexican people because it was hoping to raise a huge sum at the privatization (which it did).

Mukesh and Anil Ambani are unlikely to reach Slim's level of wealth. Carlos Slim had won a license (a *national* government-granted monopoly) that exceeded even the dreams of the political entrepreneurs of the robber baron era. While Reliance does have a (natural) monopoly on domestic production of one or two types of specialty chemicals, the Ambani brothers are not likely to reach a monopoly position in any market that matters.

Yet long before Carlos Slim's monopoly was even a gleam in his eye, Dhirubhai had shown the way. Dhirubhai was an outsider, facing a system that was spectacularly hostile to the success of outsiders. Most Indians of his position might have thought that they could never hope to scale the heights reached by the Tatas or the

Birlas and assumed that such titans of industry were a class apart. Most Indians might have thought that the country's bureaucratic maze offered only dead ends, posing an insurmountable obstacle to their dreams of becoming obscenely rich.

Dhirubhai proved that this was untrue. He showed that the wealth of the Tatas and the Birlas was achievable by anyone who had sufficient ambition, understood the system, and could make it work for them. Dhirubhai understood that the Tatas and the Birlas were not rich in spite of the system; they were rich, in part, because of it.

Dhirubhai's success in India also provides a perfect demonstration of the general principle that the more hostile a country's economy is to the growth of private business, the more profits are available to any business that survives. That is his wealth secret. It is also Carlos Slim's wealth secret. It is part of Mukesh's and Anil's wealth secret even today. Indeed, it is the wealth secret that dominates the *Forbes* list of global billionaires. Dhirubhai said: "If one Dhirubhai can do so much, just think what a thousand Dhirubhais can do for this country. There are easily a thousand Dhirubhais, if not more." And indeed he was right: today people have followed in Dhirubhai's footsteps all over the world.

Not long ago, the *Forbes* list of U.S.-dollar billionaires around the world was a relatively short list and consisted primarily of billionaires from rich countries (which seemed, at the time, logical). As recently as 1991, there were only 273 billionaires worldwide, and the five countries home to the largest number of billionaires were all among the world's richest (the United States, Japan, Germany, France, and Canada). By 1993, Mexico (with 13 billionaires, including Slim) and Hong Kong had forced their way into the top five. By 2000, there were 470 billionaires; by 2005, there were nearly 700 billionaires; by 2010, there were more than 1,000, and by 2014, there were 1,645 billionaires. Among these 1,645 are 152 Chinese, 111 Russians, 65 Brazilians, 56 Indians, and 16 Mexicans. In other words, those five emerging market countries alone are now home to almost one in four of all the billionaires in the world. In 1991, there were only about 55 emerging market billionaires; in 2014, there were 729.

In sum, there has been a vast expansion in the number of billionaires, and this is attributable in large part to the rise of the emerging markets. It is in these countries where the conditions that produced the American robber barons—rapid economic growth, weak regulation, and difficult business environments—combine to create superprofits in the modern day. In fact, if one calculates how many billionaires a country has per dollar of economic output and then ranks the nations of the world on this scale, twenty-two of the top twenty-five countries where billionaires are most concentrated are in the emerging markets (including India at twenty-second). The only advanced economies in the top twenty-five are Cyprus (which some would call an emerging market), Sweden (think IKEA and H&M), and Switzerland.

Dhirubhai showed that emerging markets, especially those where the business environment is challenging, are the places to look for billions. This strategy applies even *within* economies: the industries where Dhirubhai found his wealth secrets were those where it was *most* difficult to establish a new business. In Dhirubhai's day, this meant the industries where production and import licenses were required. These obstructions enhanced profits because a clever businessperson could use these licenses to prevent competitors from entering—whether by applying for licenses and then holding them in reserve (as the titans of the license raj tended to do) or by applying for licenses on a scale that would ensure cost advantages at the very least, and ideally industry dominance (as Dhirubhai often did). Mukesh and Anil, of course, followed in their father's footsteps, investing heavily in the most highly regulated sectors of the Indian economy. Slim, of course, went one better, obtaining (for several years) an exclusive license covering an entire industry. But there are political battles for Slim as well. As of this writing, Slim has responded to the threat of antitrust action by the Mexican government by preemptively breaking up his business empire.

Dhirubhai showed why today's *Forbes* Global Rich List looks like it does and why, counterintuitively, if your ambition is great wealth, you are better off moving to a poor country. He also showed that, given sufficient determination and good luck, an outsider can break into even the most closed system. Perhaps you are a citizen of a rich country and are reading these words with despair, as you now worry that the thriving, open economy of your home country may bar you from obtaining the billions you deserve. But do not lose hope: you can still try your hand at emerging market riches. Foreigners are by no means prevented from making a play for these opportunities. Sonia Gandhi, who served as president of India's ruling political party for almost two decades and thus became the most powerful person in Indian politics, was born an Italian (she married an Indian man who would become the country's prime minister). Carlos Slim is the son of a Lebanese immigrant to Mexico. One of Brazil's billionaires is named Ming Chung Liu (he is ethnically Chinese); one of Hong Kong's billionaires is named Michael Kadoorie (he is the grandson of an immigrant from Iraq). Even in emerging markets, immigrants can rise to the top, so do not let your citizenship block your ambitions. (The billionaire CEO of the U.S. fund management company BlackRock, Larry Fink, recently opined that U.S. millennials might be better off trying their luck in Mexico.)

But perhaps this kind of thing seems risky to you. Or perhaps you don't like Indian food. In that case, you will appreciate the next chapter, which brings the story to the cutting edge of wealth secret innovation—the global technology sector, responsible for about a quarter of the twenty largest fortunes in the world, and one remarkable man whose wealth secret started it all and who three decades later is, remarkably, still in the lead.

6

Dot.com Wealth Secrets

THE HOUSE OF THE FUTURE

There are many reasons to envy the billionaires of Silicon Valley. They are rich and young. They are cultural icons. When their life stories are made into movies they are played by Justin Timberlake. But what I envy most are their houses, which inevitably achieve something many of us can only dream of. Even in such august company, though, the dot-com billionaires on the West Coast stand out. They have not only $50 million or so in petty cash to spend on a house but also creative flair and fascinating neuroses.

For instance: what teenage boy has not dreamed of being a samurai? The brave charges into battle, the shining swords, the red-lipped geisha, the ritual suicides. Oracle founder Larry Ellison has reconstructed a samurai villa on twenty-three acres in California, based on the architecture of sixteenth-century Japan. It is a feudal fantasy of wooden beams and earthen plaster. No cement here. Just gravel, manicured grass, a tea house, a moon pavilion, and an archery range (in a nod to progress, the rice-paper doors are covered with glass). It is his second Japanese-style dwelling, the first having been based on an imperial residence in Kyoto.

But the house of which I am most jealous is the Gates mansion in the Seattle suburbs. Its underground garage has been compared to the Batcave. Lit by natural light via tubes coming up through the ground, it has space for about thirty cars and "transforms" into a basketball court. The house itself is built into a hillside (visitors enter at the top), and on construction was appraised at $53 million. Those millions were spent on quality, not scale—initially, the main house had one bedroom and one bath. Regardless, so many beams of rare, recycled old-growth Douglas fir up to seventy-five feet in length were used in the building's construction that dealers in boutique wood had trouble sourcing the material until the leftovers from the project were eventually put up for sale.

The feature of the Gates home that received perhaps the most press attention (and was profiled in Gates's book *The Road Ahead*) is a tracking system that enables the house to follow and respond to residents' and visitors' movements. You tell the house once what kind of lighting and temperature you would like and carry an identity pin on your person. These settings then follow you unobtrusively as you move from room to room. Let us say you want some music. This follows you as well, transitioning seamlessly from speaker to speaker (including underwater, in the pool). From your perspective, it appears that music is playing throughout the house; from the perspective of others, it appears that you are accompanied by your own personal theme music. ("[Microsoft cofounder] Paul Allen is a Jimi Hendrix fan," wrote Gates, so "a head-banging guitar lick will greet him whenever he visits"; Gates's own favorite is U2.)

Artwork, on high-definition screens, also changes in response to your preferences. As Gates's company Corbis has acquired the rights to more than seventeen million pictures and images, you are unlikely to tire of the selection. "We'll have to have hierarchy guidelines, for when more than one person goes to a room," said Gates when the house was under construction. One presumes that in his own home Gates ranks at the top, a constant salve to any feelings of social anxiety he may have had in high school. Thus I imagine him stepping into a crowded room: the temperature and lighting shift subtly, the art on the walls begins to change, and from the speakers one hears the pealing bell-like riffs favored by U2's guitarist, the Edge. (In my dreams, of course, it is my own arrival that is heralded with such drama.)

Essentially it is the House of the Future, but since Gates is the world's richest man, it probably really *is* the house of the future, in an exhilarating and slightly scary way. Most of the details related here date back to the mid-1990s, just after construction was completed. Indeed, many could today be replicated by an average homeowner using an Apple iPhone and a few connected accessories. Not, however, in the Gates household: "There are very few things that are on the banned list," explains Melinda Gates. "But iPods and iPhones are two things we don't get for our kids."

In recent years the Gates house has undergone a major upgrade and expansion, and has been valued at $109 million, more than twice the original appraisal. A 17-by-10-foot video wall composed of multiple screens would now seem quaint and has presumably been upgraded. The identity pin has, one assumes, been replaced by something more seamless, such as face-recognition technology. There are many rumors about the upgrades, which are deliciously enticing (the Gates family now tightly controls access to the house). The media has made much of the trampoline room, and the fact that one can swim in the lap pool from indoors to outdoors by ducking under a glass wall. But the detail that most captures my imagination is the interior doors, each made of solid wood and reported to weigh more than 300 pounds, not driven by motors but rather so perfectly counterbalanced that they can be moved with the push of a finger. The shower door for the spa is reportedly the pièce de résistance of these grand portals, made of granite and clocking in at some 4,500 pounds, again counterbalanced so that it seems all but weightless.

It is this last detail that to me reveals the scope of Gates's vision. I imagine Bill Gates ready to leave the spa, his glasses steamed up, placing a finger against the shower door, knowing that it will move but thrilled by the delicious possibility that it will malfunction, thus entombing him forever within his hillside like a pharaoh of old. The temperature perfectly as he likes it; the greatest hits of U2 playing on repeat for eternity.

THE WORLD'S RICHEST MAN

Bill Gates is, as of this writing, the world's richest man. He has been very rich for a very long time, first reaching the top spot on the *Forbes* list of the world's billionaires in 1995. He stayed there for about a decade before ceding his position to the Mexican billionaire Carlos Slim and then regaining it. Microsoft operates roughly at the epicenter of the dog-eat-dog, rags-to-riches-to-rags world of high technology, where many companies (MySpace, BlackBerry) dominate markets one day and teeter on the verge of bankruptcy the next. So how does Gates stay on top?

The story of Gates's wealth secret is simultaneously the story of the wealth secrets of a lot of other technology-related names near the top of the Global Rich List—such as Steve Ballmer and Paul Allen at Microsoft, Larry Ellison at Oracle, Larry Page and Sergey Brin at Google, and Mark Zuckerberg at Facebook.

It is also a story of the bleeding edge of wealth secret innovation. As a result, in the early years no one understood what was going on—probably not even Gates himself. As Gates was earning his fortune, the U.S. government spent millions of dollars of taxpayers' money in antitrust litigation, based largely on misconceptions. In 1999, a U.S. court ruled that Microsoft was a predatory monopolist and in 2000 that the company should be broken up— a ruling that fortunately was not implemented, as in retrospect it would have been largely pointless. New microeconomic theories invented in an effort to explain Microsoft's costs to society were subsequently discovered to be wrong, misinterpreted, or both.

And at the center of all this misunderstanding is a puzzle. Microsoft is almost certainly a monopoly, having reached at one point a more than 90 percent share of the operating system market for personal computers globally. This monopoly position would seem to imply that Microsoft has hardly any effective competition, tremendous pricing power, and little need to innovate. And yet Microsoft is clearly an innovative company, pouring money into research and technology acquisitions and rolling out an unending stream of new products—some successful (the Xbox, Internet Explorer), some less so (Bing, Zune). It often charges a pittance for its products (offering the Windows 8 upgrade, for instance, at $40 in early 2014). Microsoft is, and always has been, making a huge effort to remain competitive—against competition that does not appear to exist. Why?

If solving this puzzle—of why a near monopolist makes such huge efforts to innovate against phantom competition—had been the focus of inquiry from the beginning, a vast amount of economic theorizing and lawyers' fees could probably have been saved.

But then, wealth secrets are difficult to understand. If they were not, they would not be wealth secrets.

IN THE RIGHT PLACE

Bill Gates was always interested in making money. He came up with a variety of moneymaking schemes while still in high school. Some were simple, if clever—reselling political campaign buttons and computer memory tapes—but most were impressively complicated operations for a high schooler. For instance, together with eventual Microsoft cofounder Paul Allen, Gates attempted to create a small business offering traffic-flow measurement services to local government.

To help on another such initiative, the development of a computer program that would automate high school class scheduling, Gates hired a couple of fellow students as subcontractors. One recalls Gates confidently asserting, "I am going to make $1 million by the time I'm twenty." Another high school friend recalls the same prediction, but with a target age of thirty; yet another recalls the predicted age as twenty-five. It was evidently an oft-repeated forecast. At Harvard University, from which he famously dropped out, Gates's favorite hobby was poker. Even for Harvard students these were high-stakes games, with players winning or losing several hundred dollars a night. Gates liked making money, and he liked competing for it.

Even after he had become wealthy ("I have an infinite amount of money," he once proclaimed), Gates remained interested in the topic, perhaps mainly for the competitive aspects. Flying home from a successful meeting with IBM in 1986, he impressed his colleagues by reciting from memory the percentages of their company's stock owned by each of the technology industry's CEOs ("to the decimal point," recalled former Microsoft executive Mike Slade). Needless to say, Gates's share was the largest in the industry. He was by then a billionaire. As Jim Conner, a program manager at Microsoft's Office Product Unit, said of his boss: "This guy is awesomely bright. But he's unique in a sense that he's the only really bright person I've ever met who was 100 per cent bottom-line oriented — how do you make a buck?"

While his success was far from preordained, when Bill Gates cofounded Microsoft in 1975, he was already positioning himself to make a fortune, merely by choosing the technology sector. As we saw in chapter 5, the list of the world's 1,600 or so billionaires is currently dominated by individuals from the emerging world (including India, China, and Russia). In the modern-day United States and Europe, well-crafted and well-enforced law and regulation make it increasingly difficult to earn a billion dollars. But among the top 100 people on the *Forbes* Global Rich List, the developed economies still dominate, even if only barely: 61 of the top 100 billionaires in the world are European, American, Japanese, or Australian.

It turns out that most of these 61 fortunes fall into two main categories. The first of these is the financial sector, broadly defined—8 of the 61 arise from money management, including hedge funds, private equity, and fund management. The other category is intellectual property, also broadly defined to encompass copyrights (which prevent you from copying this book), trademarks (which prevent you from opening a store called "Best Buy"), and patents (which prevent you from hiring a Chinese factory to produce a tablet computer, or anything else for that matter, using the patent-protected technologies embodied in Microsoft's Surface).

Companies that are based in large part around intellectual property assets account for about 40 of the 61 rich-world fortunes among the world's top 100. I would contend, admittedly somewhat arbitrarily, that these firms include consumer goods companies (LVMH, Mars—which tend to own valuable trademarks and brands), media companies (Disney, Bloomberg—which tend to own valuable copyrights), retail companies (Walmart, Aldi—also valuable trademarks), and, of course, technology companies (including Microsoft—which tend to own valuable patents). Basically, to oversimplify the situation somewhat: hedge funds and intellectual property ownership have produced more than 75 percent of the largest fortunes in Europe and North America today. And the vast majority of this 75 percent comes from intellectual property ownership.

So why is intellectual property so lucrative?

Well, it has a great deal to do with monopoly.

THE JOYS OF COPYRIGHT

Two economists at Washington University in St. Louis, Michele Boldrin and David Levine, recently caused a stir in the worlds of jurisprudence and academia with a book called *Against Intellectual Monopoly*, which argued that all intellectual property rights ought to be abolished. In the three years following publication the book has already been cited by more than five hundred academic studies—many of them critical of the book's central arguments, including the contention that patents and copyrights should be known as "intellectual monopoly" instead of "intellectual property." This would be more accurate, Boldrin and Levine contend, because "currently patents and copyrights grant producers of certain ideas a monopoly." And monopolies, as we all know, are bad (or very, very good, depending on your point of view).

This proposed rebranding is perhaps a bit too ambitious. If intellectual property is a monopoly, it is at most a limited monopoly. Unlike legislated monopolies, intellectual property monopolies do not apply to a market (like steamboat services in New York or telephone services in Mexico), but to an idea. And in fact a patent does not really protect an idea, but only a particular implementation of an idea. The intellectual property rights associated with the Microsoft Surface tablet, for instance, do not give Microsoft a monopoly on tablet computers, or even a monopoly on the narrower category of so-called convertibles (laptop computers that convert into a tablet form, like the Surface or the Lenovo Yoga). There are plenty of similar technological toys on the market, from the iPad to touch-screen laptops. That said, as a result of intellectual property rights protections only Microsoft can produce something that is called the "Surface," stamped with the Microsoft logo, or which uses the patented technologies that Microsoft developed or purchased in order to create the device. And thus Microsoft does have, in effect, a legal monopoly on a few potentially important things, including the Surface brand name and many of the device's component technologies. A law that prevents you from copying Microsoft, when the company is doing something obviously lucrative, has a wealth secret ring to it.

Indeed, while Boldrin and Levine are extreme in their views, the existence of intellectual property laws is not always easy to justify. The theoretical case for some kind of government intervention is open-and-shut. Ideas are "non-excludable," meaning that once an idea is made public, anyone can use it. And free markets tend to fail at providing "non-excludable" goods, because if anyone can use any idea that you come up with, there is no financial incentive for someone to come up with ideas. Hence ideas are what is known as a "public good." This aspect of market failure is unfortunate, because new ideas are very valuable (including new ways of doing business, new technologies, and of course, most valuable of all, new books).

But is providing a limited monopoly to a person or corporation, via a patent or copyright, the best way to encourage the production of new ideas? It is a problem that has long troubled legal thinkers. In the early 1800s, Thomas Jefferson, the principal author of the Declaration of Independence and the third president of the United States, fretted that the state-backed monopolies of intellectual property were an "embarrassment" to American ideals of free competition.

The usual argument in favor of intellectual property laws is that they reward creativity and innovation, and that, on balance, the extra costs consumers pay for these limited monopolies will be justified by the benefits of greater innovation. Consumers may pay more for Microsoft's Surface, but if there were no intellectual property rights, would Microsoft have developed it? If there were no copyright on this book, and anyone could copy it at no charge, would I have bothered to write it?

But oddly, it is very difficult to find real-world evidence that intellectual property laws do in fact encourage creativity or innovation. For instance, many crucial historical innovations (the cotton spinning machine, the power loom) did not benefit from patent laws, and countries and industries that were historically the most innovative do not appear to have registered more patents than other, less innovative countries and industries. While strengthening *general* property rights does appear to increase a country's rate of economic growth, strengthening *intellectual* property rights does not appear to have the same effect. Even businesses themselves rarely report that intellectual property rights—specifically, patents—are a benefit to either competition or innovation (except in the pharmaceutical sector).

One possible reason that intellectual property laws might not work as intended is that progress in innovation over time is cumulative. Isaac Newton's famous quote "If I have seen further it is by standing on the shoulders of giants" may well apply to innovation. If this is true, then patents, which limit people's ability to use new ideas, could actually slow down the innovation process. For instance, after the Wright brothers obtained patents relating to their development of the airplane, progress in airplane technology temporarily stalled until the U.S. government coerced the brothers into licensing their patents to others.

One does not need to look back so far to find similar examples; some of the fastest innovation in the software industry has happened on "open platforms" such as Linux (the basis for the Google Android operating system). When Microsoft was creating a mobile phone version of Windows, it invested hugely and expected to be rewarded accordingly. But Linux was developed via repeated small innovations by thousands of users, largely uncompensated, who were immediately able to piggyback on each other's unpatented innovations. Just as Newton stood "on the shoulders" of previous great scientists (by using their ideas), perhaps inventors work best when they do the same. The limited monopolies of intellectual property may serve to slow this process. There are, to be sure, many more arguments regarding the potential benefits of intellectual property rights, but most also suffer from a lack of strong evidence.

So why do intellectual property laws exist? An alternative way to think about this question is to look back at the era in which they were created. The origins of modern patent laws can be traced back to the British patent system of the early seventeenth century, specifically the Statute of Monopolies of 1623. This law was implemented, in part, at the behest of an increasingly powerful merchant class, which had grown tired of the habit of the English monarchy of awarding lucrative monopolies to favored friends (a practice that persisted for years thereafter in other countries, as we saw in chapter 3). England's Elizabeth I, for example, had issued monopolies for "innovations" such as starch and salt. The new law made royal monopolies obsolete, replacing them with patents that were to be awarded based solely on the merit of an invention — not the inventor's political connections. In a similar vein, laws for the protection of trademarks were implemented in the United States in response to merchant demands. Initially, businesses seeking to protect their brands had to resort to legal action using the preexisting laws against fraud. For example, it was fraudulent for some unscrupulous person to mix up sugar, water, and caramel coloring and claim it was a product of the Coca-Cola company. But this approach became unwieldy as companies like Campbell Soup, H. J. Heinz, and Procter & Gamble sought to grow their businesses across the United States in the late 1800s (Coca-Cola, for instance, was by that time seeking to protect its trademark with separate initiatives in forty-three states). These consumer goods companies demanded — and received — the first effective national trademark protection law in 1905.

In the United States, copyright law came into being along with the first patents, in 1790. At the time, authors enjoyed a copyright term of fourteen years (and the option to renew for an additional fourteen). This term has since been extended many times, partly at the request of authors, playwrights, and musicians, but mostly due to lobbying by media companies seeking to increase the value of their assets. The European Union recently extended copyright protection for music from fifty to seventy years and applied the extension retroactively—that is, to works already created. This aspect of the decision is particularly difficult to justify on public interest grounds. Such a retroactive extension *could* encourage the production of more music—for instance, the Beatles might decide to stay together longer—but only if someone can go back in time and tell them about it.

And thus, we can provide an alternate answer to the question of why intellectual property law exists. That is: intellectual property law is a tool for making money. Indeed, intellectual property law was created at the behest of people who wanted to make more money. Now, that is a motive we can relate to. The limited monopolies of intellectual property, deployed properly, spin laws into gold.

And, as the dominance of intellectual-property-rich companies on the Global Rich List suggests, this is one of the few blunt instruments for moneymaking remaining to seekers of wealth in the United States and Europe today.

BILL GATES, SUPERMAN

Many tales of Bill Gates's exploits ascribe to him almost superhuman abilities. This is only natural: he has amassed an absurd fortune and is now in the process of giving it away via a charitable foundation that takes on superhuman challenges, such as attempting to rid the world of polio and improve the American educational system. One expects that even in the company of geniuses, Gates will stand apart.

The various stories of Bill Gates's feats of brainpower tend to support this. He is reported to have read the *World Book*

Encyclopedia, in its entirety, at the tender age of nine. To this day, people close to Gates report on his high-speed reading habits. An ex-girlfriend recalled that he read four weighty newsmagazines over a short lunch they had together. Some other tales of Gates's genius may be apocryphal, such as the rumor that he had, on a whim, memorized the license plate numbers of all of Microsoft's roughly four hundred employees in the early 1980s.

Gates's ability to function without sleep for days on end is also the stuff of legend—and was crucial to a number of Microsoft's early business successes. These included the firm's first real project, a piece of software that Gates and his colleague Paul Allen claimed was nearly complete, when in fact it did not exist and therefore had to be developed in a marathon of all-day–all-night coding.

Gates was also, without a doubt, an excellent computer programmer, personally contributing to many products over the years. In 1983, when Microsoft already had more than a hundred programmers on its staff, Gates wrote the last piece of Microsoft code he would produce himself—a text editor for an underpowered computer that his staff had said was "impossible" given the constraints. Gates reportedly did it overnight. In 1986, in a bold but typically self-confident move, he challenged journalists at a press conference to a timed onstage programming competition, the nature of the program to be selected from audience submissions. Gates was hoping to demonstrate the power of the company's new QuickBASIC software. At that point several years had passed since Gates had moved from programming into executive management. He did not win, but he came surprisingly close. Few other technology CEOs would undertake such a challenge.

While Gates is without doubt a genius, there are many geniuses in the world. Indeed the reason, according to Gates, that he decided not to go into academia was the realization that a number of his Harvard classmates were better at math than he was. We've seen that he was a gifted programmer, but he was far from the world's greatest. He also demonstrated a good head for commerce, but his initial approach to leadership at Microsoft was chaotic, and projects were repeatedly saved by heroic feats of all-night programming.

Gates did, however, have one personal advantage that was almost certainly unique among technology executives, and this would be crucial to his success.

That is, his father was a lawyer.

THE DEAL OF THE CENTURY

At one point during a 1994 interview with *Playboy* magazine, Gates leapt to his feet and strode theatrically across his office to the bookshelf. "Let's look around these bookshelves and see if we find any business books," he told the interviewer, scanning the books' spines. "Oops. We didn't find any."

True enough. The secrets of Microsoft's success were not to be found in business books. The unruly start-up companies competing to define the fledgling information technology marketplace fought over two issues in particular. The first was which company would come up with the greatest market-leading innovations. The second was which company would make money from the innovations. These turned out to be two entirely distinct issues. Some companies were very good at innovating but bad at making money from that innovation. Xerox was perhaps the most infamous of these. Its PARC laboratories came up with the mouse, laser printing, Ethernet networking technology, and the graphical user interface (the predecessor to both the Macintosh and Windows operating systems). But Xerox made next to no money out of any of these (and many of Xerox's top researchers would eventually defect to either Microsoft or Apple). Other companies were, by contrast, very good at making money from innovations, regardless of the source of those breakthroughs. Microsoft was the leader of this latter pack.

In the mid-1970s, when Microsoft was starting out, the application of intellectual property law to software was uncertain. There were a number of categories of software that could potentially be covered. First was the operating system, which, roughly speaking, allowed a computer's brain to interact with its body, controlling access to disk drives, memory, and any other devices connected to the computer (monitors, printers, networks, keyboards). Windows, Android, and OS X are examples of operating systems. There were then programs (today usually called applications, or apps) that ran on top of the operating system. If there was more than one program running (say you were pretending to work on a word processing document but switching to Angry Birds whenever the boss looked away), the operating system would allocate the computer's resources (such as memory) between the different programs. In the early days of personal computing, users had to make their own apps, using a programming language like BASIC (computer hobbyist magazines contained page after page of listings of exceedingly simple apps the user could type in). A programming language was essentially an app that allowed the user to build other apps. Today, most programs are still written in programming languages, but they are compiled and sold in formats that can be run directly (called "executables"), so the user never needs to know in what language the app was originally written.

When the first software patent case (for, in effect, a piece of code that could be used in many different programs) went before the U.S. Supreme Court in 1972, the patent was ruled invalid. The judges believed that, like all scientific principles, software could not be patented, as it was "pure mathematics." Copyright laws, by contrast, did offer software companies at least some protection for their programs or operating systems, although nothing was really formalized until the 1980s. Indeed, in the late 1960s and early

1970s, software was thought to be uncopyrightable as well as unpatentable. Certainly, computer software consisted of written text in many cases, but this text was purely utilitarian, and ultimately translatable into a string of 1s and 0s. How did this software code bear any relation to the novels, poems, or plays that copyright laws were intended to protect? In the mid-1970s, however, Congress established a commission to study the issue of software copyright, and by the 1980s making direct copies of someone else's computer code was considered illegal. By 1981, the beginnings of patent protection for software had been established, but it was not until a series of federal circuit court of appeals decisions more than a decade later that patent protection for software could truly be relied upon. Hence, when Microsoft started out, direct plagiarism of software was discouraged, but producing code that did exactly the same thing as a competitor's code was entirely legal.

As a result, in 1975, Bill Gates was entering the high-technology equivalent of the Wild West. This is where the lawyer's son had his chance to shine. From an early age Gates had been imitating his father's legalese. In 1966, for instance, aged ten, Gates drew up a formal contract for unlimited but nonexclusive use of his sister's baseball glove, complete with "on acceptance of terms" and "witness sign here," such legalese mixed endearingly with kidspeak: "When Trey [Gates's nickname] wants the mitt, he gets it."

On cofounding Microsoft, at the ripe old age of nineteen, Gates was immediately preoccupied by the problem of how to make money from products that could be copied freely. He first became well known in the computing industry—indeed, achieved a degree of infamy—for writing an open letter to the industry magazine *Computer Notes* in 1976. He was irate, he said, that "less than 10 percent" of the people he assumed were using the BASIC programming language (BASIC was Microsoft's first product) were paying for it. The rest were copying it. "As the majority of hobbyists must be aware, most of you steal your software," wrote Gates, refusing to mince words. At the time, of course, most software was freely copied, and it was not clearly illegal to do so. But Gates was having none of it. "Who can afford to do professional work for nothing?" he asked. To make such assertions required some chutzpah, as Microsoft's own product, BASIC, was explicitly based on the feature set of RSTS-11 BASIC, which had been developed by Digital Equipment Corporation. No problem with that, of course, as software was years away from being patentable, and RSTS-11 BASIC was unpatented. But still.

Many of the magazine's readers did not agree with Gates. Indeed, there was a miniature deluge of hate mail. "Defamatory and insulting," wrote one reader. But Gates stuck to his guns. That same year, in his first speech to an industry conference, he again railed against people who were "ripping off" his software (he was now twenty and, contrary to his most optimistic prediction, yet to earn his first million). It was ultimately a lost cause. The apps of the day, written in BASIC, were instantly copyable. The programming languages themselves, such as BASIC, were harder to replicate, but many tech-savvy hobbyists could do it. Eventually Gates wrote another open letter in *Computer Notes,* entitled "A SECOND AND FINAL LETTER," which included something of an apology. In it, Gates noted that the majority of computer users were "intelligent and honest individuals who share my concern about the future of software development."

But the young Bill Gates was not going to abandon his efforts to extract money from his computer software as easily as that. There was an alternative: he could write up contracts. With each sale of a Microsoft product would come a legal agreement which, provided buyers were willing to sign, would establish rights enforceable in court. Even in the corporate sector, this was something of a novel approach. "We never tried to patent CP/M [the industry-standard operating system prior to Microsoft's DOS]," explained an employee of Digital Research, the company that had developed

CP/M. "Nobody was patenting software then; it was almost unethical."

But this did not stop Gates. At first he tried to draw up legal agreements with personal computer users—the end users of his software. Initially, anyone wishing to receive a copy of Microsoft BASIC had first to return a signed secrecy agreement affirming that he or she would not share the software (an approach that has recently become popular again, with websites demanding that users click "OK" or "Agree" to lengthy user agreements that few people bother to read). An article in *Computer Notes* warned that Microsoft "will prosecute anyone who violates their license agreement." Sadly for Gates, this approach turned out to be impractical, since the fledgling company lacked the resources to prosecute hundreds of users for such paltry fees. Indeed, the administrative burden of sending, receiving, and filing the user agreements was so onerous that the practice was soon abandoned, over Gates's objections.

Gates had better luck with corporations. By selling his software to corporations, which would then sell it on to end users, Gates could create proprietary rights, via legal contract, that were practical to defend. Unlike a sale of one copy of software to a user, the sale of a single software license to a company would bring in, at a stroke, tens or even hundreds of thousands of dollars, so threats of legal action were realistic. The company's first agreement, a contract with one of the first personal computer manufacturers, MITS, was reportedly drawn up by Gates himself, with help from his father and another attorney recommended by his father. In the years to come, Microsoft would rarely produce an industry-leading breakthrough (lagging competitors in the development of graphical user interfaces, networking, the web browser, and then mobile computing). But in contract law, the company repeatedly led the field. According to two technology journalists, the contract Microsoft had signed with MITS would, in years ahead, "serve as a model for

The MITS Altair 8800 computer that ran Microsoft's (at the time "Micro-Soft") BASIC software. The contract with MITS was Microsoft's first. (Michael Holley. Licensed under public domain via Wikimedia Commons)

future software licensing agreements in the growing microcomputer industry, and it helped set industry standards."

And the agreement would soon be tested in court. Microsoft wanted to sell BASIC to other companies, but MITS had little interest in helping out, and so Microsoft's efforts were floundering. Happily for Gates, in the contract with MITS, Microsoft had included a provision stating that MITS would use its "best efforts to license, promote and commercialize the program (BASIC). The company's failure to use its best efforts...shall constitute sufficient grounds and reasons to terminate this agreement." Gates was not shy about legal confrontation—his first contract dispute over software had taken place in high school. Microsoft sent a legal letter to MITS informing them of the intent to terminate their companies' relationship if "best efforts" (and other issues) were not corrected within ten days. MITS responded by taking Microsoft to arbitration. Fortunately, Gates's legalese was first-rate: Microsoft won the dispute.

But this contract, though it set industry standards, was far from the most brilliant that Microsoft would draw up. That prize goes to the paperwork surrounding Microsoft Disk Operating System (MS-DOS, or just DOS), released in 1981. By the mid-1990s, MS-DOS was running on roughly 140 million of the 170 million personal computers worldwide. Yet Microsoft created neither DOS nor most of the ideas behind DOS; nor did it pay for the development of DOS. Hence the contracts that gave Microsoft proprietary rights to sell DOS were later hailed as the "deal of the century" or the "bargain of the century." Of course, those accolades came with the benefit of hindsight. At the time, not even Gates realized how big DOS was going to be. Yet he drew up an indisputably first-rate set of contracts.

There were four potential claimants to ownership of DOS. The first was Digital Research, which had produced CP/M, the industry-standard (but unpatented) operating system on which DOS was loosely based. The second was Seattle Computer Products, which developed Q-DOS, the software that became DOS. The third was Microsoft, which bought a license from Seattle Computer Products to distribute DOS. (Microsoft paid $75,000 for these rights. In the next two years alone, Microsoft would earn $10 million from DOS sales.) The fourth was IBM, which had paid Microsoft to develop DOS.

The most likely winner in any contract-drafting battle was IBM, a whale among minnows. The money it was spending on the development of DOS entitled IBM to at least claim ownership of it, but in a departure from usual practice, IBM didn't. It is unclear why not. It is possible that Microsoft negotiated rings around IBM. While the contract, in theory, gave IBM a license to sell DOS, in fact, the cleverly worded document stated elsewhere that IBM could not "publish or disseminate the source code"—with potentially unlimited liability for violations. As dissemination of the code would be necessary for such a sale, in practice, IBM could not license DOS to third parties, even if it had the theoretical right to do so. And yet it seems unlikely that IBM's large legal team would have failed to read the fine print on the contract. Jack Sams, the IBM executive who oversaw the deal, later contended that IBM left sales of DOS in Microsoft's hands because the company did not want to deal with the legal disputes over software ownership that would inevitably arise. We had "a terrible problem being sued by people claiming we had stolen their stuff," said Sams.

Indeed, confirming IBM's fears, both Digital Research and Seattle Computer Products eventually threatened legal action regarding DOS, with the former claiming that DOS was a copy of CP/M. "Ask Bill why function code 6 [in DOS] ends in a dollar sign. No one in the world knows that but me," Gary Kildall, CP/M's developer, later complained. Despite such complaints, in the end the threats from Digital Research did not achieve much. Lawsuits from the various heirs to Seattle Computer Products, however, timed to coincide with Microsoft's IPO in 1986, managed to extract roughly $2 million from Microsoft.

But it could have been worse—much worse. Seattle Computer Products had initially wanted $20 million. By that time, Microsoft was earning more than $30 million *each year* from sales of DOS. The company's total revenues were above $197 million, and Microsoft's value at IPO was $520 million and rapidly rising.

The reason Microsoft, despite its apparent underpayment, had a strong claim to nearly all the revenues from DOS was, once again, Bill Gates's contract magic. An attorney who had seen the original

1981 agreement with Seattle Computer Products noted that Gates, in handwritten alterations, changed key language to specify a *sale* of DOS rather than an exclusive *license to distribute* DOS. "That was a brilliant masterstroke on his part," the attorney later commented, since it meant that Microsoft's claim to the ownership of the intellectual property surrounding DOS was ironclad, regardless of DOS's origins. Indeed, Microsoft arguably had no need to pay anything at all to Seattle Computer Products, and Gates confidently took the case to trial. Unfortunately, after some pointed references to Gates's $550 million fortune during cross-examination (Gates claimed, on the stand, to be unaware of how much he was worth), the jury seemed to turn against him, and eventually Microsoft swallowed its pride and settled.

All told, despite this minor setback, the set of agreements surrounding DOS put Microsoft on the path to riches. Nineteen eighty-one, the year of the IBM PC release, was the year that Gates reportedly earned a million dollars for the first time. He was twenty-six — so his high school forecasts for his future success were roughly accurate. As Gates's interviewer from *Playboy* would write, with verve and some hyperbole, "IBM thought they had Gates by the balls. He's just a hacker, they thought. A harmless nerd. What they actually had by the balls was an organism that had been bred for the accumulation of great power and maximum profit, the child of a lawyer, who knew the language of contracts, and who just ripped those IBM guys apart."

Of course, in years to come, there would be many more contracts, and many more lawsuits. But Microsoft was always ready to fight. In 1982, for instance, Microsoft sued Advanced Logic Systems (ALS) for copyright infringement. Gates continued the suit even after the company agreed to change its code, explaining that he wanted to set a legal precedent. In the view of one ALS executive, this was an attempt to "litigate a competitor out of existence," but most likely it was a matter of principle — an attempt to firm up the then uncertain application of copyright law to software. If Microsoft wanted to make money from software, Gates would need to be a pioneer. Indeed, many more software companies would in time benefit from his efforts. As he would later explain: "Microsoft is an intellectual property company. We have no factories of any consequence or natural resources. Indeed, we have no physical assets of any kind that are important to the success of the company. Our products instead consist almost entirely of information we create."

NETWORK EFFECTS

So why was it worth Microsoft spending so much time drafting contracts and conducting elaborate courtroom battles, when such diversions of management time and resources at times threatened to undermine the young company's financial viability? Why did it make commercial sense for Gates to attempt to set legal precedents at his company's own expense? After all, Microsoft was not a law firm — it was not making money off these court cases directly. Wasn't all the time spent on contracts and lawsuits just a waste?

In one sense, of course, Microsoft did benefit from its legal maneuvering. In the late 1970s, software that had been developed without patent (such as CP/M) was being claimed by private owners. Microsoft capitalized on this moment, using clever contracts to acquire some valuable software technology at little cost. Arguably, the company thus saved itself a substantial sum of money that otherwise would have had to be invested in software development.

More importantly, by the early 1980s, Gates had managed to establish for his company the "miniature monopolies" of intellectual property rights protection for its key software products.

But this fact alone does not fully explain Microsoft's success — how the company was able to turn these "miniature monopolies" into a very real and nearly global monopoly on computer operating systems. For that, one needs to know something about the economics of software. As Gates himself explained to an industry conference in 1981: "I really shouldn't say this, but in some ways it leads, in an individual product category, to a natural monopoly: where somebody properly documents, properly trains, properly promotes a particular [software] package and through momentum, user loyalty, reputation, sales force, and prices builds a very strong position in that product."

He was absolutely right, of course: he shouldn't have said it. Never, ever, mention the word "monopoly" in mixed company. Having a monopoly in a market is a red flag, because gaining one through improper means and abusing its power to thwart competition are both illegal in the United States, Europe, and most other advanced economies. Antitrust legislation generally requires in these cases some kind of remedy, which may involve one's precious, beautiful, mother-of-all-wealth-secrets monopoly being broken up.

But what Gates was talking about—the almost magical force that turned his hard work, clever contracts, and borrowed software into billions of dollars—was economies of scale. It was a principle that would not have been unfamiliar to Andrew Carnegie, John D. Rockefeller, or Dhirubhai Ambani. But in the software business, these effects would be multiplied.

First, software companies benefit from a phenomenon known as "network effects" (which also aided the telephone and telegraph network-building of Vanderbilt, mentioned briefly in chapter 3—I'll come back to that again in chapter 7). Positive network effects are the additional value each user derives from a product as more individuals use it. Network effects are perhaps easiest to understand in the case of the telephone. If your telephone is not connected to a network, it is pretty much worthless. If it's connected to one other person's telephone, the connection is more valuable (assuming that person is someone you want to talk to). If it's connected to everyone else's telephone, it is hugely more valuable. So this means that the more people who are connected to a network, the more you would be willing to pay to join that network—as long as they are people you might conceivably want to talk to. The same is true, more or less, with railroads. The more cities and towns and farms that are connected via a rail network, the more valuable your connection to that network is.

In software, network effects apply in more than one way. Some of these effects are direct, and come from setting an industry standard. For instance, if you write documents in Microsoft Word, you can share them easily with other users of Microsoft Word (as I did, many times, with my editors while writing this book, while they made excessive use of Word's "comment" feature). [It was for your own good.—Ed.] If you are attempting to collaborate closely with other individuals on the joint development of a document, using the same software is important. Swapping back and forth between different word processing programs (or even between Word on a PC and Word on a Macintosh) usually leads, after a few iterations, to a document so bug-ridden that it crashes everyone's computers, and the intern has to retype it from scratch. So the more people use a program, the more valuable that program becomes to other potential buyers.

In software, there are also indirect network effects, which exist because some types of software, notably operating systems, become more valuable when used with complementary products. Consider an operating system like Microsoft Windows. The more applications written for Microsoft Windows, the more you would be willing to pay to own a copy of Microsoft Windows so you can use all those applications. This type of network effect is more subtle—it sometimes takes thousands of users before the pool is large enough to attract applications developers. But these indirect network effects are also powerful, because they attract not only consumers but companies, and companies make investments. If Microsoft Windows is the dominant operating system, companies writing application programs will tend to write programs for Microsoft Windows first. Each time they do, they are — in effect — adding the value of the money they invested in developing their own application to the value of Windows.

To be sure, the direct network effects in software are not as powerful as in many other industries. An unconnected telephone is pretty much useless, and so is a train track that doesn't go anywhere, but a single copy of Microsoft Word is still an improvement on a typewriter. But there is another crucial point to note about the economics of software: it costs almost nothing to make an additional copy. While making another computer or iPhone is expensive, software can be copied almost infinitely at no cost. (Especially in an age when it is increasingly downloaded, rather than packaged in boxes.) As in most industries, at some point diseconomies will tend to set in (mostly having to do with adding features and lines of code, which makes software more prone to crashing, security flaws, and bloated development costs). But once a piece of software has been written, making more copies of it is nearly costless. As Steve Ballmer, who took over as CEO of Microsoft from Bill Gates, put it: "Software businesses are all fixed-cost businesses. And so volume is absolutely everything."

This means that the economies of scale in software apply not only on the demand side, like railway and telephone networks, but also on the supply side, like oil refining and steel production. The more you produce, the more profit you will tend to make on each sale. This combination is very, very exciting.

As Bill Gates said, the exceptional economies of scale in software businesses should lead, under certain circumstances, to natural monopolies. The clever cartel maneuverings of Rockefeller, the Morgan-sponsored bailout of Carnegie, or the rearranging of the license maze by Dhirubhai — all these schemes to gain monopolies would be unnecessary in software. Indeed, the software business is perhaps unrivaled in the scale economies it enjoys. The company that sells the most in the market will gain an advantage not only in the appeal of its products but also in production costs. The more it sells in comparison to its competitors, the greater each of these advantages becomes. Once in a dominant position, a software company's profitability and competitive advantage are all but unassailable. One would have to be a moron not to make money in this type of business. And Bill Gates was not a moron.

A BITE OUT OF APPLE

At the beginning, however, it was far from obvious that Gates was making good choices. In the 1970s and 1980s, Microsoft—as its name suggests—made only software, and very few people were paying for software (many end users were pirating it). The companies that made hardware (which had strong patent protection) were the ones doing well, at least at first. In 1981, Apple was making profits of $39.4 million on sales of $334 million. Microsoft's sales at the time, at $15 million, were less than Apple's *profits*.

There was a good reason for this, of course. In the early days of DOS, Microsoft was giving its products away (literally, in the case of the first MS-DOS contract, with Seattle Computer), or selling them very cheaply. Soon Microsoft was also running a publishing company, Microsoft Press, at a loss, churning out computer programming manuals and training materials. The goal was, as Gates said, to nurture a user base and community of application developers, so that network effects could begin to apply. But in the early days, the potential strength of these effects in the software industry was not obviously apparent.

Yet Microsoft very likely understood the potential gains that could come from setting a compatibility benchmark for the industry. The company's first success with this approach, albeit on a small scale, came in the 1970s, with the programming language BASIC. The applications of the day were programs written in

BASIC and shared freely (as was the ethos of the time), but to run them you needed to have BASIC on your machine. Despite the initial difficulty of getting people to pay for software, Microsoft soon began to make money. "This is a very personal business, but success comes from appealing to groups," said Gates. "Money is made by setting de facto standards."

And yet, even by the mid-1980s, Microsoft's strategy was still not a clear winner. In contrast to Microsoft's products, each new generation of Apple computers was a thing of beauty—robust, secure, and easy to use. In an iconic 1984 Super Bowl commercial, Apple introduced the Macintosh, the first widely used computer system based on a graphical user interface. In the commercial, a sprightly female hammer thrower liberated a legion of drones from the grip of—you guessed it—the industry standard.

Microsoft's response seemed ham-fisted. Its new graphical user interface, Windows, tended to crash frequently. (Older users will recall the "blue screen of death.") Each time Windows crashed you may have (as I did) wished the suffering you experienced could somehow be visited upon the person of Bill Gates, in a form of karmic justice. Perhaps you were, as I was, mildly surprised when Gates eventually became the world's richest man despite producing such terrible software.

But when I thought these uncharitable things, I was merely demonstrating my lack of vision. There was a method in Microsoft's apparent madness. As Gates explained in an internal Microsoft memo from 1995: "Aspects of the [IBM] PC were arbitrary or even poor. However, a phenomena [sic] grew up around the IBM PC that made it a key element of everything that would happen for the next 15 years. Companies that tried to fight the PC standard often had good reasons for doing so but they failed because the phenomena overcame any weakness that resistors identified." What Bill Gates was trying to say (he is not a gifted communicator) was that the existence of network effects—the mysterious "phenomena"

The Windows "blue screen of death" strikes a high-tech billboard in London. Those who are surprised that Gates became so rich selling buggy software fail to understand his wealth secret. (Allan Hailstone)

he referred to—made it more important for a technology product to be widely used than for it to have the best features.

In his book *The Road Ahead*, Gates explained more clearly why this was the case: "A positive-feedback cycle begins when, in a growing market, one way of doing something gets a slight advantage over its competitors. It is most likely to happen with high-technology products that can be made in great volume for very little increase in cost." This was, of course, an exact description of the economics of the software industry, although it appears to conflate economies of scale on the supply and demand sides (fortunately, Gates was not trying for an economics degree). "One of the important lessons the computer industry learned," he continued, "is that a great deal of the computer's value to its user depends on the quality and variety of the application software available for it. A positive feedback cycle began driving the PC market. Once it got going, thousands of software applications appeared, and untold numbers of companies began making add-in or 'accessory' cards, which extended the hardware capabilities of the PC.... Although buyers of a PC might not have articulated it this way, what they were looking for was the hardware that ran the most software, and they wanted the same system the people they knew and worked with had."

Microsoft's strategic decisions constantly reflected an understanding of this trade-off—that it was acceptable for a product to be "arbitrary or even poor" if that was what it took to increase the user base. It meant getting new products to the market fast, perhaps before they had been thoroughly debugged, in the hope that they would establish a leading position. It meant pricing low, especially for new types of products, even if that meant making less money in the early phases than the insufferable hipsters at Apple. But most of all, it meant ensuring that each generation of Microsoft products was compatible with what had gone before. When major technological advances came along—multitasking, graphical user interfaces, networking, 32-bit operating systems, multithreading— this required messy compromises. Older readers will recall with fondness (or perhaps annoyance) the various workarounds used to make programs designed for prior operating systems work with the latest Microsoft software (starting a Windows PC in "MS-DOS mode" for instance).

This approach had real costs. Windows 95, Microsoft's 32-bit operating system, had a 16-bit subsystem (Win16 Mutex) hidden inside it, in order to operate Windows 3.0 and 3.1 applications. It crashed a lot. These problems were not unexpected because Windows 95 had to be compatible not only with earlier applications written for Windows 3.0 but also a huge variety of computer hardware. And Windows 3.0 itself was already a mess, in large part because of efforts to retain compatibility with its own predecessor, MS-DOS. Brad Silverberg, who headed Windows development, admitted that "[Windows] 3.0 was pretty big and pretty slow." But, he explained, this was a necessary trade-off: "You can't break compatibility.... In some ways, if we could do them over again, we know how you can do it so you could write the system faster.... But once you have those interfaces, you are pretty much locked."

Still, the launch delays, and the bugs, and the crashes, were worth it. Any applications developed for prior Apple generations generally did not work on the newest machines. Hence the number of Apple users was inherently limited, not only to Apple products but to a single generation of Apple products. The Apple Macintosh, however cool it may have been, lacked applications, and sales were slow (after a year on the market, the Macintosh was selling a mere 20,000 units a month).

Bill Gates may not have been cool, but it did not matter. The number of users of Microsoft's uncool, bug-ridden, user-unfriendly, but (mostly) compatible software grew and grew. Finally, the logic of increasing returns to scale began to produce the inevitable conclusion that Bill Gates had predicted. By 1988 there were 40 million computers in the world that were compatible with MS-DOS. By 1990, 50 million. By 1995, 140 million (by then, about 70 million of these were running backward-compatible versions of Microsoft Windows). At that time, there were only 30 million computers running anything other than DOS. The cumulative network effects were by this point so powerful that Apple could not hope to compete, no matter how trendy Steve Jobs's pullovers were. If you owned an MS-DOS computer, there were superb applications for whatever you might imagine, from writing, to spreadsheets, to video games, to music composition, to turning your computer screen into an aquarium.

By 1995, Microsoft was making profit margins of 35 percent, while Apple languished at 6 percent. Adding insult to injury, the most popular applications on Macintosh computers were applications written by Microsoft. Apple's CEO, Gil Amelio, was fired. In 1997, Apple was forced to negotiate a $150 million bailout in order to survive. The bailout was provided, humiliatingly, by Microsoft.

That must have felt really, really good.

A MODERN MONOPOLIST?

There was potentially a problem—a serious problem, threatening Microsoft's very survival. Microsoft was by this point a near monopoly, with a 95 percent share of the operating systems market in the United States. And there are very few privately owned monopolies in business in the modern day.

This is because the great monopolies of the robber baron era have mostly been broken up. The last holdovers from the age of "monopoly capitalism" (so called because the government allowed private profit-generating businesses to operate without competition) were public utilities. These businesses were most efficient at a large scale. It was thought that consumers would benefit most if these businesses operated as the only provider in the market, or at the very least were protected from competition so they could grow to the largest scale possible. Examples included electrical power and telephone utilities, which were allowed to operate as monopolies (in fact, often required to operate as monopolies) subject to regulation of the prices they could charge. Eventually even these became an endangered species. A few survived as public companies (the U.S. rail network Amtrak; the German rail network Deutsche Bahn), but the private operators were mostly gone. The network businesses were split up. Electric power plants, railroads, and telephone service providers were made to compete over electric transmission lines, railway tracks, and local networks owned by other parties (sometimes by the government, at other times by regulated private businesses). Just about the only place one can still find unfettered monopoly capitalists is in the emerging world (although even Carlos Slim has recently had to break up his empire).

But once intellectual property rights had been established as applying to software, Bill Gates had a new kind of monopoly—a legitimate one, enshrined in law, meaning that it would be very difficult to break up. Arguably, Microsoft's monopoly rights were enshrined in the U.S. Constitution and European Union law.

Since the 1990s, courts and government regulatory authorities have attempted to square this circle, without much success. From the lofty perspective of theory, the problem is that Microsoft operates at the intersection of two market failures: the "public good" nature of ideas, and the "natural monopoly" nature of software businesses, which are characterized by very strong economies of scale. In attempting to solve the first problem (by creating intellectual property laws), governments gave rise to the second. Efforts to solve the second problem will inevitably undo the solution to the first. Correcting both market failures simultaneously may be all but impossible.

And that is why all the lawyering was worth it. By establishing intellectual property rights in an economy-of-scale business, Gates had given himself not only a monopoly, but an *untouchable* monopoly. This was put to the test in the 1980s and 1990s when the company exploited its dominance in operating systems in order to gain a market-leading position in other software products (notably word processing programs, and then spreadsheets). Microsoft's efforts in this regard reached their zenith in the "browser wars" of the 1990s, when the company crossed what many perceived to be a red line. In an effort to take market share from Netscape, Microsoft integrated the code for Internet Explorer into Windows so that it could not be uninstalled. This initiative was perfectly within Microsoft's rights, of course. Microsoft owned the intellectual property behind Windows and could modify Windows however it wished. But it began to look as if Microsoft would be able to exploit its dominance in operating systems in order to own the Internet. A lawyer working for Microsoft's competitors submitted a white paper to the U.S. government arguing that it was now "a realistic (and perhaps probable) outcome" that "a single company could seize sufficient control of information transmission so as to constitute a threat to the underpinnings of a free society."

This contention was a little over the top, but something needed to be done. In 1999, a U.S. judge ruled that Microsoft was a predatory monopolist, such that some sort of legal remedy was needed. This finding was confirmed by a second U.S. court in 2001. A few years later, in 2004, the European Commission reached the same conclusion. These were more or less open-and-shut cases. In court, Microsoft claimed that it did not really have monopoly power and gave various explanations for its behaviors—arguing that it was trying to benefit consumers, and that there was no way to separate the Internet Explorer code from the Windows code. These arguments generally failed to hold up, especially after document discovery turned up various incriminating e-mails (Brad Chase, Microsoft's head of marketing for Windows, wrote in one presentation: "The Internet is part of Windows. We will bind the shell to the Internet Explorer, so that running any other browser is a jolting experience"). Microsoft's anticompetitive behavior was ruled to be abuse of its monopoly position by courts on both sides of the Atlantic.

The problem was what to do about it. U.S. courts had noted that the "most effective" antitrust remedy is to break up a monopoly business. The problem was, Microsoft's monopoly was rooted in an intellectual property right granted by law, not in a physical network that could be dismembered or a portfolio of factories that could be divided. In the remedy phases of antitrust trials in both the United States and Europe, Microsoft argued that the limited monopoly enshrined in intellectual property rights would be violated by any attempt to change the company's structure.

At the turn of the twenty-first century, Microsoft's anticompetitive behavior was ruled to be abuse of its monopoly position by courts on both sides of the Atlantic—but finding a remedy has proved much harder than identifying the problem. (U.S. Department of Justice)

Nonetheless, in 2000, a U.S. court ruled that Microsoft should be broken up—perhaps into an applications company and an operating systems company. Another suggested solution was that Microsoft be forced to disclose the code for Windows, so that clones of Windows could be created by other companies.

It seemed to be a watershed moment, but the courts backed off from imposing a breakup, in part because of concern that this would harm consumers. While Microsoft's ownership of the Windows standard was a license to print money, it was also genuinely valuable to consumers, as Microsoft's setting of an industry standard had fostered the development of a vast market for software applications. Moreover, because Microsoft was purely an intellectual property company, remedies that would enable the creation of Windows clones would have struck fundamentally at the company's rights. A U.S. judge wrote that forcing the company to disclose "vast amounts of its intellectual property" to other companies was simply a bridge too far—it would amount to "an intellectual property 'grab' by Microsoft's competitors."

In the end, the courts on both sides of the Atlantic, despite ruling that Microsoft had engaged in illegal anticompetitive behavior, settled for so-called conduct remedies. That is to say, Microsoft's monopoly would be left untouched, but the courts would monitor Microsoft's actions and seek to force it to behave in a way that created a level playing field for competitors. For instance, Microsoft was forced to allow computer makers and consumers to remove easy access to Internet Explorer, so that competing browser producers could displace Microsoft's browser with their products. These conduct remedies, while a burden for Microsoft, amounted to acceptance by regulatory authorities that Microsoft's monopoly was untouchable. The company's stock soared. Microsoft's right to "own the standard" was upheld.

It was big news for wealth secrets. One hundred years after the great monopolies created by Morgan, Rockefeller, and Carnegie had fallen or at least been tamed by trustbusters and regulators, monopoly capitalism was back—and without any of the regulation of profits or prices that had applied to public utilities.

That meant Bill Gates was going to have serious, house-of-the-future money. It meant that he would one day be able to realize his quirky vision of swimming from outdoors to indoors with his favorite music following him all the way. "Be careful of what you do in there, since the boats on the lake can see inside," a security guard admonished as Gates showed off his pool to a reporter from *Time* magazine. Gates doubled over with laughter. He spent time in there at night with Melinda, he explained.

He was living the dream.

THE LESSON IN BILL'S DOLLARS

There is always the risk, of course, that a government regulator could decide to limit Microsoft's profitability. But there is a practical reason why this is unlikely. And it has to do with the nature of competition in the technology industries.

Microsoft's efforts to "set the standard" to leverage network effects are an early example of what has since come to be known as a "platform strategy." When Windows became a standard—or "platform"—it attracted an ecosystem of application developers, computer developers, chip developers, and developers of computer peripherals. The value of Windows then became not only the value that Microsoft had invested in the software's development, but also the value that all of these companies had invested in all of their products. Once a platform takes off, its value increases exponentially. The key question in platforms (think *Field of Dreams*) is "If you build it, will they come?" And, as with Microsoft's DOS/Windows standard, in the end, because of network effects, one platform usually dominates.

In the early days, the U.S. government worried that Microsoft's monopoly would strangle innovation in the technology sector. But this concern proved to be misplaced. The government did not at first believe that Microsoft faced competition, but this was an error. The nature of competition in industries where platform strategies are used is very different from that in "normal" industries.

In most "normal" industries, companies battle over market share. In these sectors, the various competitors will tend to gain or lose market share against each other over time (think Ford vs. GM vs. Honda vs. Toyota). In platform competition, by contrast, the participants expect that one platform will emerge as dominant and eventually "own" the market. They also expect that with monopoly market share will come huge, marvelous profits. In industries where there are platforms, companies tend to compete *for* the market, rather than *in* the market.

Hence there is genuine competition in platform industries, even for monopolies like Microsoft's, although that competition may be hard to see. Investors will be willing to put up a huge amount of capital, and take large initial losses, if they think they can create a new platform. Indeed, the more protection from competition a dominant position in a given market offers, the more incentive there is for other companies to attempt to achieve that position themselves, and the greater the potential rewards for investors willing to back the upstarts. Such markets for technology products and services are characterized by what has come to be called "catastrophic entry," or "waves of creative destruction," where a new competitor arises as if from nowhere, and seemingly overnight gains a dominant share.

This may be why Gates believed that Microsoft was vulnerable despite its overwhelming share of the operating systems market—there was always someone working away in a garage who could invent a platform that would knock Microsoft into oblivion. The dynamics of platform competition explain why Apple, following its humiliation at the hands of Microsoft in the mid-1990s, was able to stage a comeback. Investors bet hugely on the mere possibility that Apple would somehow manage to displace Microsoft's platform. Against the odds, this bet appears to have come off: Apple introduced tablet computers and smartphones, and these devices are now cutting into global sales of personal computers, which suffered their worst decline in history in 2013. (Steve Jobs relished this turnaround. When asked why he was offering a version of iTunes that ran on Windows PCs, he explained that it was "like offering a glass of ice water to someone in hell.")

That may be bad news for Microsoft, but it is actually great news for Gates's personal fortune. Apple's recent success demonstrates that the principle of platform competition applies to Microsoft, which implies that if the government were to attempt to regulate Microsoft's profitability or the prices it can charge (as is usually the case for regulated monopolies), it would inadvertently remove the incentive for companies like Apple to attempt to displace Microsoft. Microsoft's immense profitability year after year after year is the lure that draws competitors like Apple into the market, backed by the investment dollars of people determined to take a punt on gaining a fortune for themselves. It is what drives inventors in Silicon Valley garages and college dorm rooms to create innovative new platforms, ignoring their parents' constant refrain to get a proper job. If the U.S. government had capped the amount that Gates could earn, the huge sums Apple threw into the fight to displace Microsoft would never have been invested, the garage and dorm room inventors would have gone into investment banking instead, and Microsoft's monopoly would likely have persisted forever (or at least for a very long time).

For seekers of wealth secrets, this is the most marvelous of Catch-22 situations.

Beneath the domed ceiling of the library in the Gates home is engraved a quote from *The Great Gatsby:* "He had come a long way to this blue lawn, and his dream must have seemed so close that he could hardly fail to grasp it." Gates had once dreamed of being a millionaire. He was a long way past that now.

NET NEUTRALITY

Did Bill Gates intend, when he set out, to exploit the extraordinary economies of scale in software—which, unlike perhaps any other type of business, occur on both the supply and demand sides? It seems likely. In the 1970s, his corporate motto was "We set the standard," and at the beginning of the 1980s, he forecast that a "natural monopoly" was possible. It appears that Gates at least intuitively understood this principle of software economics before anyone else.

Did he also know that by basing his monopoly on intellectual property rights he would render it all but immune to effective antitrust remedies? This seems less likely. After all, having a monopoly is the secret ambition of every right-thinking businessperson. Probably Gates, in his eagerness, simply did not consider that, a decade later, governments would act against him. Indeed, when they did, Gates was outraged because he believed that the antitrust laws were designed to protect consumers and that he was giving consumers better products at no additional cost. If Gates had anticipated the governments' attack, surely he would not have used the words "natural monopoly" in a public forum.

Still, Gates's exploitation of economies of scale was without a doubt a stroke of wealth secret genius. It would not take a genius to copy Microsoft, of course. But then, because of intellectual property laws, no one *can* copy Microsoft; that is the whole point. Still, a very smart person could probably emulate Bill Gates, applying his approach in another market. And in Silicon Valley, very smart people are not in short supply. Among the wealthiest individuals in the world, platform strategies—usually based on intellectual property rights protections—are well represented. Nearly all of the dot-com billionaires in the top fifty spots have gained limited monopolies or appear likely to gain such monopolies in the future, and investors are backing them generously in the hope that they do so. Most of their companies (Apple, Oracle, Google, Facebook, Amazon) have been accused of antitrust violations. But even when the antitrust cases have gone against them, the basis of these monopolies in intellectual property has limited the effectiveness of remedies. Many have been forced to pay fines or disclose key technical details to competitors, but none in a way that would enable direct replication of their core products or services.

First among the companies that rule the dot-com roost is still Microsoft, which produced not only the $76 billion fortune of Bill Gates and the $19 billion fortune of Steve Ballmer but also (narrowly outside the top fifty) the $16 billion fortune of Paul Allen—about $111 billion in personal wealth in total. Google comes next, exploiting the network effects inherent in search and developing the web's premier advertising platform (producing the $32 billion fortunes of Larry Page and Sergey Brin in the process). Google is followed by Oracle, whose founder, Larry Ellison, has a fortune of $48 billion. Oracle's platform is in business software and hardware (where Microsoft is uncharacteristically an underdog, although gaining rapidly even as it cedes share to Apple on the consumer side). Mark Zuckerberg's Facebook follows, with perhaps the most straightforward network-effects strategy (the more people who join Facebook, the more valuable the site is as a place to connect—and to advertise within). But simple strategies can be good, and his fortune is now estimated at $29 billion.

Of course, there are many other such strategies used by famous names in the technology sector. In the 1990s eBay boomed with a network-effects business model that increased in value the more buyers and sellers it attracted (and despite recent difficulties, the site continues to monopolize the online auction space). Twitter's social messaging network was one of the leaders of the second wave of Internet companies, and more recently the messaging network WhatsApp famously landed itself a $19 billion valuation in only five years (by virtue of its 450 million users, which acquirer Facebook evidently judged to be an insurmountable "network effects" lead in online instant messaging).

Amazon, the famous name in high technology I have omitted until now (founder Jeff Bezos's fortune is $32 billion), initially struggled to attain profitability. It was a retail operation, so there were no network effects to speak of, and while its virtual storefront meant its costs were lower than those of many retail competitors, the company did not benefit from the snowballing economies of scale of companies like eBay. However, user ratings (now ubiquitous on websites) did provide a platform for buyers to create value.

And by 2005, after many twists and turns, the company was widely recognized as a leading exponent of platform strategies. For instance, Amazon enables third-party sellers to reach buyers on its website and third-party marketers to be compensated for advertising products sold on Amazon. Moreover, in recent years, the supply-side economies of scale inherent in retail (essentially, the ability to use one's size to squeeze the profits out of suppliers, as with Circuit City) have also begun to kick in, enabling Amazon to both undercut its competitors and (occasionally) turn a profit.

Amid these rising fortunes, the debate on what to do about these modern monopolies created by intellectual property law continues to rage. One approach, of course, is to drastically reform intellectual property law—perhaps going so far as eliminating patents, as Boldrin and Levine have advocated. Alternately, one could update antitrust remedies so that there was some way to break up intellectual-property-based monopolies (as they broke up Pierpont Morgan's Northern Securities Railroad and Rockefeller's Standard Oil). Timothy Wu, a professor of law at Columbia University, advocates a "separations principle," which would split companies into content creators, distributors, and hardware makers. And yet, because such approaches would presumably at a stroke destroy much of the stock market value of the U.S. and global high-technology sector, they seem profoundly unlikely to be implemented. Indeed, the likelihood diminishes as the value of intellectual-property-based companies continues to grow.

The only other alternative is, roughly speaking, some form of conduct remedy. If you are a monopolist and you have the misfortune to reach the remedy phase of an antitrust trial, when you hear the term "conduct remedy" you start screaming and jumping up and down and hugging and kissing your family members and especially your lawyer. Because a conduct remedy means your monopoly stays essentially intact.

The approach with the greatest backing is usually called

"neutrality." The idea is to pass laws that give everyone equal access to the networks of the new monopolists. For instance, Google could be prevented from manipulating its search formula to disadvantage competitors, which is called "search neutrality." Policies to make social media accounts portable to other providers are called "social media neutrality" (in a world of social media neutrality, you could move your Facebook account seamlessly to Google+ or LinkedIn as easily as you move your telephone number). While President Barack Obama threw his weight behind these approaches, and some "neutrality" measures seek to undermine network effects, in general the more effective they might be, the more challenging they would be to implement. And so, in all likelihood, the billions will continue to roll in (the most successful effort thus far has focused on "net neutrality," which targets old-school telecoms and cable companies, not dot-com companies).

So the real question is, how can you get your own intellectual property monopoly worth billions of dollars?

Of course, if there were a simple answer to that question, I would not be writing this book, I would be strangling competitors and consumers with my monopoly and rolling around naked on gold coins like the emperor Caligula. That said, there are a few pointers that can be gleaned from the successes and failures of others:

• To make money in software, you need a platform. There are lots of application developers, but they don't tend to make too much money (remember Corel WordPerfect? Remember Lotus Notes? Remember—and you are really dating yourself here—VisiCalc?). Microsoft's breakthrough was to create one of the first software *platforms*—initially DOS, and then Windows—which brought together users on one side with application developers on the other. Platforms enjoy indirect network effects, because the money other companies invest in creating applications for your platform add to the value of your platform. These network effects, along with economies of scale in software production, are what lead, joyously, to monopoly.

- Displacing a platform is hard; complementing one is easier. If you have a lot of money (like Apple) you may well want to try to take on Microsoft directly. The advantage of displacing a platform is that you know there is a lot of money there—Bill Gates's house proves it. It's tempting to just go straight after that monopoly. The problem is, you are then competing not just with the money and technology embodied in Windows but also that embodied in all the applications written for Windows. So you might instead want to try building a complement to an existing platform that then becomes a platform in its own right. For instance, the Internet browser Google Chrome runs on Microsoft Windows, but then itself runs various applications. Even Apple eventually decided that it was better off attacking Microsoft with complements (the iPad, the iPod, the iPhone, the iWatch) than via a full frontal assault.

- Software is not the only area where platform strategies apply. For instance, credit cards are a classic example of a non-software-based platform. Credit cards bring together consumers on the one side and merchants on the other, and network effects apply: the more consumers use a card, the more merchants will want to join the card's network; and the more merchants accept the card, the more consumers will want to use it. The thing you must be careful of is that people generally carry more than one credit card. This means that the market doesn't tend naturally toward monopoly. It's better than perfect competition, but it's still sort of competitive. The same is true of video game systems, where no single company has a monopoly (because the average gaming household has some- thing like 1.4 video game machines). This is also what killed MySpace—people could create more than one profile, which was fun but meant no monopoly (in contrast to Facebook, where each person generally has only one profile). If you want to pursue platform strategies, it's best if each user uses only one of your type of product (Facebook can be a little relentless in trying to force you to use your real name, but you would be too if your monopoly depended on it). The fact that most people use only one personal computer is what made Microsoft's monopoly possible and makes Microsoft so hard to displace.

• Until a monopoly sets in, competition in platforms is unbelievably complicated. It used to be that everyone in the software business thought first mover advantage was the key—the platform that got the largest number of users, and therefore the greatest network effects, most quickly, would win. It turned out that this wasn't the case. One reason is that platforms have two sets of customers. For instance, Microsoft's customers for its Windows operating system are both computer users and application developers. The application developers aren't suppliers, as you'd expect in a traditional business, because Microsoft must attract them to develop applications for Windows. The winning platform is the one that manages to simultaneously appeal to both sets of customers, which is a delicate balancing act. Hence platform markets tend to evolve more slowly, and earlier advantages are more vulnerable, than you might expect. Creating a winning platform is therefore a bit like playing a game of three-dimensional chess while blindfolded.

Well, that was complicated (in 2014, Jean Tirole, a French economist, won the Nobel Prize in part for his work on platform competition—which produced some of the above insights—and in general, the Nobel Prize isn't awarded for doing things that are simple).

Isn't there a more direct way to make money off of intellectual property rights?

THE PATENT PARTIES

In 2006, a reporter from *Bloomberg Businessweek* happened upon an unusual scene — what one commentator later dubbed a "patent party." Nathan Myhrvold, the former chief technology officer of Microsoft, had gathered a small group of very smart people and provided them with an unlimited supply of coffee, beef jerky, and nuts. In return for the nuts, and of course some money, these people were required to brainstorm ideas for possible inventions. In the back of the room sat patent lawyers from Intellectual Ventures, Myhrvold's new company. They took notes, recorded the conversation, and snapped photographs of the room's whiteboard. At the end of the day the lawyers turned some of the brainstormed ideas into patents, not with the intention of producing and selling any actual products using the patents, but with the intention of selling the patents themselves. On the day the *Businessweek* reporter dropped by, the topic was the future of surgery.

It doesn't sound like much of a party to me, but according to one of the day's participants, neurosurgeon Dennis J. Rivet, the appeal is not moneymaking but "the opportunity to interact with a diverse group of thinkers purely for the sake of invention." "This is really cool! This is really damn cool!" said Myhrvold at one point in the brainstorming session, taking the party atmosphere up a notch.

Since the 1990s, when a series of court decisions made it increasingly possible to enforce patents on things like software and business processes, patenting has become very, very popular. In a way, Myhrvold's "patent parties" were a logical outgrowth of this brave new world of patenting: instead of making a piece of software and then obtaining a patent to protect it, why not come up with the idea for the software first, patent it, and *then* make it — or perhaps sell it to another company that would then make it? Myhrvold's company is not itself really in the "making" business. It has created few actual inventions, aside from a mosquito-killing laser (yes, really). Mostly it produces, or buys, patents. The *Businessweek* reporter called it "Myhrvold's Mysterious New Idea Machine." Since the 1990s, these kinds of companies have become increasingly common. They are called "non-practicing entities."

Myhrvold's "idea machine" is actually a rare breed among non-practicing entities in that it produces ideas at all (it has reportedly spun off two start-up companies so far). Most non-practicing entities only buy patents from other patent holders (Intellectual Ventures does this as well). Most companies in this new sector claim their business model is the following. An inventor comes up with an idea and pitches it to a major company. The company likes the idea but does not like the inventor. The company commercializes the idea without paying the inventor. Along comes a non-practicing entity, buys the patent from the inventor, sues the company, collects a settlement payment, and thus the inventor is made whole for his or her intellectual property losses.

The problem is, the inventing process is complicated, and it is generally difficult to trace the "real" story of a patent. When pressed by National Public Radio to give an example of an inventor that Myhrvold's company was protecting, the company came up with the name Chris Crawford. Crawford, it emerged, had a patent granted in 1998 for connecting to an online service provider to do things like back up data or purchase software (services that are offered by numerous companies, including Microsoft, today). According to a patent lawyer contacted by NPR, a number of organizations were already doing this even in 1998, and so the patent should never have been issued. Furthermore, the ideas that led to the patent had emerged during a series of regular Saturday meetings involving four colleagues at a technology company. Because the technology of the day (computer modems that connected over phone lines) was not up to the task of online backups, the project was eventually abandoned. Crawford was the notetaker for the group, and some time later took his notes down to the patent office and obtained a patent for the not-yet-implemented idea (crucially, he obtained the patent only for himself, although his colleagues should probably have been listed as co-inventors).

All of this information emerged during a lawsuit, after a firm called Oasis Research sued eighteen companies using Crawford's patent. Most of the companies settled out of court, but two cases went to trial. Eventually the patent claim was disallowed, partly on the grounds that Crawford had not credited his co-inventors. During the trial it emerged that Oasis Research was likely a shell company of Myhrvold's company, Intellectual Ventures. Ninety percent of the money from the Oasis Research settlements would be paid to Intellectual Ventures, and 17.5 percent of that would in turn be paid to Crawford.

Even though Intellectual Ventures (via Oasis Research) lost the lawsuit, it may still have made money from this scheme because of the sixteen out-of-court settlements. The settlements are covered by nondisclosure agreements so there is no way to know precisely how much money was made. According to a company that took the case to trial, Oasis Research was initially asking for a payment of $20 million. Another company, which had settled and therefore could not speak on the record, complained bitterly, albeit anonymously, to NPR: "We were hit hard by this lawsuit. Infringement on our part seemed completely bogus, but we could not afford to fight it. Even with the settlement, we were forced to lay off employees." The story was complex. Like many patent lawsuits, even after the details were made public the roles and motives of the various actors remained unclear. But however one tells the tale, the resemblance of this story to the tale of non-practicing entities standing up for the rights of the small inventor whose invention is then stolen by a big company appeared tenuous at best.

Google has another name for Myhrvold's company: a "patent troll." Intellectual Ventures has reportedly purchased some 70,000 patents from companies and inventors, and claims currently to own some 40,000 "intellectual assets" (presumably including brain-stormed ideas it hopes to turn into patents). Intellectual Ventures says that it is licensing ideas to companies that need them. Compa-nies say they already have these ideas and are already commercial-izing them, and the tactics used by Intellectual Ventures are a shakedown. A licensing "offer" from a non-practicing entity can quickly turn into a lawsuit. A Google spokesperson claims that Intellectual Ventures uses "low-quality patents to extort money from companies that actually innovate and make real things." A Motorola spokesperson claims that Myhrvold's lawsuits are "based on overbroad patent claims meant to tax innovation." (Of course, since these companies are on the opposite side of lawsuits from Myhrvold's firm, such comments should be taken with a grain of salt.)

Regardless of which side of this particular debate one takes, it is clear that we are back in the world of Marcus Crassus. The expan-sion of intellectual property rights has resulted in outright wars to seize the property of others. Conquest is once again a wealth secret. The centurions in these battles are lawyers, and the property over which the modern legions battle is ideas.

The U.S. patent office takes the understandable view that it should err on the side of permissiveness when granting patents. Would you really want government bureaucrats deciding whether ideas are too far-fetched to be patented? Moreover, going through prior patents to decide whether or not a new patent overlaps with existing inventions would require hundreds of hours of highly skilled labor. Hence the U.S. patent office grants a lot of silly pat-ents. To wit, patent number 5,443,036: "a method for inducing cats to exercise consists of directing a beam of visible light pro-duced by hand-held laser apparatus onto the floor or wall or other opaque surface in the vicinity of the cat, then moving the laser so as to cause the bright pattern of light to move in a regular way fascinating to cats." The idea is to give the benefit of the doubt to the patent applicant and then let the legal system sort out issues of infringement.

And that is precisely what is happening. With most physical property, such as buildings or land or your car, the boundaries of what is owned are fairly clear. Now that it is possible to own ideas, the boundaries are rarely clear. Hence fighting over the gray area can be very profitable. Since the 1990s, battles over the ownership of ideas have become astonishingly frequent. The U.S. International Trade Commission reports that the number of intellectual property investigations increased by more than 530 percent between 2000 and 2011. Non-practicing entities like Intellectual Ventures function in these battles like Rome's legions: because they do not produce anything themselves, they are almost immune to countersuits.

Essentially, non-practicing entities are built for war. While a lawsuit (especially the document discovery phase) will be an expensive distraction for a technology company's executives, for executives at a non-practicing entity it is their core business. By 2012, non-practicing entities accounted for a majority (60 percent) of patent lawsuits filed, up from only 29 percent two years earlier. In 2011, the total costs associated with lawsuits from non-practicing entities were estimated at $29 billion, with more than 5,000 companies or individuals named as defendants. The number of lawsuits by non-practicing entities quadrupled between 2005 and 2011, and then doubled again between 2011 and 2012. Large corporations have fought back fairly effectively, licensing their own patents to NPEs, enabling them to monetize patents that they own but that are not otherwise being used. (Indeed, ironically enough, Intellectual Ventures appeared to be one such company, with initial backing from Microsoft, Intel, Apple Computer, Sony, and Nokia.) The main victims of the wars to seize intellectual property are small businesses, which can ill afford litigation costs and therefore tend to settle. The median company sued by a non-practicing entity in 2011 had $10.8 million in annual revenue. The median legal cost for a patent infringement suit with a value above $1 million is $2.5 million. For an infringement claim over $25 million, total litigation costs average roughly $5 million. That is half a year's revenues for the median company being sued, in many cases the difference between profitability and bankruptcy.

Myhrvold's public persona is not quite like Bill Gates's. Myhrvold is clearly a genius and perhaps a bit of a nerd, but unlike Gates he appears more interested in ideas for their own sake than in earning money. When Myhrvold served as chief technology officer at Microsoft, he was famous for writing a series of prescient memos, including one, "Road Kill on the Information Highway," in which he argued that Microsoft would have to make drastic changes to adapt to the rise of the Internet (and Microsoft did so, confounding skeptics who said no large company could be so agile). Myhrvold also coauthored Bill Gates's book *The Road Ahead*, which includes an enticing description of the Gates mansion.

Unlike Gates, simultaneously with his commercial ventures Myhrvold pursues a wide range of seemingly random intellectual interests at a professional level. He coauthored an article for the peer-reviewed journal *Paleobiology* regarding the physiology of the brontosaurus dinosaur (arguing that its tail could break the sound barrier). He has produced a 2,438-page cookbook, *Modernist Cuisine: The Art and Science of Cooking*, which won two awards, including a cookbook of the year award. He is clearly a person who is happiest when thinking deep thoughts. "The diplodocus was not like any existing animal," he solemnly informs a reporter from the *Washington Post* as they stroll around the Smithsonian Natural History museum. Yet Myhrvold is also rich: as of 2013, he was reportedly worth more than $650 million, and Intellectual Ventures had earned more than $3 billion from its patents. "People misunderstand our business and how we do it," said Myhrvold.

"Nathan Myhrvold is a very, very, very smart man. He may be the wealthiest man on earth when all is said and done," says Jonathan Schwartz, former CEO of Sun Microsystems. "Congratulations on arbitraging the patent system."

7

Seven Secrets of Spectacularly Rich People

NOT LONG AGO, following a difference of opinion with my company's CEO that didn't exactly go my way, I found myself with what is known in the business as "gardening leave," which is to say a few months during which I was being paid not to work (more of that, please). I decided to celebrate by taking a three-week cycling trip in Germany, much of which was spent dodging German retirees on e-bikes wobbling amiably down the bicycle path (wine tasting is also popular). On this trip I whizzed through, or more accurately wheezed through, a somewhat forgotten town on the Danube close to the border with Austria named Regensburg.

During the Holy Roman Empire, from 1663 to 1806, Regensburg became the permanent seat of the imperial parliament. At its peak, it was a sizable empire, covering most of modern-day Germany, Austria, the Czech Republic, Switzerland, the Netherlands, Belgium, Luxembourg, and Slovenia (not to mention significant parts of France, Italy, and Poland). As such, Regensburg could have staked a plausible claim to being Europe's political capital.

The name does not trip off the tongue now because, following the empire's collapse in the 1800s, the town slipped into obscurity. Today, its medieval city center remains a monument to a historical moment. The streets are thick with ancient architecture; more than 1,000 medieval buildings cluster in the center along with towers and gates from the Roman fortress that gave the town its name. Another legacy of Regensburg's past is that it is home to the family of Thurn and Taxis, one of Germany's wealthiest, and most improbable, family dynasties.

The Thurn and Taxis dynasty is an improbable one because its origins were in the postal system. Few things are more prosaic than the postal service, but in medieval Europe delivering the mail, over bad roads plagued by bandits, was a high-stakes venture— including for the sender, as the greater the value of the posted item, the greater the temptation for your courier to sell it, vanish, and live off the proceeds. The Taxis family, perhaps better described as a clan, given their numbers, specialized in courier services in medieval Europe and enjoyed a reputation for bravery and reliability. So much so that one Roger Taxis became a member of a royal court in the early fifteenth century. But it was another Taxis family member, Francesco, who in 1489 secured the family's fortunes by graduating to the management of postal routes extending from Brussels out to modern-day Austria, France, and Spain for the Hapsburgs. Over time, this became a contract to run key postal routes for the emperor. Meanwhile other Taxis clan members had obtained key postal positions in Innsbruck, Venice, Milan, and Spain.

At some point—it is difficult to say precisely when—the Taxis clan in effect produced the first recognizably modern postal service, based on the posthouse relay system: fresh horses stabled at intervals along key trunk routes enabled postal delivery riders to switch horses and continue journeys at speed. This approach was not new, of course. The Roman Empire had created a public post, *cursus publicus*, of great efficiency more than a thousand years before, based on a similar scheme. But the Taxis system was novel in combining two elements that today define our expectations for a proper postal service: first, it was available to the general public (not just the government); and second, the sender entrusted his or her letter to Taxis couriers (most previous systems required users to provide their own couriers). It was a great breakthrough, one that modern historians believe came about for the most prosaic of reasons. Essentially, the Holy Roman Empire was quite unreliable when it came to paying its bills (telling the emperor you are about to cut off his credit is a delicate business). The Taxis family wanted new, more obedient customers. Hence one member of the family, who had added "Thurn" to his last name (because the Taxis clan were so numerous), came up with the idea of selling postal services to the public. It was an idea whose time had come: for perhaps the first time in history, widespread literacy meant that members of the public wanted to send letters. The Holy Roman Emperor backed the idea, and a member of the Thurn and Taxis family was made postmaster general of the empire in 1543, a position that granted the family an effective monopoly over postal routes in large portions of Europe. The postal monopoly of Thurn and Taxis was made hereditary in 1574.

If there is one.thing we know for certain, it is that a legislated monopoly is a wonderful thing. And a government-awarded monopoly that spans not just a province or a country but an *entire empire* is even more wonderful. For the Thurn and Taxis it was, predictably, fabulously lucrative, "the well into which all streams flow" in the rather poetic phrasing of one count belonging to the family. In 1800, more than two hundred years later, it was still paying the family an annual income of nearly $9 million (in today's money) — which was lamented as a comedown from the truly fat years.

One reason for its longevity was that the postal monopoly helped fund the empire, since the family paid an annual fee into the imperial treasury for each region where their monopoly was protected. From a mere service provider, this family business had graduated into an important source of imperial income. Yet the clan served another crucial function. Total control of the mail provided the opportunity for espionage of hostile correspondence while ensuring the security of imperial correspondence—a benefit the family emphasized in making their case to the Hapsburg emperors for the monopoly's continuation.

The Thurn and Taxis were made princes of the Holy Roman Empire in 1695, and thus became a new and very modern kind of nobility. While most nobles of the medieval era were landed gentry, the Thurn and Taxis had the postal service as their fiefdom. (Through creative genealogy, they were also granted a noble history and a coat of arms that, none too subtly, featured a post horn.) At the height of their power, the family took key political offices, even serving as the emperor's representative at the imperial diet in Regensburg.

But there was trouble ahead. The power of the Holy Roman Emperor was on the wane, and the family's monopoly depended on royal protection. The Peace of Westphalia in 1648, which ended the Thirty Years' War, gave the territories within the Holy Roman Empire almost complete sovereignty. It was by then an empire in name only. As their political protection faded, the Thurn and Taxis began to lose postal territories to competitors. A hundred years later, following catastrophic military defeat by Napoleon at the Battle of Austerlitz, the empire was formally dissolved. It was 1806. The Thurn and Taxis family, who by then had been the imperial postmasters general for generations, were placed in spectacular peril. With the imperial *Reichspost* disbanded, the family's income would collapse—a fortune on the scale of a nation-state's dissolved, to be replaced by a few side businesses such as beer brewing. (As my tour guide to the family's castle in Regensburg, an enthusiastic young German, noted with understatement, the illustrious postmasters urgently needed to find "a new economic basis.")

Showing considerable bravery, Princess Therese, the wife of the last postmaster general, traveled down the Danube to Pressburg (modern Bratislava, the capital of Slovakia), where the carving up of the defeated empire was being negotiated. She had a weak hand to play. The family had a fortune but no army, and were more likely to become targets than to set terms. And yet, Therese charged in, parlaying the advantage she had—chiefly, good taste and connections in elite society—into a role hosting informal discussions on the margins of the formal negotiations at Pressburg. She must have served some marvelous cocktails. By the end Therese had somehow secured a private monopoly over a postal service connecting several successor states to the empire. This new monopoly included France, by specific order of Napoleon, even though it was Napoleon's army that had brought the empire to its end. If they had been rich before, this new arrangement more than secured the family's "economic basis."

Of course, the feudal era eventually came to an end. But by this point the Thurn and Taxis family were so rich there was no

The Thurn and Taxis family's ancestral castle. The family either sold, or were forced to give up, more than twenty-five castles, but they still own six in the vicinity of Regensburg, including this one. (Werner Böhm)

stopping them. All told, in the twentieth century they either sold or were forced to give up more than twenty-five castles throughout Europe. They also once owned the spectacular Villa Serbelloni at Bellagio in the Italian lake district (today it is owned by the Rockefeller Foundation). That is only what they lost. In the vicinity of Regensburg, they continue to own six castles to this day. On visiting the city, one can admire their astonishing collection of gilded carriages and gem-encrusted snuffboxes. They are still among the largest private landowners in Germany. In 2014, Albert von Thurn und Taxis appeared on the *Forbes* Global Rich List with a fortune of $1.6 billion. He was by then a veteran of the list: his first appearance had been at the tender age of eight. At present he is thirty-two and single. He enjoys society parties and motor racing.

Which brings us to the first secret of spectacularly rich people:

SECRET #1: DON'T BE THE BEST. BE THE ONLY.

Any good book on business strategy will tell you that profits are determined by a vast array of external and internal factors. Circuit City rode a wave of increasing consumer demand for electronics, and fell amid rising competition. LTCM was likewise pummeled by industry rivals. Reliance Industries nearly came to grief in a commercial and political battle against Bombay Dyeing, and its performance is currently threatened by new refineries in Asia and the Middle East as well as a fall in demand from China. Microsoft struggled to come to grips with technological advances such as networking and the rise of the Internet, and now the rise of the tablet and smartphone.

One of the most famous representations of such challenges, and how they impact an industry's profitability, is Michael Porter's "five forces": (1) the threat of substitute products, (2) the threat of new entrants, (3) competition among existing players in the industry, (4) the bargaining power of suppliers, and (5) the bargaining power of buyers. Usually the first two forces and the last two are depicted as external pressures acting upon the key question of rivalry among existing players. The "five forces" approach is a powerful tool for identifying lucrative commercial opportunities and can offer substantial insight into how profitable a given industry is likely to be.

Of course, if you follow the first habit of spectacularly rich people, you can forget all of this.

In 1659, the city of Antwerp attempted to set up a rival postal service to challenge the house of Thurn and Taxis. It could have been a cheaper service, or perhaps a higher quality one. The world would never find out. The Holy Roman Emperor dispatched troops to defend the monopoly. Antwerp mounted a token defense but capitulated quickly. Five would-be postmen were hanged.

To be sure, even with such powerful friends, the Thurn and Taxis family did need to worry about some "five forces" issues—their supply of horses; substitute services such as people carrying their own letters; customers complaining if their letters went missing. But frankly, they did not have to worry about any of these things very much, because their business was going to be hugely profitable, no matter what. It was, after all, a legislated monopoly, and it persisted for hundreds of years. When Circuit City made a strategic mistake or two, it resulted in a fire sale. When LTCM made a mistake or two, it nearly precipitated a global financial collapse. When the house of Thurn and Taxis made a mistake or two, it really didn't matter.

Economists will tell you that even legislated monopoly businesses, facing no competition—not even the threat of competition—will tend to seek an optimal price point (not optimal for the consumer, of course, but optimal for the monopoly's revenues). But if the Thurn and Taxis family got a little greedy and missed that optimal price point by a lot, what was going to happen to them? They might miss out on a couple of gem-encrusted snuffboxes that year, but they were still going to make so much money that, more than fourteen generations later, no one called Thurn and Taxis would have to work for a living if he didn't want to.

At a conference I recently attended, the technology CEO Meg Whitman was asked about the lessons she had learned while serving first as head of eBay and then Hewlett-Packard. She responded: "Always, always, *always* start with the customer." It is a commonly heard refrain from business executives. And there is good reason for it. Whitman's point was that when things go wrong companies instinctively tend to focus on analyzing and correcting internal problems, rather than looking at what is happening in the marketplace. She was telling the audience, in effect, that when you are seeking to correct underperformance, you have to look at your customers first.

That may be true, but only if you have competitors. The only rationale for paying attention to your customer is that there is a risk your rivals will pay *more* attention to them. In the absence of any competitors, simply ignore your customers and all will be fine. The director of India's state-owned telephone monopoly, C. M. Stephen, once defended his company against complaints that its service was terrible by noting that there was an eight-year waiting list to get a telephone in India. If so many people wanted a phone that there was an eight-year waitlist, he reasoned, the service they were offering must be really great. He had confused the wonders of a government-awarded monopoly with consumer acclaim. If any company in a competitive market ignored would-be new customers for eight years, believe me, it wouldn't last long.

A lot of experts on personal financial success will exhort you to be the best. They will advise you on routes to self-improvement and personal growth. Business books will tell you how to make your business "great" or perhaps "excellent." Self-help gurus will tell you how to transform your mental attitude and realize your inherent potential. These are all pretty much dead ends. The geniuses at LTCM were the best. And really, it got them nothing. Circuit City was the best as well—one of only eleven "good to great" companies in America, and far and away the top performer among them—and its assets ended up in a fire sale.

You don't want to be the best; you want to be the only.

Unfortunately, finding a government that will award you a monopoly is, in the modern day, a challenge. The emerging markets are a good place to look. Carlos Slim accomplished it in Mexico, to great effect. In Algeria, well-connected businesspeople known locally as the *"mafia-politico-financiere"* do very nicely off government-protected trading monopolies. The Russian oligarch Vladimir Potanin for a time owned part of the telecom monopoly Svyazinvest.

There are even a few examples in the rich world—the three rating agencies, for instance, divide a legislated monopoly among them, which is at least better than free-market competition. Anything requiring government licensing or involving government suppliers or buyers is a good place to start looking for these kinds of opportunities. An example from the United States is the company Pitney Bowes, which eventually gained a 100 percent share of the metered mail market thanks to its close relationship with the U.S. Postal Service. By the end of the 1950s, about half of all U.S. mail was processed using Pitney Bowes machines. Perhaps unsurprisingly, the company's profit margins at the time exceeded 80 percent, and better yet, it maintained its monopoly position for roughly forty years.

And then, of course, there is the technology sector. Technology gurus will often say things like "Technology companies are very profitable because they are very innovative." That is only a small part of the story. Companies in many sectors are innovative (the financial sector, for example, with its deployment of Nobel Prize–winning mathematicians). But companies in the financial sector cannot patent their innovations, so they must look for profits in other ways. Moreover, even in the technology sector, the most profitable technology companies are not necessarily the leading innovators (Microsoft, for instance, lagged on graphical user interfaces, multitasking, networking, the Internet, mobile devices...). Technology companies are profitable because they have patents; and patents give them miniature monopolies. If any competitor attempts to imitate a technology company in a way that is protected by patent, the government will come around and rough them up a bit.

Of course, the house of Thurn and Taxis had already proved the underlying principle several hundred years earlier. Growth isn't the ultimate achievement of business strategy; having one's competitors hanged is the ultimate achievement of business strategy.

SECRET #2: BIGGER IS STILL BETTER

Classic wealth secrets never go out of style, and the next one is something of a throwback.

The famed business book *In Search of Excellence*, by Tom Peters and Robert H. Waterman, Jr., published in 1982, documented an important shift in business fashion. Its findings were based on a comprehensive analysis of the factors that led to exceptional business performance, drawing on structured interviews conducted with about fifty high-performing organizations. Like Porter's "five forces," this study, undertaken in the late 1970s, produced a framework with seven nodes and a checklist with eight attributes describing exceptional organizations. These nodes and attributes included things like "structure," "skills," "style," "shared values," "productivity through people," and "close[ness] to the customer."

In other words, they were a bit touchy-feely. At the time, it was revolutionary stuff. Prior to this point, U.S. businesses had largely focused on gaining scale, because scale offered an insurmountable barrier to competition. Think Vanderbilt, Rockefeller, and Carnegie. Even after they (especially Carnegie) started to face competitors, being in an economies-of-scale industry was still usually good for some decent profits, if not perhaps robber baron profits.

Peters and his colleagues had a new message. They said it was better to be focused and specialized—to "stick to the knitting," in their chosen phrase—than to be big. (Today one might hear that a business should focus on "core competencies.") Peters and Waterman claimed that business advantage was produced not by scale economies but by soft factors like the motivation of employees, and that some companies were better at these things than others. "All that stuff you have been dismissing for so long as the intractable, irrational, intuitive, informal organization *can* be managed," they claimed.

Peters and Waterman cited a lot of evidence that bigger wasn't better. Larger companies were plagued by labor disruptions, for instance. Factories with more than a thousand employees lost an average of two days per employee per year to labor disputes, including strikes and walkouts. Factories with between ten and twenty-five employees, by contrast, lost less than 0.02 days per employee, on average. The McKinsey consultants also argued that larger organizations were less innovative. They offered vivid descriptions of giant companies mired in bureaucratic paralysis (at one firm they studied, they found 325 separate task forces and that "not a single task force had completed its charge in the last three years"). Peters and Waterman approvingly quoted the "tough-minded" president of Motorola, who said: "Something just seems to go wrong when you put more people under one roof."

These problems are called, as I have noted before, "diseconomies" of scale, and have plagued businesses for decades. The largest operations of the robber barons also posed management challenges, and in fact were probably less well run than the factories of the 1970s that Peters and Waterman studied. Carnegie's Edgar Thomson steelworks employed five thousand workers and suffered extraordinary labor disruptions, including one infamous strike that was brutally suppressed, resulting in ten deaths and thousands of injuries. In the modern day, killing striking workers is frowned upon.

So, yes, Peters and Waterman were onto something. By the

1970s the simple pursuit of scale was no longer a great wealth secret—at least, not in most sectors of the U.S. economy. In the robber baron era, scale had been the basis of the largest fortunes the world had ever seen, largely because it was difficult to achieve and because the robber barons came up with schemes to turn scale economies into wealth secrets. Carnegie's massive Edgar Thomson steelworks required so much investment that no one else could come close to matching it for years. U.S. stock markets were plagued by manipulation and conflict-of-interest schemes, which made people reluctant to invest, and hence it was hard to raise the funds that would have been necessary to take Carnegie on (at least until the early 1900s, which is when Carnegie started to get into trouble with competition and benefited from the assistance of Morgan). Furthermore, at the time, the absence of antitrust law meant that one could freely use one's scale to bludgeon suppliers and competitors. Rockefeller's aborted but spectacularly successful agreement with the South Improvement Company was perhaps the most extreme example.

In the United States of the 1970s, however, these advantages had all but vanished. Comprehensive antitrust law was by then strongly enforced. Large competitors were springing up around the world and shipping their goods globally. Furthermore, capital markets were by then so well developed that it was possible to fund operations large enough to challenge just about any commercial venture (LTCM, after all, started with more than $1 billion in the bank). In this environment, in which large-scale companies were legally constrained from exploiting their scale and faced competition from other companies of a similar size, the better-run company just might win, as Peters and Waterman had contended.

But there was a problem: the seven nodes and eight attributes revealed in In Pursuit of Excellence were not wealth secrets either. Business executives who followed these directives were once again chasing pipe dreams of being the best, which perhaps earned them a couple of percentage points of profit before their competitors copied them. "Soft is hard," wrote Peters and Waterman, but of course it really is not. If you have a motivated and innovative workforce, that is wonderful, but there is nothing to stop your competitors from finding out how you did it and doing the same thing. Having scale is different. A company may know it needs scale but be unable to obtain the financing to do it. Having intellectual property rights is also different. A company may know what you are doing and be able to do what you are doing, but not be allowed to do what you are doing. Just knowing that your competitors are living each day with this kind of frustration may be worth more than any amount of money. But in case it is not, the profits from such hard advantages are very nice too.

Many business leaders chased the rainbow of being better at "soft" management. But a few visionaries understood that bigger was still better, because it was still a wealth secret; you just had to find a way to make scale advantages apply. In Dhirubhai's India, for instance, scale was the secret to winning in the licensing regime. Scale efficiencies could be used to convince bureaucrats to grant licenses for production capacities so large that it became very difficult for any competitor to enter. Indeed, scale is still a wealth secret in most emerging economies—including modern-day India—in part because in most of these countries, domestic capital markets are not yet developed to the point where they could fund a truly huge, unprofitable enterprise for the years or even decades that are necessary for it to grow.

After the United States adopted a light touch approach to antitrust law, retail became another sector where scale created hard advantages, because retailers could use their size to bludgeon their suppliers (as we saw in chapter 1). No one understood this point better than Sam Walton, and Walmart is today the source of four of the twelve largest personal fortunes on earth (each of the four fortunes belongs to a member of the Walton family). Walmart's low prices are legendary, but they come from squeezing suppliers' profits, not the company's own profits, which are healthy. Amazon .com has a similar idea, and despite its low profitability throughout most of its existence, Wall Street has been eager to pour money into the company, on the off chance that it does become—as its slogan suggests—the "Everything Store," large enough to squeeze the profits out of every producer in the world and into its (and its investors') pockets.

I exaggerate somewhat, but these megastores offer the possibility of realizing, on a national or even *global* scale, the vision that one of Circuit City's CEOs, Richard Sharp, articulated: the virtuous cycle of market dominance creating lower prices that lead to even greater market dominance. At the end of this rainbow is—whisper it softly, lest speech put this fragile hope to flight—a natural monopoly. The very thought of it, as you can tell, makes me a little giddy. Perhaps one day there will be a global retail monopolist. I'm sure there are diseconomies of scale in retail, but the megaretailers don't seem to have reached their upper limit yet. Buy Amazon stock, and hope.

The problem is, as Peters and Waterman noted, in most industries diseconomies of scale start to set in fairly quickly. In steelmaking, for instance, there is not one giant mother-of-all-steel-factories producing all the world's steel. Making small operations larger makes them more efficient only up to a point, after which they become less efficient. As a result, while the global steel market is far from perfectly competitive, there are lots of steel companies worldwide battling intensely with each other.

Indeed, I am struggling to think of many industries where there is a truly global "natural monopoly." One that comes close is an industry I have mentioned before—jumbo jets, where there are really only two companies in the industry worldwide: Airbus and Boeing. Both of these companies have been subsidized heavily by their governments. Perhaps, in the absence of subsidies, there would be only one. Another industry with very strong scale economies is asset management: managing a large sum of client money generally costs about the same, in terms of overhead, as managing a small sum of client money—you make the same investments, just with more money. Yet at some point diseconomies start to set in, because the amount of money under management becomes so large that one's investments start to move markets—a problem that bedeviled LTCM at its peak, and pushed the fund to adopt trading strategies outside its core model-based expertise.

Really, the only industry I can think of where economies of scale are strong enough to produce a global natural monopoly is computer software, where Microsoft at one point enjoyed a more than 90 percent share of the world market for personal computer operating systems. Some might say computer software is not a "real" industry—it exists in its current form only because of intellectual property law. Most "real" products can't be copied infinitely at no cost, and therefore don't enjoy such spectacular scale economies. (Until recently, local newspapers, another intellectual-property-law-based business, also tended toward monopoly, although only of the town or city where they were published.)

But the profits of these industries—retail and software—are real enough. For modern-day seekers of wealth secrets, it is the most obvious place to focus.

That said, sometimes it pays to go for something that's not obvious.

SECRET #3: THE WORST PLACE TO DO BUSINESS IS REALLY THE BEST

The difficulties facing large-scale businesses in the advanced economies of the 1970s were one symptom of a broader problem. Basically, most countries in North America and Europe were becoming increasingly business-friendly. Corporate governance standards were improving, capital markets were developing, legal systems were becoming increasingly predictable, corporate tax rates were falling, bureaucratic interference was being reduced. This process accelerated in the 1980s, especially in the United States and the United Kingdom, with privatization and the downsizing of government. These changes were, generally speaking, a disaster for wealth secrets because they allowed competition to flourish. New businesses could be started easily, and successful medium-sized companies could grow quickly to challenge established titans of industry.

There were many places, though, that remained a wealth secrets paradise. Perhaps the most famous—or rather infamous—of these was post–communist Russia. The advent of democracy and extensive privatization during the 1990s was widely expected to birth a new Russia. It did, but the New Russians who popped out of the proverbial birth canal weren't who anyone was expecting. The world waited on a Russian George Washington or perhaps a Mahatma Gandhi; instead, it got Russian Silvio Berlusconis and Bernie Ecclestones by the dozens—a new class of businesspeople who were ruthless, pragmatic, colorful, and did not play by the rules.

Also contrary to expectation was that democracy and privatization produced economic catastrophe in Russia. Communism had been a nightmare for the country's people. Capitalism, it turned out, was worse. Roughly eighteen thousand of Russia's industrial enterprises were privatized between 1991 and 1996. The economy responded ungratefully, by contracting to roughly half its former size. The life expectancy of the average Russian fell from sixty-nine years to sixty-four.

This economic contraction should also by rights have been nearly fatal for anyone hoping to make money in Russia. Any business that somehow managed to turn a profit became the prey of corrupt bureaucrats and a rising mafia. The New Russian industrialists who survived came to be known as the "oligarchs." Many were forced to rely on underhanded tactics, including defrauding some major foreign investors, to survive. These oligarchs soon became famous globally for their unscrupulousness and their nouveau riche tastes.

The oligarchs were also, it emerged, laughing all the way to the bank (in most cases, a Swiss or Cypriot bank). Russian businesses had stumbled across a mother lode of wealth secrets. By the year 2004 Moscow was home to more U.S.-dollar billionaires than New York.

When this statistic came to light, many people were dumbfounded. The Russian economy had imploded, capped by a debt default in 1998 (the one that brought down LTCM), and by 2004 was a fraction of the size of the U.S. economy. So how could there be so many Muscovite billionaires?

Those left in stunned surprise simply did not understand wealth secrets. What matters in business is not having a big market; what matters is dominance. What matters is the absence of competition. And here, the oligarchs were having a field day. Some of their moneymaking schemes were little better than the proscriptions of Marcus Crassus. For instance, some managers of state-owned enterprises came up with a plan through which they could buy Russian oil from state firms at the state-controlled price of 30 rubles per ton (30 rubles was, at the time, about the cost of one pack of cigarettes) and sell the oil abroad at market prices, where it was worth millions of dollars. This particular scheme was so popular that in 1992, when reformers attempted to close this loophole, they were rebuffed by the managers, politicians, and government officials who were growing rich off the scam. As late as 1999, the scheme was still going. That year, the newly privatized Yukos oil company purchased oil from its subsidiaries at $1.70 a barrel even though the market price was about $15. In total, Yukos paid a total of $408 million for something that arguably should have cost $3.6 billion. It then exported about a quarter of that oil to world markets, earning a tidy $800 million in thirty-six weeks. Scholar Anders Aslund estimated that the total take from reselling underpriced natural resources, a scheme that went well beyond Yukos, approached $24 billion—a staggering 30 percent of Russia's annual economic output.

But most oligarchs relied on other wealth secrets to get rich—secrets more in line with Dhirubhai's way than Crassus's. To get started, they needed some start-up capital, and this was often obtained in creative ways. Mikhail Khodorkovsky—later jailed and then exiled following an apparent falling-out with Russian president Vladimir Putin—reportedly got his start by converting worthless accounting rubles into real rubles in the confusion of the 1980s, and then converting these rubles into dollars. Vladimir Potanin—who today ranks among the world's top 100 billionaires—allegedly used his connections to win control of a state bank and then entice several Russian government ministries to do their banking with him. But once these oligarchs had start-up capital, they tended to make money in more conventional ways. The problems of the Russian business environment—corruption, crime, inability to access capital, bureaucratic interference—made it nearly impossible for anyone who was not an oligarch to start a business. Hence the oligarchs spent years dominating their respective industries.

Oligarchs in the natural resources sector got all the headlines, but even oligarchs doing fairly mundane things like producing fertilizer, chemicals, candy, or tobacco made a killing. According to the research and advisory firm Oxford Analytica, one popular tactic used by oligarchs to deal with their competitors is so-called asset-grabbing: based on a tip, an entrepreneur is arrested for some sort of "economic crime" such as embezzlement or tax evasion and placed in pretrial detention. Usually, the desperate entrepreneur will cut some kind of deal to secure his release, which involves the loss of his company (sometimes into state hands, sometimes into bankruptcy). The entire process is usually instigated and even guided by a well-connected competitor. There are many variations on the theme: in one, corrupt police raid a company, seize its books, and illegally alter the ownership in the official register. In another, a rival businessperson acquires a target company's debt and then bribes a judge to declare the company insolvent. The business association Delovaya Rossiya estimates that there have been three million such raids over the past ten years. In 2012, there were about 150,000 cases started, with 3,000 closed and 30,000 taken to court—many of the remainder, presumably, having been settled by the entrepreneurs involved through the loss of their businesses.

This makes Russia a difficult place to do business, but mostly for the medium-sized companies that are usually the targets of such tactics. Large, well-connected companies tend, as a result of such tactics, to face little market competition. Perhaps unsurprisingly, it turned out that at least some of Russia's oligarchs appeared to rather like the system that made them rich. President Putin certainly believed this to be the case. Gathering his country's business leaders, he told them: "I only want to draw your attention straightaway to the fact that you have yourselves formed this very state, to a large extent through political and quasi-political structures under your control." Of course, Putin was not an entirely disinterested party. Shortly afterward he was to launch a ruthless campaign to imprison, exile, or impoverish any oligarch who failed to pledge unconditional political support. But it was undeniable that Russia's oligarchs had taught the world a lesson in wealth secrets.

The New Russians changed the way a great many people think about poor and middle-income countries. These places might be relatively impoverished, but they are also, counterintuitively, a land of opportunity for wealth secrets. "Oligarchs," or people like them, today thrive in a lot of places, including not only Russia, Mexico, and India, but also the Philippines, Egypt, and Venezuela. The well-connected children of Communist Party officials have become captains of industry in China. And, as I discussed at the end of chapter 5, such individuals today dominate the *Forbes* list of the world's billionaires. Their hard-won fortunes are testimony to Dhirubhai's wealth secret: the worst places to do business are really the best. Most businesspeople are instinctively attracted like moths to a flame to the largest, most lucrative markets. They see a number with a lot of zeros at the end and it overwhelms their common sense. They think that if they can get even a little bit of that huge sum of money, they will be rich. Following this line of reasoning, they conclude that going global is the ultimate achievement of business strategy, because going global increases the number of markets they are in.

They are totally wrong. Yes, going for a huge market is tempting, but then you will be forced to price competitively and probably won't make much money. You might have a small share of a huge market, but it won't be worth much. It is much better to go for a large share of a tiny market. There, you can turn the screws.

And that is why it's good to go where no one else wants to go. Take, for instance, the humble synthetic fiber business of Reliance, Dhirubhai Ambani's company, back in the 1990s when it was a tiny operation by global standards. Between 1989 and 1991, Reliance's operating margin in its synthetic fiber business was between 14 and 15 percent. At the time, Reliance exported next to nothing. Indeed, as recently as the early 2000s, 97 percent of Reliance's sales were in India, and India was a tiny market by global standards. By contrast, the titans of the synthetic fiber industry were global chemical companies like AkzoNobel of the Netherlands, Hoechst of Germany, and ICI of the United Kingdom. All of these companies operated factories around the world and had sales operations in about 100 countries worldwide. And they were making no money doing it. While Dhirubhai was turning in margins of 14 to 15 percent, AkzoNobel's margins languished between 2 and 5 percent and ICI's were even lower, at between 2 and 4 percent. Hoechst barely made it to half of Dhirubhai's level.

Being a global competitor may be glamorous and exciting and

get your picture in gray dots on the front cover of the *Wall Street Journal*, but it is bad for profits. Dhirubhai, having stitched up India's domestic market, was rolling in rupees. There were probably some other Indian businesses that tried to become global players. Perhaps some even tried to take on the international giants. But there was no money in it, and so history does not record their names. It was Dhirubhai, doing business where no one else wanted to go, who built India's largest company, lived in his own personal skyscraper, and raised one son who married a movie star and another son who lived in an even larger personal skyscraper. It's okay to admit you are a little jealous.

SECRET #4: WHEN LENDERS CAN'T LOSE, YOU WIN

When describing the previous few secrets of spectacularly rich people, I have often used the rather anodyne phrase "access to capital." For instance, I have noted that scale economies are a wealth secret when access to capital is difficult (because one needs a lot of cash to build large-scale operations), and that doing business in a difficult place is a wealth secret (because when other people are unable to raise capital, they cannot compete with you).

All very logical, but perhaps a little dull. Let me jazz it up a bit: access to capital is another way to say "people giving you money." Seen this way, unlimited access to capital is the most exciting of all wealth secrets. If people just gave you money no matter what, then you would not have to worry about the five forces determining your profitability, about scale no longer being a wealth secret, or even about competition. You would just take your investors' money and run. Or better yet, you would take their money and then ask for more. The problem is—and I hope you will not take this personally—in most cases, people are going to be reluctant to give you money, unless they are reasonably sure they are going to get it back.

Of course, you can fool some of the people some of the time. Think of the conflict-of-interest dealings of Rockefeller's railroad, or the foreign investors who were defrauded in Russia. There are ways to make people think they are going to get their money back, or even (in the case of Bernie Madoff, for instance) to make people think they *are* getting their money back, when in fact they are not.

But really, these aren't wealth secrets. We've already seen that one reason competition was limited in Russia and the robber baron–era United States was that access to capital was very constrained, largely because after their money was stolen a few times, people wised up and didn't hand over any more. Stealing investors' money might make you a few rubles, but it's hardly sustainable. Even Bernie Madoff eventually came to a bad end.

Overcoming this challenge — finding reliable ways to misuse people's money and still attract more of it — is a modern wealth secret breakthrough. American S&Ls were, of course, masters in this regard. Indeed, the money they were stealing was being managed by some of the most sophisticated financial institutions on Wall Street. What the S&Ls had discovered was that if lenders and depositors are all but guaranteed to get their money back (in this case, thanks to deposit insurance), they will happily give you their money even *after* it becomes obvious that you are probably stealing it. The extraordinary cases of S&L fraud emerging from Texas and California did not, after all, cause mass withdrawals from brokered accounts — because the deposits were guaranteed.

The same secret was then exploited by those Wall Street banks that became too big to fail. One might expect that in the wake of the global financial crisis, banks would have fallen on hard times. If anyone was under the illusion that risk management systems in banks were working, they probably don't harbor that illusion anymore. But then, that was never the point. The point was that the banks were invincible. While you might expect the global financial crisis to have drained money from banks like J.P. Morgan by publicly demonstrating that they were taking extraordinary risks, in fact the crisis and its aftermath had the opposite effect. The crisis proved unequivocally that some banks were too big to fail. So people (and other banks) became even more eager to entrust their money to those banks.

Are there other examples of government guarantees, where investors and lenders cannot lose? Happily, yes. In England during the 1700s, the government bailed out both the South Sea Company and the East India Company (although some directors of the former were sent to the Tower of London, which was unpleasant). During the Great Depression, the U.S. government bailed out numerous banks and railroad companies, although it imposed harsh conditions of oversight on these companies. In more recent years, governments have become more sympathetic to the need for wealth secrets. In the 1970s, the U.S. government bailed out Lockheed Aircraft, a major defense contractor, with fewer strings attached.

The U.S. auto sector is a more recent example. Chrysler, when it was headed for bankruptcy in 1980, was bailed out by the U.S. government. The auto sector was rescued again during the global financial crisis. Broadly speaking, the sector is too political to fail, as its workforce is a major source of campaign support (although U.S. automakers haven't really made much use of this potential wealth secret, preferring to overpay their executives and unionized workers).

A more go-getting approach to the government guarantee was taken by two government-sponsored enterprises: the Federal National Mortgage Association, nicknamed "Fannie Mae," and the Federal Home Loan Mortgage Corporation, nicknamed "Freddie Mac." These institutions were created in 1938 and 1970, respectively, to buy mortgage loans from banks and sell them on to investors. Both Fannie Mae and Freddie Mac eventually became quasi-public institutions. That is to say, they had private shareholders and operated to some degree as private companies, but both operated according to government-directed business models and with implicit government support.

Initially, these semipublic organizations operated much as you would expect a government bureaucracy to operate. They employed people who did not make much money, but nor did they work very hard. (Think of the U.S. Postal Service, or Amtrak.) But then, in the 1990s, a new CEO, James Johnson, took charge of Fannie Mae. He realized he was sitting on a gold mine. Fannie's debt was, in effect, U.S. government debt, so it was rated AAA (a point the rating agencies took the trouble to make explicit when there was talk of a law that might make it possible for Fannie to go bankrupt). So, like the too-big-to-fail banks, no matter how much risk these quasi-public companies took, people would continue to hand Fannie Mae money. Johnson and his predecessor, David Maxwell, brought in a new hard-charging work ethic. They brought the capital held in reserve against losses down to next to nothing (specifically, 2.5 percent of assets, as against roughly 8 percent for even the most gung-ho banks) and threw everything they had into taking lots of risk in mortgage securitization. Investors didn't worry: Fannie had a government guarantee.

And that was extraordinarily lucrative. A Congressional Budget Office study quantified the value of the implicit U.S. government guarantee at $7 billion annually in 1995. The study also alleged that one-third of the subsidy (about $2.3 billion) was retained in the form of larger profits and higher staff salaries. Between 1993 and 2000, bonuses for Fannie executives more than quadrupled, from $8.5 million to $35.2 million. Johnson himself made $5.1 million in 1995, which was comparable to the CEO of Chase Manhattan Bank—not bad for government work. When the global financial crisis came, both Fannie Mae and Freddie Mac collapsed and required a government bailout. In contrast to the U.S. bank bailouts, the conditions of this bailout were fairly harsh. Still, it was a great wealth secret while it lasted.

SECRET #5: YOU'VE GOT TO OWN IT, BABY, OWN IT

There are any number of books on the topic of how to get rich. The good ones—those with some basis in economics—will tell you that rather than working for a salary or investing in a broad portfolio of stocks, to get rich you need to own your own business.

This is sage advice, based on sound economic logic. You may recall that in chapter 1, I said that in perfectly competitive markets, economists expect that firms will earn no *economic* profits. I also mentioned that economists look at business profits a little differently than most people do. An economist would not be surprised to see a business earning profits roughly equal to its cost of capital, because to an economist the cost of capital is part of the cost of doing business (along with wages, production machinery, and so on).

In most cases, this observation doesn't tell you anything really interesting about getting rich. The cost of capital for large firms in advanced economies might justify profit margins in the single digits—nowhere near wealth secrets territory. But say that you're running a business that is exceptionally risky. If most businesses of a particular type fail, in order to attract investors, these businesses will need to offer the possibility of significant returns. Even in perfectly competitive markets, these businesses can earn substantial paper profits because investors will only back new entrants if they are earning a return that justifies the risk. This means that if you start such a business, and put all of your money into that business, and keep reinvesting in that business as the profits roll in, you could end up reasonably rich, even in a competitive market. Of course, if you do that, it's much more likely that you are going to lose everything. This strategy involves putting all your money into one very risky basket. It's not really a wealth secret. It's getting an appropriate return on the incredible risks you're taking. That's an outcome of a well-functioning market, while the wealth secrets described in this book tend to involve the engineering of catastrophic breakdowns of market competition. (Being rewarded for the risks you took is not a wealth secret—being rewarded for the risks borne by *someone else* is a wealth secret.)

Nonetheless, owning things is, in fact, a very good way to get rich. The key is to think about the bigger picture.

In chapter 6, I talked about how intellectual property rights are the basis for miniature monopolies. That's actually a special case of a more general rule, which is that "All private property is, in a sense, a monopoly," to quote Harvard professor Lloyd L. Weinreb. That is to say, private property rights generally give you the exclusive right to something—the right to use something, to make money from it, and to exclude others from using it. As noted in a briefing prepared for a U.S. Senate subcommittee, "'property' and 'monopoly' are one and the same thing from an economic point of view.... The 'owner' of an invention has a monopoly of its use just as the owner of a house has a 'monopoly' of its use."

Once you own something, it's yours, exclusively. As with intellectual property rights, so with broader property rights: you have a miniature monopoly, not over a market but over an asset. So if an asset produces ongoing revenues—say, the "numberless" silver mines that Crassus acquired via proscriptions—then any revenue streams from that asset will be yours in perpetuity, guaranteed. No competitor is going to take that from you (as long as you can defend your property rights). In practical terms, this is why Marcus Crassus's wealth secret worked so well, and why the Russian oligarchs, in the early days of post-Soviet collapse, were able to get so rich so quickly. It is why people who inherit a lot of assets don't need to work particularly hard, or indeed at all, to continue to do well.

When climbing the greasy pole to the top, each piece of property that produces a stream of revenues offers a secure handhold. Real estate produces tenant rents; mines produce revenues from minerals. Of course, as with intellectual property rights, the value of the associated revenues can vary (as many people in the

United States and Ireland, who had assumed that house prices would go up indefinitely, learned the hard way).

You might think that property rights are so fundamental to capitalism that pointing this out is a little silly. But actually, property rights vary quite a bit. In Mongolia, land was until recently held communally, although the herds of animals that grazed the land were privately owned. In Germany, property rights don't generally include subsoil rights (the rights to exploit what's under the ground), so unlike North Dakotans, who have been falling over themselves to invite shale gas companies onto their land, Germans, who wouldn't personally see any revenues from fracking, have been largely opposed. Hence understanding what kinds of monopolies private property rights can produce for you is crucial to exploiting this wealth secret.

John D. Rockefeller, even after he had rolled up more than 90 percent of America's refining capacity into Standard Oil, might in theory have been vulnerable to future competition. His monopoly was, after all, a natural monopoly, and so the spectacular profits he was earning might eventually have attracted determined, well-funded competitors.

And indeed they did. In the early 1870s, Russia began developing its oil fields in Baku (today part of Azerbaijan) and began exporting oil globally. Since the Pennsylvania fields were starting to run dry, meeting this competition from overseas required Rockefeller to make a large bet on new oil fields to supply his refineries. He chose the oilfields near the Ohio-Indiana border, which were rich with oil but of a type that could not be refined using the technology of the day. It was risky: Rockefeller had to offer to put up several million dollars of his own money to convince his reluctant board of directors to make major investments in this region. But the bet was made good after a German chemist Rockefeller had employed discovered a way to process the oil. Standard Oil then unleashed its acquisition machine in oil production. By 1891, in addition to 90 percent of America's refining capacity, the company controlled a quarter of the country's oil production.

A quarter does not sound like much of a monopoly. But Standard Oil's position was now based on property rights: it owned the oil fields, free and clear. As long as the oil fields continued to produce oil, and as long as oil remained a mainstay of global energy supply, Standard Oil would be assured a steady stream of revenues via its property rights on the output of these fields.

The benefit in this was demonstrated when Standard Oil was broken up by government antitrust regulators in 1911. Once the pieces of the former monopoly began to compete with each other, Rockefeller no longer dominated oil refining. But it didn't matter: his oil production companies, with their value based in part on property rights, weren't going to be undone by a little competition. The successor companies to Standard Oil included Exxon, Mobil, Chevron, Amoco, ARCO, and Marathon Petroleum, among others. Delightfully, in the year of the antitrust breakup, the value of Rockefeller's personal fortune actually grew. Property rights tend to be resilient in the face of market competition.

In the modern era, most property rights are acquired the hard way: by buying them. Conquest and theft are risky and increasingly challenging in a world of well-functioning legal systems. However, when legal systems suddenly break down due to well-intentioned but poorly conceived liberalization schemes (in post-Soviet Russia, for instance), the way is thrown open to the minting of new fortunes. And there is at least one modern arena that harkens back to the valor and glory of ancient Rome, when the assets of others were ripe for the taking: intellectual property rights. In the world of intellectual property, armies of lawyers (often employed by non-practicing entities, as I mentioned in chapter 6) do battle to seize the property of others—usually small businesses that are relatively defenseless.

Taken together, property rights are the basis for a wealth secret that appears often on the *Forbes* Global Rich List. In chapter 6, we discovered that among the top fortunes in advanced economies, 75 percent are attributable to either fund management or intellectual property rights. On the broader *Forbes* list, of over 1,600 billionaires, including emerging markets fortunes, there is more diversity. But fortunes attributable to property rights in general nonetheless appear frequently. For instance, about 130 of the roughly 1,600 fortunes are in real estate. A further 40 or so are in oil and gas or mining. About 120 are in fashion or retail, where companies often own not only valuable brands but valuable properties. Roughly 65 are in pharmaceuticals or health care, 90 or so are in technology, and about 70 more are in media. In other words, on a rough estimate, at least a third are property rights fortunes of some kind. And that is without trying to factor in the fortunes gained in the post-Soviet collapse. Own it, baby, own it.

SECRET #6: SPIN LAWS INTO GOLD

Remember those nineteenth-century farmers from chapter 3? While you were busy mocking their silly accents and off-trend clothing, they became wealth secret masters. There was a time when they couldn't organize themselves out of a paper bag. In the robber baron era, every piece of legislation the farmers wanted seemed at the last minute to go wrong somehow. They demanded a bill restraining railroad pricing, and instead got one that enabled the railroad presidents to create a cartel. The farmers demanded antitrust laws, and got something so vaguely worded it was used to prosecute labor unions (at least at first).

Today, the tables are turned. Almost no one pays any attention to agricultural programs like the U.S. Farm Bill (which is updated every five years). And the farmers, now a cohesive and effective lobby group, have turned the program into a cash bonanza. Lobbying expenditures on the 2008 Farm Bill alone amounted to $173.5 million—more than $500,000 for every day that the 2007–2008

U.S. House of Representatives was in session. The lobbyists employed in this cause included 45 former members of Congress and 461 former congressional and executive branch staffers. And the lobbying paid off: by the early 1990s, direct federal farm subsidies amounted to more than $20 billion per year. The 2008 Farm Bill alone directed about $307 billion in federal spending.

U.S. sugar beet farmers in particular have acquired an almost legendary status among political science researchers. During the 1980s, it turned out American sugar beet farmers (there were only 11,000 of them at the time) were receiving benefits from the U.S. government equivalent to about $1.5 billion in annual gross income. That's more than $100,000 per farmer (about $217,000 today). Now, even among readers who have one or two wealth secrets of their own, there are probably few who would scoff at a guaranteed annual payment of $217,000 from the government. It sure beats welfare. (The cost, incidentally, was about $6 per year in higher sugar prices for every U.S. household.)

Of course, the subsidy for sugar beet farmers did not appear in the form of a simple U.S. government budget line item ("$1.5 billion payment to farmers" or similar). Rather, it involved a complex mix of moving parts including country-by-country import quotas for foreign sugar exporters, government loans to U.S. sugar producers, and a related program to support U.S. sugar prices based on an esoteric formula.

And there you have the key to spinning laws into gold. It is what the American humorist P. J. O'Rourke called "dictatorship by tedium." As he put it, government officials can do "anything they want, because anytime regular people try to figure out what gives, the regular people get hopelessly bored and confused, as though they'd fallen a month behind in their high school algebra class."

O'Rourke was referring to the S&L bailouts rather than agricultural subsidies, but the same principle applies in both cases. Indeed, it applies to just about every wealth secret explored thus far in this book. You might call it "hiding things in plain sight." Wealth secrets are hidden in laws and regulations so complex and boring that even though they are publicly accessible, it is unlikely that anyone will ever find them, and even more unlikely that anyone will do anything about them. The Dodd-Frank Act, for example, which was supposed to put an end to too big to fail in the United States, ran to 848 pages, and required regulatory agencies to produce about 400 further rules and clarifications, producing 30,000 pages of rule making in total. A rough estimate was that postcrisis financial reform in Europe would double this figure, requiring 60,000 pages of new regulations. And one more example: at the end of chapter 6, we saw how the seemingly boring topic of intellectual property law has enabled the existence of "non-practicing entities" that exploit patents to wrest profits away from other companies. While reading that section on "patent parties" you may have thought, "This is really abstract and convoluted and I don't see how it applies to me." Which is precisely the point.

While "dictatorship by tedium" has a great ring to it, in reality, hiding things in plain sight works just as well in democracies. The reason is that each regulation that produces wealth secrets (like intellectual property law) has only a tiny impact on most of the public. On top of that, each member of the public, by voting, has only a tiny impact on these regulations (try to recall the last time you changed your vote because you didn't like your country's agricultural policy).

Understanding complex issues takes a lot of time. Understanding which politicians are likely to adopt positions on the issues that are aligned with a voter's own views takes even more time. Monitoring politicians to make sure they actually do what they said they would is perhaps most time-consuming of all. Hence most people not only don't vote based on issues like agricultural subsidies or banking regulation—they don't pay any attention to what is going on. Why should they, if there is no benefit in doing so? As a result, voters tend to be — in the phrase favored by political scientists — "rationally ignorant" on complex policy topics. The more complicated an issue is, and the less direct impact it has on each individual voter, the more likely it is to be, in effect, invisible.

In the wake of the global financial crisis, many people tended to assume that bankers were incompetent or foolish. "Jimmy in Virginia" called in to CNN's *Lou Dobbs Tonight* to claim that "what we have in this bailout of the banks is the inept, corrupt politicians trying to save the incompetent, corrupt CEO's." On the campaign trail, Barack Obama blamed the crisis on the fact that "too many people in Washington and Wall Street weren't minding the store." U.S. senator Claire McCaskill was more colorful, blaming the crisis on "a bunch of idiots on Wall Street."

I have bad news: there were some idiots involved in the global financial crisis. But it wasn't the bankers. It was us.

Or, more accurately, we were not idiots, but rational ignoramuses. We may well be smart, but we definitely were not paying attention. I'm not sure how many of the academic volumes on too-big-to-fail issues you read prior to the global financial crisis (how about *Too Big to Fail,* edited by Benton Gup, published in 2004?), but I didn't get through many of them. And I was writing research papers on the global financial sector.

For seekers of wealth secrets, these complex regulations — whether they are the Farm Bill, intellectual property law, or financial sector regulation — are hugely important. They may be boring, but they are well worth studying, because they are worth lots of money to a few beneficiaries. When it comes to spinning laws into gold, therefore, the battle between beneficiaries of complex laws and the general public is a very uneven fight.

And the best part: if you are caught red-handed (as the sugar beet farmers eventually were), fixing the laws will inevitably require *a lot more laws.* With any luck, and some determined lobbying, you'll be able to spin those laws as well.

SECRET #7: IF YOU WANT TO SUCCEED IN BUSINESS, NETWORK, NETWORK, NETWORK

In the mid-1860s, Cornelius Vanderbilt took control of the New York & Harlem Railroad, one of only two railroads with direct access to Manhattan. To do so was no easy task. The New York & Harlem was, at the time of the takeover, on the verge of gaining a connection via streetcar all the way to Battery Park at the south tip of Manhattan. Vanderbilt had to counter insider trading schemes by politicians exploiting their control over the streetcar-line approval process not once but twice. When he had finally, by virtue of his vast fortune, triumphed over the market manipulation efforts of the New York legislature, he was exultant: "We busted the whole legislature and scores of the honorable members had to go home without paying their board bills!"

Selling off his steamboat empire to raise the necessary funds, Vanderbilt went fully into railroads, next adding the Hudson River Railroad to his collection. Both the Hudson River Railroad and the New York & Harlem were short lines (144 miles and 130 miles, respectively), but by controlling both, Vanderbilt had gained a monopoly over rail traffic into Manhattan. He next took control of the New York Central, a 500-plus-mile trunk line that, by linking Buffalo to Albany (where Vanderbilt's two New York lines began), controlled crucial links in the connection between New York and the Midwest. The New York Central was a much larger company, and its track length far exceeded that of the two lines Vanderbilt owned, yet he was able to seize this large prize via clever use of his two smaller lines. He made the New York Central an offer it could not refuse, by imposing an embargo. He ordered his lines to stop accepting any New York–bound traffic coming off the New York Central. Because Vanderbilt controlled rail access to Manhattan while the New York Central was only one of several trunk lines, Vanderbilt had greater leverage. The New York Central had to give in, and by the end of the 1860s, Vanderbilt had assumed control.

It was an early and marvelously effective application of "network effects" in business strategy. Most railroads in the 1860s were point-to-point operations (like the New York Central, which stretched from Buffalo to Albany). These railroads generally used incompatible track gauges, and freight would need to be unloaded and then reloaded when it reached the end of each line. This inconvenience was in many cases entirely deliberate. Local merchants did not want passengers and freight to ride right past them; they wanted to make money at the transfer points.

What Vanderbilt had discovered was that the value in railways could come from controlling network connections, not just the traditional focus of point-to-point routes. In effect, he was able to control New York's connection to the nation's rail network.

It was a wealth secrets breakthrough. By 1870, Vanderbilt's merged railroad was paying the largest dividend of any company in U.S. history. Following a market crash in 1873, most railroads were no longer making profits, but Vanderbilt's line kept up the dividends. Although they did not perhaps quite understand it, people knew that something had changed. The *New York Times* was a little scared by Vanderbilt's unsurpassed control: "We already begin to feel the first grindings of the approaching tyranny of capitalists or corporations. . . . Every public means of transit is in the hands of the tyrants of modern society."

Even today, network effects can be a little scary. The industries most likely to develop into natural monopolies on a local or even global scale tend to be network businesses of one kind or another. Even after its government-awarded monopoly ended, Carlos Slim's empire showed little sign of succumbing to competition until Mexican antitrust authorities threatened to break it up. In the United States, AT&T eventually came to dominate telecommunications in the early 1900s (it made the nation's smaller networks acquisition offers they could not refuse, by threatening to turn away any calls their customers made to AT&T customers). AT&T maintained that dominant position until it was finally broken up in 1982. And of course the computer software industry, with its platform strategies (exploiting indirect network effects) and its social networks (exploiting direct network effects), is the home of numerous monopolists, or at least companies that dominate their subsectors.

Governments today attempt to limit such advantages by forcing companies to interconnect their networks. The laws that do so are called "common carrier" laws, and these require companies such as railroads, airlines, taxicabs, and telephone companies to serve members of the public without discrimination (which means, in effect, that they must accept travelers, freight, or callers originating from other networks).

Sometimes these laws have the effect of almost completely undermining network effects. Take the case of airlines. The major airlines that operate global hub-and-spoke networks tend to be unprofitable. The airlines strive mightily to reintroduce these effects—for instance via frequent flyer programs that reward travelers for staying on their network (even if it's a little more costly or less convenient than other flights on offer)—but it doesn't seem to work. Travelers tend to book the lowest-cost, fastest flight. The airlines that are profitable tend to be budget airlines that operate point-to-point networks, and they appear to make their money on those routes that face little direct competition (not unlike the point-to-point railroads of Vanderbilt's day, with their local monopolies).

However, some network businesses continue to do well. U.S. railroads, for instance, tend to be reliably profitable—although one could argue that this is because regulatory barriers limit the number of operators per region. There are a lot of telecoms-related fortunes on the *Forbes* global billionaire list, especially in emerging markets. Most stem from companies you have probably never heard of: HKT in Hong Kong, Digicel in the Caribbean, Orascom in Egypt, Investcom in Lebanon, Turkcell in Turkey, MTS in Russia, Airtel in India, and Maxis in Malaysia, among others. All of these companies have made people billionaires. So have the package shipping networks FedEx and DHL.

You see, even in the modern day, the mail can be really exciting.

SO YOU'D LIKE TO BE A MASTER OF WEALTH SECRETS?

This book has so far not said much about the personal qualities of those profiled. As noted before, it is not a book about inevitable success; it is a book about the strategies people have used to become rich. However, while undertaking the research for this book, I did come across a few characteristics that many of history's überrich seem to have in common.

The first is a love of math. I don't mean abstract math (the kind of math that helped the geniuses at LTCM). I mean basic figures, accounting, bookkeeping, and balance sheets. In most cases, the wealth secrets practitioners profiled here had an almost alarming fondness for this kind of thing. Pierpont Morgan may hardly have said a coherent sentence in his life, but he was a whiz with numbers. The same can be said of Dhirubhai Ambani, with his "razor-sharp brain for finance," and also of Bill Gates (even if Gates realized that others in his Harvard math class would surpass him in the esoteric world of theoretical math).

For these men, math was not only a passion but a primary means of communication. None, aside from perhaps Carnegie, were particularly comfortable with writing or speaking, as the incoherent quotations from Gates and Morgan (the most "reserved" man his minister had ever known) indicate. A family friend said of Dhirubhai: "When he talks, he doesn't bother about mundane things like correct sentences, grammar, etc." But in the language of figures—the language through which businesses describe their current health and future prospects—these men were undeniably fluent. Even Carnegie, a writer and public intellectual, was most at home in the world of numbers. When one of his factory employees saw him walk by, he said: "There goes that damned bookkeeper."

It was John D. Rockefeller who perhaps best expressed the quality I am trying to describe. His first job (literally as a book-keeper) was, he said, "delightful to me—all the method and system of the office." Later, after he had become stupendously rich, he claimed: "I chartered my course by figures, nothing but figures." If you have ever looked at a balance sheet and thought you saw a bit of poetry there, you may have wealth secrets potential.

Another personal characteristic common to many successful people profiled in this book is an abiding love of money and the desire, expressed from a very early age, to possess it. Not just money as an instrument to obtain something, but money itself. Bill Gates is one example, repeatedly informing his school friends that he would be worth $1 million by the time he was in his twenties. Rockefeller made a similar pledge from an equally young age. In his case the amount was $100,000—which may appear more modest, but that would be equivalent to about $3 million today. As a young man, Dhirubhai dreamed of oil refineries, one presumes for financial reasons rather than based on their inherent beauty. Once again it falls to Rockefeller to express this trait most fully, with his tale of repeatedly opening the office safe to gaze open-mouthed at the first high-denomination banknote he had ever seen. One detects an almost erotic fascination.

Another characteristic is a willingness to throw out one's early business partners. (I hesitate to even mention this, lest your business partners take the hint and guess what's coming.) John D. Rockefeller banished one of the business partners who had joined him in starting his Cleveland refinery and then tricked his other partners, the Clark brothers, into agreeing to auction off the business, while secretly lining up enough capital to outbid them and thus obtain sole control. Dhirubhai Ambani founded Reliance Commercial Corporation in partnership with Chambaklal Damani, and not long afterward took sole control—although the split was reportedly amicable, and Dhirubhai paid for his partner's share. The departure of Bill Gates's early business partner in Microsoft, Paul Allen, was somewhat acrimonious—or at least Allen felt that Gates had plotted to dilute his equity holdings, and then later attempted to underpay for his share of the company. If you are going to be rich, it pays not to divide the loot—especially not with those who were there at the beginning.

A final characteristic, not wholly unrelated to the above, is that wealth secrets masters tend to be ruthless.

I don't think it's a coincidence that a lot of the people profiled in this book are rather unpleasant, hard-as-nails kinds of people. Marcus Crassus, killing off Rome's richest citizens in order to build his own fortune, was in that respect less an outlier than an exemplar. Vanderbilt, the brawler competing for monopolies, was nearly as rough-and-tumble. Although most individuals profiled in this book were more civilized than these two, I think many of them have a mean streak. For instance, a retired Indian industrialist said to me: "One thing that made Dhirubhai successful was that he was brutal. I wouldn't have wanted to compete with him." Gates, recalling the ownership percentages of his peers to the decimal point, clearly was not deficient in his desire to win—his competitive instincts so well honed he wanted to challenge even those people who weren't his commercial competitors. Wealth secrets often involve winning in a market where there is only one victor. It stands to reason that people who would choose such a career path would need to be a little ruthless.

There are, however, a couple of exceptions. Both, I must admit, come from the financial sector. Although I am loath to endorse any aspect of the lifestyle of the moneyed herd, one must acknowledge that despite all their macho one-upmanship, they aren't trying to wipe anybody out. They are just a little annoying. The author Kevin Roose crashed a meeting of the Wall Street secret society Phi Beta Kappa in 2012 (membership roster at the time: the CEO of AIG, the CEO of Bear Stearns, a former chairman of Goldman Sachs, a former CEO of Lehman Brothers, etc.). It turned out that they weren't plotting world domination. Instead, they turned out to be doing exactly what you might expect: enjoying an overgrown frat party involving lots of alcohol, men in drag, and various parody songs about receiving government bailouts sung spectacularly off-key (the audio is posted on *New York* magazine's website). At least with these guys you know what you're getting. And, generally speaking, it's a more-the-merrier situation, because my government guarantee doesn't preclude your government guarantee. Unlike most of the people profiled in this book, the traders and executives of the moneyed herd operate at some remove from their wealth secret. The government guarantee is inherent to their industry, not something they have labored personally to put in place.

The other exception to the winner-takes-all wealth mentality so frequently profiled in this book is, of course, Pierpont Morgan. Perhaps this was because he, almost uniquely among the masters of wealth secrets described herein, was rich from the day he was born to the day he died. As a result, while he certainly had a taste for the finer things, he didn't seem to care about money. But more importantly, his relaxed attitude — like the good-natured fraternity hijinks of Phi Beta Kappa — stemmed from the economics of the financial sector. Morgan, as a lender, didn't covet the huge profits that came with victory in winner-takes-all contests; he just wanted everyone to pay their bills on time. And indeed, Morgan's most dramatic monopolization efforts (U.S. Steel, Northern Securities Railroad, International Harvester) tended to make other people rich.

Now, isn't that nice?

There is also one characteristic that I did *not* find among the masters of wealth secrets profiled here: they did not appear to be superhuman. In daily life, one tends to find that smarter, luckier, or more determined people tend to do better than others. Hence it is natural to extend this logic and assume that the superrich must have achieved their position by being *so much* smarter, or more determined, that they are essentially superhuman.

But that isn't what I found. The superrich profiled in this book are certainly impressive, and compelling, individuals. But their outsize wealth comes from the economics of what they have done. The best competitor in a highly competitive industry will earn a little bit more profit, and therefore be a little bit better off than everyone else; the best competitor in an industry that tends toward natural monopolies (like software) will end up with huge profits and, over time, a colossal fortune. The difference between the two is not that one is superhuman and the other is not. It's in the economics.

INVESTIGATING WEALTH SECRETS

I must admit, there are many millionaires and billionaires whose wealth secrets I don't understand. The Koch brothers, for instance. Of course, they have scale economies on their side, but why have these been so exceptionally lucrative for the Kochs? Such straightforward, heavy-industry scale economies were supposed to have died out in the 1970s. Or the great investor Warren Buffett. Of course Buffet is a genius, but on the surface he doesn't appear to have any more protection from competition than the geniuses at LTCM. And yet he doesn't seem set to crash anytime soon.

While I don't understand Warren Buffett's personal wealth secret, he does have a technique for evaluating other people's businesses that, as I mentioned in chapter 5, is not entirely out of keeping with a wealth secrets perspective. This technique is his concept of a "moat," which he says is something that will keep competition at bay for a "decade or two." From Buffett's perspective, a business with a moat is a good business.

While a moat is not a perfect analogue to a wealth secret, there are similarities. After all, a decade or two is a long time in business, so if a moat is not quite the equivalent of having your competitors hanged, it is still a pretty effective way of getting and staying rich. Something along the lines of throwing sand in your competitors' eyes, tripping them, and then kicking them repeatedly while they are down.

Buffett rarely talks about the particular businesses in which he invests. But some of his moat businesses are companies I would credit with having wealth secrets. I mentioned in chapter 4 that Buffett invested in Moody's, which is protected by a government policy that essentially limits competition in the industry to three companies. Buffett repeatedly emphasizes that maintaining the moat is the most important thing a business can do. Short-term goals in business matter, of course — maintaining earnings, most notably. But Buffett says that "when short-term and long-term conflict, widening the moat *must* take precedence."

If you don't have a moat, there is nothing you can do about it, no matter how good you are. One example Buffett gives is the U.S. textile company Burlington Industries. They were once the dominant company in American textiles. Between 1964 and 1985, they invested about $3 billion in improving their business — dwarfing the expenditure of any other U.S. textile company.

But the U.S. textile market (like oil refining in India today) is open to global competition, and so, Buffett says, Burlington's proactive strategies did them no good. Burlington Industries stock lost, in effect, about two-thirds of its value by the mid-1980s, and by the early 2000s the company was bankrupt. They are the best in the industry, they tried hard, they did all the right things, and the result was the destruction of shareholder value. In sum, Buffett contends, the performance of any business "is far more a function of what business boat you get into than it is of how effectively you row (although intelligence and effort help considerably, of course, in any business, good or bad)."

The businesses that Buffett likes — the "good" businesses — are in many cases businesses that I might recognize as having a wealth secret or two. An example is MidAmerican, an electric utility operating mainly in Iowa, Wyoming, and Utah. Buffett's company owns 89.8 percent of MidAmerican. Buffett writes: "With few exceptions, our regulators have promptly allowed us to earn a fair return on the ever-increasing sums of capital we must invest." Basically, the government decides how much they will earn, and it's a lot. Yes, MidAmerican is well run. But most importantly, its profits aren't determined by market competition. Now that's the kind of business I could really start to like.

Perhaps Buffett's wealth secret is knowing about wealth secrets?

GUTS AND LUCK

When Dhirubhai was asked about the keys to success, he said: "Two things: guts and luck."

At first, it seems like a singularly unhelpful remark. But in the context of what we know now about wealth secrets, it makes more sense. As a financial analyst I met at an investment bank in India put it: "Dhirubhai had a tremendous capacity for risk. And the risks he took paid off. Had they not paid off, he would have been just another failed entrepreneur."

Framed in typical business language, this is a warning for seekers of wealth secrets. Entrepreneurship is generally seen to be risky because entrepreneurs are not diversified: they tend to throw everything they own into a single business venture (which, as noted above, justifies a higher return). Hunting wealth secrets — at least those that don't involve a government guarantee — tends, if anything, to be even more risky. Not only are you putting everything you own into a venture, but it's a venture from which, ideally, only one winner will emerge. How many failed contenders risked everything in operating systems before Windows emerged as the sole winner? I can think of at least five that came close to challenging Microsoft. Presumably there were many more that tried and failed catastrophically. Four hundred Indian companies applied for that crucial polyester-filament yarn production license in 1980. Dhirubhai was one of only two winners. Two out of four hundred is not good odds.

That, I believe, is what Dhirubhai was trying to say in his "guts and luck" comment. He had the guts to risk everything on a game that he appeared to have little chance of winning and the good fortune to see it pan out.

The good news is, there are probably more wealth secrets in the world than there ever have been before. I can't prove this, but the rise of the emerging markets and the explosive growth of the *Forbes* list of global billionaires make it almost a given.

Even in the United States, it seems that wealth secrets are on the rise. Take the data on corporate profits, for instance. After-tax corporate profits in the country have generally fluctuated between about 5 and 7 percent of total U.S. output since the 1950s. Then, in the 1990s, corporate profits began to climb. There have been fluctuations here as well, most notably during the global financial crisis, but by 2011 (the latest year for which data are available) after-tax corporate profits had doubled to about 11 percent of U.S. output. While the financial sector played a large role in this growth in profits, I can't help but think that other relatively new wealth secrets—intellectual property laws, for instance, or economies of scale in retail—played their part as well. And so far there is no sign of this trend coming to a halt. If one draws a straight line from the 1990 data plotted on a graph through the 2011 data, after-tax corporate profits should triple, as a share of output, by about 2016. Of course, drawing a straight line is generally a stupid way to forecast any economic indicator. But the popularity of almost every wealth secret discussed in this book—OK, perhaps not military conquest—seems to be on the rise.

A more sophisticated analysis of performance data by the consultancy McKinsey, covering 5,000 nonfinancial companies in the United States since 1963, finds a spike in companies with "very high returns on capital" since 2005. Superhigh returns were at one time extremely rare: in the 1960s, only 1 percent of companies in McKinsey's database achieved returns of 50 percent or more. By the mid-1990s, the figure had climbed to about 5 percent. By the 2005–2007 period, the most recent period for which data are available, 14 percent of companies were making these kinds of superreturns. They were winning the wealth secrets way.

Think of the world's population as standing before a cliff face. To achieve wealth, one must climb it, but the face is sheer and each person who makes progress is soon dragged back by others seeking to raise themselves. The ground is a little higher under the lawyers and doctors. The bankers have a ramp, built with the taxpayers' money, although it doesn't go all the way up.

And then there are a few people who walk straight up, ascending the cliff face, defying the forces of economic gravity. One might think they are superhuman, and indeed this is a narrative one often hears. But really, there are hidden ladders. These ladders are wealth secrets. It is not quite fair to say that only one person is allowed on each ladder. One can invest in companies with wealth secrets, and climb up behind the company's founder. Or one can work for a company with wealth secrets, and climb partway up the ladder while the founder stands on one's head.

There are only a few people standing at the top of the cliff, drinking champagne and partying with Brazilian supermodels (or, if they are straight women, strolling around the party in stunning couture with a Ryan Gosling look-alike on each arm).

But there are more ladders now than ever before. So grab a rung.

Acknowledgments

The moment I heard from my agents, Sally Holloway and George Lucas, that Little, Brown and Hodder Sceptre were going to publish the hardcover edition of my book under the title *Wealth Secrets of the One Percent*, I realized there was shakedown potential. I called up my successful friends, threatening to feature them in the book unless they provided various favors, such as reading and commenting in detail on early drafts, or allowing me to stay for days in their palatial homes while writing or researching the book.

The victims of such schemes, to whom I am very grateful for the comments and hospitality, even if provided under duress, include: Matthew Canepa, Raphael Gamba, Dan Goldstein, Mo Henderson, Larry Jones, Peter Jordan, Jeff Lang, Dan Lefkovitz, Jordan Matus, Kara Murphy, Laurence Williams, Michio Wise, and Marvin Zonis. My parents, Judy and Peter Wilkin, also provided their review and comments.

My editors, John Parsley at Little, Brown, and Drummond Moir at Hodder Sceptre, not only reviewed and significantly improved the multiple drafts they read, but contributed several of the best lines. The same goes for Sally Holloway of Felicity Bryan Associates and George Lucas of InkWell Management, my agents mentioned above. Sally also reshaped the book at the proposal stage, from yet another dreary academic text into the fun and useful guide to wealth it is today. The amusing and shocking U.S. cover is by Ploy Siripant. The U.K. market demanded a more subtle cover, by Natalie

Chen. I'd also like to thank Chris Jerome, the copy editor, production editor Ben Allen, and associate editor Malin von Euler-Hogan.

I asked a panel of academic reviewers to look at each chapter from a specialist's perspective. The reviewers were: Helen Garten, Professor Emeritus, Rutgers University; Matthew Gibbs, Assistant Professor, University of Winnipeg; Richard R. John, Professor, Columbia University; John Lopatka, A. Robert Noll Distinguished Professor of Law, Penn State University; and Surajit Mazumdar, Professor, Jawaharlal Nehru University. Richard and Surajit were particularly generous with their time and insights. The demands of a readable narrative meant that I was not always able to take their good advice; any remaining oversimplifications or outright errors are my own. Look to the sources in the bibliography (including their own works) for more nuanced tellings.

As I made progress on the book, it became clear that I would need to do a number of interviews where the available academic research was a little thin. Luis Miranda was extraordinarily helpful in providing contacts for this purpose, as well as giving me a useful background briefing on Indian business (as he did some fifteen years ago when I first met him in Mumbai). Marvin Zonis, Dan Lefkovitz, Stephanie Hare, Nigel Singh, and Alison Taylor also provided useful contacts in India. Vicky Mehta provided an excellent introduction to Mumbai. Hriday Kant provided capable research assistance.

I must also thank my teachers in economics, particularly Diana Fuguitt. Having spent much of my career in a "macro" frame of mind, I was grateful for having stumbled, with her assistance, into a teaching assistant role in Eckerd College's microeconomics course many years ago.

Finally, my partner, Carrie Nordlund, gamely provided her comments on not one but several drafts, and handled my year of complaining about money issues with equanimity. Writing is not as lucrative as economic research. Although the copyright available to authors *is* a miniature monopoly, and thus a (very small) wealth secret.

Notes

On the Introduction

I was at a pub in Oxford, complaining to a friend about the difficulty of writing about the one-percenters and how their fortunes were made. The brave exploits and personal victories of people like Andrew Carnegie, Dhirubhai Ambani, and Bill Gates make great stories, and their wealth secrets are fascinating. But assessing the broader impacts of these individuals on society is complicated. Such complex assessments were detracting from the stories.

My friend said: "Well, have you read Schopenhauer's *The Art of Always Being Right*?"

"No," I said.

"Well," he said, "it's written as if Schopenhauer is celebrating other philosophers' arguments, but actually he's demonstrating the flaws in their logic."

(This is the kind of conversation one has with surprising frequency at pubs in Oxford.)

It turned out that my friend was oversimplifying for rhetorical effect (another fairly frequent occurrence in Oxford). But the conversation did become an inspiration. Rather than writing the stories of the one percent and then attempting to assess the impacts on society, I have just written about how the fortunes of the world's richest were made. Whether you read the book as a guide to earning great riches or a social critique is your choice.

In case you would also like to bring up Schopenhauer at the pub, the details for a recently published edition: Schopenhauer, Arthur, A. C. Grayling, and Thomas B. Saunders. 2005. *The Art of Always Being Right*. London: Gibson Square.

The quote on the robber barons and their inevitable rise that appears early in the chapter is from: Morris, Charles R. 2005. *The Tycoons: How Andrew Carnegie, John D. Rockefeller, Jay Gould, and J. P. Morgan Invented the American Supereconomy*. New York: Henry Holt. (This book is also extensively cited in chapter 3.)

As noted in the text, Malcolm Gladwell's book is: Gladwell, Malcolm. 2011. *Outliers: The Story of Success*. New York: Little, Brown.

I also quote a few statistics from the *Forbes* list of the world's billionaires, both in this chapter and throughout the book. In case you have not yet discovered the fascination of sorting and searching the list, the website is at: http://forbes.com/billionaires/. The references in this book refer to the list as it appeared in late summer 2014 unless otherwise noted (it's updated daily).

Lately, the *Forbes* list has become so popular it has attracted imitators (the fate of most successful business ventures...). For instance: http://www.bloomberg.com/billionaires/.

On Chapter 1

During the research for this book, I conducted a number of interviews. Most of these interviews were with analysts of one kind or another. I am an economist, not a journalist, and so tripping up billionaires into revealing their wealth secrets on tape is not my forte. Hence the wealth secrets described in this book are mostly based on economic analysis, and supporting evidence comes from academic or commercial research sources cited in these notes. By contrast, the quotes and biographical details that round out my pen portraits of one-percenters are often from books for the general reader. Because it is hard to make a living as a writer, I have tried to name-check the authors of such works in the main body of this book. If there is someone I have left out, I apologize — the citation will at least appear in these notes.

If you loved the Circuit City story, you'll love the documentary: *A Tale of Two Cities: The Circuit City Story*, directed by Tom Wulf. It was the 2010 official selection for the Virginia Film Festival.

The description of the fire sale that opens the chapter is based on the documentary as well as blogs such as Technologizer and popular media including, as noted in the text, the *Guardian*.

Most of the financial details and quotes regarding Circuit City are from Wurtzel, Alan L. 2012. *Good to Great to Gone: The 60 Year Rise and Fall of Circuit City*. New York: Diversion Publishing. This book was written by one of Circuit City's CEOs, who was also the son of the company's founder. Hence it is an insider's account, and many of the details are based on confidential company documents.

A few other details, as noted in the text, come from Collins, Jim. 2001. *Good to Great: Why Some Companies Make the Leap . . . and Others Don't*. New York: Harper Business. I tried to refrain from picking on Collins too much for selecting Circuit City as a "great" company shortly before its failure, as I certainly would not want my own words to be judged with the benefit of hindsight.

The profitability figures are from Yardeni, Edward, and Joe Abbott. 2014. "S&P 500 Sectors & Industries Profit Margins." Yardeni Research, August 13, 1–13.

The quotes and biographical details for LTCM's rise and fall largely come from the following books:

Dunbar, Nicholas. 2000. *Inventing Money: The Story of Long-Term Capital Management and the Legends Behind It*. Chichester, UK: John Wiley & Sons. This book focuses on the mathematics and science behind LTCM, and attempts an explanation of LTCM's wealth secrets that is different from my own (of which, more below).

Lewis, Michael. 1999. "How the Eggheads Cracked." *New York Times Magazine*, January 24, 24–35. Lewis's article is based on an interview with LTCM's founders, and therefore presents the management's own views on why they failed. The quotes from Meriwether and Haghani describing these views are from this article.

Lowenstein, Roger. 2000. *When Genius Failed: The Rise and Fall of Long-Term Capital Management*. New York: Random House. This well-written book focuses on the personalities and events associated with LTCM's rise and fall. Except as noted above, this book is the source of most of the quotes and financial and biographical details I present in the section regarding LTCM's founders and the fund's business activities.

An alternate (and popular) explanation of the success of hedge funds in making people rich is that hedge funds are gambling, with leverage. The argument goes something like this. There are relatively few comprehensive studies of hedge fund performance, and many shortcomings in the data (only a minority of the hedge funds choose to report performance data). But a not uncommon finding is that, on the whole, the industry produces returns roughly equivalent to broader market indices (or slightly below). This finding suggests that, on balance, hedge funds would perform better if they bought stocks at random. (Here I am being a bit glib, because high performance is not the only thing investors want from a fund.)

But even if they are essentially picking stocks at random, there are enough hedge funds in existence (at least eight thousand worldwide in 2014, the majority in the United States) that the sheer laws of chance will produce a few outsized winners—a few funds that strike it lucky for several years in a row. And, given enough leverage, a few good years are all it takes to produce a really sizable fortune. This is very different from most industries, where making serious money requires decades of hard graft (consider Circuit City—its financial performance was astonishing, but the company still took decades to reach the heights of the Fortune 500). So, at least in theory, the existence of hedge fund fortunes may be attributable to the combination of lots of gamblers with lots of leverage.

A couple of examples of papers on hedge fund returns are:

Ackermann, C., R. McEnally, and D. Ravenscraft. 1999. "The Performance of Hedge Funds: Risk, Return and Incentives." *Journal of Finance*, 833–874.

Capocci, Daniel, and Georges Hübner. 2002. "Analysis of Hedge Fund Performance." *Journal of Empirical Finance*, 55–89.

Indeed, in the book I cite above, Nicholas Dunbar contends that LTCM was, in essence, just another gambler. But LTCM's partners were gambling in a sophisticated way: their clever math enabled them, in effect, to bet that volatility in financial markets would remain low, Dunbar says. This kind of bet will tend to pay off most of the time (because most of the time, volatility is low). But whenever there is a market shock (like Russia's debt default), the bet is likely to go bad in a spectacular fashion. Dunbar compares this approach to "system" gambling techniques — for instance, the system whereby one bets a small sum consistently on a game that offers roughly 50/50 odds, and then doubles one's bet if one loses (known as the "Martingale"). This system produces a consistent return until one loses several times in a row, at which point the gambler is completely wiped out.

I also mention Daniel Kahneman's views on "regression to the mean" and its applicability to daily life, which are explained in this book: Kahneman, Daniel. 2013. *Thinking, Fast and Slow*. New York: Farrar, Straus and Giroux.

On Chapter 2

While the rest of the world may have forgotten about Rome's wealth, the locals have not. The breakdown of political order in Iraq and Syria as a result of civil wars in the region has led to widespread looting of archaeological sites. It's a double blow: because these sites are often in relatively undeveloped regions with arid climates, these were some of the world's best-preserved ancient remains—until the recent looting. While the area includes archaeological sites from the era of Gilgamesh onward, "they [looters] mostly go for the Roman sites, because that's where the gold is," notes Jesse Casana, professor of archaeology at the University of Arkansas. The U.S. government has publicized the damage done to archaeological sites by the Islamic State of Iraq and the Levant (ISIL, which is infamous for blowing up religious sites). Unfortunately, the damage by looters has been far more widespread, impacting most of the unstable regions of these countries—including regions controlled by groups supported by the U.S. government.

This book began life as a fairly serious commentary on the policy implications of recent research on oligarchy, but spent a long time in gestation and emerged as something rather different. If you are curious about the original argument in the book, and would be interested to hear me credit one-percenters with driving economic progress in some of the world's best-performing economies, you can find it here:

Wilkin, Sam. 2011. "Can Bad Governance Be Good for Development?" *Survival*, 61–76.

Two of my three favorite books on (modern) oligarchy start with chapters on ancient Rome, and so, continuing the tradition, my book does the same. These three books are:

Acemoglu, Daron, and James A. Robinson. 2012. *Why Nations Fail: The Origins of Power, Prosperity and Poverty.* New York: Crown Publishers.

Rajan, Raghuram. 2003. *Saving Capitalism from the Capitalists: Unleashing the Power of Financial Markets to Create Wealth and Spread Opportunity.* New York: Crown Business.

Winters, Jeffrey A. 2011. *Oligarchy.* Cambridge: Cambridge University Press.

The broad line of argument regarding the fall of Rome is from Winters. A related argument is made by Acemoglu and Robinson, although in their view Roman decline was inevitable as a result of its "extractive institutions," rather than—as I argue—being set in motion by the actions of Rome's richest citizens (like Marcus Crassus).

Early on in the chapter, I made some comparisons of ancient Roman wealth to modern wealth. These are based on: Milanovic, Branko. 2011. *The Haves and the Have-Nots: A Brief and Idiosyncratic History of Global Inequality*. New York: Basic Books. The figures on wealth inequality within Rome and Greece are from Winters, cited above.

For my perspective on the ancient Roman economy, I have largely adopted the view of Temin, Peter. 2013. *The Roman Market Economy*. Princeton: Princeton University Press. Temin is a leading exponent of the view that the ancient Roman economy operated in some respects as a market economy, and that data, such as price records, from ancient Rome are therefore susceptible to analysis using modern economic techniques. Temin's view is, however, far from the only view. For an alternative perspective emphasizing the debilitating costs of doing business in ancient Rome—which tended to undermine the operation of markets—see Bang, Peter Fibiger. 2008. *The Roman Bazaar: A Comparative Study of Trade and Markets in a Tributary Empire*. Cambridge: Cambridge University Press.

My various illustrations of the sophistication of the Roman economy are from a number of sources (in addition to Temin). My explanations of Roman slavery and business operations are largely from Temin. On oil lamps: Harris, William V. 2011. *Rome's Imperial Economy: Twelve Essays*. Oxford: Oxford University Press. Note that some scholars have argued that the reason for the prevalence for the Fortis brand throughout the empire was due to unauthorized copying (which certainly occurred), rather than, as I have suggested, production by an extended business enterprise. Indeed, recent papers have indicated that the branch production model broke down over time, being displaced by widespread copying.

On garum production and other businesses in Pompeii: Beard, Mary. 2008. *Pompeii: The Life of a Roman Town*. London: Profile. This is only one of numerous books by Beard on Roman society and literature, which are always good reads and packed with telling, human details. On Herculaneum: Dorment, Richard. 2013. "Pompeii Exhibition: Life and Death in Pompeii and Herculaneum, British Museum, review." *The Telegraph*, March 26. The comment on rhinoceroses is from: MacGregor, Neil. 2010. *A History of the World in 100 Objects*. London: Penguin.

Research on the Roman economy is a growth industry, if you'll pardon the expression, so I'll list only a few of the texts covering various business sectors in ancient Rome. I thank Matt Gibbs for his guidance in finding these sources, although the blame for any misinterpretation falls on me. Gibbs also provided a very useful critique of an early draft of this chapter. Some texts on Roman business sectors:

Andreau, J. 2000. "Commerce and Finance." In *The Cambridge Ancient History*, Vol. XI. 2nd ed., by A. K. Bowman, P. Garnsey, and D. Rathbone, 769–786. Cambridge: Cambridge University Press.

Bradley, K. 1994. *Slavery and Society at Rome*. Cambridge: Cambridge University Press.

Edmondon, J. C. 1987. *Two Industries in Roman Lusitania: Mining and Garum Production*. Oxford: BAR.

Greene, K. 1986. *The Archaeology of the Roman Economy*. Berkeley: University of California Press.

Hirt, A. 2010. *Imperial Mines and Quarries in the Roman World: Organizational Aspects 27 BC–AD 235*. Oxford: Oxford University Press.

Malouta, M., and A. Wilson. 2013. "Mechanical Irrigation: Water-Lifting Devices in the Archaeological Evidence and in the Egyptian Papyri." In *The Roman Agricultural Economy: Organization, Investment, and Production*, by A. Bowman and A. Wilson, 273–306. Oxford: Oxford University Press.

Saller, R. 2012. "Human Capital and Economic Growth." In *The Cambridge Companion to the Roman Economy*, by W. Scheidel, 71–88. Cambridge: Cambridge University Press.

Wilson, A. 2002. "Machines, Power and the Ancient Economy." *Journal of Roman Studies*, 1–32.

———. 2001. "Timgad and Textile Production." In *Economies beyond Agriculture in the Classical World*, by D. J. Mattingly and J. Salmon, 271–296. London and New York: Routledge.

For the biography of our hero, Marcus Crassus, I have relied mostly on:

Adcock, Frank E. 1966. *Marcus Crassus, Millionaire*. Cambridge: W. Heffer. Despite the fun title, it's an academic book.

Cadoux, T. J. 1956. "Marcus Crassus: A Revaluation." *Greece & Rome*, 153–161. Cadoux argues that Crassus, with better luck, could have been Rome's first emperor.

Marshall, Bruce A. 1972. "Crassus' Ovation in 71 BC." *Historia: Zeitschrift für Alte Geschichte*, 669–673.

———. 1976. *Crassus: A Political Biography*. Amsterdam: A. M. Hakkert.

Ward, Allen Mason. 1977. *Marcus Crassus and the Late Roman Republic*. Columbia: University of Missouri Press.

Most details of Crassus's life cited in the chapter are from both Adcock and Ward, cited above, although they disagree on some points (noted in the text). These books, and especially Marshall, also cover Crassus's political career, which is something I don't discuss in much detail, as I have focused on revealing his wealth secrets instead.

If you happen to speak German, there is a more recent academic book on Crassus: Weggen, K. 2011. *Der Lange Schatten von Carrhae: Studien zu M. Licinius Crassus*. Hamburg: Kovac. Let me know if it's any good.

I have also thrown in a few details on Crassus—particularly his political maneuvering—from Holland, Tom. 2005. *Rubicon:*

The Last Years of the Roman Republic. New York: Anchor. Holland offers an excellent introduction to the politics and history of ancient Rome, based primarily on ancient sources and aimed at the general reader.

As noted in the text, to place Crassus's fate in context after he "met the Parthians," I interviewed Matthew Canepa at the University of Minnesota. The details in that section are mostly from the academic biographies of Crassus as well as Canepa's comments. Appropriately, when I interviewed Canepa, he was living in a reconstructed Roman villa—the Getty Villa in Los Angeles.

One last note on Crassus: a romantic tale is often told of the fate of one of Crassus's legions in the battle of Carrhae. Unfortunately, it is probably false. A Cambridge historian by the name of Homer Dubs announced in the 1950s, to general bewilderment, that he had found one of the lost legions of Marcus Crassus in a town called Liqian, in western China. He argued that, following their defeat at the hands of the Parthians, some of Crassus's men had escaped and fled east into central Asia. From there they had perhaps offered themselves up as mercenaries in the service of some central Asian warlord and then been captured, and ultimately resettled, by the Chinese, following a haphazard journey eastward of some 3,500 miles. To the general delight of the news media, when China began to open and news photographers traveled to Liqian, they indeed found a number of villagers who had strikingly Western features, such as green eyes and blond hair. Genetic testing on some of the most Western-looking of these individuals appeared to confirm that they were Caucasian in origin. Of course, Liqian was on the Silk Road, the ancient trade route that stretched from China to Europe, and the ancestors of these few villagers could have been traders. Canepa, for one, is a skeptic. "The whole theory is based on the mistranslation of some Chinese characters," he says. "It is pure fantasy."

That said, the story lives on. The U.K.'s *Daily Mail* in 2010 published an article arguing that new genetic tests "show Chinese villagers with green eyes could be descendants of [a] lost Roman Legion." These new tests suggest that some two-thirds of the villagers are indeed of Caucasian origin. But this evidence must be taken with a grain of salt: modern China is an increasingly commercially minded place, and the villagers of impoverished Liqian have realized that proof of Roman origins would not do their tourism business any harm.

On the unfortunate would-be imitators of Crassus in the modern day, whose exploits conclude the chapter, the main sources are:

Boffey, Daniel. 2013. "Margaret Thatcher 'gave her approval' to her son Mark's failed coup attempt in Equatorial Guinea." *The Observer*, April 13.

Buckley, Neil. 2013. "A Day in the Life of Mikhail Khodorkhovsky." *Financial Times Magazine*, October 24.

Throughout the chapter there are also a number of references to ancient texts (Pliny the Elder, Caesar Augustus, Plutarch...). All of the texts I quote are now available online, so if you search for the quote or fact in question and the name of the ancient author, you should be able to find the reference. The descriptions of ancient Roman parties are all from such sources, although I tended to mix and match translations for rhetorical effect.

If you are looking for just the dirty bits of Roman history, you might enjoy the following book—but keep in mind most of it is (ancient) political propaganda: Farrington, Geoffrey, and Dorian Murdoch. 1994. *The Dedalus Book of Roman Decadence: Emperors of Debauchery*. Cambridge: Dedalus.

On Chapter 3

What is a monopoly? It is a surprisingly controversial question. Throughout the book I use the term "monopoly" frequently, to refer to businesses with a dominant share of their market.

Technically, one could argue—and indeed economists often argue—that the only time the word "monopoly" should be used to describe a business is when that monopoly is awarded by a government, i.e., when it is a legislated monopoly (like the steamboat monopoly that Vanderbilt challenged). To an economist, the word "monopoly" indicates that a business faces no competition in its market. This condition probably applies only to legislated monopolies. Hence, many scholars would contend that to call Standard Oil a monopoly is inaccurate—even though it had a nearly 100 percent share of U.S. oil refining. Instead of saying that such a company has a monopoly, these scholars would prefer to say that a company "dominates its markets," that it has "pricing power" or that the market is characterized by high "concentration."

Why not just say monopoly? The reason is that a business that is a legislated monopoly might be expected to behave very differently from a business that achieves a 100 percent market share. For instance, while Rockefeller's Standard Oil (or Bill Gates's Microsoft), at the peak of its powers, might have faced little apparent competition, in fact, the behavior of these companies was probably very different from what a business with a legislated monopoly might have done. Had Standard Oil operated inefficiently, some new competitor might have entered the market. To be sure, Standard Oil made a lot of money. But that did not mean it was uncompetitive; rather, one could argue, it was so competitive that it scared off potential rivals (who didn't want to run the risk of being bankrupted).

In a nod to such views, in the text I try to distinguish between "legislated monopolies"—awarded by governments—and "natural monopolies"—companies that come to dominate their markets based on the operation of economic principles. (Lawyers also tend to use the term "monopoly" a bit more loosely, often calling any business with a market share greater than 25 percent a monopoly.)

One reason economists tend to get upset about people throwing around the term "monopoly" is that there has been a sea change in mainstream views on whether or not monopolies (dominant businesses) are bad. The old view, which became popular in the regulated world that Pierpont Morgan inadvertently ushered in, was that all monopolies should be closely regulated. Monopolies that faced little obvious competition (like Rockefeller's) were seen as facing no competition, and therefore, to protect the consumer, public oversight was required.

The new view, which came into vogue in the 1980s, was that even a business like Rockefeller's faced competition—simply from the *threat* of new entrants. This threat ensured that companies with natural monopolies, if left unregulated, would operate efficiently and even spur innovation as other firms sought to replace the current monopolists. So consumers might not suffer, even if a market was dominated by a single firm. Moreover, efforts to regulate natural monopolies could, in that case, backfire. Limits on monopoly profits would have the unwanted effect of discouraging any potential competitors from entering the market—so, ironically enough, a regulated monopoly might face *less* competitive pressure than one left free to dominate its market.

As I write, it appears that this new view is likely to be challenged. I imagine that policy—if not necessarily the views of economists—will begin to swing back toward the earlier view, with, for better or worse, utility-style regulation coming back into vogue for dominant businesses.

Anyone interested in further reading on the robber barons will benefit greatly from the fact that these men are something of an American obsession. As a result, the robber barons are the subject of numerous books for the general reader, written by top-notch historians. Many of these biographies are based on unrestricted access to the personal papers of the robber barons themselves, and so offer exceptionally intimate portraits. These books are the primary sources I used for biographical information and quotations from the robber barons:

Brands, H. W. 2010. *American Colossus: The Triumph of Capitalism, 1865–1900*. New York: Doubleday. This book is the source for much of the background information on the U.S. economy during the 1800s.

Chernow, Ron. 1990. *The House of Morgan: An American Banking Dynasty and the Rise of Modern Finance*. New York: Atlantic Monthly Press. Along with Strouse (below), this book is a main source for details on Morgan cited in the text. Both books are excellent. Overall, I relied more heavily on Strouse, who focuses more on Morgan's business dealings.

———. 1998. *Titan: The Life of John D. Rockefeller, Sr*. New York: Random House. This book is the source for nearly all the personal details for the section on Rockefeller. Many business details and some quotations are from Brands (above), Morris (below), and the academic sources listed below.

Collier, Peter, and David Horowitz. 1976. *The Rockefellers: An American Dynasty*. New York: Holt, Rinehart and Winston. Largely used for information on Rockefeller's estate and heirs.

Krass, Peter. 2002. *Carnegie*. Hoboken: John Wiley & Sons, Inc. I used this book for a few details on Carnegie's later acquisitions, but mostly relied on Nasaw (below), who includes more on Carnegie's personal life.

Morris, Charles R. 2005. *The Tycoons: How Andrew Carnegie, John D. Rockefeller, Jay Gould, and J. P. Morgan Invented the American Supereconomy*. New York: Henry Holt. Morris explains the relationships among the various robber barons—with Carnegie and Rockefeller eager to forge ahead, and Morgan serving as "the regulator." I have taken a similar view, although I characterized Morgan's actions as being rather self-interested and based on the economics of banking.

———. 2012. *The Dawn of Innovation: The First American Industrial Revolution*. New York: PublicAffairs. Morris's book deals with the period before the rise of the robber barons. The sections of the chapter on early innovations in the U.S. economy are based largely on details from this book.

Nasaw, David. 2006. *Andrew Carnegie*. New York: Penguin. This book is the source for nearly all the personal details on Carnegie, with business details from Morris (above) and the academic sources listed below.

Stiles, T. J. 2009. *The First Tycoon: The Epic Life of Cornelius Vanderbilt*. New York: Alfred A. Knopf. Vanderbilt's life makes a fascinating story, and this book tells it well. With his investments in steamboat lines, railways, and telegraph companies, Vanderbilt was one of the pioneers of network effects businesses — a subject of chapter 6. However, as the chapter was already getting long, I cut most of Vanderbilt's story (as well as that of Jay Gould, an equally fascinating character).

Strouse, Jean. 1999. *Morgan: American Financier*. New York: Random House.

A muckraking review of the robber barons written after the Great Depression provided some interesting tidbits: Josephson, Matthew. 1934. *The Great American Capitalists, 1861–1901*. New York: Harcourt. A short synopsis of the robber barons, written for British readers, provided a useful reference (although it is mostly based on the above books): Derbyshire, Wyn. 2011. *Six Tycoons: The Lives of John Jacob Astor, Cornelius Vanderbilt, Andrew Carnegie, John D. Rockefeller, Henry Ford and Joseph P. Kennedy*. London: Grosvenor Group.

The evidence on the wealth secrets of the robber barons mostly comes from academic sources:

Behn, Richard J. 2014. *The Founders and the Pursuit of Land*. April 4. http://lehrmaninstitute.org/history/founders-land.asp. For Washington's wealth secret.

De Long, J. Bradford. 1991. "Did J. P. Morgan's Men Add Value? An Economist's Perspective on Financial Capitalism." In *Inside the Business Enterprise: Historical Perspectives on the Use of Information*, by Peter Temin, 205–249. Chicago: University of Chicago Press.

Folsom, Burton W., Jr. 1987. *The Myth of the Robber Barons: A*

New Look at the Rise of Big Business in America. Herndon: Young America's Foundation. Details on corruption in the Union Pacific Railroad are mainly from this book, which offers a right-wing perspective on the robber barons and their battles with political entrepreneurs and legislated monopolists.

Granitz, Elizabeth, and Benjamin Klein. 1996. "Monopolization by 'Raising Rivals' Costs:' The Standard Oil Case." *Journal of Law and Economics*, 1–47. This paper is the source of my argument regarding Rockefeller's "South Improvement Lite" quasi-cartel. While the argument has reasonably wide acceptance among scholars as an explanation for Rockefeller's success, it is not the only view.

John, Richard R. 2010. *Network Nation: Inventing American Telecommunications*. Cambridge, MA: Harvard University Press. John provides a nuanced and often surprising perspective on the rise of network businesses. This book is the source for details relating to telegraph and railway consolidation (it also covers telephones, which I don't really address). John also provided a very useful critique of an early draft of this chapter, for which I am grateful.

Khan, B. Z. 2011. "Antitrust and Innovation before the Sherman Act." *Antitrust Law Journal*, 757–786. This article is the source for many of the quotes explaining early U.S. attitudes toward monopoly.

Ramirez, Carlos D. 1995. "Did J. P. Morgan's Men Add Liquidity? Corporate Investment, Cash Flow, and Financial Structure at the Turn of the Twentieth Century." *Journal of Finance*, 661–678.

The story of the rise of the Grangers is also mostly based on academic research. I thank Richard John for suggesting many of these sources, although the blame for any misinterpretation is my own:

Anderson, Kym, ed. 2009. *Distortions to Agricultural Incentives: A Global Perspective, 1955–2007*. Washington and New York: The World Bank and Palgrave Macmillan.

Dickson, Peter R., and Philippa K. Wells. 2001. "The Dubious

Origins of the Sherman Act: The Mouse that Roared." *Journal of Public Policy & Marketing*, 3–14. This article is the source of the view that the Sherman Act obtained wide support because it had been watered down.

James, Scott C. 2000. *Presidents, Parties and the State: A Party System Perspective on Democratic Regulatory Choice, 1884–1936*. Cambridge: Cambridge University Press.

Miller, George H. 1971. *Railroads and the Granger Laws*. Madison: University of Wisconsin Press. This book and James (above) describe how the Grangers were repeatedly thwarted by gifted lobbyists.

Olson, Mancur. 1971. *The Logic of Collective Action: Public Goods and the Theory of Groups*. Cambridge, MA: Harvard University Press.

All conversions to modern currency in the chapter were performed using Samuel H. Williamson's helpful online tool "Seven Ways to Compute the Relative Value of a U.S. Dollar Amount, 1774 to Present," MeasuringWorth, 2014. The purchasing power comparison was used. The U.S. economic growth statistics cited in the chapter are from the same source. The data on agricultural subsidies are from the World Bank World Development Indicators.

Lastly, when Rockefeller writes powerfully about the "heartache and misery" that is introduced by competition, that is from: Rockefeller, John D. 1909. *Random Reminiscences of Men and Events*. New York: Doubleday, Page & Company.

On Chapter 4

Naturally I must begin the notes on chapter 4 with a plug for my own edited volumes on risk management in the banking sector:

Wilkin, Sam (ed.). 2004. *Country and Political Risk: Practical Insights for Global Finance*. London: Risk Books.

———. 2015. *Country and Political Risk: Practical Insights for Global Finance* (2nd ed.). London: Risk Books.

The first volume is largely from academic contributors and consultants, while the chapters in the second volume are mostly contributed by bankers. Although expensive, these books make great gifts for the financial sector executives in your life.

The description of the debauchery involving bankers that opens the chapter is mostly from the popular media, as noted in the text, as well as: Freeland, Cynthia. 2012. *Plutocrats: The Rise of the New Global Super-Rich and the Fall of Everyone Else.* London: Allen Lane.

The review of the rise of deposit insurance is mostly based on academic sources:

Garten, Helen A. 1994. "A Political Analysis of Bank Failure Resolution." *Boston University Law Review*, 429–479. Garten also contributed a valuable critique of an early draft of this chapter, for which I am grateful. Garten's own view on the causes of the global financial crisis is rather different from my own (see a discussion of some alternate views below).

Johnson, Simon, and James Kwak. 2010. *13 Bankers: The Wall Street Takeover and the Next Financial Meltdown.* New York: Pantheon. This book was written to explain the global financial crisis but goes into historical detail as well. It is excellent on the degree to which banks were able to shape the regulation of their sector to their financial advantage, a point also made, bravely, in: Johnson, Simon. 2009. "The Quiet Coup." *Atlantic Monthly*.

Reinhart, Carmen M., and Kenneth S. Rogoff. 2009. *This Time Is Different: Eight Centuries of Financial Folly.* Princeton: Princeton University Press. This is the classic account of financial crises and their (economic) causes (of which, more below).

Sprague, Irvine H. 1986. *Bailout: An Insider's Account of Bank Failures and Rescues.* New York: Basic Books. This book is remarkable in that it was written by a banking regulator who was present, and a key decision maker, in many of the early banking bailouts.

In contrast to the robber barons, and to the global financial crisis, it is hard to find good books about the S&L crisis written for a general audience. The main sources for the quotes and financial details used in the section on the S&L crisis are:

Day, Kathleen. 1993. *S&L Hell: The People and the Politics behind the $1 Trillion Savings and Loan Scandal.* New York: W. W. Norton. This book has everything you need to know about the S&L crisis, but out of order, possibly because it is based on a compilation of the author's articles. The book is the source for most of the human-interest stories I quote (Jeffrey Levitt, Spencer Blain).

Lowy, Martin. 1991. *High Rollers: Inside the Savings and Loan Debacle.* New York: Praeger.

Mayer, Martin. 1990. *The Greatest-Ever Bank Robbery: The Collapse of the Savings and Loan Industry.* New York: Charles Scribner's Sons. This book deals confidently, but somewhat idiosyncratically, with the main economic causes of the S&L crisis (a topic I don't go into in much detail in the chapter, focusing instead on incidents of fraud).

The section of the chapter that deals with the costs of the S&L crisis, and then the origins of too big to fail, is based on many of the above sources used in tracing the rise of deposit insurance (such as Reinhart and Rogoff, Johnson and Kwak, and especially Sprague—who is often quoted in the main text). In addition:

Boss, Maria, and Gary Watson. 1991. "The FDIC's Special Defenses: Before and After FIRREA." *American Business Law Journal*, 309–334.

Class, Edgar. 1995. "The Precarious Position of the Federal Deposit Insurance Corporation after O'Melveny & Myers v. FDIC." *Administrative Law Journal*, 373–402.

Dabos, Marcelo. 2004. "Too Big to Fail in the Banking Industry: A Survey." In *Too Big to Fail: Policies and Practices in Government Bailouts,* by Benton E. Gup, 141–151. Westport, CT: Praeger. Long before the global financial crisis, scholars had understood that too big to fail was a problem and were publishing books on the issue, but they were generally ignored. This volume is one example.

Dymski, Gary A. 2011. "Genie out of the Bottle: The Evolution of Too-Big-to-Fail Policy and Banking Strategy in the U.S." Unpublished paper (UC Riverside, Riverside, CA), 1–47. If you are looking for a Marxist (but very interesting and well-documented) view on the causes of the global financial crisis, this is it.

FDIC. 1997. *History of the Eighties—Lessons for the Future*, Vol. I. Washington, DC: FDIC.

Hetzel, Robert L. 1991. "Too Big to Fail: Origins, Consequences, and Outlook." *Economic Review*, 3–15.

Stern, Gary H., and Ron R. Feldman. 2004. *Too Big to Fail: The Hazards of Bank Bailouts*. Washington, DC: Brookings Institution Press. This book offered another advance warning of the issues that would (in my view) lead to the global financial crisis. It was also ignored.

In contrast to the S&L crisis, the global financial crisis brought out the A-list talent and induced them to spend a lot of time and effort crafting excellent, well-written books. In addition to the Johnson and Kwak book and Dymski chapter cited above, the main sources I used for the details quoted in this section of the chapter are:

Martin, Iain. 2013. *Making It Happen: Fred Goodwin, RBS, and the Men Who Blew Up the British Economy*. London: Simon & Schuster. Used for the section on the global game.

McLean, Bethany, and Joe Nocera. 2010. *All the Devils Are Here: The Hidden History of the Financial Crisis*. New York: Portfolio. This is the most comprehensive book on the financial crisis, covering all the players from the banks to the rating agencies. It was crucial for the sections on the rating game and the risk management game.

Morgenson, Gretchen, and Joshua Rosner. 2011. *Reckless Endangerment: How Outsized Ambition, Greed and Corruption Led to Economic Armageddon*. New York: Times Books. This book focuses on the U.S.-government-supported entities Fannie Mae and Freddie Mac, as well as securitization—two important aspects of the crisis that, for space reasons, I do not cover in much detail in the chapter (although I returned to the story in chapter 7). Used mostly for the section on the winnings.

Sorkin, Andrew Ross. 2009. *Too Big to Fail: The Inside Story of How Wall Street and Washington Fought to Save the Financial System—and Themselves*. New York: Viking. This is the book (now a movie) that brought too big to fail into the popular lexicon. It is a good book, although it is not really about the too-big-to-fail problem. Rather, it is a play-by-play account of how the banks were saved during the global financial crisis.

Tett, Gillian. 2009. *Fool's Gold: How the Bold Dream of a Small Tribe at J.P. Morgan Was Corrupted by Wall Street Greed and Unleashed a Catastrophe*. New York: Free Press. This well-written book focuses on the creation of credit default swaps and is the main source for the section on the risk swapping game, as well as some parts of the rating game and risk management game.

To explain the wealth secrets of the bankers (including the section on the winnings, the global game, and the game going on), I have once again turned to academic research. In addition to the sources cited above in reference to the origins of too big to fail, the main sources are:

Bebchuk, Lucian A., Alma Cohen, and Holger Spamann. 2010. "The Wages of Failure: Executive Compensation at Bear Stearns and Lehman, 2000–2008." *Yale Journal on Regulation*, 257–282.

Bijlsma, Michiel J., and Remco J. M. Mocking. 2013. "The Private Value of Too Big to Fail Guarantees." CPB Discussion Paper 240, 1–43.

Brewer, Elijah III, and Julapa Jagtiani. 2013. "How Much Did Banks Pay to Become Too-Big-To-Fail and to Become Systemically Important?" *Journal of Financial Services Research*, 1–35.

Cunliffe, Jon. 2014. "Ending Too Big to Fail: Progress to Date and Remaining Issues." The Barclays European Bank Capital Summit. London: Bank of England, 1–10.

Karmel, Roberta S. 2011. "An Orderly Liquidation Authority Is Not the Solution to Too Big to Fail." *Brookings Journal of Corporate Finance and Commercial Law*, 1–46.

Keister, Todd, and James McAndrews. 1990. "Why Are Banks Holding So Many Excess Reserves?" Federal Reserve Bank of New York Staff Reports, 1–13.

Santos, João. 2014. "Evidence from the Bond Market on Banks' 'Too-Big-to-Fail' Subsidy." *Federal Reserve Bank of New York Economic Policy Review*, 1–22.

Seelig, Steven A. 2004. "Too Big to Fail: A Taxonomic Analysis." In *Too Big to Fail: Policies and Practices in Government Bailouts*, by Benton E. Gup, ed., 219–229. Westport, CT: Praeger.

van Rixtel, Adrian, Yupana Wiwattanakantang, Toshiyuki Souma, and Kazunori Suzuki. 2004. "Banking in Japan: Will Too Big to Fail Prevail?" In *Too Big to Fail: Policies and Practices in Government Bailouts*, by Benton E. Gup, ed., 253–283. Westport, CT: Praeger.

The data for the section on the earnings of the bankers and their relationship to the one percent are from:

Bakija, Jon, Adam Cole, and Bradley T. Heim. 2012. "Jobs and Income Growth of Top Earners and the Causes of Changing Income Inequality: Evidence from U.S. Tax Return Data." Working Paper, Williams College.

Piketty, Thomes, and Emmanuel Saez. 2013. "Top Incomes and the Great Recession: Recent Evolutions and Policy Implications." *IMF Economic Review*, 456–478.

Tomaskovic-Devey, Donald, and Ken-Hou Lin. 2011. "Income Dynamics, Economic Rents and the Financialization of the U.S. Economy." *American Sociological Review*, 538–559.

Wójcik, Dariusz. 2012. "The End of Investment Bank Capitalism? An Economic Geography of Financial Jobs and Power." *Economic Geography*, 345–368.

If you have read Thomas Piketty's well-regarded book, *Capital *in the Twenty-First Century* (Belknap Press, 2014), you'll notice a difference in emphasis regarding the rise of the one percent. This isn't because I disagree with Piketty. Piketty's book mostly focuses on inequality in Europe, which is in many countries increasingly attributable to differences in inherited wealth. In the United States, by contrast, and as Piketty notes, the main driver of income inequality in the present day is salary differentials, the focus of my chapter. While Piketty forecasts that differences in inherited wealth eventually will come to drive U.S. income inequality, this is not at present the case.

Piketty would probably disagree with my focus on the importance of the financial sector in driving the rise of the one percent. Piketty points out that the largest share of the increase in income inequality in the United States is attributable to increases in managerial salaries, with the rise in financial sector compensation accounting for only a minority of this. The point that I emphasize is that financial sector employees, while a minority, are the segment of the one percent—indeed, the only segment of the one percent—whose share of one-percent incomes has grown materially over time. In other words, while general increases in managerial salaries may be the main explanation for the rising fortunes of the one percent (as Piketty notes), it is the particularly meteoric rise of the financial sector that has made everyone else feel they are falling behind (or so I argue).

After reading the chapter, you may come to the conclusion that too big to fail was not only a wealth secret for the bankers, it was a major cause of the global financial crisis. Not only did the too-big-to-fail subsidy help to make the bankers rich, but the existence of a government guarantee helped to encourage the bankers to take more risks (this problem, known as moral hazard, arises when the parties taking risks do not bear the consequences of their actions, but rather these consequences are passed on to another group—in this case, the taxpayer). Furthermore, as I tell it, when the government guarantee was suddenly and unexpectedly withdrawn (when Lehman Brothers was allowed to fail), this touched off the financial crisis.

Let me provide a brief introduction to some other views on the causes of financial crises. My friends in the financial sector who reviewed early drafts of this chapter generally favored hubris as an explanation for the crisis. They argued that bankers did not plan to create banks that failed—they genuinely believed they could manage the risks. And it is true that even though many bankers walked away from the financial crisis very rich, they would have been much richer if their banks had not failed. So it is fair to say that the bankers suffered serious personal losses in the crisis.

The classic view on the economics of banking crises comes from Reinhart and Rogoff, cited above. Two more recent books by economists with similar views on the underlying economic causes of banking crises are:

Admati, Anat, and Martin Hellwig. 2013. *The Bankers' New Clothes: What's Wrong with Banking and What to Do about It.* Princeton: Princeton University Press.

Wolf, Martin. 2014. *The Shifts and the Shocks: What We've Learned—and Have Still to Learn—from the Financial Crisis.* New York: Penguin.

I also interviewed Wolf and Hellwig for the preface to the second edition of my own edited volume on country risk management in banking.

Generally speaking, the view of each of these economists is that the repeated occurrence of financial crises is inherent in the economics of banking. A principal function of banks is "maturity transformation." That is, banks accept depositor funds that are instantly exchangeable for cash, and they lend funds on longer terms (a bank will probably get its money back from mortgage lending, for example, but only over time, and there is no way the bank can instantly call in its loans). The classic manifestation of the risk inherent in maturity transformation is a bank run: depositors lose confidence in a bank and rush to withdraw their money. But the money is tied up in mortgage loans, and so if enough depositors withdraw simultaneously, the bank fails. While banks hold some assets in reserve against withdrawals, there comes a point when any bank, no matter how well run, will fold in the face of a loss of its depositors' confidence.

In fact, a bank run is only one way in which the risks inherent in maturity transformation can manifest themselves. For instance, during the U.S. S&L crisis, there weren't many runs. Rather, the problem was that the S&Ls' long-term mortgages were paying about 6 percent interest (remember 3-6-3?) but then, after interest rates were deregulated, S&Ls had to offer much higher interest rates to attract short-term depositors—in some cases as high as 15 percent. The difference between outgoings of 15 percent and incomings of 6 percent is a lot, so most S&Ls were losing huge amounts of money. The solution, of course, would have been to raise mortgage interest rates to 15 percent—but many mortgages were long-term, with fixed rates, so the 6 percent rates were locked in for years or even decades. Hence: a risk from maturity transformation.

There are lots of schemes that seek to offset such risks. The most popular is deposit insurance—where banks insure each other, often via a government program, against the risk of failure. But fundamentally, such schemes do not eliminate the risk, which is, as I have said, inherent in maturity transformation. The risk has to go somewhere. For instance, there was still the risk that the deposit insurance fund itself would be overwhelmed. Ultimately, in the global financial crisis, so many banks were impacted at the same time by a real estate collapse, and by their simultaneous "fire sale" efforts to sell assets to raise capital (which led to asset price collapses), that the deposit insurance scheme would have run out of money had there been no bailout. Deposit insurance had hidden the risk, but it was still there.

In the view of the economists I cite above, resolving "too big to fail" would not eliminate the risk of systemic financial crises — any financial system in which leveraged institutions, whether large or small, engage in maturity transformation is inherently at risk. That's a little worrying, from a policy perspective.

Fortunately, this is not a book about policy. A far more interesting question is: Does this mean there are wealth secrets in finance beyond too big to fail? If the whole system is inherently at risk, that implies there is a lot of money to be made, because risks tend to be rewarded by high returns (a topic covered in chapter 7). Of course, it's no fun bearing the consequences of financial risks oneself (think LTCM), so masters of wealth secrets who take serious risks generally find a way to have someone else pay.

It certainly seems that there are some further wealth secrets to be found. For instance, securitization involved the passing on of maturity-transformation risks throughout the financial system. Subprime mortgages were packaged together, assigned AAA ratings, and sold on to investors (such as pension funds) that had been excluded from running such risks. The question is whose wealth secret this was. Did the pension funds understand they were in fact running large hidden risks and accept these risks in exchange for higher returns? Or did the well-paid bankers who structured the deals pass the risks off on the unsuspecting funds? Or, amid all the hubris, did no one realize that large, unmanaged risks were being hidden and passed around?

If no one knows it's a wealth secret, is it still a wealth secret?

On Chapter 5

This is another chapter that has a movie version: *Guru*, directed by Mani Ratnam. *Guru* is a standard Bollywood epic — complete with song and dance numbers — but Anil Ambani was tangentially involved in the production, so it is generally taken to be loosely based on Dhirubhai's life. Because it is Bollywood, some details are changed: Dhiru (Dhirubhai's nickname among friends and family) becomes "Guru," the young man travels to Turkey rather than Yemen, the company is called "Shakti Trading" rather than Reliance, and so on. The movie is both well acted and surprisingly moving, and you might enjoy it even if Bollywood song and dance routines are not your thing.

Although there are a number of excellent English-language books on Dhirubhai Ambani — to be discussed in a moment — compared to the Romans, the robber barons, the bankers, or the technology billionaires, coverage of Dhirubhai's business dealings, particularly in the English-language academic literature, is relatively thin. For this reason, to evaluate Dhirubhai's wealth secret, I traveled to India and interviewed a number of analysts of, as well as current and former competitors of, Reliance.

The interviewees included: Ashish Chauhan, CEO, Bombay Stock Exchange; Gurcharan Das, author of many well-regarded books (including those cited below) and former CEO of Procter & Gamble India; Chirag Dhaifule, Research Analyst, LKP Securities; Subir Gokarn, Director of Research, Brookings India; Piyush Jain, Equity Research Analyst, Morningstar India; Surajit Mazumdar, Professor, Jawaharlal Nehru University; Ashok Sinha, Chairman, 4i Advisors and former Chairman and Managing Director, Bharat Petroleum Corporation Limited; and Rahul Tongia, Fellow, Brookings India. I thank them, as well as several interviewees who preferred to remain anonymous, for their generosity with their insights.

The backstory about the Indian economy under the license raj, and the analysis of the wealth secrets of the firms that thrived during that era, are based on the following sources, as well as McDonald and Mazumdar (cited below):

Bhattacharya, Debesh. 1989. "Growth and Distribution in India." *Journal of Contemporary Asia*, 150–166.

Das, Gurcharan. 2002. *India Unbound: The Social and Economic Revolution from Independence to the Global Information Age.* New York: Anchor Books. This book is a well-regarded popular economic and business history of India aimed at the general reader.

Forbes, Nashuad. 2002. "Doing Business in India: What Has Liberalization Changed?" In *Economic Policy Reforms and the Indian Economy,* by Anne O. Krueger, 129–158. Chicago: University of Chicago Press.

Kochanek, Stanley A. 1996. "Liberalisation and Business Lobbying in India." *Journal of Commonwealth and Comparative Politics,* 155–173.

Majumdar, Sumit K. 2004. "The Hidden Hand and the License Raj: An Evaluation of the Relationship between Age and the Growth of Firms in India." *Journal of Business Venturing,* 107–125.

Mukherji, Rahul. 2009. "The State, Economic Growth, and Development in India." *India Review,* 81–106.

Panagariya, Arvind. 2008. *India: The Emerging Giant.* Oxford: Oxford University Press.

For the personal details regarding the life of G. D. Birla, the main sources are:

Birla, Ghanshyam Das. 1986. *Nehru Family and Ghanshyam Das Birla: A Unique Collection of Living Letters.* New Delhi: Vision Books. This book records the correspondence of G. D. Birla with India's first prime minister, Jawaharlal Nehru. Although I cited only one or two details from it in the chapter, it makes for interesting reading.

Kudaisya, Medha M. 2003. *The Life and Times of G. D. Birla.* New Delhi: Oxford University Press. This is the main source for the details I cite on Birla's life.

Most of the personal details about Dhirubhai, as well as the quotes from him, come from the excellent English-language biographies available:

Ambani, Kokilaben. 2007. *Dhirubhai Ambani: The Man I*

Knew. Mumbai: Reliance Industries. This large-format picture book by Dhirubhai's wife contains, in addition to excellent photographs, a number of charming personal details, such as Dhirubhai's habit of sleeping on his clothes to "iron" them, and his swim through shark-infested waters to claim a reward of ice cream.

Bhushan, K., and G. Katyal. 2002. *Dhirubhai Ambani: The Man Behind Reliance*. New Delhi: A.P.H. Publishing Corporation. This book includes a long list of quotes from current and former Reliance employees, and is thus the source for most such quotes in the chapter.

McDonald, Hamish. 2010. *Ambani & Sons: The Making of the World's Richest Brothers and Their Feud*. New Delhi: Roli. This detailed, well-written but unauthorized biography of Dhirubhai is the source for most of the material on Dhirubhai's personal life and business dealings quoted in the chapter. Much of the material in the book was originally published as: McDonald, Hamish. 1998. *The Polyester Prince: The Rise of Dhirubhai Ambani*. Sydney: Allen & Unwin. The earlier book also contains a number of stories that I have largely overlooked in preference to focusing on Dhirubhai's wealth secret, including Dhirubhai's innovative capital-raising strategies, and the extraordinary battle between Mukesh and Anil Ambani for control of their father's empire after his death.

Piramal, Gita. 1996. *Business Maharajas*. New Delhi: Penguin Books India. This book contains biographies of a number of Indian business leaders including Dhirubhai. Because it focuses on Dhirubhai's business activities, it was a surprisingly useful resource, including some details missing from longer biographies.

Thakurta, Paranjoy Guha, Subir Ghosh, and Jyotirmoy Chaudhuri. 2014. *Gas Wars: Crony Capitalism and the Ambanis*. Delhi: Paranjoy Guha Thakurta. This is a surprisingly evenhanded book, despite the fact that the authors' extreme distrust of Mukesh and Anil Ambani shines through on every page. The authors have taken the approach of interviewing a series of commentators on the oil and gas dealings of the Ambani family and presenting the views of each commentator in sequence. The effect is sort of an oil and gas Rashomon—you get all the angles, despite the authors' evident bias. But by the third time you read about the decision to change the administered gas price, it becomes a little annoying. Mostly the book focuses on the Ambanis' investments in oil and gas exploration, which is something I don't cover very much in the chapter.

Most of the evidence for Dhirubhai's wealth secret comes from the interviews I conducted in India and the academic literature. The interviewees are cited in the text (for those who wished to be quoted). Academic sources are the following, along with Nashuad Forbes (cited above):

Capelli, Peter, Harbir Singh, Jitendra Singh, and Michael Useem. 2010. *The India Way: How India's Top Business Leaders Are Revolutionizing Management.* Boston: Harvard University Press.

Chandrasekhar, C. P. 1999. "Firms, Market and the State: An Analysis of Indian Oligopoly." In *Economy and Organization: Indian Institutions under the Neoliberal Regime,* by Amiya Kumar Bagchi, 230–266. New Delhi: Sage.

Heston, Alan, and Vijay Kumar. 2008. "Institutional Flaws and Corruption Incentives in India." *Journal of Development Studies,* 1243–1261.

Mazumdar, Surajit. 2011. "The State, Industrialisation and Competition: A Reassessment of India's Leading Business Enterprises under Dirigisme." *Economic History of Developing Regions,* 33–54. Mazumdar has also conducted his own research on Reliance, and provided a very useful critique of an early draft of this chapter.

Vachani, Sushil. 1997. "Economic Liberalization's Effect on Sources of Competitive Advantage of Different Groups of Companies: The Case of India." *International Business Review,* 165–184.

Most of the sources for the review of Carlos Slim and other

emerging markets billionaires that concludes the chapter are cited in the text. See http://stats.areppim.com/ for similar, and alternate, calculations on the prevalence of emerging markets billionaires in the *Forbes* list. The OECD study mentioned is: OECD. 2012. OECD Review of Telecommunication Policy and Regulation in Mexico. http://dx.doi.org/10.1787/9789264060111-en, OECD Publishing.

Finally, a word about the use of Dhirubhai's first name. In most of this book I refer to people by their last names. However, the English-language books about Dhirubhai Ambani generally use his first name, so I have adopted the same convention (and for his sons Mukesh and Anil as well). I hope I do not cause offense by sounding overly familiar.

On Chapter 6

The description of Bill Gates's house comes from blogs and the popular media, as well as Gates's own description from his book: Gates, Bill. 1995. *The Road Ahead*. London: Viking.

If you want more on the house, photographs of the interior appear in books on architecture, including:

Morrow, Theresa. 1997. *James Cutler*. Gloucester: Rockport. This is a small volume, in color, with the sections on the Gates house labeled "Guesthouse," "Garage," and "Swimming Pool."

Ojeda, Oscar Riera, ed. 2005. *Arcadian Architecture: Bohlin Cywinski Jackson — 12 Houses*. New York: Rizzoli. This is a large coffee-table book with the Gates house labeled as "Pacific Rim Estate."

The general feeling of the house is rustic and even cozy, although the use of thick beams of old-growth fir on a large scale and with minimalist precision creates a templelike effect in many rooms — a bit like constructing a house from the torii gates outside the Fushimi Inari Shrine in Kyoto. The garage, taking the form of a huge arch molded from concrete, looks like the inside of an enormous underground bunker.

As usual, most of the "color" in the chapter comes from popular books, in particular a few biographies of Bill Gates and business histories of Microsoft:

Cringely, Robert X. 1992. *Accidental Empires: How the Boys of Silicon Valley Make Their Millions, Battle Foreign Competition, and Still Can't Get a Date.* New York: HarperCollins.

Cusumano, Michael A., and Richard W. Selby. 1998. *Microsoft Secrets: How the World's Most Powerful Software Company Creates Technology, Shapes Markets, and Manages People.* New York: Touchstone. This book takes a look at business strategies adopted by Microsoft, as well as providing a business history.

Manes, Stephen, and Paul Andrews. 1994. *Gates: How Microsoft's Mogul Reinvented an Industry—and Made Himself the Richest Man in America.* New York: Touchstone. This is the best of the Gates biographies, in my view.

Rensin, David. 1994. "The Bill Gates Interview." *Playboy,* July, 63.

Toulouse, Stephen. 2010. *A Microsoft Life.* Self-published e-book. Though I used it for only one detail, it was an interesting window into the life of a "Microserf" (and Microsoft true believer).

Wallace, James, and Jim Erickson. 1992. *Hard Drive: Bill Gates and the Making of the Microsoft Empire.* New York: Wiley.

In the chapter, I introduced intellectual property rights as "tools for making money"—probably not the way most people are used to thinking about the subject. That said, from the earliest days of intellectual property rights in the United States, they were used for precisely this purpose. William Thornton, the Commissioner of Patents during the era of the robber barons, inserted himself into key patents for firearms and steamboats by pretending to have invented "improvements" (which did not work) and refusing to grant the patent until he was added as a co-inventor. This detail is from Morris (cited in the notes to the robber barons chapter). The evidence supporting the review of intellectual property law in the current chapter, as well as the intellectual property rights aspects of Bill Gates's wealth secrets (for instance, the deal of the century section), are from:

Bessen, James, and Michael J. Meurer. 2008. "Do Patents Perform Like Property?" *Academy of Management Perspectives,* 8–20.

Boldrin, Michele, and David K. Levine. 2008. *Against Intellectual Monopoly.* Cambridge: Cambridge University Press. This is the controversial book arguing that intellectual property rights should be abolished.

Devlin, Alan, and Michael Jacobs. 2009. "Microsoft's Five Fatal Flaws." *Columbia Business Law Review,* 67–108.

Easterbrook, Frank H. 2001. "Who Decides the Extent of Rights in Intellectual Property?" In *Expanding the Boundaries of Intellectual Property: Innovation Policy for a Knowledge Society,* by Rochelle Dreyfuss, Diane L. Zimmerman, and Harry First, 405–413. Oxford: Oxford University Press.

First, Harry. 2006. "Microsoft and the Evolution of the Intellectual Property Concept." *Wisconsin Law Review,* 1370–1432.

Gilbert, Richard J. 2011. "A World Without Intellectual Property?: Boldrin and Levine, Against Intellectual Monopoly." *Journal of Economic Literature,* 421–432.

McManis, Charles. 2009. "A Rhetorical Response to Boldrin & Levine: Against Intellectual (Property) Extremism." *Review of Law and Economics,* 1081–1100.

Merges, Robert P. 2000. "One Hundred Years of Solicitude: Intellectual Property Law, 1900–2000." *California Law Review,* 2187–2240. As the title suggests, this offers a historical perspective and was crucial for my discussion of how intellectual property law evolved.

———. 2001. "Institutions for Intellectual Property Transactions: The Case of Patent Pools." In *Expanding the Boundaries of Intellectual Property: Innovation Policy for a Knowledge Society,* by Rochelle Dreyfuss, Diane L. Zimmerman, and Harry First, 123–165. Oxford: Oxford University Press.

Seltzer, Wendy. 2013. "Software Patents and/or Software Development." *Brooklyn Law Review*, 929–1131.

Gates's understanding of the benefits that enforceable rights could have for his computer business started early. In his sophomore year of high school, Gates and several friends took on a project to write some payroll software for a company called Information Services, Inc. (ISI). The work was badly done, so ISI refused to provide the students with the valuable computer time they had been promised in exchange for their coding. Gates immediately got his father to write a threatening lawyer's letter. Impressed, ISI agreed to negotiate a formal legal contract with the students: for delivery of a quality product, a set amount of time on the ISI computers would be provided. Gates altered some details of the contract to his liking and signed; the altered details enabled Gates and his friends to use the ISI computers to work on a second contract project, earning about $4,200. Not bad for a bunch of high school students (with some legal assistance).

The following articles, as well as Cusumano and Selby (cited above), are the basis of the section on the application of network effects and platform strategies to Gates's wealth secrets:

Bresnahan, Timothy F. 2001. "Network Effects and Microsoft." Department of Economics, Stanford University Working Paper. This professor had the excellent idea of trawling through the documents released in the Microsoft case to find out how much Microsoft itself understood about the theory of network effects. Amusingly, Bresnahan is transparently surprised to find that Microsoft clearly understood each of the major implications of the theory (momentarily forgetting that businesses tend to catch on to leading-edge strategies before academics do). However, Bresnahan does give credit where due, noting that "the firm's analysis...shows that we [academic economists] have missed an important way in which partial equilibrium and general equilibrium diverge."

Cusumano, Michael A. 2010. "The Evolution of Platform Thinking." *Communications of the ACM*, January, 32–34.

———. 2010. "Platforms and Services: Understanding the Resurgence of Apple." *Communications of the ACM*, October, 22–24.

———. 2011. "The Platform Leader's Dilemma." *Communications of the ACM*, October, 21–23.

Evans, David S., Andrei Hagui, and Richard Schmalensee. 2006. *Invisible Engines: How Software Platforms Drive Innovation and Transform Industries*. Cambridge, MA: MIT Press. This book offers a relatively precise economist's view of business strategies in platform businesses. It is mostly accessible to a general reader, if perhaps a little dry.

Gawyer, Annabelle, and Michael A. Cusumano. 2002. *Platform Leadership: How Intel, Microsoft, and Cisco Drive Industry Innovation*. Boston: Harvard University Press. This book (as well as Cusumano's articles, cited above) provides an engaging introduction to the strategies of platform businesses, at the expense of some oversimplification in comparison to Evans et al. (above).

Liebowitz, Stan, and Stephen E. Margolis. 1998. "Dismal Science Fiction: Network Effects, Microsoft, and Antitrust Speculation." *Policy Analysis*, 1–38.

In 2014, the French economist Jean Tirole was awarded the Nobel Prize in economics in part for his work done on platform competition. His work is the basis for some of the above texts (in general, the formula for creating a classic management text is to find some work by economists, translate it into comprehensible language, and add a diagram or two):

Rochet, Jean-Charles, and Jean Tirole. 2006. "Two-Sided Markets: A Progress Report." *RAND Journal of Economics*, 645–667.

Tirole, Jean. 2008. "A Fine Balance." *Business Strategy Review*, Winter, 94–95. This short article is accessible to a general reader.

The sources cited above provide some of the detail regarding the government's antitrust case against Microsoft. In addition I relied on:

Boniwell, Ann. 2012. "The Implications of Network Effects for Competition Law." *Sibergramme*, 2–8.

Gilbert, Richard J., and Michael L. Katz. 2001. "An Economist's Guide to US vs Microsoft." *Journal of Economic Perspectives*, 25–44.

Lopatka, John, and William H. Page. 2009. *The Microsoft Case: Antitrust, High Technology, and Consumer Welfare.* Chicago: University of Chicago Press. This is the authoritative review of the Microsoft trial and its implications. Lopatka also provided a useful critique of an early draft of this chapter, for which I am grateful.

Thierer, Adam. 2012–2013. "The Perils of Classifying Social Media Platforms as Public Utilities." *CommLaw Conspectus*, 249–297.

The story about Nathan Myhrvold is taken from the above sources as well as: Orey, Michael. 2006. "Inside Nathan Myhrvold's Mysterious New Idea Machine." *Bloomberg Businessweek*, July 2.

This chapter was written in its entirety using Microsoft Word 2013 on a computer running Microsoft Windows version 8.1.

On Chapter 7

As I was finishing this manuscript, two books were published that independently arrived at some of the conclusions I review in this chapter (there are also, naturally, a few points of disagreement). These books are:

Brilliant, Heather, and Elizabeth Collins. 2014. *Why Moats Matter: The Morningstar Approach to Stock Investing.* New York: Wiley.

Thiel, Peter, and Blake Masters. 2014. *Zero to One: Notes on Startups, or How to Build the Future.* New York: Crown Business.

Interestingly, the authors of both of these books appear to have had no interaction with each other, and I did not know of either of them when I was writing this book. We also started from very different places. My objective was to tell the story of the world's richest people and how they actually made their fortunes. Brilliant and Collins set out to describe the results of their company's efforts to operationalize Warren Buffett's concept of a "moat" to forecast stock market returns. Thiel and Masters set out to record the personal experience of Peter Thiel, who is himself a billionaire and venture capitalist with a track record of identifying and backing several successful start-up companies, including PayPal and Facebook.

Brilliant and Collins list five factors that produce moats with staying power: (1) cost advantages, (2) intangible assets, (3) network effects, (4) customer switching costs, and (5) efficient scale. Thiel and Masters come up with a list of four factors that build monopolies: (1) proprietary technology, (2) network effects, (3) economies of scale, and (4) branding.

Compare those lists with my list of seven habits of spectacularly rich people, and you'll notice some of the points of agreement. The first thing you'll notice is that we all agree on network effects. These are a clear winner. If you want to be rich, go out and get yourself some.

There is another, also relatively clear, point of agreement: intellectual property rights. I group both brands and patented technologies into this category. Brilliant and Collins lump them together with government licenses (calling them "intangible assets"). For Thiel and Masters they are points 1 ("proprietary technology") and 4 ("branding"). There is also some overlap on the concept of scale economies. On most other points, the three books tend to disagree with each other, although a little disagreement is always healthy.

I think both books are very much worth reading. The book by Thiel and Masters is short, provocative, and a good read, with lots of memorable catchphrases that are genuinely enlightening. It also features a comparison of hipsters to the Unabomber that on its own justifies the book's cost. Thiel also, rather bravely, admits that the sources of his fortune, and Google's success, are monopolies (so he knows the first secret of spectacularly rich people: don't be the best—be the only).

However, as the book is based on Thiel's personal experience in the rarefied world of the technology sector (where, thanks in part to Bill Gates, almost everyone enjoys a miniature monopoly from patent protection these days), it has some blind spots. For instance, Thiel unfairly criticizes the financial sector for failing to be innovative. This is a little odd: the financial sector has been innovative to a fault. Not only the structure of the industry (for instance, the rise of hedge funds) but the financial instruments in use today would be all but unrecognizable to a time-traveling banker arriving from the early 1980s. The difference between the financial sector and the technology sector is not that financial firms are not innovative; it is that financial firms, by and large, cannot patent their innovations, while technology firms can. This is a big difference, and is why technology firms become monopolists. But it has very little to do with innovation itself.

Thiel writes: "By 'monopoly,' I mean the kind of company that is so good at what it does that no other firm can offer a close substitute." Well, no. There is no such monopoly. LTCM was exceptionally good at what it did. But there is no possible scenario one can imagine under which LTCM, by being even better than it was, ends up with a monopoly. Monopolies don't come from being the best, they come from wealth secrets such as barriers to competition. There were few such restrictions on competition in the hedge funds business, and being superior, no matter how superior, wasn't going to change that.

The book by Brilliant and Collins is longer and more comprehensive. Because it covers many business sectors and is based on more than a decade of experience in applying the framework to assess companies' prospects, it is rich with detail and case examples. That said, like most business books, you will feel entirely justified in reading it at work, as it is sometimes hard going. There are also a few square peg–round hole moments, where elements that are necessary for stock analysis but don't really relate to moats are shoehorned into the moat framework. There are also some philosophical issues one could raise (why is a government's refusal to allow other competitors into the industry sometimes an example of efficient scale and sometimes a type of intangible asset?). In terms of value for money, though, it's a great book.

I spoke with Elizabeth Collins, head of Morningstar's North America equity research, about the book. "What matters for equity valuation is not the next few years, but the next five to twenty years," she explains, which is why the moat is important. If a company is earning a lot of profits now but doesn't have a moat, these profits are likely to vanish abruptly as competitors, attracted by the high earnings, pile into the market and shamelessly imitate what the company does well.

Morningstar currently assigns Microsoft a wide moat rating (the best possible), although on a negative trend, as the company is playing catch-up in key areas including search, mobile, and cloud computing. In particular, the Office software suite could be threatened by cloud-based products. But then, technological innovation was never really Microsoft's wealth secret; so I'm not sure we should be all that concerned. By contrast, many U.S. investment banks covered by Morningstar appear to have weak moats. As I've mentioned, there are few barriers to competition in banking. But erecting competitive barriers was never the wealth secret of the bankers, so I don't think we should panic about that either.

After a decade of assigning moat ratings, Morningstar claims to have found that the ratings are useful not just for forecasting profitability, but for forecasting equity returns (particularly for undervalued stocks). If you'd like to get in on the moat action yourself, the company offers a Wide Moat Focus Index, composed of what it believes are the most undervalued stocks with good moats.

A very interesting question is: why is it that three books, with different starting points, and from authors with diverse backgrounds, have come to at least a few of the same conclusions, at roughly the same time?

I would argue that this has to do with the point I make at the end of the chapter: there are more wealth secrets now than ever before. If you are going to analyze stocks based on a traditional framework that does not focus in the first instance on barriers to competition, you are going to miss something important. Morningstar has achieved an impressive track record of forecasting equity returns based on this realization. Similarly, if you are going to invest in the technology sector using one of the traditional frameworks for understanding business profitability (like those I review in this chapter), you are not going to do very well. Thiel, to his credit, saw this early on and developed a new approach based almost entirely on the pursuit of monopoly. He has, partly as a result, been greatly successful and become very wealthy.

With regard to this book, I would make a similar claim: if you are going to understand the rise of the one percent in the modern era, you are going to need to look beyond the standard explanations, like globalization, technology, and increasing returns to education. You're going to need to understand wealth secrets. The expansion of wealth secrets—like intellectual property rights and government guarantees for the banking elite—has helped to inflate the salaries of both top managers and financial sector executives, as well as contributing to the dramatic expansion of the *Forbes* list of the world's billionaires. While it would be hard to quantify the contribution of wealth secrets to inequality, I do think it's hard to get ahead in stock market investing, or venture capital, or just to get ahead of the Joneses, without them.

Apologies for getting a little carried away—I almost forgot about the notes. Returning to the beginning of the chapter, the facts behind the story of the Thurn and Taxis dynasty are mostly sourced from: Puttkammer, E. W. 1938. "The Princes of Thurn and Taxis." Chicago Literary Club. Some dates are adjusted in accordance with more recent sources, notably: Grillmeyer, Siegfried. 2005. *Habsburgs Diener in Post und Politik: Das "Haus" Thurn und Taxis zwischen 1745 und 1867.* Verlag Philipp von Zabern. A few facts about the modern family are from either their profiles on the *Forbes* billionaire list or: Colacello, Bob. 2006. "The Conversion of Gloria TNT." *Vanity Fair,* June. You can contribute to the Thurn and Taxis cause by hiring a room in their castle for your next corporate event. Visit http://www.thurnundtaxis.de/events/vermietung/vermietung.html.

The two iconic business books to which I compare wealth secrets are:

Collins, Jim. 2001. *Good to Great: Why Some Companies Make the Leap...and Others Don't.* Harper Business. Also cited in chapter 1, and the source of the Pitney Bowes anecdote.

Peters, Thomas, and Robert Waterman, Jr. 1982. *In Search of Excellence: Lessons from America's Best-Run Companies.* New York: Harper & Row.

I was pointed to this book as a potential foil: Harford, Tim. 2012. *Adapt: Why Success Always Begins with Failure.* London: Picador.

The information on Russian billionaires is from: Zonis, Marvin, Dan Lefkovitz, Sam Wilkin, and Joseph Yackley. 2011. *Risk Rules: How Local Politics Threaten the Global Economy.* Agate B2.

With a few additions from: Wilkin, Sam. 2011. "Can Bad Governance be Good for Development?" *Survival,* 61–76. (Also cited in chapter 2.)

As well as the private briefing service offered by Oxford Analytica, at www.oxan.com.

The quote on the joys of monopoly in the Indian telecommunications is from: Chandrasekhar, C. P. 1999. "Firms, Market and the State: An Analysis of Indian Oligopoly." In *Economy and*

Organization: Indian Institutions under the Neoliberal Regime, by Amiya Kumar Bagchi, 230–266. New Delhi: Sage Publications. (Also cited in chapter 5.)

Most of the quotes and data for the stories of Fannie Mae and Freddie Mac are from: Morgenson, Gretchen, and Joshua Rosner. 2011. *Reckless Endangerment: How Outsized Ambition, Greed and Corruption Led to Economic Armageddon*. New York: Times Books. (Also cited in chapter 4.)

The quotes and data for the section on spinning laws into gold come from:

Gwartney, James, and Richard E. Wagner. 1988. "The Public Choice Revolution." *Intercollegiate Review*, 17–26.

Pollock, Rufus. 2009. "Forever Minus a Day? Calculating Optimal Copyright Term." *Review of Economic Research on Copyright Issues*, 35–60.

Wise, Timothy A. 2005. "Identifying the Real Winners from U.S. Agricultural Policies." Global Development and Environment Institute Working Paper No. 05-07.

The section on Vanderbilt and network effects draws on: Stiles, T. J. 2009. *The First Tycoon: The Epic Life of Cornelius Vanderbilt*. New York: Alfred A. Knopf. (Also cited in chapter 3.)

An example of a book on getting rich that draws on economic principles: Fridson, Martin S. 2000. *How to Be a Billionaire: Proven Strategies from the Titans of Wealth*. New York: John Wiley & Sons.

Dhirubhai is quoted in: Bhushan, K., and G. Katyal. 2002. *Dhirubhai Ambani: The Man Behind Reliance*. New Delhi: A.P.H. Publishing Corporation. (Also cited in chapter 5.)

Piramal, Gita. 1996. *Business Maharajas*. New Delhi: Penguin Books India. (Also cited in chapter 5.)

Lastly, the quotes regarding Carnegie are from: Brands, H. W. 2010. *American Colossus: The Triumph of Capitalism, 1865–1900*. New York: Doubleday.

Index

About the Author

SAM WILKIN is a senior advisor to Oxford Economics, one of the world's foremost global forecasting and research consultancies, where he previously served as head of business research. He is also a senior advisor to Oxford Analytica, a strategic analysis and advisory firm that counts among its clients many global companies and more than twenty-five world governments. Wilkin received his B.A. in economics from Eckerd College, where he was the 2004 alumni fellow and his M.A. in international relations from the University of Chicago. He lives in New York and Oxford.

Sam Wilkin's views as expressed in this book, via social media, or at dinner parties are his own and not necessarily those of Oxford Analytica or Oxford Economics.